People Powered Radio

Heather Anderson

People Powered Radio

Fifty Years of Australian Community
Radio Station 4ZZZ

Heather Anderson
Griffith University
Brisbane, QLD, Australia

ISBN 978-3-032-05688-7   ISBN 978-3-032-05689-4 (eBook)
https://doi.org/10.1007/978-3-032-05689-4

© The Editor(s) (if applicable) and The Author(s), under exclusive license to Springer Nature Switzerland AG 2025

This work is subject to copyright. All rights are solely and exclusively licensed by the Publisher, whether the whole or part of the material is concerned, specifically the rights of translation, reprinting, reuse of illustrations, recitation, broadcasting, reproduction on microfilms or in any other physical way, and transmission or information storage and retrieval, electronic adaptation, computer software, or by similar or dissimilar methodology now known or hereafter developed.
The use of general descriptive names, registered names, trademarks, service marks, etc. in this publication does not imply, even in the absence of a specific statement, that such names are exempt from the relevant protective laws and regulations and therefore free for general use.
The publisher, the authors and the editors are safe to assume that the advice and information in this book are believed to be true and accurate at the date of publication. Neither the publisher nor the authors or the editors give a warranty, expressed or implied, with respect to the material contained herein or for any errors or omissions that may have been made. The publisher remains neutral with regard to jurisdictional claims in published maps and institutional affiliations.

This Palgrave Macmillan imprint is published by the registered company Springer Nature Switzerland AG.
The registered company address is: Gewerbestrasse 11, 6330 Cham, Switzerland

If disposing of this product, please recycle the paper.

People Powered Radio *is dedicated to all the 4ZZZ folk who no longer walk this mortal coil. We treasure your memories in our collective heart*

Foreword

Radio, live music, activism—by their nature they are experienced in person and live on through oral history. This book demonstrates the major challenge of transforming an oral medium into a written one. It goes a good way towards meeting that challenge (although it definitely needs a second volume—probably more. But one mustn't get greedy—one good book at a time).

This book does not purport to be a complete history. It's not a history told by an outside observer, it is a history as told by a myriad of voices at different times, coming from and being in different places. It is told by people who were part of it, people who were there. Most importantly, those people speak with a sense of collective achievement and events, not as individual disconnected stories or reminiscences.

For every single person quoted or mentioned here, there would be well over a hundred other people not named who were and are an essential part in making 4ZZZ all that it is. Even a hundred more written histories like this one would still be incomplete. (That's not an excuse not to have at least a second volume though).

To me, a key aspect of the book—perhaps it happens intrinsically rather than by deliberate design of the author—is how it organically gives clear meaning and life to a slogan 4ZZZ often uses to describe itself—"people powered radio".

The station wouldn't have survived without the people who subscribed, and this book is a mark of thanks to each and every one of them—whether they provided that show of support (and money!!) just once or fifty times. The punters who turn up at gigs, those who provided grants or donated equipment or music, the musos, the artists, the activists, and those who have just listened and passed on the word or bought and worn one of what must now be more than hundred different designs of 4ZZZ t-shirts– all those people played a part.

But most of all, the book tells the story of the thousands and thousands of people—the vast majority of them volunteers—who helped out at 4ZZZ over those years because they believed in the place, because it was a fun thing to do (sometimes), because they were just exploring or looking for something—which sometimes they didn't find and other times they found that and so much more—or because they believed in the power and magic of music, of changing their community or their world, of the importance of ensuring excluded voices are heard, or just the overall idea and vision of 4ZZZ, however fuzzily or varyingly it's been described over the years.

Every one of those volunteers built the place. In a physical—and financial—sense, they have built and rebuilt it multiple times. But more importantly they built (and are still building) community and are continually (re)creating something much bigger and deeper than just a radio station.

4ZZZ isn't for everyone. That's part of the point of it—not in a snobbish, exclusionary sense, but in the sense of being a place for those looking for something different from the establishment-controlled mainstream; looking for something more—whether it be music, ideas, voices, connections—and people—that are often ignored.

This book doesn't hide from the fact that 4ZZZ hasn't always done things well. It has at times been cliquey, unaware or unwilling to examine its own social biases. And while so many people have very fond and often deeply precious memories and feelings about ZZZ, the book doesn't neglect the reality that some people's experiences and memories were not so great. You can't have people-powered radio without people, and people are imperfect and don't always work well together. That's a simple fact, but it's no excuse not to strive to do better. I think this book will be part of helping to make that happen —it's too easy to forget the past and forget where we've come from, the mistakes and missteps made, but also the wonderful efforts, vision and commitment of those who paved the way. Good books help remedy that.

It sometimes feels like a miracle that 4ZZZ has survived for fifty years (so far). In some ways, it still seems a miracle it was able to come into being in the first place. The institutional, political, technical, financial and human obstacles that were overcome in the early 1970s were incredible and merit a book in its own right. But the relevant chapter in this book gives a good flavour of that, and hopefully pays proper tribute to those who literally made it all happen all those years ago, many of who are no longer with us in person—but whose spirit very much lives on in ZZZ.

The book also details a few of 4ZZZ's near death experiences along the way. It's possible that one or two of those came about in part because people may have got a bit too comfortable with the assumption that ZZZ would survive just because it always has. Assuming immortality is not known to have a good track record. ZZZ living for fifty years should not lead to the hubris of assuming ZZZ will always survive just because it has always managed to do so thus far.

I hope this book provides a warning to guard against that—and if the book doesn't, then hopefully this Foreword makes it crystal clear. We are all custodians of something very special and we have a responsibility to make it even better, not fuck it up. The efforts and love of the many thousands of people who have kept breathing life into 4ZZZ should not just be honoured, they should be respected in the best way possible—by building on their legacy to touch even more communities and people's lives with the unique magic of 4ZZZ. There is genuinely no other radio like it in all the world. So, the people's work is never done. It's just as well being part of a ratbag radio station is so much fun (or for those who aren't really into fun, then just as well it's also a deep source of inner fulfillment). I am confident that *People Powered Radio* fits that bill on both counts, so please read on and find out for yourself.

Meanjin/Brisbane
April 2025

Andrew Bartlett

4ZZZ Volunteer: 1982–1991; 2008–forever
4ZZZ Chairperson: 2014–2017
4ZZZ Board Director: 1980s; 2010s & 2020s
Senator for Queensland: 1997–2008; 2017–2018

Acknowledgements In 2015 I mentioned to my husband Thomas that I wanted to write a book that shares the story of 4ZZZ. This was during the leadup to the station's 40th anniversary, and I decided that if I spoke the words aloud to the Triple Zed community then I'd have to follow up on the claim. It has taken me nearly ten years to see it through, and the support I've received along the way has been magnificent.

If I were to list every person who contributed to *People Powered Radio*, the book would be twice the size (I quote nearly 200 individuals within these pages). I could not have pulled together these stories without the generosity of each person who granted me an interview, responded to a message or email, contributed to an online discussion, or forwarded me an interesting titbit. I have been awash with 'warm inner glow', thanks to the 4ZZZ community.

There are a few individuals that need singling out. The brilliant Nicki Clarke —who I spent ten years presenting *Locked In* with—has been by my side the whole time, copy-editing every chapter with never-ending patience for my often-questionable grammatical choices. This book would be a lot more difficult for readers to digest without her talented 'massaging' of my sometimes-clumsy expression. Lucas Moore, my *13-23* partner in crime, has also been a lifeline, proofreading every chapter and ensuring my footnotes were accurate: an unglamourous but vital task. My *Megaherz* sister, Kirstyn Lindsay, stepped up with invaluable research assistance, ensuring that I had contributions from the current suite of 4ZZZ Coordinators. I also had a small team of readers beta testing chapters for me—former Zed volunteers Warinkil Aunty Glenice Croft, Anita Earl, David Lennon, Ilana Tulloch, Jim Beatson, John Stanwell, Linda Rose and Terry 'Oofus' O'Connor—not only proofing but providing feedback on what did and didn't work. Thank you for sustaining me with your encouragement. Andrew Bartlett, possibly the most honest man to enter a House of Parliament since Guy Fawkes, didn't miss a beat in accepting my request to write the Foreword. Thank you, Andrew. It's a true privilege to be a part of the Zed family with you. And finally, 4ZZZ Station Manager Jack McDonnell has answered every single one of my requests with enthusiasm and a welcoming smile.

This book has been written on the unceded lands of both the Jagera and Turrbal people across a city now known as Brisbane. I am a migrant to these lands although my mother was born on Darumbal Country in Central Queensland. First Nations[1] people have been caring for the lands that make up so-called Australia for tens of thousands of years, which includes

---

[1] I use the term 'First Nations' to refer to Indigenous Australians and 'Murri' to refer specifically to Indigenous Australians from the Queensland area. I recognise that 'First Nations' is an imposed, generic and contested term, and there isn't universal agreement on referring to the diverse groups of Indigenous Australians living across mainland Australia and its surrounding islands—these are colonial concepts in themselves. I recognise that First Nations Australians represent diverse communities, cultures, language groups and kinship systems throughout Australia. Other terms, such as 'Aboriginal and Torres Strait Islander People' and 'Indigenous Australians' are used when included in original sources.

stewardship of knowledge and communication systems that have survived the impact of colonialism. Their sovereignty remains intact and unbroken.

I would like to acknowledge the support I received from the Queensland Memory Awards through a Rainbow Research Fellowship, which provided me with access to the archives and staff support at the State Library of Queensland (SLQ). If you have any 4ZZZ memorabilia that you're not sure what to do with, please consider donating it to the John Oxley Collections at SLQ. This will, no doubt, greatly assist the next person who writes about 4ZZZ. Thank you also to the staff at the Fryer Library and The University of Queensland Archives, where I accessed a variety of primary resources.

I'd like to recognise the assistance afforded to me by the School of Humanities, Languages and Social Science at Griffith University who supported my application for time away from my teaching duties to work on this manuscript; without this I don't think the book would ever have reached completion. I am also extremely grateful to Robin James, Editor for Music, Sound, and Audio Media Studies and the team at Palgrave MacMIllan, New York for believing the story of 4ZZZ was one worth putting into print.

My greatest of thanks of all go to Thomas. If not for him, I'd probably still be weeping in a corner convinced I'd never get this done! Thank you for your unwavering faith in me, and for calling me an author.

Heather Anderson

Please be aware that the names of people who have passed away are mentioned throughout this publication, some of whom I also quote. I hope I have done their words and memories justice. For the most part, I use the full names of people I interviewed unless they have asked otherwise, or I was unable to determine if they were comfortable for me to use their complete name.

Contents

Part I	Home Is Where the Heart Is	1
1	Introduction: You're Listening to 4ZZZ	3
2	If We Build It, They Will Come	11
3	Decisions, Decisions, Decisions	31
4	The Early Bird that Didn't Catch the Worm	47
5	Shelter(s) from the Storm	65
6	Our House (In the Middle of Two Streets)	79
Part II	Music Runs Through Our Veins	95
7	More Than Just a Radio Station	97
8	Market Dazed	117
9	The Police Riot Formerly Known As 'Cybernana' Market Day	137
10	Our Core Business Is Community Radio	159
11	Community Radio Is Hot Stuff	181
Part III	Without Community There Is No Soul	187
12	A Kaleidoscope of Communities	189
13	Where Your News Isn't Limited	209
14	They Can Starve for All I Care	225
15	A Living History	243
Index		251

List of Figures

Fig. 1.1	4ZZZ logo, designed by Matt Mawson; circa 1980	7
Fig. 1.2	Photo of the studio floor of Zed Towers, Fortitude Valley, taken by Ezarco Dos Santos; 2023	10
Fig. 2.1	Early flyer advertising an aspirant 4ZZ. Note the launch date of Dec 1, which was delayed due to the sacking of the Prime Minister by the Governor General.	19
Fig. 3.1	Photo of televisions ready to be smashed as a fundraising activity at a Radiothon held at the University of Queensland, St Lucia; photographer unknown; circa 1982	37
Fig. 3.2	Aerial photo of Zed Towers and neighbours in Fortitude Valley, taken by Robert Broeders; 2018	44
Fig. 4.1	Photo of 4ZZZ premises, University of Queensland, St Lucia, taken by David Lennon; 1985	50
Fig. 4.2	Photo of 4ZZZ studio, University of Queensland, St Lucia, taken by Andrew Dent; 1989	63
Fig. 5.1	Cartoon by Sean Leahy depicting the attempted eviction of 4ZZZ from the St Lucia studios; 1988	68
Fig. 5.2	Poster for a Joint Effort concert held in Sydney to raise funds for 4ZZZ and Radio Skid Row, designed by Matt Mawson; 1989	70
Fig. 5.3	Photo of 4ZZZ's caravan studio, Mt Coot-tha, taken by David Lennon; 1989	75
Fig. 6.1	Photo of 4ZZZ's first transmitter tower being erected at Mt Coot-tha; photographer unknown; 1978	84
Fig. 6.2	Cover of *Radio Times* magazine celebrating 4ZZZ's full-power licence; designed by Matt Mawson; August 1978	85
Fig. 6.3	Photo of Zed Towers front facade, Fortitude Valley, during revamp by artist Beastman, taken by Julian Schmitt; 2010	89
Fig. 6.4	Photo of Zed Towers front facade, Fortitude Valley, post-revamp, by artist Beastman, taken by Julian Schmitt; 2010	90
Fig. 7.1	Poster for 4ZZZ Octobanana celebrations, designed by Sally Hart; 1985	108
Fig. 7.2	Poster for the 4ZZZ event 'Dub Day Afternoon', designed by Basmati; 2012	110

Fig. 7.3	Poster for the 4ZZZ event 'Brain Banana', designed by Sam Kretschman and Benjamin Constantine; 2008	111
Fig. 7.4	Poster for the 4ZZZ event 'Rumble Rock', designed by Nyssa Elliott; 2012	113
Fig. 7.5	Poster for the 4ZZZ event 'Return of the Joint Effort', designed by Nathan Smith; 2014	114
Fig. 8.1	Poster for 4ZZZ's 'Promised Land' Market Day, designed by Dean McInerney; 1992	119
Fig. 8.2	Poster for 4ZZZ's 'Bananageddon' Market Day, designed by Adrian from Rinzen; 2002	133
Fig. 9.1	Poster for 4ZZZ's 'Cybernana' Market Day, designed by Will Serantak; 1996	138
Fig. 10.1	Album cover for 4ZZZ compilation 'State of Emergence', designed by Cora Lansdell; 1986	176
Fig. 11.1	Poster for 4ZZZ's Hot 100, designed by Josh Murphy; 2021	182
Fig. 12.1	Poster for 4ZZZ show *Megaherz*, designed by Nyx (Nancy) Westerman; 1985	192
Fig. 12.2	T-Shirt artwork for 4ZZZ show 'Murri Time', designed by Shellah M Ballesteros; 1983	198
Fig. 13.1	Poster for 4ZZZ Solidarity Drive to support First Nations protests during 1988 Bicenterary, designed by Sally Hart; 1988	214
Fig. 14.1	Poster in support of Boggo Road Gaol rooftop protests, produced by 4ZZZ's Prisoners' Show; 1988	232
Fig. 15.1	Photo of 4ZZZ's current transmitter tower at Broadcasting Park, Mount Coot-tha, taken by Gavin Unsworth; year unknown	248
Fig. 15.2	Photo of 4ZZZ's reception area at Zed Towers, Fortitude Valley, taken by Robert Broeders; 2025	250

PART I

Home Is Where the Heart Is

CHAPTER 1

Introduction: You're Listening to 4ZZZ

If ever there's a perfect time to experience the quirky and vibrant essence of the 4ZZZ community, it's on New Year's Day at the station's annual Hot 100 Countdown Hangout Party. Since its first broadcast in 1977, the Hot 100 tradition has evolved to showcase the most popular of each year's new songs, as voted by 4ZZZ listeners. While you could choose to tune in from anywhere in the world, attending the Hangout Party in person is the quintessential way to immerse yourself in the local flavour of Brisbane's oldest community radio station. That's the magic of 4ZZZ. It's not just a radio station, it's a living, breathing community—a space for self-expression, activism, and the love of music.

But I don't want to get ahead of myself and assume you're familiar with our station, so let's start with the basics.

4ZZZ (pronounced "Four Triple Zed" or simply "Triple Zed") has been a cultural cornerstone of Brisbane since it hit the airwaves in December 1975. Nestled in Fortitude Valley—an eclectic, inner-city suburb of Queensland's capital—this independent radio station broadcasts across the Greater Brisbane area on 102.1fm. Accessible online via live streaming, radio on demand and podcasting, 4ZZZ also operates a digital station (ZedDigital) that, for the most part, broadcasts content unique to the channel and acts as an incubator for new programming. With an estimated audience of "over 160,000 loyal listeners each month,"[1] 4ZZZ is a local institution with a global reach. But Triple Zed is more than this—it's also a hub for community voices, subcultures, and activism—a place where people can both make and hear the important stories and music that mainstream media so often ignores.

Independent and local music are important to the 4ZZZ ethos. Unlike many radio stations, 4ZZZ has no set playlists. Volunteer announcers are

---

[1] 4ZZZ. '4ZZZ Audience Overview' [Internal document supplied to author], 4ZZZ, Brisbane, QLD.

given freedom to curate their own shows so long as they meet certain quotas. These ensure a significant portion of airtime is dedicated to Australian artists, local and new releases, and tracks by women and First Nations musicians. As such, the station's sound is highly eclectic, covering everything from jazz to punk, electronica to country. And then there are the community-based programs with shows for specific social groups, including LGBTIQ+ listeners, people with disabilities, and incarcerated audiences.

Let's circle back to where we started: the Hot 100 Hangout Party of 2025.

For nearly ten years, 4ZZZ has broadcast its Hot 100 live from The Triffid. Co-owned by the bass player of one of Brisbane's most successful musical exports, Powderfinger, this venue is set in what was once a WWII aircraft hangar. It's no surprise that The Triffid, with its lush open-air beer garden, child and dog-friendly policies, and wheelchair accessibility, is the Hot 100's regular home. The kitsch indie decor, featuring cassette tape covers from a variety of Brisbane bands, provides the perfect finishing note to this vibrant space.

I arrived at the party half-way through the countdown and the atmosphere managed to be both bustling and relaxed. The beer garden was full, with people seated casually on low built-in benches and cushions, animated in lively conversations, catching the occasional breeze. Others stood closer to the outside broadcast area, straining to hear the 4ZZZ announcers introduce each track from the makeshift studio just metres from the bar. In a second, quieter space, adults and children played Giant Jenga, handball, and a variety of board games, while vintage documentaries screened silently on a TV screen in the background.

As I joined the crowd, I couldn't help but smile. Somehow, it had been twenty years since I last attended a New Year's Day Hangout Party, yet it felt like no time had passed. Many of the faces had changed, but the spirit of community, rebellion, and creativity remained. These were my people from all walks of life, bound together by their love for community radio and a shared belief in alternative media, who had chosen to spend the first day of the year together under the Triple Zed banner.

The only other tangible thread connecting this eclectic gathering was its sheer, almost defiant, diversity. Fashion choices were varied but leaned toward casual, reflecting a mosaic of alternative subcultures. Band logos and activist slogans adorned t-shirts and sleeveless jackets, while an eye-catching assortment of 4ZZZ merchandise—caps, bandanas, shirts, pins, tote bags—was proudly displayed, not just by the human attendees, but also their canine companions.

Ages within the crowd were equally diverse, a quality reflected in the countdown itself. This year's number two spot was claimed by a band made up of four high school students, The Distained, while seasoned performers Mick Medew and Ursula secured number three with a track celebrating the milestone of becoming a "punk grandma". Both acts hail from the greater Brisbane region, as do many of the bands and musicians featured in this year's Hot 100. This local dominance is no anomaly; for decades, the countdown has been led by Brisbane, Queensland, or Australian independent artists. In fact, a local song has claimed the number one spot every year since 2012.

This year that streak was broken when the top honour went to Melbourne punks Amyl and the Sniffers. With their fierce, high-energy style and super-charged songs about rebellion and self-expression, their winning track, *U Should Not Be Doing That*, seemed a fitting anthem for the free-spirited anti-establishment ethos of 4ZZZ. Singer Amy Taylor says finding out Amyl and the Sniffers made number one was "massive," a highlight of the year for their album, *Cartoon Darkness*. "As a band, when the listeners of community radio support you it means the world," she says. "It's a hard-earned respect because they listen to so much good music!"

The Hot 100 crowd certainly didn't seem to mind Amyl and the Sniffers taking out the number one spot. They're hardly outsiders; Amy Taylor grew up in Mullumbimby, a small town roughly 130 kilometers south-southeast of Brisbane. She remembers driving home from Brisbane when she was a teenager, listening to 4ZZZ and feeling "so happy to hear alternative music on the radio". "At a time when everything is homogenised," she says, "having access to different music and different people's perspectives is mad".

* * *

In 2025, 4ZZZ celebrates fifty years of championing independent bands like Amyl and the Sniffers. The Hot 100 Countdown kicked off the station's fiftieth birthday celebrations with a bang, but what the end-of-year party will look like is currently undecided. 4ZZZ has thrown quite a few grand birthday parties in its time. The tenth was held at the Rialto Theatre—"a magnificent night," according to announcer Liz Willis, who was part of a lip-synching drag performance duet that won the night's talent contest. 4ZZZ band The Black Assassins also played, making a dramatic entrance in borrowed classic cars. "Of course, half the newsroom starts egging us," says drummer and announcer Tony Biggs. "Not the paintwork!" At some point during the night, a hapless soul discharged a fire extinguisher inside the venue, coating everything in white powder. Station Coordinator at the time Nyx (Nancy) Westerman remembers the theatre's owner was furious and even threatened to sue 4ZZZ. "We cleaned, and we cleaned, and we cleaned," they say.

As fun as (most of) all that sounds, I'm hoping 4ZZZ will host an old-fashioned reunion, much like our unforgettable gathering to mark the station's 40th milestone. After all, if there's an event that captures the true essence of 4ZZZ more closely than even the Hot 100 Hangout Party, it's a reunion of Zed volunteers and staff from across the decades, as was the case on December 5th, 2015.

Nearly 150 former and current staff and volunteers gathered for the 4ZZZ 40th Reunion Dinner at Souths Leagues Club in Brisbane's West End. We were a motley crew, ranging from teenagers to seniors, some in their seventies. Among the party were at least three of the station's founding members, along with a few others who had literally helped build 4ZZZ's first studio. Though indistinguishable from the rest of the Triple Zed family, the attendees also included a former Senator and a future Lord Mayor aspirant.

Three local bands from the station's past dusted off the cobwebs to perform a few songs, filling the night with music and nostalgia. Video messages played from those who couldn't attend, and a slideshow of old photos stirred long-buried memories. Tears were shed for those no longer with us, and glasses were raised—and emptied—in their honour.

Michelle Brown, the station manager at the time, and I had the pleasure of co-hosting the Dinner. One of our greatest challenges was planning the night's awards. How would we acknowledge just a handful of people from such a long and rich history, knowing that inevitably many deserving contributors would go unmentioned? There simply wasn't enough time to thank every single person who had played a role in setting up or sustaining 4ZZZ over the decades. Nearly ten years later, I found myself grappling with a similar dilemma as I planned out the structure for this book. There are as many stories to tell about 4ZZZ's fifty-year journey as there are people who have survived them. I can only apologise in advance for everyone and everything I've missed.

Back in 2015, Michelle and I solved our dilemma with a suite of theme-based categories that neatly captured the fundamental nature of Triple Zed. First up, there was staying power—because people come to 4ZZZ, and they just don't leave! Acknowledgements such as 'Growing up at Zed' and 'Longest Contributing Zedder' celebrated the unwavering dedication of those who had stuck with the station through thick and thin, working both on-air and behind the scenes. We also recognised the long-running programs that have become stalwarts of Triple Zed's identity. Some shows such as *Queer Radio*, *Eco Radio*, and the *New Zealand Show*, had been on-air in one form or another for close to thirty years, providing the station with a clear, enduring community identity across the decades.

The 'Agitate Educate Organise' award acknowledged the radical and alternative perspectives that 4ZZZ brings to its spoken word content. 'Agitate Educate Organise' is a (slightly modified) Fabian[2] slogan that was unofficially adopted by 4ZZZ in the mid 1980s and was synonymous with the station up until the early 2000s.[3] From the stations' very formation, inspired as a response to the lack of independent media in Brisbane, 4ZZZ has consistently produced critical commentary on the issues of the day. Flip the 4ZZZ coin, and you'll find an equally strong commitment to alternative and independent music, particularly local artists. This was recognised at the 40th celebrations with the 'Local Music Knowledge' award honouring the promotion of homegrown talent.

Less obvious roles are also vital to the station's survival. For example, the 'Techies Award' went to three generations of audio technicians, who reluctantly came forward to accept their prize. The youngest, Patrick King, gave a heartfelt speech that perfectly summed up their often-thankless task, ending with the cry,

---

[2] The Fabian Society is an organisation of socialists aiming to achieve socialism by gradual rather than revolutionary means.

[3] P. Pugh, *Educate, Agitate, Organize: One Hundred Years of Fabian Socialism*, Routledge, Oxfordshire, 2013.

Fig. 1.1 4ZZZ logo, designed by Matt Mawson; circa 1980

"it's really hard!". I'm happy to report Pat is now 4ZZZ's Tech Manager, passing on his extensive knowledge to new volunteers in a decades-old tradition. We also acknowledged the invisible but vital labour needed to keep the station operational, and the volunteers behind the scenes at reception, raising funds for the station, and in other 'less glamorous' roles far removed from the spotlight of broadcasting. Without them, the station simply wouldn't survive.

Each acknowledgement came with a kitsch prize that paid tribute to the station's long-standing mascot—the humble Queensland banana. No-one knows where the original design for the Triple Zed banana-dude came from, besides vague memories of a couple from Canberra who "popped out [to the station] to subscribe" in the very early days, according to founding member Jim Beatson. "The woman worked for ABC[4] Radio News and her partner was a graphic artist," he says. Co-founder John Stanwell remembers being told "there's a guy here who says he has a logo for the station; are you interested?". The Disney-esque style, microphone wielding banana immediately won the hearts of station workers and 4ZZZ has been obsessed with banana graphics ever since (Fig. 1.1).

---

[4] The ABC (Australian Broadcasting Corporation) is Australia's main public service broadcaster, fully funded by the federal government.

For the 2015 awards, we used a Styrofoam replica, decorated with a handwritten 4ZZZ logo and skewered onto a trophy base. It was a deliberate nod to the low-key, grassroots spirit of the station, putting the focus on fun rather than formality. Little did we know that our Lifetime-Subscriber award recipient, Jim Beatson, had already accepted a banana trophy once before, way back at the station's first birthday party in 1976. That one? An actual piece of fruit jammed onto a stick. Michelle and I had considered a similar design during the frantic preparations for the night, but it was quickly scrapped—it didn't exactly scream longevity. In fairness, the 1976 birthday planners probably weren't thinking that far ahead.

Then again, who could have imagined 4ZZZ would still be going strong in 2025?.

* * *

People Powered Radio explores what has kept Brisbane's oldest community radio station alive and thriving for the past fifty years. How has 4ZZZ managed to keep radio relevant in a world that's becoming more digitalised and individualised? To find out, I've delved into the music, politics, and events that have shaped not only the station itself, but the lives of those who've dedicated their time and energy into ensuring 4ZZZ's survival. Taking inspiration from the 40th birthday awards, I've opted for a thematic approach rather than a straightforward, linear timeline.

Section One: Home Is Where the Heart Is focuses on the physical, technical, and organisational aspects of 4ZZZ's history, broken into five chapters. *Chapter* 2: *If We Build It, They Will Come* looks at the construction of the original station—physically, technically, and ideologically. It is the 4ZZZ origin story leading to the first broadcast in December 1975, at its original location on the University of Queensland (UQ) campus. The campaign to establish community radio, not just in Brisbane but across the whole country, could fill a book of its own. *Chapter* 3: *Decisions, Decisions, Decisions* outlines the organisational nuts and bolts of Triple Zed, focusing on how it is funded and managed. *Chapter 4: The Early Bird That Didn't Catch the Worm* is a deep-dive into the dramatic events of December 14th, 1988, when 4ZZZ was forced off-air after receiving an immediate eviction notice from the UQ Student Council, which was delivered in the wee hours of the morning. 4ZZZ wouldn't fully leave UQ until July 1989, but that night marked the beginning of the end of its relationship with the university as a landlord. This is where *Chap.* 5: *Shelter(s) From The Storm* picks up, as Triple Zed prepares to move out into the big wide world, broadcasting from a makeshift studio in a caravan at its transmission site and then renting a commercial property for the first time. Section One concludes with *Chap.* 6: *Our House (In The Middle Of Two Streets)*, which documents 4ZZZ's move to, and purchase of, its current home at Zed Towers, the former Brisbane headquarters of the Communist Party of Australia, in Fortitude Valley.

Section Two: Music Runs Through Our Veins covers 4ZZZ's contribution to local and independent music. *Chapter 7: More Just a Radio Station* highlights some of the key live music venues, events, and gigs that Triple Zed has organised over the years. At various times the station has acted as more than just a broadcaster—it became an events organisation as well. Closely related is *Chap. 8: Market Dazed* which documents the hey-day of 4ZZZ's Market Day, from 1992 to 2006. One of the station's most memorable events, Market Day was an essential entry in the Brisbane alternative musical calendar, drawing thousands of festival goers and leaving a lasting mark on the city's cultural landscape. This leads into *Chap. 9: The Riot Formerly Known As 'Cybernana' Market Day*. In October 1996, 4ZZZ's 'Cybernana' Market Day was thrown into chaos when it was forcibly shut down by the Public Safety Response Team, better known as the Riot Police. 4ZZZ lodged a formal complaint against the Queensland Police Service, citing ongoing harassment, but the case went nowhere. *Chapter 10: Our Core Business Is Community Radio* covers 4ZZZ's relationship with music and how it has shaped the sound of the station over the years, while *Chap. 11: Community Radio is Hot Stuff* looks at 4ZZZ's Hot 100, the New Years' Day countdown discussed at the top of this chapter.

Section Three: Without Community, There Is No Soul turns its attention to the community engagement that has made 4ZZZ a vital part of Brisbane's social movement media over the past fifty years. *Chapter 12: A Kaleidoscope of Communities* focuses on the ways that 4ZZZ has amplified marginalised voices over the years drawing on but a few of the communities represented through 4ZZZ's activities both on and off the air. *Chapter 13: Where Your News Isn't Limited* charts the station's history of news and current affairs programming and the activist journalism that has set 4ZZZ apart from other news outlets. *Chapter 14: They Can Starve for All I Care* reflects on the station's legacy of supporting people affected by the criminal justice system, and to wrap things up, *Chap. 15: A Living History* reminds us that the story of 4ZZZ is still being told, with a look at the station as it operates today.

* * *

I am one of the thousands of people who have powered 4ZZZ over the past five decades. I started volunteering at the station in 1991, drawn by its unique mix of musical and political freedom. Back then, I was 21 years old and deeply involved in the Brisbane punk scene, booking gigs, producing a fanzine, and looking for new ways to support and promote local music. Naturally, Triple Zed seemed like the perfect outlet.

My first substantial on-air gig was presenting *The Punk Show* with friend and co-host Richard Stanley, who later founded Aarght Records, described by Vice Media as "one of the most important independent record labels in Australia".[5]

---

[5] T. Hernandez, 'Aarght Records: Ten Years of Absurd and Psychotic Underground Music', *Vice Magazine*, September 18. 2017, https://www.vice.com/en/article/aarght-records-ten-years-of-absurd-and-psychotic-underground-music/ URL, (accessed 11 Jan. 2025).

Fig. 1.2 Photo of the studio floor of Zed Towers, Fortitude Valley, taken by Ezarco Dos Santos; 2023

My interest in social justice issues eventually pulled me into a more formal role in the newsroom, and the longer I stayed, the more involved I became—from delivering announcer training to developing policy and a bunch of other roles that I've long since forgotten.

Even after I moved out of town, I made the two-hour journey most Sundays to present the feminist show *Megaherz* and the shorter-lived *Kidzone*, often bringing my young son along for the ride. I continued to help remotely with grant writing, documentaries, and community engagement projects, for a while scraping together a living from those. In 2013, I took on the role of Chairperson of 4ZZZ's Board of Directors, a position I held for two years despite living over 2000 km away in Adelaide for work.

Fast-forward to 2025, and I've been back in Brisbane for five years. While I don't spend most of my time at 4ZZZ anymore, I keep a foot in the door, mainly through writing for and about the station and occasionally contributing to the long-form interview show *Talking Zeds*. What I love most about my time with 4ZZZ is that my experiences aren't unique or unusual. I'm not the station's longest-serving volunteer, and I haven't given more of my time than many other dedicated supporters. I'm sharing my history simply as a way of introducing myself and to give a friendly warning that my own stories are inextricably woven into the pages ahead.

This is only a partial history of 4ZZZ (Fig. 1.2). There are too many people, programs, songs, and events for one book to capture. These are but a few of my favourites.

CHAPTER 2

If We Build It, They Will Come

It's Monday December 8th, 1975—a warm summer's day in Brisbane, Queensland, Australia. As the clock approaches noon, John Woods sits at the panel of a brand-new radio studio on the University of Queensland campus in the riverside suburb of St Lucia. Lightly bearded with curly dark hair, 4ZZZ's[1] first DJ looks calm and concentrated in a photo taken at the time, but there must have been some nerves as he switched the microphone on at midday to begin the inaugural broadcast.

> You are listening to 4ZZ-FM in Brisbane bringing you stereo FM rock on a frequency of 105.7 MHz. 4ZZ-FM is Brisbane's first new radio station in over thirty years, and first ever stereo FM station.

After years of dedication, a group of volunteers with a passionate belief in the power of independent media had helped changed the face of Australian broadcasting. This wasn't 'just' about securing a community radio licence in Brisbane but establishing an entire national community broadcasting sector. Later in his opening statement, John explains the philosophy behind this movement for a more democratic media. "It is essential that as many people as possible have access to the media," he says, adding that "fairness in broadcasting is not achieved by all stations seeking the lowest common denominator in programming, but by diversity".

Before moving to Brisbane as one of 4ZZZ's first hires, John Woods had been sacked from his position as a television presenter in Adelaide, South

---

[1] 4ZZZ originally broadcast under the callsign of 4ZZ-FM (pronounced Four Double Zed). In February 1976, this was changed to 4ZZZ-FM following a decision by the Broadcasting Control Board that all FM stations would have a three-letter callsign. For simplicity's sake, I refer to the station as it is now known, 4ZZZ, unless citing other people's words.

© The Author(s), under exclusive license to Springer Nature Switzerland AG 2025
H. Anderson, *People Powered Radio*,
https://doi.org/10.1007/978-3-032-05689-4_2

Australia, for taking part in the city's first Gay Rights demonstrations. He'd been told this would happen, and that he'd never work in broadcasting again, but that didn't stop John from joining the front lines of the protest. Listeners didn't know this at the time, but I like to think it was a nice flourish to 4ZZZ's first broadcast—led by a gay man who'd been sacked for standing up for basic human rights.

Not that Brisbane was a more progressive city than Adelaide. The uberconservative Australian Country Party—Queensland (better known as the Country Party)[2] had held power in Queensland since 1957, governing in coalition with the Liberal Party, and from 1968, Johannes (Joh) Bjelke-Petersen was at the helm. Joh would go on to become Queensland's longest-serving Premier, infamous for his authoritarian rule and law-and-order stance. He was a divisive character. To his supporters, he was a strong leader, but to his critics, he ran a police state.

The political climate of late-1960s and early-1970s Queensland and the corruption rife within its police force have been well-documented.[3] As much as I want to avoid rehashing old stories, it's impossible to map the origins of 4ZZZ without providing some context. So, we'll begin by looking at the political and cultural backdrops that gave birth not only to Brisbane's first community radio station, but the entire Australian community broadcasting sector.

* * *

Before the 1970s, Australian radio had just two main sectors: commercial stations, like those in the U.S., and the national government-run broadcaster, the Australian Broadcasting Commission (now Corporation, ABC), which was heavily influenced by the British Broadcasting Corporation (BBC). The push for a third broadcasting sector in Australia came from four distinct but unrelated groups, each with a different perspective on the broader movement for greater media diversity, access, and representation. These groups can be loosely described as multicultural and ethnic communities, universities and educators, grassroots left-wing political activists, and fine music enthusiasts—the latter being perhaps the most surprising early advocates.[4]

Fine music supporters were particularly interested in FM radio because of its superior sound quality and stereo output. Music Broadcasting Societies (MBS)

---

[2] The Australian Country Party—Queensland changed its name to the National Party of Australia—Queensland in 1974 (E. Whitton, *The Hillbilly Dictator: Australia's police state*, ABC Books, 1989, p. 23).

[3] See, for example, Matthew Condon's true-crime series, starting with *All the King's Men*; Mark Bahnisch's *Queensland: Everything You Ever Wanted to Know, But Were Afraid to Ask*; Anne Richards' memoir, *A Book of Doors*; and Andrew Stafford's *Pig City*.

[4] D. Melzer, 'The future of community radio', *Arena*, 2010, https://arena.org.au/the-future-of-community-radio/ (accessed 4th December 2024).

were formed to lobby the government to expand FM frequencies for public broadcasting, especially after experimental FM stations had been shut down to make space for television. This campaign was consumer-driven, shifting the debate on broadcasting policy into the general public for the first time.[5] Before this, media policy was mostly shaped by commercial radio industry players and focused on technology rather than audience access. By encouraging public involvement in discussions about new radio services, the fine music movement helped lay the groundwork for broader community radio access. However, in Queensland, it was almost exclusively grassroots activists and progressive music fans that led the campaign for community broadcasting.

It's hard to overstate the impact of the Bjelke-Petersen regime, especially on youth countercultures and marginalised communities. In Queensland during the 1950s and '60s, moral panics surrounding youth and their music reflected broader societal anxieties about changing social norms and values. As rock 'n' roll, the hippie movement and surf culture gained popularity, authorities and conservative groups viewed these trends as a challenge to traditional morality and social order. This was amplified in Queensland, where parliamentary discussions would often focus on "protecting children against pollution of the mind and defilement of the spirit as one of deep and urgent concern".[6] This pollution, according to many elected officials, came from a variety of threats including movies, books and—of course—contemporary music. The rise of youth music venues, particularly those hosting rock music, became focal points of concern, with fears they encouraged delinquency, drug use, and promiscuity. As author Anne Richard explains, "if you're a muso [musician], if you had long hair, if you were in any way different … you were a target … music was a moral panic situation".

Many adults responded to rock 'n' roll "as if told they had a terminal disease"[7] and media coverage often amplified these concerns, depicting young people as rebellious and disrespectful of authority. The Queensland government, under Premier Bjelke-Petersen, reacted to this newly emerging youth culture with strict policing and censorship measures, aiming to curb what was perceived as a cultural threat. This period of moral panic illustrated a generational clash as the younger population embraced global youth movements while conservative institutions sought to preserve established societal norms.

Anne Richards remembers that police—when not making arrests—would "hand out white shirts to bodgies or to mods or whatever … [saying] put on a nice white shirt … get your hair cut". Queensland even had its own

---

[5] Radio Adelaide, 'A history of community broadcasting', *Radio Adelaide*, https://media.adelaide.edu.au/radio/intro/history_com-radio.pdf (accessed 4th December 2024).

[6] Queensland, Parliament, *Queensland Parliamentary Debates [Hansard]*, Brisbane, Friday 19th November 1971, p.2030.

[7] M. Sturma, 'The politics of dancing: When rock'n'roll came to Australia.' *Journal of Popular Culture*, vol.25 no.4, 1992, p. 124.

legislation—the *Objectionable Literature Act of 1954*—used to outlaw the distribution of 'questionable publications'. In the early 1970s, students were arrested for circulating *The Little Red School Book*, a Danish publication that gave advice to young people about contemporary topics such as drugs, sex, democracy and resisting authority. 4ZZZ founding member, Sue Horton, remembers this and other aspects of Australian popular culture being restricted in the State. "Some things would be illegal, not illegal in Australia generally, but illegal to distribute in Queensland," she says. "That's very hard to explain if you weren't there at the time. I can remember, as a kid, [the musical] *Hair* came out; it was banned in Queensland."

* * *

By the late 1960s, Brisbane was also notorious for its harsh restrictions on protesting and free speech. Public demonstrations were often banned, with police given sweeping powers to arrest activists simply for assembling in the streets. This crackdown disproportionately targeted marginalised groups such as Indigenous activists, trade unionists, feminists, and anti-conscription Vietnam War protesters, who faced heavy surveillance, intimidation, and police violence. The State Government justified these measures under the guise of maintaining law and order when, in reality, they served to suppress dissent. As 4ZZZ founding member, Alan Knight describes, "in Queensland in those days, it really was living in a state of siege".[8] Despite these oppressive conditions, activists found creative ways to resist, including underground publications, guerrilla theatre, flash protests designed to evade police crackdowns and—later in the 1970s—community radio.

At this time, the University of Queensland (UQ) was a central point for activism, with many future political leaders and change-makers emerging from this period. Radicals on campus hosted countless public forums, movie nights and rallies introducing students to a broad range of political ideologies and social justice concerns. According to Sue Horton, it was easier to effectively mobilise, "because we were all actually there … and studying was almost peripheral to the university experience". Sue's close high school friend and fellow 4ZZZ founder, Marian Wilkinson, remembers the first time she heard First Nations speakers on campus, "trying to tell us what it was like living on an Aboriginal reserve in Queensland," she describes. "All these ideas, cultural and political, were percolating at the time … it was very exciting." It was within this haven of political expression, supported by a radical Student Union, that 4ZZZ found its first home on the UQ campus. But I'm getting ahead of myself.

In 1968, student activists launched an underground newspaper called *The Brisbane Line*—a name that would later be revived by 4ZZZ's news and current affairs program. *The Brisbane Line* was hounded by authorities, with

---

[8] Alan Knight passed in 2017, after I interviewed him for this book.

street sellers regularly arrested, and newsagents refusing to stock it. The harassment escalated to the point where swastikas were spray-painted on the building where it was produced,[9] the Queensland Communist Party headquarters that 4ZZZ now calls home. *The Brisbane Line* became a symbol of defiance, even though it only lasted three issues. One of the printers for *The Brisbane Line* was Jim Beatson, who was well-known as an active member of the radical movement and would later play an indispensable role in establishing not just 4ZZZ but the Australian community broadcasting sector.

Important social clubs also developed in response to conservatism in Brisbane, which fostered alternative music, political discussion and countercultural expression. The FOCO Club, established in the late 1960s, was a radical youth venture jointly run by the Society for Democratic Action (SDA) and the Young Socialist League, based at the Trades Hall in South Brisbane. Taking its name from Che Guevara's Foco theory of revolutionary warfare, FOCO became a hub for folk, rock, and psychedelic music, as well as poetry readings, political debates, and experimental theatre. While "decidedly and very openly, political,"[10] the club was "also a place where you could let your hair down and have a bit of fun".[11] It attracted progressive youth and countercultural figures, but its radical politics led to intense police scrutiny and surveillance. HARPO (How About Resisting Powerful Organisations) emerged as a successor to FOCO, aiming to continue its legacy of music, activism, and underground arts. John Stanwell—an early and active member of HARPO—would become another influential contributor to 4ZZZ's establishment.

* * *

Political tensions in Queensland hit boiling point in 1971 when Premier Bjelke-Petersen ordered a month-long State of Emergency in response to protests against the Springbok Rugby team's tour of Australia. The all-white South African team had been selected based on apartheid policies, and anti-racist activists across the country were determined to disrupt the tour. Protests and marches became illegal under the State's emergency measures, and according to Police Union President Ron Eddington, the Premier promised police immunity from prosecution for any forceful measures they took to control them.[12]

On Thursday July 22nd, around 6:00pm the Springbok Rugby Union team arrived at the Tower Mill Motel on Wickham Terrace, inner city Brisbane. Across the street, a vigil gathered—approximately 400 anti-racism protestors

---

[9] 'Alan Knight Interview' [radio], Brisbane, 4ZZZ, 2015.

[10] P. Gray and F. Neilsen, 'Australia's most evil and repugnant nightspot', *Radical Times*, Brisbane Discussion Circle, 2012, http://radicaltimes.info/PDF/FOCO.pdf (accessed 14 November 2024).

[11] P. Gray and F. Neilsen, 'Australia's most evil and repugnant nightspot'.

[12] M. Condon, 'Three Crooked Kings', UQ Press, p. 249.

faced a cordon of over 500 police, including hundreds brought in from regional Queensland to bolster numbers. There were also 50 or so members of the riot squad on the front line and plain-clothed police milling undercover with the protesters. According to Raymond Evans in the book *Radical Brisbane*, the day before, a 'sanctioned' march of over 2,000 protesters ended in violent arrests, and as a result, numbers were less than expected at the Thursday vigil. It wasn't long before police moved forward, under orders to clear the footpath.

> The demonstrators have little choice but to turn and flee into the pitch-dark, down the abrupt descent of Wickham Park. They are followed, shoved, knocked down and attacked with fists, batons and boots ...[13]

Some protesters, including future Queensland Premier Peter Beattie, fled to the protection of Trades Hall, pursued by police. Beattie was badly beaten—eventually taken to hospital under police guard for suspected spinal injuries and then charged with disorderly conduct and resisting arrest. As described at the time in the UQ Student Union newspaper, *Semper Floreat*, "the systematic brutality" of that night left little doubt in the "minds of anyone who experienced it or witnessed it as to what the State of Emergency meant for the rights of dissent in the State of Queensland in 1971".[14]

The following day, approximately 3000 students gathered at the University of Queensland and voted to strike as a political statement against racism, the State of Emergency, and police violence against Springbok protesters. A silent vigil held outside the Tower Mill Motel that night went ahead without incident, however, a third, much larger, demonstration on Saturday July 24th (after game day) was again met with police violence. About a thousand gathered at the Tower Mill that evening and when the lines of police moved forward to clear the footpath, they charged the demonstrators in a similar manner to Thursday. John Stanwell, who'd been an active participant against the Springbok tour, describes the police reaction as "totally offensive, and totally predictable" while Anne Richards recalls the panic that ensued as protesters once again fled into the park below.

> It was a really, really big crowd. They just pushed us into the park ... they were throwing punches and wielding their batons and doing whatever damage they could on whomever, you know, whether it was woman, male, big guy, little guy, kid, didn't matter. So, it was basically running from chaos, from sheer chaos.

The extensive police violence at the Tower Mill Motel vigils was mostly dismissed or reframed by the mainstream media. Brisbane's leading newspapers

---

[13] R. Evans, 'Springbok Tour Confrontation', in R. Evans and C. Ferrier (eds) in *Radical Brisbane: an unruly History*, Carlton North, The Vulgar Press, 2004, p. 280.

[14] S. Roger, 'History of the Strike', *Semper Floreat*, St Lucia, University of Queensland Student Union, vol. 41, no. 11, 1971, p. 4.

ran the government's version of events as straight news, with no mention of police brutality. Alan Knight participated in the protests and, years later when he was a Professor in Journalism, analysed newspaper coverage of the tour. He found the reportage focused on confrontation and was "strongly skewed by vitriolic government sources," treating politicians with deference and stereotyping demonstrators as anarchists or hippies.[15]

Media apathy towards these stories of police violence and their place in the broader contexts of free speech and anti-racist action only strengthened calls for an alternative media outlet. Jim Beatson had recently returned from two years in London where he had witnessed the rise of "cheap-to-establish pirate radio stations". He says the impetus for 4ZZZ grew out of "local media indifference to State Government corruption, violence, incompetence and insensitivity".[16] As Alan Knight describes it, "we were appalled at the way *The Courier Mail* covered the Springbok tour … Largely it did the work of police public relations". Newspapers and pamphlets clearly weren't enough. According to Alan, what became glaringly obvious during the Springbok tour were the limitations of the offset printing technology being used by political activists at the time, "so we started thinking about different ways, more effective ways of communicating". Marian Wilkinson also remembers when the idea of an independent radio station in Brisbane was raised. "We thought, 'we're writing for student newspapers and things like that so why weren't we using the new technology?'" she says. "And the new exciting technology was FM radio, believe it or not, back then … FM radio where you could play fantastic music as well as discuss ideas."

Some suggested a pirate radio station, but Jim Beatson quickly questioned the idea. Pirate stations, he argued, were too easy to shut down. Unlike some countries, Australia didn't have a strong history of pirate radio. Jim knew that during the Vietnam War, anti-draft activists and their supporters attempted to operate illegal radio in Sydney and Melbourne, which were quickly intercepted by authorities. Besides, the short-range style of broadcast synonymous with pirate radio wouldn't have the desired impact. What Brisbane needed, according to Jim, was a full-time licence. "We didn't just want a pirate radio station," he explains. "We wanted something legal, permanent, and powerful enough to reach people across Brisbane."

* * *

Telecommunications in Australia are managed federally, meaning the community broadcasting movement—including activists in Brisbane—had to lobby at

---

[15] A. Knight, 'Police, radicals and the media in the 1971 springbok protests', *Labour History*, no.110, 2016, p. 179–185, https://www.jstor.org/stable/10.5263/labourhistory.110.0179 (accessed 14 May 2024).

[16] J. Beatson, 'The Importance of Locally-Owned Media', *Radical Times*, 2012, http://radicaltimes.info/PDF/Beatson.pdf (accessed 14 May 2024).

a national level. This made radio an even more attractive option for Brisbane as the Queensland Government would have limited control, both at the decision-making stage and with any radio licence granted. But first, the Federal government needing convincing that Australia warranted a third type of broadcasting, beyond that of the commercial and government sectors. In the early 1970s, Australian national politics were dominated by two major parties: the Liberal-National Coalition (conservative) who had been in power for over twenty years, and the Labor Party (centre-left). Both (especially the latter) ended up playing a role in shaping what became Australia's three-tiered broadcasting system.

It seemed unlikely that a community group would be granted a licence to broadcast across Brisbane while a conservative Federal government remained in power. Furthermore, the campaign for a third sector of broadcasting was pushing for a home on the almost non-existent FM spectrum. FM radio was already highly popular in America and Europe and many student campuses in the United States had FM radio stations, albeit mostly low power.[17] An early flyer for the aspirant 4ZZZ (Fig. 2.1), with the tagline "Steroe Rock", outlined why FM radio was the ideal location for a new suite of non-commercial licences.

> FM transmissions consist of two signals transmitted simultaneously which are decoded by an FM receiver to give a stereo sound of the quality of a good hi–fi stereogram … Because it has a wider frequency bandwidth the transmission has greater clarity and better base and treble response … FM is not nearly as prone to atmospheric and similar interference as AM.[18]

In December 1972, Gough Whitlam's federal Labor party was elected, breaking the Coalition's 23-year streak of governance. Buoyed by Whitlam's pro-media and more liberal agenda, the University of Queensland Media Committee (UQMC) formed in March 1973 to lobby for an experimental on-campus licence. According to early committee member, Sue Horton, student-run radio "was a vehicle by which we could challenge what was happening around us". As mentioned, the University of Queensland was central to the protest movement of 1970s Brisbane, and, as such, a logical home for an aspirant community radio station.

In addition to Sue Horton, the UQMC featured a roll call of 4ZZZ alumni including (but not limited to) Jim Beatson, John Stanwell, Marian Wilkinson, Alan Knight (who was also editor of UQ student paper *Semper Floreat*), Stephen Stockwell (Snr),[19] Ross Dannecker (an engineering student who

---

[17] K. Jewell. 'The History of College Radio', *Unsung History* [podcast], https://www.unsunghistorypodcast.com/college-radio/, 2024, (accessed 2nd December 2024).

[18] *4ZZ-FM Stereo Radio: Why FM Radio?* [Flyer], Brisbane, 4ZZ, n.d.

[19] There are two "Stephen Stockwells" who have worked in significant roles at 4ZZZ, where we informally distinguish them as Stockwell Snr (a UQ Media Committee member prior to 4ZZZ being licensed and then an announcer, producer, journalist and Promotions Coordinator in the

Fig. 2.1 Early flyer advertising an aspirant 4ZZ. Note the launch date of Dec 1, which was delayed due to the sacking of the Prime Minister by the Governor General.

became 4ZZZ's technical adviser), and future announcer Helen Hambling.[20] Helen was a first-year English and politics student at the time, and remembers being attracted by a notice on campus, advertising for people to come together and talk about applying for a radio licence.

early 80s) and Stockwell Jnr (a journalist and announcer from 2007 and then Station Manager in the early 2020s).

[20] This isn't the full UQ Media Committee. I have limited this list to (some of) the people I have spoken with directly, and those whose names were on 4ZZZ's original licence proposal.

I was a complete outsider and newbie and started going along to those meetings. And just got drawn in ... I loved it, it was so exciting ... we thought we could just do anything, you know, it was amazing.

Members met regularly, discussing all aspects of establishing a new radio station on campus, most notably programming, community involvement, technical requirements, finance and staffing.

The Committee constantly lobbied for a licence through a variety of channels. Delegations would travel to Canberra to meet with politicians and public servants who, according to Helen Hambling were open to hearing their arguments. "There were people that wanted things to be different ... that was a ... [reformist] Labor government at that time ... they were open to it," she says. However, Jim Beatson was soon told by an insider within the Media Department of the federal government that the Brisbane campaign for a broadcast licence had not gained much traction. As such, the friendly informer suggested as many community organisations in Brisbane as possible should be sending letters of support to the federal government. Quick to respond, committee members wrote countless personalised letters to every community organisation in Brisbane they could identify, from the Girl Guides to the Trade Unions Council, to gather statements of support. "We wrote letters to government departments, community organisations, and unions—anyone we thought could help us build momentum," Jim Beatson says. Marian Wilkinson similarly remembers "spending hours and hours and hours and hours on Triple Zed work to get the station started ... It was full on. It consumed our lives".

The hard work paid off. Soon after, the UQMC was considered number one on the list of radio licence aspirants. So serious was this recognition that, in May of 1973, Jim Beatson flew to the nation's capital, Canberra, to discuss the possibility of an educational AM licence which he rejected because music couldn't be played.

Also in 1974, the Whitlam government tabled a report from an *Independent Inquiry into FM Broadcasting*, that recommended both the introduction of FM and the establishment of a public broadcasting sector (later renamed community broadcasting). Soon after, the Public Broadcasting Association of Australia (PBAA, now CBAA) formed to represent the myriad interest groups wanting to engage in the sector. Its mission was to oversee community radio's development and ensure it was shaped by community demand, rather than dictated by the government.[21]

* * *

---

[21] P. Thornley, The early days of community broadcasting: Elites, ordinary people and 'community of interest', *Blur and Focus: Community Broadcasting Association of Australia (CBAA) Annual Conference*, Coolangatta, CBAA, 2000.

In a step closer to formalising a third sector of broadcasting in Australia, the Sydney-based Media Department's Working Party on Public Broadcasting (WPPB) was established and tasked with developing a community broadcasting policy on behalf of the federal government. Jim Beatson was one of its seven members, who worked full time for two months to determine how the new sector would be established, funded and regulated. According to Jim, through his work with the WPPB he discovered Whitlam's Media Minister, Moss Cass, was impressed by the work of the UQMC and agreed they should be granted a licence as quickly as possible.

By this time, the UQ Media Committee, using the call sign 4ZZ-FM, had been granted an experimental licence to test broadcast across the UQ campus during Orientation Week. From February 17th to 21st 1975, the station was on air from 10:00 am to 5:00 pm, playing a mix of specialist and modern music, student news, and current affairs.

The UQMC submitted its *Formal Application for Issuing of a non-Commercial Frequency Modulation (F.M.) Stereo Broadcasting Licence* to the Cabinet of the Australian Government, the Australian Broadcasting Control Board and the Department of the Media in the same month, February 1975. The submission was prepared by Jim Beatson, Ross Dannecker, Susan Horton and Marian Wilkinson and began with a clear statement of intent: "The union seeks to broadcast to an audience of predominantly tertiary and secondary students in FM stereo throughout metropolitan Brisbane at approximately 5 kW e.r.p. [effective radiated power]."[22]

The 16-page application detailed the Media Committee's arguments for a student radio station:

> For some years a considerable number of university students have been dissatisfied with much of the present radio programming and have lacked any method by which they could transmit radio programs themselves. With the advent of public broadcasting in Australia this has changed.

The submission was explicitly critical of mainstream radio, stating its aim was to create a station that wasn't constricted by the limitations of its commercial counterparts.

> Examples of the limitations of commercial radio are their reliance on the 2-to-3-minute disc to accommodate advertising demands; the use of the 'top 40' and its consequent disregard of music trends indicated by album sales concerts, rock films etc.; the censorship of songs with controversial social or political comment; the artificial promotion of certain artists, record companies, concerts, etc, evident at various times.[23]

---

[22] J. Beatson et al, *Formal Application for Issuing of a non-Commercial Frequency Modulation (F.M.) Stereo Broadcasting Licence*, 1975.

[23] J. Beatson et al, *Formal Application for Issuing of a non-Commercial Frequency Modulation (F.M.) Stereo Broadcasting Licence*, 1975.

It also explained that a higher power licence was required to reach the target (student) audience, scattered throughout Brisbane and its suburbs. It justified the need to be licenced on the FM spectrum in detail, noting the higher incidences of interference with AM broadcast in tropical regions.

An alternative new service was outlined, that would provide an hourly news bulletin during the breakfast timeslot slot, together with news and information from a variety of sources throughout the day. These would be produced by full-time station employees and a group of volunteers from the university's journalism department. Programming (including general and specialist music programs from on and off campus), finance, technical and management structures were also described and the full-time positions to be created at the station were listed. With the formal application submitted, the UQMC had done all it could possibly do to be considered for a broadcasting licence.

In late June of 1975, the WPPB's report was tabled in Parliament and a future Australian community radio sector seemed assured. UQ's Student Union took the plunge and ordered a high-power transmitter and antenna from the United States. In August, the UQMC conducted another test transmission from the Park Royal Motel, to coincide with the Brisbane Hi-Fi Show. Ingeniously, a transmitter was set up in the bathroom of the station's motel room—an early indicator of the seemingly limitless workarounds implemented by 4ZZZ's volunteer technical team at the time (and to this day).

One of 4ZZZ's future technical engineers, Marc Jackson, remembers hearing the test broadcasts as an eight-year-old, attending the Hi–Fi Show with his father. Marc's dad also volunteered with the team who built 4ZZZ's first transmitter, with his son often tagging along. Dan Flannery—who would become a 4ZZZ journalist a few years later—distinctly remembers tuning in to one of the early test transmissions, lucky enough to be sharing a house with a friend who'd brought "a really good FM set up" over from South Africa. Exactly which test broadcast Dan picked up is still being debated, but he recalls enjoying the music.

* * *

In September 1975, Media Minister Cass named twelve potential licences that would be offered, almost exclusively to universities. As Jim Beatson explains[24]:

> Only one, (later known as) 4ZZZ, was offered - not to the University like the other eleven - but to the Student Union. And while all twelve quickly said 'yes please', only 4ZZZ was close to being ready to broadcast.

Construction of the 4ZZZ studio and office complex began almost immediately. The UQ Student Union provided space for the studios, and made

---

[24] J. Beatson, 'The Importance of Locally-Owned Media', *Radical Times*, 2012, http://radicaltimes.info/PDF/Beatson.pdf (accessed 14 May 2024).

a substantial cash grant for the purchase of equipment and building materials.[25] A volunteer team—many of whom juggled other responsibilities such as university studies or jobs—worked quickly to build three studios in the basement of the University Refectory building, led by architecture student, Kevin Hayes, his second-in-charge, Don Little and "a couple of brickies from the Building Workers Industrial Union of Australia," according to Jim Beatson. It was a monumental task to convert the empty space into a functioning broadcast facility.

John Stanwell describes an "army of energy, of people who saw that this thing had potential" working tirelessly, often in gruelling summer-hot conditions, to ensure the station was completed on time.

> You'd just go up to the refectory and put out a call ... 'brick line at Double Zed now' ... and people would come down and just stand there and throw hundreds of bricks from out the front ... 20 people throwing bricks at a time, which is the old-fashioned way of moving [them].

He recalls announcer John Woods arriving from Adelaide, "resplendent in Cuban heels and a bad hangover ... pressed straight into bricklaying"[26] and that Marian Wilkinson was also particularly skilled at masonry, surprising even herself. "I like to think I was probably a bit neater than some of the blokes that were on at that time," she agrees. "It was all heaps of fun ... everyone would do everything ... it was a great way for us all to bond together." Early 4ZZZ journalist, Margot Foster was one of many volunteers who joined the station during the construction phase, arriving each day on her "little motorbike," puffing on a pipe she still has today. "I was quite a practical person and an outdoorsy type ... but also, my dad was a plumber and so I was used to tools and stuff like that," Margot says. "I did brickwork and did the studios ... it was just thrilling to be, you know, pulled into a group." Gordon Curtis also began volunteering around this time, attracted by 4ZZZ's radical potential, but not as adept in construction.

> If you needed to hold a wooden frame up, you'd get called in, and people would just pitch in to help ... you had people like Margot who were good at brick laying and you'd help her out, I could see that my brick laying was appalling, and I got out of the way!

Regardless, Gordon fondly recalls the growing camaraderie among the volunteers as they built walls, painted floors, and fabricated furniture for the studios. The physical construction became a rallying point for the

---

[25] The Queensland Institute of Technology's Student Union also pledged a capital cost contribution to the venture, recognising the station's benefits for all students, not just those at the UQ.

[26] J. Stanwell, 'The Pocket Oxford History of 4ZZZ-FM', *Radio Times*, December 1979, p. 3.

community, bringing together people who shared a common vision for independent media.

Things didn't always go smoothly for the amateur building team. Jim Beatson recalls the crew "removing two walls in the Student Union Building's first floor before discovering its floor would not support the weight of soundproof cavity-brick walls". This forced the station to change locations to the basement. Other times, questionable actions were taken to overcome financial and logistical challenges. One example involves finding a solution for the rubble generated during the studio's construction. Instead of paying for disposal, the team repurposed it to improve the station's surroundings. Anyone who visited the station after its construction may recall an area in front with a mound at the grassy knoll. "That was actually mountains of blue stone and brick and rubble that we'd smashed out of the old cellar," explains John Stanwell. "We couldn't afford to take it to the tip!" However, the Zed construction crew didn't have permission from the University or the equipment for the job.

> Basically we 'borrowed' a front-end loader down on a building site. One of our volunteer builders was a Vietnam Vet, and he jump started it and brought it up … just dug all the rubble out and built the mound and then we bought some topsoil, and we put that over the rubble and then we put turf on that. And then we took the front-end loader back and put some petrol or diesel in the tank, and no one was any wiser.

At first, university officials were not happy with the renovations, accusing 4ZZZ of stealing land from the Student Union. However, they were soon placated. According to John, "we'd created this quite attractive area which they eventually agreed was probably a good thing … looking out on a green instead of a car park".

The station also 'acquired' a baby grand piano from elsewhere on campus. The small Steinway had been neglected, and the team saw an opportunity to repurpose it for live music broadcasts. As one station worker recounts, "it was sitting gathering dust in the Schonell Theatre and effectively being used as a drinks table … so someone suggested we should probably liberate it". The baby piano was lugged to its new home. "It was quite bold," another volunteer recalls. "I was just caught up in that 'nothing's impossible' kind of headspace. What do we want? We need this, this and this." Although the acquisition didn't follow proper protocol, the team believed the piano would be better utilised at 4ZZZ. Volunteer and musician Irena Luckus likes to think "it's still there, haunting its position".

> I walked into a space filled with busy student builders. Long haired. Messy haired. Happy faces. They were building a radio station. The problem was the layout. How would they get the baby grand piano in after the studios were built. Solution - take it in now then brick it in. And so they did and there it stayed.

While Kevin Hayes' crew of amateur builders worked on the physical space, Ross Dannecker, David Aberdeen and "his team of boffins"[27] built a 1 kW FM transmitter from scratch. It was modelled from one used by 2MBS-FM in Sydney, a modified 2-m transmitter giving a theoretical output of 500 W (although the actual output was less).[28] This 'Do–It–Yourself' (DIY) attitude and success is mightily impressive especially given it was the mid-1970s, and FM technology in Australia was in its infancy. Gordon Curtis agrees. "These were all very clever people who decided to have a go at something new," he says. "Students made the original transmitter, students made most of the components that went into the studio desks and all that sort of thing." A final successful pre-transmission was conducted from the studios on Saturday, November 1st, to test the newly built transmitter on a 'non-university day' when few students would have been on campus.

* * *

It's important to note that, despite all this activity, the Federal government had only issued licence *offers*, which weren't yet formalised. Under usual circumstances, this technicality may not have caused much concern. However, by November 1975, Australian federal politics were in turmoil and Whitlam's position as Prime Minister was tenuous. The crisis stemmed from a standoff between the elected Labor government and the opposition-controlled Senate which repeatedly blocked supply bills, denying the government the funds needed to function effectively. The opposition, led by Malcolm Fraser, refused to pass the annual budget unless Whitlam called an election. Whitlam, however, would not concede, arguing that the government had been democratically elected, and the Senate was overstepping its authority. To complicate matters further, the *Broadcast Act 1942* made no provision for FM radio services, causing internal political disagreement as to which department had jurisdiction to issue the licences.

Meanwhile, the high-power transmitter and antenna on order from the United States had gone missing. Given the political insecurity of the time, Jim Beatson thought it prudent "to get that transmitter ASAP" and started "harassing the company" through which it had been ordered some months earlier. According to Jim:

> The Student Union has already paid for the thing and at that point we were told it had been lost on the New York docks. Well, I imagine the New York docks are enormous so it's absolutely conceivable that it was lost. It's also conceivable that given the political records of the lot of us and the extraordinary political atmosphere of the time that ASIO [Australian Security Intelligence Organisation],

---

[27] J. Stanwell, 'The Pocket Oxford History of 4ZZZ-FM', *Radio Times*, December 1979, p. 3.

[28] 'A Brief History of Brisbane Radio Station 4ZZZ-FM', *Radical Times*. http://radicaltimes.info/PDF/4ZZZhistory.pdf (accessed 5th October 2024).

[and] the CIA [may have been involved] ... but that's pure conjecture on my part.

As the deadlock between the Prime Minister and the Senate dragged on, Australia's Head of State representative, the Governor-General Sir John Kerr, made the unprecedented decision to dismiss Gough Whitlam on November 11th, 1975. Rather than temporarily appointing Whitlam's Deputy, the Governor-General installed the leader of the Opposition Malcolm Fraser as caretaker Prime Minister. Kerr justified his actions by citing his constitutional duty to ensure the government could function, but critics saw it as an abuse of power and a violation of democratic principles. The dismissal sparked public outrage, with protests across the country. Although Fraser went on to win the subsequent election, the dismissal remains one of the most contentious moments in Australian politics, fuelling debates about the role of the Governor-General and the limits of Executive power.

None of the twelve new radio licences promised by Whitlam's government had been signed off on, and a conservative Opposition party were now in Caretaker mode. This was a definite blow to the fledgling community broadcasting sector; however, Helen Hambling recalls the resilience of the Brisbane campaigners. "The whole thing was such an outrage ... the government being sacked and whatnot," she says.

> And yes, in amongst all of that was ... fear that it wouldn't come off. But ... I remember feeling like we could do it, you know, we could still do it ... And we set about doing that, so I didn't despair ... It was just, 'well, let's get to work'.

When Whitlam was sacked, a few people closely associated with (the still aspirant) 4ZZZ used the UQ Student Union truck—a key contribution to the station's construction—to participate in a rally protesting the dismissal. This was a choice John Stanwell describes in hindsight as "unwise," given the decision to honour the new licences now sat with a more conservative (albeit caretaker) government. More seriously, around the same time, a sympathetic senior officer in the Department of Media called Jim Beatson with alarming news.

> He rang me to say 'Jim, I doubt that you will get the licence, as I've just come out of the [Media] Minister's office, and the Queensland Police Special Branch's files are on his desk. All have been read ... you're also at the top for having the highest number of arrests by the Special Branch.[29] But many of the leading figures at your proposed station are in that pile'.

The station was also notified that a senior government official was coming to Brisbane to investigate 4ZZZ. To survive the growing political scrutiny, the

---

[29] Special Branch was an intelligence-gathering body within the Queensland Police Service tasked with investigating subversive organisations.

station purged anyone with a police record from its official board or staff, including Jim Beatson and John Stanwell.[30] "In the poisonous atmosphere in Canberra at the time, it was clear ... we needed to look like clean skins," explains Jim. "Ross Dannecker (the station's technician) was appointed Station Coordinator, though in name only. 4ZZZ survived the visit."[31] Station staff also postponed 4ZZZ's launch by one week, a short delay as they didn't want to give the caretaker government too much time to rule against honouring the licence offer. "We thought if we only made it a week," says John, "we'd keep the pressure on, and in fact, we succeeded and we got our licence signed literally on the day we went to air".

According to Jim Beatson, it was thanks to a pledge made by then Deputy Prime Minister Doug Anthony to his Lismore electorate that its university would soon have a community radio station, that the licence-promise was ultimately implemented. Many others give the highest of praise to Beatson himself for his relentless lobbying, and somewhat one-minded support for the establishment of a community radio sector. After spending hours in The University of Queensland Archives reading correspondence and other documents from the 'lobbying phase' of 4ZZZ, I absolutely agree.

Unfortunately, 4ZZZ were only offered a 1 kW licence rather than the much more powerful one they'd been originally promised (5 kW was asked for in the formal application, however, later documentation claims a 10 kW licence had initially been offered). This was incredibly disappointing for the founding members, who'd always agreed the station needed a strong transmission to reach a large audience and survive financially. There had already been a fair deal of handwringing over whether or not to broadcast on low power if the new transmitter didn't arrive in time. According to Jim, "we believed once 4ZZZ showed its hand on-air at low power [that is, as part of the radical left] we would never be granted a full-power licence". That decision was taken out of 4ZZZ's hands when they were only offered a smaller licence, a situation that would cause significant rifts at the station about its on-air sound.

The interim transmitter was positioned behind the movie screen in the Schonell Theatre, which Marc Jackson remembers helping to install with his father. According to Jim Beatson, the antenna on a tower atop the Schonell, was barely above sea level. This meant the station could only be heard clearly in the nearby suburbs close to the university, a situation Jim was never satisfied with.

> [It was] too small an area for us to generate an audience base to support our ambitious income generation plans: memberships; 4ZZZ events; sponsorships ... Yes, you could hear 4ZZZ almost anywhere in Brisbane but only if listeners

---

[30] A. Stafford, *Pig City: From The Saints to Savage Garden*, Brisbane, University of Queensland Press, 2014.

[31] J. Beatson, 'The Importance of Locally-Owned Media', *Radical Times*, 2012, http://radicaltimes.info/PDF/Beatson.pdf (accessed 14 May 2024).

purchased an expensive radio and antenna. So, the decision to start broadcasting was very difficult.[32]

Meanwhile word was getting out about a new radio station in Brisbane. Later volunteer Mark Louttit learnt about 4ZZZ from his physics teacher, who told his class about forthcoming test broadcasts and explained the station would use new Frequency Modulation technology for its high-quality stereo broadcasts. Mark says his final physics class of the year included practical advice from the teacher about buying a Hi–Fi FM stereo system—"allocate at least half of your budget to your speakers; awesome advice"—and a final reminder about the imminent launch of the station

* * *

Broadcast day—Monday December 8th, 1975—was met with an understandable mix of emotions amongst the volunteers and staff—excitement, relief and, according to Gordon Curtis, some inevitable nerves. "There'd been test broadcasts, so we knew that everything worked, but of course that's nothing like the day that it actually all happens," he says. "There was tremendous excitement and trepidation … the buildup had been going for six months." Gordon remembers a large gathering outside the front of the studio area, "and of course the speakers were on … It was a euphoric day because a lot of work and a lot of emotion had gone into this". 4ZZZ staff struggled to keep people out of the building, with too many trying to get inside to watch John through the soundproofed windows. Marian Wilkinson was one of those listening outside. "We were all just amazed that the whole thing had come together, and we were on air, after all the battles, all the hard work, all the setbacks," she says. "It felt like youth and optimism had won the day."

Margot Foster describes the day as momentous. "It was fantastic … to see us actually go to air was just so exciting." She also notes she wasn't aware of "all the background stuff that was going on with the licence," which tempered the emotions of those who had hoped for a full-power licence. John Stanwell explains:

> Obviously, we were all excited that we had finally got the new radio station on air. However, we were exhausted from the huge and relentless effort that we had undergone to create and physically construct the station; disappointed that we were only transmitting from a self-made transmitter on low power; and intimidated by what we knew would be an even greater challenge to run and pay for the station we had created.

---

[32] J. Beatson, 'The Importance of Locally-Owned Media', *Radical Times*, 2012, http://radicaltimes.info/PDF/Beatson.pdf (accessed 14 May 2024).

At midday, John Woods kicked off the broadcast—"the perfect first on-air announcer for 4ZZZ," according to Gordon Curtis, with a "beautiful voice and just a beautiful personality". John's opening statement highlighted 4ZZZ's role in expanding media diversity beyond commercial and government-controlled stations. It acknowledged the other public broadcasters who had also received licences and credited the Labor Government's policies for enabling those independent voices. While steering clear of overtly political talk, John also acknowledged resistance from established media powers and government figures, emphasising the importance of free speech and the necessity of independent broadcasting.

> While some people may not enjoy some of the material we put to air, we certainly don't deny them the right to switch us off. To attempt to impose limitations or restrictions on public broadcasting is to seriously threaten a fundamental liberty, that of free speech.

With references to political tensions surrounding new radio licences, he framed 4ZZZ as a crucial part of a broader movement for media access and diversity.

The first song to ever be played on 4ZZZ didn't come from a local, or even an Australian artist. John Woods' statement was instead followed by The Who's rock anthem, *Won't Get Fooled Again*. A critique of power and revolution, the song reflects lyricist Pete Townshend's disillusionment with the '60's countercultural experiment and its so-called societal changes.[33] The song served as a fitting metaphor for the new station. "We were thrilled when we heard the opening track," says Marian Wilkinson. "It just seemed to sum up 1975, the political chaos, the fall of Whitlam, the disaster of Bjelke-Petersen regime." For Margot Foster, every time she hears *Won't Get Fooled Again*, "it takes [her] straight there," back to the UQ studios. Sue Horton describes similar emotions:

> For many years, I could not hear that song without wanting to jump up and dance. And it's not my kind of music at all. But anyway, I still have a very fond regard for it.

Not everyone was happy with the choice. John Stanwell notes the song was less-than ideal, "but the best of a bad lot" that fit the criteria of a rock anthem with a non-party statement about the political atmosphere of the time.

* * *

In December 1975, the UQ Media Committee's dream became a reality. In a media landscape that hadn't added a new radio station for thirty years, 4ZZZ was both Queensland's first and only community radio station and its first

---

[33] C. Charlesworth, *Townshend: A Career Biography*, London, Proteus Publishing Company, 1984.

stereo FM station. It employed 12 full-time staff on wages of $100 per week[34] and broadcast from 6:00 to 1:00am, seven days a week. As a mark of independence, the station chose not to seek sponsorship revenue, hoping instead to cover costs through donations from student unions, membership fees and fundraising events. But the work was far from finished and the battle to stay on air wasn't over. 4ZZZ was only licenced for low-power transmission and reached a fraction of its potential audience. The station would travel a long and, at times, hostile road to reach its status as Queensland's *oldest* community radio and stereo FM station.[35]

---

[34] J. Beatson, 'The Importance of Locally-Owned Media', *Radical Times*, 2012, http://radicaltimes.info/PDF/Beatson.pdf (accessed 14 May 2024). Jim also notes that "by week two, the weekly wage was cut from memory, from $100 pw to $25 pw plus [unemployment benefits], if you were eligible".

[35] I can't resist but add that Helen Hambling and John Stanwell became a couple during these early days of 4ZZZ's establishment—a relationship that continues to this day.

CHAPTER 3

Decisions, Decisions, Decisions

In 1986, volunteer David Lennon made a mistake that could have sunk 4ZZZ's Radiothon before it even began. Radiothon is the station's annual fundraising appeal, and a tradition almost as old as Triple Zed itself. Working late in the production studio, David accidentally bulk-erased every pre-recorded endorsement for the upcoming event. Gone. All of them. Just like that.

Steve Sharp, the station's production coordinator, was quite understandably cheesed off. Those endorsements were vital messages of support from musicians, artists, and fellow broadcasters urging listeners to subscribe and keep the independent spirit of 4ZZZ alive. Without them the Radiothon was in serious trouble.

Faced with the fallout, David didn't make excuses. Instead, he jumped into full critical response mode, making call after call, desperately trying to salvage the situation. One of the first people he reached was Andy Nehl—a Triple Zed staff member of old, who'd moved to Sydney to work at Triple J. Andy didn't hesitate and what he sent through wasn't just any spot. It was *the* spot.

> You could stuff your face on your favourite food.
> You could blow your whole dole cheque in a day.
> You could take all kinds of weird drugs.
> You could get into heaps of hot passionate sex.
> You could win the Golden Casket[1] and break the bank at the casino.
> You could even see Joh lose the next election.
> But nothing, yeah, nothing is gonna give you that same warm inner glow as a new subscription to Triple Zed.[2]

---

[1] A form of lotto ticket.

[2] A copy of this promotion can be found at https://soundcloud.com/lemonfresh27/warm-inner-glow.

Dripping with satire, the 30 second monologue coined a phrase that became synonymous with 4ZZZ: the 'Warm Inner Glow'. For decades, the station has used it to define the intangible but unmistakable satisfaction that comes from supporting community radio.

That endorsement also lit a fire in David Lennon. His frenzied effort to salvage the campaign led to more and more production work, and he never looked back. David would go on to produce some of the most creative and iconic promo spots in 4ZZZ's history.

Radiothon 1986, officially named Radiothon Priority 102.1, ran from March 14th to 16th and raised around $33,000. It was promoted with the station's signature grit and humour: "For 72 hours we batter your eardrums, consciences and purses for donations and pledges of subscriptions."[3]

The Warm Inner Glow lives on today, pulsing through the decades of Radiothons, promotional spots and passionate Zed testimonials. It's the only rise in temperature that doesn't negatively affect climate change and the only one you can get by simply subscribing to Triple Zed.

* * *

4ZZZ doesn't exist in a vacuum; it's one of over 500 community radio stations in Australia, which together make up the largest independent media sector in the country. In contrast to much of the world, Australia has a mature and well-established third tier of broadcasting. Around the country, nearly six million people tune in to community radio stations each week—that's one in four Australians, according to the sector's National Listener Survey.[4]

Unlike 4ZZZ, most community radio stations—over three quarters—are based outside major cities.[5] In this respect, Triple Zed is not typical. In many places around the country, you're more likely to hear Top 40 classics than independent releases, or the local horseraces rather than a protest for trans kids' rights. But wherever people listen to community radio, the most common reasons given are to hear local news and information, connect with local voices and enjoy specialist music genres.[6]

Community radio stations operate on a not-for-profit basis, serving the interests of their communities rather than shareholders, unlike their commercial counterparts. Some stations cater to a specific community; there are stations for First Nations Australians, young people, seniors, ethnic and multicultural communities, religious groups, LGBTIQ+ audiences, fine music lovers and people with print disabilities. Other stations serve a broader

---

[3] 4ZZZ. 'Radiothon Priority 102.1fm', *Radio Times*, February 1986, p. 3.

[4] McNair Yellowsquares. '2024 Community Radio Listeners Survey', Audience Details, Wave 2', Community Broadcasting Association of Australia, 2024, n.p.

[5] Community Broadcasting Association of Australia. 'Roadmap 2023', Community Broadcasting Association of Australia, 2023, p. 15.

[6] McNair Yellowsquares. '2024 Community Radio Listeners Survey'.

audience—this is the case for 4ZZZ guided by the mission statement "connecting and amplifying the voices of our local communities".[7]

4ZZZ is unique in many ways, but it is also part of a much larger social movement for both media diversity and local media. Guided by the *Broadcasting Services Act 1992* and the *Community Radio Broadcasting Codes of Practice*, it's overseen by a peak body called the Community Broadcasting Association of Australia. Triple Zed is operated by a not-for-profit company and registered charity called Creative Broadcasters Ltd, meaning donations to the station are tax deductible.

This may seem a world removed from the ideals motivating 4ZZZ in the early 1970s and in some respects the station has changed dramatically, particularly with regard to the way it is managed. But there are still some familiar structures within the station. For example, listeners can still be card-carrying members through an annual subscription which gives them voting rights at 4ZZZ's Annual General Meeting. From an organisational perspective, Triple Zed has moved from consensus-based collectivism to a traditional management structure overseen by an active Board of Directors, elected at Annual General Meetings. This chapter explores the decisions about fundraising and governance that are the foundations of the station.

* * *

Once on air, the 4ZZZ founders had to make some serious decisions about how to financially sustain the station. The UQ Student Union had been generous with its initial support and pledged an annual budget, but with up to 12 staff members on a full-time (albeit low-paid) salary and a growing wish list of resources, Triple Zed would need to raise additional funds. Sponsorship had already been ruled out, as a statement in the first edition of 4ZZZ's magazine, *Radio Times* explains:

> The most striking difference about 4ZZ-FM is that the station won't be funded by endless commercials nor will it be like the A.B.C and funded by the government, so we will be relying on you, our listeners, for financial and moral support.[8]

Plans were already underway for Triple Zed to hold fundraising concerts at the UQ Student Union Complex (discussed in Chap. 7) The early 4ZZZ staff were also aware that independent radio stations in the United States had found success with a 'listener-supported' model. The Pacifica Radio Network's first station, KPFA in Berkeley, launched in 1949 as the United States' first listener-supported radio outlet.[9] At the time, the idea of a station funded directly by its

---

[7] 4ZZZ, 'Station Policy 1.5', 4ZZZ, 2025, p. 1 https://jeff.4zzz.org.au/sites/default/files/media/4ZZZ%20Station%20Policy%201.5.pdf, (accessed 26 Feb 2025).

[8] 4ZZZ, 'Why become a subscriber', *Radio Times*, Dec 75/Jan 76, p. 2.

[9] A. L. Phillip, 'Riding the waves at Pacifica radio', 3 August 2013, https://andrewlesliephillips.blogspot.com/2013/08/riding-thewaves-at-pacifica-radio-by.html#more (accessed 3rd April 2024).

audience was untested and many doubted a broadcaster could survive without corporate ads or government grants.[10] Yet Pacifica's founders moved forward with this subscription model, explicitly rejecting revenue from advertising to avoid commercial influence. This new approach presented a visionary alternative to commercial radio and challenged the era's dominant funding models by relying on its listeners for support. By proving that listener contributions could sustain a station, Pacifica opened the door for others to finance media through memberships and donations rather than ads.[11]

Seeing a clear parallel between Pacifica and 4ZZZ, the station decided to follow the American model of listener-supported radio. "We will be making ourselves self-supporting in a number of ways," continues the *Radio Times* article cited above. "But the most important means of fundraising will be the 4ZZ-FM Subscription. Basically, your Subscription is to help keep the station on air".[12]

Founding 4ZZZ member John Stanwell says that while the station offered discounts and a free copy of *Radio Times* to financial members, "we always knew that we were asking people to subscribe because they wanted to support the station not because they'd get discounts". While not articulated as such, 4ZZZ's main fundraising arm capitalised on the warm inner glow generated by supporting a worthy cause. "You subscribed because it was the right thing to do to," John says.

A 4ZZZ subscription is an annual commitment that, according to 4ZZZ's Constitution,[13] equates to being a financial member of Creative Broadcasters Limited. 4ZZZ subscribers have the right to attend, vote at, and be heard at all general meetings held by the station, and to run for election to the Board of Directors. They receive discounts on Triple Zed merchandise, at registered 4ZZZ discount outlets, and at events hosted by the station. There are a range of subscription types. Besides the regular membership (with a discounted option for low-income earners and under-18s), there are options for bands, artists, households, businesses and community groups. There are also Passionate and Super-Sub options for those who have the means to give a little more. You can even subscribe your pet, although they don't get to vote at the Annual General Meeting (which, given the bad attitude of our cat Tegan, is probably for the best).

* * *

To encourage listeners to subscribe, the station adopted the Radiothon model—a fundraising tool that evolved from early twentieth-century radio

---

[10] M. Lasar, *Pacifica Radio: The Rise of an alternative network*. Temple University Press, 2000.

[11] D. K. Dunaway, 'Pacifica Radio and Community Broadcasting'. *Journal of Radio Studies*, 12(2), 2005, pp. 240–255.

[12] 4ZZZ, 'Why become a subscriber', *Radio Times*, Dec 75/Jan 76, p. 2.

[13] 4ZZZ, 'Constitution of Creative Broadcasters Limited ACN 009 950 958 (a company limited by guarantee): Approved by members at AGM November 25, 2020', 2020, https://jeff.4zzz.org.au/sites/default/files/media/4ZZZ%20Constitution_McCulloughRobertson.pdf, (accessed 7th December 2024).

charity events.[14] These were usually short appeals rather than marathons, but after World War II the success of long-form televised fundraisers, especially Milton Berle's 16-h 1949 telethon that raised over $1 million for cancer research,[15] inspired radio stations to create their own extended on-air drives. The term 'radiothon', combining 'radio' and 'marathon', describes multi-hour or day/week-long broadcasts that keep audiences engaged with music, interviews, and appeals for pledges.

4ZZZ's first Radiothon was held early in 1978. John Stanwell says the Zed team "dreamed up the Radiothon as a way to get another peak of subscriptions," and it worked. The station raised $7000 over a weekend of special broadcasting, although an article in *Radio Times* suggests there wasn't complete confidence in the venture: "On Friday afternoon near hysteria set in as we realised we have never done this type of thing before, and could we cope? It was doubtful."[16] According to the article, "various odd and not so odd people drifted in and out all weekend, donating money into [a] giant banana positioned in the foyer of Triple Z.[17] If people didn't have money to donate, they brought in presents to the station instead that ranged from "home-grown pumpkins to strange concoction of tea". A "vealing calf" was also produced as a gift (yes, you read that correctly) but no further information was provided as to the animal's fate.

Stephen Stockwell (Snr) was Promotions Coordinator in the early '80s, and responsible for Radiothon, which involved soliciting prize donations from businesses and mobilising volunteers to work phones, process payments, and promote the event. He recalls the 1980 Radiothon as a turning point, raising a record-breaking $35,000 in one weekend. "[Radiothon] would start on Friday, often with a concert," Stephen says. "There was a big Market Day on the Saturday … and then a full-on on-air pitch on the Sunday". These Radiothon Market Days featured stalls run by local businesses, artists, and community groups selling second-hand records, clothing, books, and collectibles. There were also food and drink vendors, street performances and banana sundae eating competitions to create a festival-like atmosphere. Musician Michelle Bowden remembers a Joh Bjelke-Petersen impersonator, "who also dressed as [Joh's wife] Flo, selling pumpkin scones". Most popular though, may have been the AM radio throwing competition, introduced by John Stanwell. In 1984, the competition even featured a mechanical device that

---

[14] BBC, 'Charity appeals on the BBC', 2023, https://www.bbc.com/charityappeals/governance/history (accessed 26 April 2024).

[15] B. Higgins, 'Hollywood Flashback: Milton Berle Hosted the First Star Telethon in 1949', *The Hollywood Reporter*, 9 May 2020, https://www.hollywoodreporter.com/movies/movie-news/hollywood-flashback-milton-berle-hosted-first-star-telethon-1949-1292832/ (accessed 4 Jan 2024).

[16] 4ZZZ, 'How to make $7000 without really trying', *Radio Times*, February 1978, p. 14.

[17] 4ZZZ, *Radio Times*, p. 14.

one aspiring inventor used to throw their AM radio, "but it was badly embarrassed by the strength of the human arm".[18]

Live music made its first appearance at these Market Days during the 1982 'No Choice' Radiothon, held in the UQ car park on October 23rd. Punk bands Mystery of Sixes and "a notoriously shambolic outfit called The Pits played against a wall".[19] Victor Huml, who went on to become a Triple Zed volunteer, remembers the day well. "The AM radio throwing competition was hilarious," he says. "They were also selling records on the day, and I bought both [Brisbane band] Razar 7 inches [singles]. I think they were $5 each. What a score!" In addition to the usual Market Day shenanigans, the mid '80s saw the introduction of 'TV smashing' which involved dozens of televisions decorated with photocopied faces of politicians (including the Premier, of course), lined up and ready to be destroyed (Fig. 3.1). Punters paid a dollar to buy half a brick to throw at the TVs, "and then punks moved in with crowbars".[20] David Lennon remembers preparing the televisions—donated by listeners—for their impending destruction. "We had to … cut a small hole in the back of the … tubes to let out the vacuum otherwise the TVs would implode when being smashed." Rumour has it that an ounce of green leafy material was discovered stashed in the back of one of the donated televisions, possibly an extra donation for Radiothon staff.

For the 1987 Market Day a small marquee was set up on the University oval for bands Kremlin and Groovy Things, "while the acrobatic Rock 'n' Roll Circus did their thing wherever they saw fit". In March 1988, 4ZZZ held another Market Day on the Oval. The stage was a simple mat laid out on a flat patch of grass, and the line-up included Batswing Saloon, whose band subscription had won them a generous Radiothon prize two years prior. This coveted prize of a studio recording package allowed them to record their single *Harold and Maude* and made them the first all-female band in Brisbane to release a 7-inch record.[21] Guitarist Michelle Bowden has a lot of Radiothon luck; her bands Gravelrash and The Worm Turns have also won band subscription prizes, "so Triple Zed support has always been a pretty big part of getting my musical endeavours off the ground," she says.

Correspondence held in The University of Queensland Archives reveals that University administration, including the Chief Security Officer and his team, had not been told the 1988 Market Day was going ahead, let alone given authorisation. Noise complaints were received, students' cars were towed to make room for the markets, and alcohol was sold without a permit. While

---

[18] S. Stockwell, 'Radiothon', *Radio Times*, April/May 1984, p. 2.

[19] G. Williams, *Generation Zed: No other radio like this*, Brisbane, Kingswood Press, 2000, p. 59.

[20] K. Torpy, 'Meet Market, Triple Z's annual bash bypasses the mainstream', *The Courier Mail*, 21 Oct 2002, p12.

[21] Brisbane Music Graveyard, 'Harold And Maude [Single]', https://thebmg.bandcamp.com/album/harold-and-maude-single, (accessed 23rd June 2024).

Fig. 3.1 Photo of televisions ready to be smashed as a fundraising activity at a Radiothon held at the University of Queensland, St Lucia; photographer unknown; circa 1982

4ZZZ were to organise further Market Days off-campus, there wouldn't be another one held at the University of Queensland until 1995 (see Chap. 8).

4ZZZ also organised larger Radiothon benefit gigs featuring big-name bands. During Stephen Stockwell (Snr)'s time, 4ZZZ was booking now-iconic Australian acts. "It was a time when bands like Mental as Anything and Midnight Oil, we could get them to play for Triple Zed," Stephen says. "They weren't that big that you couldn't do them in the refectory, and they would bring two thousand people out at any time they were around." My favourite Radiothon concert memory comes from a few years later when U.K. artist Billy Bragg played for Triple Zed, raising over $2200 for the station.[22] According to Billy, "when [he] returned to Brisbane in 1989, it was shortly after 4ZZZ had been ousted from the campus of the University of Queensland by right-wing student activists," speaking of events that we'll cover in the next chapter. "It was imperative that I expressed some of the solidarity that I had spoken about on my previous trip by playing a benefit for the station, back at the Easts Leagues Club." Around 2500 fans squeezed into the club, craning their necks as Billy Bragg belted out a generous collection of songs. This included *Waiting for the Great Leap Forward* with a lyric change to sing in support of 4ZZZ, which brought a roar from the crowd. "Just like in '87, it was a coming together of diverse groups of radicals and ravers, who crowded into the room to express their solidarity with 4ZZZ," Billy says. "To me, it was a definitive expression of the importance of dissenting culture in a conservative climate".

* * *

---

[22] According to Collective meeting minutes.

The heart of 4ZZZ's Radiothon has always been the on-air subscription drive, where announcers offer incentives to encourage listeners to call in (or log on to the website) and subscribe. As far as I'm aware, this has always included a suite of major prizes that each subscriber goes in the draw for a chance to win. In 1978 this included a Yamaha tuner donated by Rose Music, a light show to the value of $200 from Gridley's Lights, and donation from Cheviot Industries of a set of Mag wheels to fit any car.[23] Radiothon continues the tradition of major prizes, and local businesses still support 4ZZZ with donations. In 2024, subscribers had the chance to win prizes such as a personalised arcade-style gaming cabinet from Netherworld, an annual pass to Five Star Cinemas and a year's supply of beer from Felons Brewing Company.

Another Radiothon trick of old was the live auction, which Stephen Stockwell (Snr) says was particularly hectic. "You become this manic, crazy person and just try and drum up as much money as possible," he says. However, by early 2000, the on-air bids got a little out of control. Announcer, Quentin Ellison—who has been volunteering at Zed for over 25 years—remembers 'bidding wars' where listeners would offer a donation on top of their subscription with the prize going to the highest offer. "The announcers would [sound] like a racetrack commentator [reading] the bids that were placed," says Quentin. The problem was that people would get caught up in the hype and pledge more than they could afford, which before the days of online payments, meant that no-one would end up with the prize.

Sometimes announcers chose a stick, rather than carrot approach. *Queer Radio*'s Blair Martin instituted a "Radiothon Punitive Action" during a morning program, where he informed the audience that he would play Black Lace's song *Agadoo* nonstop until $250's worth of subscriptions was received. The total was reached in less than ten minutes, which was great for 4ZZZ but not so pleasant for one Zed announcer who later told Blair they were "trapped in their car on the way to work, unable to phone in, subscribe, and stop it!". Quentin Ellison adds he wasn't too shy to put radio guests on the spot during Radiothon and ask them if their subscriptions were up to date. "[There's] nothing like a guilt-out when they haven't," he says. "Next thing you know, they make it down to reception and subscribe."

Radiothon at 4ZZZ has never just about fundraising. It is also a communal experience that bonds volunteers and listeners alike through hard work, excitement, and a lot of fun. Many Zed Folk first entered the station's world during Radiothon, swept up by its energy: David Lennon, for instance, recalls how "Radiothon was a good time to start volunteering at 4ZZZ," describing the station at that time as "a hectic but amazing place" where camaraderie was forged under pressure. Similarly, when Charlie Woods first stepped into Zed, they had no idea it was Radiothon season. "I ended up being there nearly every day from like 8:00am till about 7:00pm just doing the Radiothon stuff," they say, eventually becoming Radiothon Coordinator themselves.

---

[23] 4ZZZ, 'How to make $7000 without really trying', *Radio Times*, February 1978, p. 14.

For many, Radiothon embodies the chaotic and joyful spirit of 4ZZZ. Speaking of the early 1990s, Alex Wightman[24] remembers how "people were virtually at the station 24/7, constantly working [but] there was a lot of partying that went alongside the franticness of the Radiothon itself," while volunteer Anthony likens Radiothon in the early 2000s to "Christmas at Triple Zed," a time when "everyone was having a great time, everyone was in it together". Even amidst the stress, there was a profound sense of collective achievement. As Danika E puts it, "Radiothon sorted things out a little bit. It brought in money quickly when we needed it most". It remains a cornerstone of the 4ZZZ fundraising calendar.

* * *

By choosing to operate without sponsorship revenue, 4ZZZ made a strong statement about its identity and values. In a similar manner, the founding members put a great deal of consideration into how Triple Zed should be managed. The station was very much the product of the '70's protest era, and its founders wanted to avoid the hierarchical approaches to decision-making typical of commercial and mainstream media. This wasn't about just running a radio station—it was about practising the kind of alternative politics that Zed folks believed in. The founders set up a system for station meetings, that ended up known as 'the Collective', where decisions were made by everyone involved in the station, not just a few people at the top. For nearly 30 years, 4ZZZ operated this way using a distinctive model of consensus decision-making.

Consensus isn't a concept that 4ZZZ invented. Dating from the anti-nuclear and feminist movements of the late '60s and early '70s, consensus decision-making was pretty much the norm in leftist and liberal organisations looking for more inclusive, non-hierarchical ways to operate. According to founding member, Jim Beatson:

> [4ZZZ] started at a time when progressives believed in workers' control ... We believed that a group of very smart people, collectively, would come up with a better solution to complex problems, than individual bosses.

Consensus decision-making also aims to foster social change from within an organisation, and while fellow founder John Stanwell admits there were some challenges at times, "the common purpose generated loyalty and tolerance".

In a consensus process, everyone in the group must agree on a decision (or at least not be opposed to it) before they move forward. It's not about majority rule but rather making sure everyone's thoughts are considered and the final decision works for the whole group.[25] Consensus decision-making is an

---

[24] Alex Wightman passed in 2015, after I interviewed him for this book.

[25] T. Hartnett, *Consensus-oriented decision-making: The CODM model for facilitating groups to widespread agreement*, Gabriola, Canada, New Society Publishers, 2011.

approach that values inclusivity, respect, and shared responsibility, and makes sure different viewpoints are heard before making a final call while recognising expertise within the group. It usually involves open discussions, active listening and tweaking ideas until there's a solution that no one strongly disagrees with. While it can take more time, consensus decision-making aims to strengthen teamwork and commitment to whatever is decided.

Stephen P joined 4ZZZ in 1978 as a volunteer. He was a big fan of radio and liked the alternative ethos of the station but had never been exposed to consensus decision-making before. As he explains, "it wasn't communism and it wasn't democracy as it's practised in the industrialised West, where one block of people argues against another and whoever gets the most numbers wins". Instead, Stephen says decisions were met when "we all sort of felt okay about [it]".

The Collective met weekly and was compulsory for paid staff. Anyone who volunteered, or even 'just' had a subscription to the station, was eligible to attend. "We'd all sit in the foyer, and discuss whatever business decisions were being made,"[26] says Linden Woodward, a journalist at 4ZZZ from 1979 to 1982. "The full-time staff would present their views and all the information they held. And things would be discussed and decisions made."[27] By all accounts, the 4ZZZ Collective functioned effectively for maybe its first ten years. According to early member, Margot Foster, the station meetings were very well attended and helped keep the station on track, even during its development phase. "Everybody was absolutely eagle eyed," she says. "Because we were deadline driven to get on air … and so the focus was really, really razor sharp."[28] Early journalist, Dan Flannery agrees, saying "people put as much effort into Collective meetings as they did the rest of the week".

Linden Woodward says Collective decisions were made "efficiently and effectively," which may have been helped by "an imperative to, if possible, finish in time to get to the Royal Exchange for a drink or two afterwards".[29] The tradition of the post-Collective drink was still in place when Andy Nehl joined the Zed team in the early 1980s. "You'd argue it out at the Station Meeting, then you'd go down … to have drinks at the RE and be best mates," he says, "and treat the thing very professionally".[30] While there's no longer a Collective in place at 4ZZZ, the weekly post-work drinks tradition continues. On a Thursday evening you'll usually find a core group of staff and volunteers at Netherworld—a nearby independent bar/arcade/diner they affectionately refer to as Studio Four.

For many Zed folk, the Collective was a welcomed education in radical political structures. Liz Willis says she felt "politically naïve" when she started

---

[26] Unpublished transcript of interview with Linden Woodward by 4ZZZ volunteer, Scott Mercer, recorded in 2020 for the A to Triple Zed podcast series.

[27] Unpublished transcript of interview with Linden Woodward.

[28] Unpublished transcript of interview with Margot Foster by 4ZZZ volunteer, Scott Mercer, recorded in 2020 for the A to Triple Zed podcast series.

[29] Unpublished transcript of interview with Linden Woodward.

[30] G. Williams, *Generation Zed*, Brisbane, Kingswood Press, 2000, p. 15.

volunteering at 4ZZZ in the early 1980s before becoming a fulltime staff member, "so it was all a bit of a mystery to me," she says. "Although I used to think it was amazing, you know, just the idea, the concept, the governance model." According to Stephen P, "formally administering something as big and concrete and functional as a radio station in that way, was a new idea". He says 4ZZZ "made you aware ... that you didn't just have to do things the way the [previous] generation did". Deb Strutt started a little after Stephen in 1982. For her, Collective was an "incredible experience". "I was young and impressionable," she says. "I'd never experienced politics before ... it was a really good way to learn politics and democracy."

However, let's not over-romanticise the early Collective days. Consensus decision-making can take a lot of time; since the goal is to get (almost) everyone on board, discussions and negotiations can drag on, slowing things down.[31] Future Australian Democrats Leader and Greens Party Senator Andrew Bartlett wasn't a fan. For him, they were "a real nightmare ... because they were so unproductive". He found the meetings were "unfocused and went on far too long," while "one or two people could stop something happening even after you had spent three hours talking about it".

Other critics of the consensus model claim that people who are regularly around an organisation (for example, the full-time staff) ultimately have more power, regardless of the decision-making processes in place. As Linden Woodward points out, the staff who were at the station full time "obviously had closer and more detailed knowledge of issues". She says it made sense for others attending the station meetings to take their opinions on board. According to Linden this didn't seem to create problems. "People would listen respectfully to their views, and I'd say mostly supported them," she says, "[but] it wasn't a case of volunteers sitting and meekly being told what would happen".[32] However, by the mid-'80s, Dan Flannery felt the Collective (and by extension, the station) had become cliquey. For collective organisations to function properly, he says, "you need some new blood, all the time". Dan even took a proposal to Collective that staff only hold a paid position for two years to discourage faction-building but says the idea didn't gain any traction.

* * *

John Stanwell admits that from the start a structure was put in place at Collective to act as "protection" so that "volunteers, including those who had only recently joined," couldn't dominate station meetings. Known as 'negative quorum' it meant a majority of Triple Zed's paid staff needed to be present for a decision to stand. "[Staff] could leave the meeting and break that

---

[31] T. Hartnett, *Consensus-oriented decision-making: The CODM model for facilitating groups to widespread agreement*, Gabriola, Canada, New Society Publishers, 2011.

[32] Unpublished transcript of interview with Linden Woodward by 4ZZZ volunteer, Scott Mercer, recorded in 2020 for the A to Triple Zed podcast series.

quorum [to stop a motion being passed]," John says. "To the best of my knowledge, that power was never required [or] used."

This defence mechanism became redundant when 4ZZZ was no longer able to pay wages. As discussed in Chap. 4, paid positions became much more difficult to sustain in the mid-'80s as 4ZZZ's financial health declined. There's a clear parallel between the radio station becoming more reliant on volunteers and growing criticism of the Collective process. Linda Carroli was Station Coordinator from 1985 to 1987. She recognises the problems that engulfed many of the meetings at that time. "I guess the elephant in the room is always the Collective," she says, "this rippling, pulsating thing". Linda saw a lot of conflicts played out, "sometimes really unpleasant ones," particularly around programming decisions and what 'good radio' should sound like.

Plenty of people I've spoken to mentioned embittered arguments about a range of issues, especially about the station's musical direction. Collective minutes of the time reveal a litany of complaints and debates about the merits and pitfalls of almost every conceivable genre of music. When the Murri[33] community became more closely involved in the station and started playing Country and Western, some members of the 4ZZZ Collective didn't know what to think. As Liz Willis explains:

> None of that stuff ever went to air on Triple Zed. It was beyond uncool. It was … so controversial, they're playing country music, they're talking about football! … People were not liking it!

Another problem with consensus decision-making at 4ZZZ was that it required people from all walks of life, of differing ages, education and personal experiences, to engage in civilised and rational conversation with one another. At times, with people working together for little or no money—and a lot of strong personalities living in each other's pockets—it was difficult to keep a level head. Debates at Collective could become very passionate and often emotional. Tony Biggs, an announcer for the first half of the '80s, admits to occasionally putting his foot through a plasterboard wall out of frustration. Fellow announcer, Sue Williamson, remembers Tony "going off his head all the time" but also admitted "it was actually good the way he stuck to his guns".[34]

It was common for the Collective format at Triple Zed to favour people who were more confident, charismatic or simply just louder. Sue started at the station when she was 17 and says she was "really shy, but by the end of a couple of years [she] was fine speaking at Collective meetings". According to Liz Willis, some people were more skilled than others at navigating the debates. "Any of those kids that had done politics at uni … let's say, they 'worked' that system a lot

---

[33] 'Murri' is a self-identifying contemporary term used by Indigenous Australians from Queensland and northern New South Wales.

[34] G. Williams, *Generation Zed*, Brisbane, Kingswood Press, 2000, p. 15.

better than I ever did or understood," she says. Alex Wightman agrees. He was around the station, on and off, for over 15 years. Initially attracted to 4ZZZ's activist roots, he brought with him a clear understanding and appreciation of consensus decision-making. However, he also recognised that dominant personalities had an impact on the way the 4ZZZ Collective functioned. "Stronger voices can cause a sort of mass conformity effect that gives the appearance *of* democracy more than it *provides* democracy," Alex says. "It's something you really need to be careful of [because] people can be as railroaded by that as much as they are by the traditional democratic voting system."

In mid-1989, Linda Carroli wrote an article for *Radio Times*, addressing critiques of the collective process.[35] In it, she suggested that a collective stops working because its members "don't participate or don't play the game fairly, or because people abuse it". Linda proposed 4ZZZ reassess its decision-making processes and "work towards a model of collectivity that is most amenable to the objectives/functions of 4ZZZ" and then support that structure. The article concluded somewhat prophetically; "If, in time, this structure proves to be restrictive and inhibitive, then it is time to change the structure and effect a new model of collective organisation".[36]

* * *

Here's a quick but necessary spoiler—4ZZZ owns the building that houses its studios and offices (Fig. 3.2). With the stability of a permanent home, and especially once paying off a mortgage, 4ZZZ folk began to take more notice of the station's legal structure. The station had always been operated by a not-for-profit company and as such legally required to have a Board of Directors. For many years, this obligation was met on paper, yet decision-making power was left to the Collective. As '90s volunteer, Darren J explains, "the board was always secondary to the Collective. They just rubber-stamped things".

During the mid-1990s, the value of an active Board of Directors gained popularity; one that could focus on more strategic long-term planning and work alongside the immediate and reactive decision-making role of the Collective. However, the Collective did, from time to time, flex its power over the Board of Directors. I remember one occasion when the Board voted to sign Triple Zed up for a Discount Voucher Book—a popular fundraising tool of the time. Under the scheme, 4ZZZ would raise money selling the books, which were basically a collection of coupons offering special deals on various services or products. Fiona P was on the Board at the time, one of the few members who didn't support the idea. "Collective did not want this fundraising idea to happen because the voucher book was full of businesses that we didn't want to have anything to do with [e.g. McDonald's and other multinational corporations]," she says. According to Fiona:

[35] L. Carroli, 'But it's a Collective', *Radio Times July/Augst*, 1988, p. 11.

[36] L. Carroli, 'But it's a Collective', p. 11.

Fig. 3.2 Aerial photo of Zed Towers and neighbours in Fortitude Valley, taken by Robert Broeders; 2018

> We had to put in a vote of no confidence in the Board essentially ... we had to do that because if the Board was doing something completely against the wishes of the entire Collective body, it didn't seem to make much sense to go with the decision.

After ten years of operating almost solely on volunteer labour, the station also began to pay a few staff again. This constancy gave the Collective a more solid membership. According to volunteer Geoff Wilson, "some real eager beaver people turned up and [pointed out] some procedures were hopelessly out of date, and the place got a bit of a revamp". Jason Pfingst was Station Bookkeeper at this time. He remembers it was "some of the younger generation" who took on roles on the Board, "fully understanding their responsibilities as Directors" and bringing "some stability and cohesion through their different personalities". For a while, a core crew of volunteers and paid staff, working alongside an active Board of Directors and a relatively well-functioning Collective, provided a strong foundation for the station. Abbie Trott was a volunteer around this time and says, "it was a really good ... training ground in how to make things work". The structure at the time also allowed coordinators to focus on their roles without too much micromanagement.

In the late 1990s the effectiveness of Collective again came under scrutiny. What was once an energetic and vigorous opportunity to test out new ideas about the goals and roles of the station, again seemed time-consuming and pointless. Part of the problem may have been that newer arrivals weren't always schooled in how the consensus model functioned. According to Stephen P, in the late 1970s "there were bits and pieces of literature around the place explaining, 'this is how we're trying to run the station'". However, when announcer Stefan Armbruster left 4ZZZ in 1991, he believed "the whole concept of a Collective was only loosely understood by people," including himself. When Peter Rohweder joined in 1994, first as a volunteer but later as Finance Officer and Station Manager, little had changed. Peter says he found Collective to be a "beast of a thing" to understand. "You grow up thinking, 'it's not my place to talk' because you're new to the organisation, so you sit and you want to learn what's going on, what's the etiquette," Peter says. "It was very combative ... people yelling across the room and stuff like that." Jason Pfingst believes Collective was also negatively impacted because members weren't familiar with 4ZZZ's history and ongoing projects yet were able to participate in key decisions. "The differing levels of engagement and knowledge made it difficult to reach consensus," he says.

The exact rules of Collective were often a hot topic of debate. My understanding of the 1990's procedure is this; if we couldn't reach a consensus after three meetings in a row the issue would be put to a vote. However, only people who had been at two of those three meetings were eligible to vote. Collective also needed a minimum number of people (quorum) for the meeting to count. Simple right? Week after endless week we'd argue about when a stalemate could be broken with 'a majority rules' vote.

Throughout the '90s, Collective meetings proved to be both loved and despised.

Darren J says he had profound admiration for 4ZZZ's governance model of that time. While he admits the meetings were often long and frustrating, he says "at the end, you felt like you'd been part of something meaningful". Darren credits 4ZZZ with shaping his views on effective collaboration, lessons he carried into his personal and professional life. "I've never had an experience like that anywhere else," he says. "It taught me how people can reach decisions collectively and equitably." However, Collective meetings were "a source of dread" for volunteer Bec Moore,[37] because of the frequent conflict. "They were my weekly nightmare," Bec says, "pure political warfare. No one had been in all week, and then they'd turn up Monday night, and war would begin". I have similar memories of volatile Collective meetings in the '90s, that volunteer Annie Winter shares.

> You could get a chair thrown at you, you could watch people hurl themselves across tables to try and strangle people, it was fucking good stuff mate! We were passionate, sometimes useless, but very fucking passionate.

Danika E joined the station in the early 2000s when still at high school. She soon noticed that people went to Collective meetings only when there was something controversial on the agenda. Meetings became forums for factions within the station. "You'd look around the room ... and try and figure out who was going

---

[37] Bec Moore passed in 2016, after I interviewed her for this book.

to be on your side," Danika says. "Most of the time I'd just sit around and watch because it was the best entertainment to watch these people just fight."

* * *

By the early 2000s, a range of changes to unemployment and student entitlements made it more difficult for people to volunteer. For others, their interests rested in the media itself rather than the organisational structures that underpinned it. In a nutshell, people simply weren't attending the Collective meetings, even after they were cut back to once-a-month affairs. Important decisions were delayed as a result. By this time, volunteer Jamie Hume had the unenviable position of Collective Chair, a role that involved organising the meetings. By 2004, Jamie found himself alone at the table. "It basically got to the point where I was the only one turning up," he says. After months of "waiting for Godot," Jamie made the decision to "pull the plug". He didn't make a big deal about it; he just stopped sending out meeting reminders. "No one noticed," he says. "No one said anything to me … it was just … 'ah, Collective is dead, okay, who wants a cup of coffee?'"

Reflecting on why people stopped attending, Jamie suggests that the shift of power towards the Board and individual coordinators may have played a role. "I guess over time, power became more concentrated in the hands of the various coordinators and committees," he explains. While Collective once had the authority to overrule the Board, its influence diminished, and volunteers seemed content to let decisions be handled by station leadership. More and more people at 4ZZZ were involved with the station as a side-project, needing to work elsewhere to pay the bills, and possibly trusting in the organisation's ability to run itself.

Current station manager, Jack McDonnell says he's reluctant to comment on the past structure, as he "wasn't there for it [and] wasn't really sure how it work[ed]" (you're not the only one, Jack!). However, he suspects "life is very busy … and it would be very hard to get a lot of people here consistently to make decisions". Jack also points out that, in the digital age, "things move a lot more quickly," which means decisions also need to be made without too much delay.

Since the Collective disbanded over twenty years ago, 4ZZZ has operated with either a Station Manager or a small management team, advised by an active Board of Directors. There have been a few occasions when volunteers and subscribers have shown their dissatisfaction with management and/or the Board by calling for Extraordinary Meetings and holding votes of no-confidence, showing that the 4ZZZ community still wants a certain level of hands-on engagement. It's been at least ten years since anyone has been ousted in such a fashion. For almost everyone at Triple Zed today, volunteer or otherwise, this is the only organisational structure they have known.

CHAPTER 4

The Early Bird that Didn't Catch the Worm

Tuesday, December 13th, 1988, had been an ordinary day. Mike Brown, one of 4ZZZ's regular announcers, set his alarm clock before bed. The station was stretched thin for volunteers, and he'd promised to cover the 9:00am shift. Like most of us at that time, his clock radio was tuned permanently to 102.1fm.

When the alarm buzzed the next morning, it was still dark. Mike half-heard something through the low hum of the radio: a mumble, a voice in the distance. Groggy, he hit the snooze button and rolled over. Five minutes later, the alarm repeated its wake-up call. The same voice, still mumbling. Same message, looping. Bleary-eyed, Mike finally turned the volume up properly. What he heard jolted him into reality.

It was an emergency broadcast. A woman's voice—the breakfast shift announcer, Anita Earl—repeating over and over that 4ZZZ had been kicked out of its studios by the newly elected conservative Student Union. "All announcers and supporters," she urged, "get out to St. Lucia right now".

Mike threw off the covers, heart pounding. 6:00am might as well have been the middle of the night back then. Still half-asleep but running on pure adrenaline, he stumbled out of his room and down the hallway of the share house he lived in with Greg Fryer, his bandmate and fellow 4ZZZ volunteer.

Without hesitation, Mike pounded on Greg's door, yelling loud enough to shake the windows. "The fascists have taken Triple Zed!" he shouted. Inside, Greg bolted upright. No questions, no second-guessing. That one sentence was all it took.

"Fuck, we're on, Comrade. Let's go!" he called back. Within minutes, they were both out the door, racing towards St. Lucia.

Later, Greg thought, "we didn't really think about it, did we? We just acted".

* * *

The second half of the 1980s were tough times for 4ZZZ and its workers, and many agree that the station's financial health became increasingly shaky during these years. A variety of factors contributed to its funding woes, with the ever-rising cost of living compounded by fluctuating levels of both university and community support. However, shifts in the local music industry had one of the most significant impacts. For Triple Zed's first ten years, a major source of its income came from live music promotion, with the station hosting gigs for local, interstate, and international bands, promoting events for either a share of ticket sales or a fixed fee (see Chap. 7). Booking bands had become dramatically more expensive, with insurance a growing financial liability. Corporate promoters and larger venues had started to monopolise the live music market, effectively squeezing out small operators like 4ZZZ. Putting on gigs became an unpredictable venture. It was also increasingly difficult for 4ZZZ to hold fundraising shows on the university campus.

Exacerbating all this, 4ZZZ was a place of employment and salaries comprised a significant component of the budget. When it first started operations, 4ZZZ employed 12 full-time members of staff, including announcers, journalists and a Station Coordinator. According to founding member Helen Hambling, "there was a very strong view that we should be able to pay salaries ... and it was good pay at the time ... let's value ourselves, you know". Station finances still appeared healthy when Dan Flannery joined the team, first as a volunteer and then as a paid journalist in the early '80s. Not only did the station receive support from the University of Queensland, but the Queensland University of Technology Student Union also made regular financial contributions. As Dan describes it, there were "radical student unions in those days all over the place". However, reflecting on 4ZZZ's early financial structure, Helen admits it may have been a little naive to expect to sustain such a large crew of paid staff. "Never mind the numbers," she says, "we just thought that's what you *should* do".

For ten years, a core team had been retained on wages equivalent to, slightly above, or double 'the dole' (standard government unemployment payment), depending on who you ask and when they were employed at the station. Anne Jones, Station Coordinator from 1982 to 1983, remembers "we weren't getting a huge wage, but we were getting the so-called basic wage ... you could afford to live on that ... it was kind of amazing". This became harder to sustain into the '80s. As revenue declined, paid staff at 4ZZZ frequently had to forgo wages to keep the station running. Amanda Collinge was employed as a journalist in 1983, but two years later it was clear the station was struggling financially.

> There was a period where ... we sort of stopped being paid because [4ZZZ] ran out of money ... It was a radical drop ... And we all had to go and get other

jobs. I remember a bunch of us ended up working at Scoops, which was the ice cream parlour ... three or four nights a week at Scoops as well as at Triple Zed ... you know, when you're young, you're very passionate. We're completely dedicated and committed. And yeah, so we really worked for peanuts.

Journalist Claire Grenet also lived through this period of constant financial uncertainty. By 1986, she says Zed staff were "going off wages more than we ever had. We'd have these periods where the station just couldn't afford to pay us, so we had to go without". Sometimes this lasted weeks at a time, with no guarantees of back pay. Andrew Bartlett was employed as Finance Coordinator for part of this time and remembers "it got pretty threadbare" with the lack of finances impacting station morale. "I think in those last few years of the decade, you know, when we just couldn't afford to have genuine paid staff, it really fell apart pretty badly," Andrew says. "Not just money wise, but sharpness, you know, focus and coherence ... it was a bit of a shambles, to be honest."

I've spoken to countless people who moved away from 4ZZZ during this period to protect their mental health and financial safety. "Thank God others stuck it out and ran with it, because 4ZZZ is still here today," Claire Grenet reflects. Folks weren't only leaving the station, but Brisbane itself, especially "those of a creative bent who confronted the petty censorship and political repression that was the Premier's stock-in-trade".[1] This extended to activists and other marginalised folk who had the means to leave. Founding member Alan Knight left for Sydney as early as 1976:

> I come from the working class. Basically, I had to make my way, such as it was, and Sydney was a much more liberal environment to work. Perhaps I should have stayed around a bit longer ... after seven years of activism in Brisbane, it does get you down a bit. And I think the people who stayed in Brisbane paid a very heavy price for it.

As employment opportunities became less stable at 4ZZZ and much of the target audience and volunteer base were leaving Brisbane in droves, 4ZZZ's relationship with the UQ Student Union also began to deteriorate. Though the station had enjoyed a long, symbiotic relationship with the Union, by the mid-to-late 1980s the relationship had become strained. 4ZZZ Finance Coordinator Stephen Davies says the relationship between the station and Student Union became increasingly tense during this time. According to Stephen, the Student Union was shifting ideologically, becoming less tolerant of the station's radical politics and unorthodox operations. This conflict was not immediate or explosive but manifested in a slow and growing hostility. "I think the Union was getting more conservative and having less patience with these radical ratbags downstairs," Stephen says. As Finance Coordinator, he found himself in an awkward position. His role was not just about managing money—it also required sensitive negotiations with the increasingly hostile

---

[1] S. Stockwell, 'Alternative Media in Brisbane: 1965–1985', *Queensland Review*, vol 14 no 1, 2007, p. 75–87.

Fig. 4.1 Photo of 4ZZZ premises, University of Queensland, St Lucia, taken by David Lennon; 1985

Student Union to ensure 4ZZZ's continued operation. Stephen's instinct was to avoid confrontation. "I wanted to do what I could not to wind them up, because *a lot* of what we did wound them up," he explains.

This seemed a logical approach; the Student Union controlled 4ZZZ's physical space (Fig. 4.1), renting the building for a nominal fee and providing free access to university resources, such as photocopying and printing. The Union also handled some payroll processing and provided small financial contributions, as well as meal vouchers for staff and volunteers. However, as Student Union leadership became less aligned with 4ZZZ's political stance, they grew more reluctant to extend this support. Claire Grenet noticed the Student Union's support gradually being clawed back, as the station started losing access "bit by bit". "First it was meal vouchers, then photocopying, and eventually the funding itself … we could see it all slipping away," she says.

* * *

The latter half of the 1980s was also proving problematic for the Queensland government. While the State's political climate was still dominated by Joh Bjelke-Petersen's long-standing rule, his leadership was unravelling as allegations of corruption within his government and the police force gained public attention. His ill-fated 'Joh for Prime Minister' campaign in 1987 backfired, weakening support even within his own party. Meanwhile, media investigations revealed widespread police corruption, illegal gambling, and vice operations protected by high-ranking officials. 4ZZZ, as one of the few media outlets willing to challenge Bjelke-Petersen's rule, played a crucial role in exposing this corruption. By providing independent, unfiltered reporting and fostering activism against corruption, 4ZZZ helped maintain public pressure for accountability. It was the ABC's national television exposé, *Moonlight State* (1987), however, that caused the most damage to the Queensland government. The documentary was written by the award-winning Chris Masters, and produced by early 4ZZZ journalist, Sean Hoyt. The documentary provided evidence that senior police officials were accepting bribes to protect illegal brothels and gambling operations, and that key Queensland political figures were complicit.

In response to the public outcry generated by *Moonlight State*, the National Party (formerly County Party) reluctantly established the Fitzgerald Inquiry, led by Tony Fitzgerald QC. The inquiry quickly exposed deep-seated corruption within both the police force and government, implicating Members of Parliament, high-ranking police officers, and senior political figures. As damning evidence mounted, internal pressure forced Bjelke-Petersen to step down from his Premier position in December 1987, marking the end of his 19-year tenure.

David Lennon was a regular volunteer at Zed for at least 20 years, starting in 1981. He was an announcer, promotions coordinator and one of the most creative producers I've heard. He sums up the bittersweet consequences of the Premier's fall from grace.

> The thorn in ZZZ's side for the last twelve years was gone! Our nemesis was gone! But that was the problem. 4ZZZ's whole identity was so tied up as the lone voice against this regime, from its beginnings in 1975 ... What does Batman do without the Joker? What does the Phantom do without evil in the world?

Even after Bjelke-Petersen stepped down, the conservative National Party still held power and was preparing for Brisbane to host the World Expo in 1988. Life in Queensland continued to be less than ideal for marginalised communities and others outside of the mainstream. Cal Crilly—a volunteer who, like David, chose to stick around—could see the city's counterculture movement struggling as police harassment continued. "All the venues ... had cops coming in, and people from Triple Zed were getting raided," Cal says.

> They were getting ready for Expo, and anyone who looked strange on the streets was getting searched. Heaps of people had gone to Melbourne and Sydney. And so Triple Zed had lost all of its listeners.

Fewer listeners renewed their subscription memberships, even if they stayed in Brisbane. Cal recalls filling in as Finance Coordinator in the later part of 1988, when months passed by without anyone subscribing to the station. Andrew Stafford summarised it well in his book, *Pig City*: selling 'warm inner glow' wasn't enough to keep the station alive in the age of economic rationalism.[2]

* * *

[2] A. Stafford, *Pig city: from the Saints to Savage Garden*, St Lucia, University of Queensland Press, 2006.

By 1988, tensions between the station and the UQ Student Union were at their peak. As former Station Coordinator Anne Jones explains:

> The student body was changing. Students were less interested in changing the world and more interested in securing a good job with an attractive wage package ... with student politics growing more conservative as well.[3]

In late March, a Student Union council meeting refused to approve 4ZZZ's quarterly administrative budget of $4300. The station quickly jumped on the offensive and produced an announcement encouraging listeners to call the Student Union and register their objections to the funding freeze. The radio spot opened with the iconic phrase, "we interrupt this broadcast," and reminded people they could also help by subscribing to the station. But as David Lennon points out, "ZZZ had been crying poverty for years and many listeners considered it as crying wolf".[4]

To rub salt into the struggling community radio station's wounds, a conservative faction called The Better Alternative (TBA) won the UQ Student Union election in September. Led by 19-year-old medical student Victoria Brazil, TBA claimed no political affiliation during its campaign. However, it was later revealed that Victoria and two other union executives were members of the National Party with another eight affiliated with the equally right-wing Liberal Party. For the first time since the station was established, 4ZZZ's key connection with the university and, more concerning, its property manager, was ideologically opposed to all the station stood for. With most of its fundraising and promotional income drying up and UQ Student Union funding reduced, it felt close to a death knell for the Triple Zed team. The radio station was limping towards the end of the year. Paid staff was an ideal of the past and volunteers were at an all-time low, as was listener support. As David Lennon describes:

> It was now twelve months since Joh was gone. A big chunk of the 4ZZZ annual subscriptions had expired. The 4ZZZ staff/volunteer base had dwindled to just a few of us who were burning out quickly. I was seriously wondering if 4ZZZ would actually last much further into the New Year.[5]

* * *

On Wednesday, December 14th, 1988, at 4:17am, two volunteer announcers, Mark Solway and Darren Tyers, were partway through their graveyard shift[6] when

---

[3] S. Jones, 'Who's getting fooled in battle for 4ZZZ'. *Financial Review* 6 January 1988, p. 8.

[4] Taken with permission from a Facebook post authored by David Lennon on December 13, 2015.

[5] Taken with permission from a Facebook post authored by David Lennon on December 13, 2015.

[6] Colloquial term for a late-night radio shift, usually 2–6am.

the UQ Student Union executed a surprise eviction. Student Union President, Victoria Brazil, accompanied by other Union members and security guards,[7] entered the 4ZZZ building. The REM song *Orange Crush* played out, as an eviction notice was served to the announcers, followed by radio silence as they were escorted away.

The Notice to Leave made clear that the new Student Union, less than a week into their elected term, wanted 4ZZZ out immediately.

> To the Directors, Managers, Servants and Employees of Creative Broadcasters Limited and of Media Facilities Pty Ltd and to all persons associated with Radio 4ZZZ.
> Whereas the University of Queensland Union is in lawful possession of the Union Building situated at the University of Queensland in St Lucia.
> I, Victoria Brazil, President and Chief Executive Officer of the University of Queensland Student Union do by this notice prohibit any person from entering that part of the Union Building currently known as 'The Offices of Radio 4ZZZ'. Any person acting in contravention of this prohibition will be trespassing upon the property of the University of Queensland Union and will be made the subject of civil proceedings at the suit of the University of Queensland Union ...[8]

Studio equipment was dismantled by the Executive and the building locks were changed. David Lennon was immediately informed. "I got a phone call around 4:30am," he recounts. "Darren told me they'd been kicked off air. And I was just sitting there in shock, you know, thinking, 'What do we need to do?'" When David arrived at the station less than ten minutes later, he was met by breakfast announcer and Program Coordinator Anita Earl, 'grave-yarders' Darren and Mark, two security guards and "two very clean-cut members of the Student Union cowering behind the front door".[9] The only person allowed into the station was Darren who grabbed a Superscope (portable tape recorder), a microphone and fresh batteries. According to David, "no explanation was given as to why we were requesting this equipment and thankfully no questions were asked".[10] Anita and David woke Station Coordinator Gordon Fletcher from his "peaceful slumber ... and after some brief amateur legal advice from Gordon,"[11] the team headed to the station's transmitter site at the top of Mount Coot-tha, 15-minutes west of the studios.

Although the eviction had severed access to its primary facilities, the station still had the capability to broadcast. Victoria Brazil and her Union Executive clearly hadn't been briefed on the transmission chain of command. "As far as

---

[7] Numbers vary.

[8] The Notice to Leave was read out in full on 4ZZZ Emergency Broadcast One which was broadcast on 4ZZZ on December 14, 1988. A copy of this recording is owned by Anita Earl, one of the speakers in the broadcast.

[9] D. Lennon. 'Silenced but not silent'. *Sounds Like a Jilted Generation*. 1995. p. 34.

[10] D. Lennon. 'Silenced but not silent'. p. 34.

[11] D. Lennon. 'Silenced but not silent'. p. 35.

radio goes, you only need the tower [which houses the transmitter]," 4ZZZ's current Technical Manager Patrick King explains. "It's just a place where the aerial will pump out the FM signal we pick up on our radios." To get as much broadcast reach as possible, the tower is located at Mount Coot-tha, the highest point in Brisbane, around 220-metres above sea level. Ideally, a radio station should be located somewhere accessible for its workers and the public, on a university campus for example, rather than atop a mountain in the outer suburbs. At the time of the eviction, 4ZZZ's broadcast audio originated from the premises at the university, with a studio transmitter link sending audio to the tower site at Mount Coot-tha via a microwave dish. But that was purely a matter of convenience. "As long as you can run [audio] into the transmitter, you're good to go … that's all you really need," Patrick King says. "Should it hit the fan, at any point, we can go up there and literally you could just plug a mic into the back of the transmitter."

Fortunately, when it hit the fan back in 1988, 4ZZZ were somewhat prepared. Months previously, volunteer tech genius Allan Herriman set up an emergency broadcasting kit at the transmitter site, building the infrastructure that allowed for the 'plug in' described above to occur. In the '80s, this meant installing a stereo generator so that an FM radio picking up the signal could still decode it back into audio (I promise that's as technical as I get). According to Allan, the set up was "so we could get by in the case of equipment breakdown [but we] hadn't thought that it would be used for an emergency of this type".[12] It's no wonder many Zed folk hold the station's technicians in such high regard. Anita Earl says she remains "in awe of the shamanic prowess of the early Triple Zed techs". Allan Herriman was the brains behind many of the ingenuities that kept 4ZZZ broadcasting against the odds. Thanks to him, the link from the studio to the transmitter may have been terminated by the Union Executive but there was nothing to stop 4ZZZ plugging directly into the mainframe!

The first emergency broadcast began around 5:15am. While it was thought to be lost to the annals of time, Anita Earl found a copy mere days before the manuscript for this book was due to be submitted to the publishers. The recording begins with Anita reading the full eviction notice followed by an explanation of the situation:

> *Anita:* … At that time, 17 minutes past 4am, Triple Zed stopped transmission when all the transmission cables were cut from the studio … we would like you to come in, in this time of need.
> *David:* It's the only way you can really help at the moment. I mean, this is fucked, I don't know what to do … it's happening … they've done it … Imagine what the place is going to be like? It's going to be yuppie radio, basically. A new conservative right has been elected to the Student Union …

---

[12] G. Williams, *Generation Zed: No Other Radio Like This*, Brisbane, Kingswood Press, 2000, p. 32.

And you can't let it happen. This is public radio ... So, please, come out to the studios.

Anita: This is not a hoax. This is really happening ... It's not early radiothon hype ... Triple Zed has been foreclosed by the University of Queensland Student Union.[13]

The unedited recording finishes with David saying "OK, let's get this on air" followed by the sound of a car engine starting, as the crew set off for Mount Coot-tha. Despite it being only a few hours since Victoria Brazil and her team claimed possession over its studios, 4ZZZ had a clear message about what was needed from listeners.

The emergency broadcasts caught Victoria Brazil and her team completely off-guard. It must have come as an absolute shock when the silence at the 4ZZZ premises was suddenly broken with the voices of familiar announcers. Urban legend has it that Zed allies later came into possession of Victoria Brazil's diary, where she'd noted "7:09am: the station's back on air, how can this be?". Darren Tyers—witness to the confusion as it unfolded—was quick to call David at Mount Coot-tha and gleefully describe Student Union members "doing impressions of 'chooks without heads', frantically wondering where the hell we were broadcasting from and how they could stop it". David says he cherishes that vision to this very day.

* * *

By December 1988 I'd been living in Brisbane for almost a year. While yet to be involved with Triple Zed, like Mike Brown I woke to its quirky charms each morning through my own radio alarm clock. On December 14th this is how learnt the news of the eviction, as did countless other listeners across the city. 4ZZZ volunteer Stefan Armbruster was sleeping at his parents' house when he found out. "My mum took the call from Gordon Fletcher," he says. "She came into my bedroom and said, 'there's something going on at your Triple Z thing' ... I grabbed the car and shot off down to the station."

Anita Greenhill kept late hours studying and says she (and her pet axolotl) heard the first emergency broadcast, but at the time thought "there's not much I can do". After some sleep, she went down to the station. "There was lots of energy, and people needed things doing, so I pretty quickly gravitated towards office work," she says. Anita was 'just' a listener when she went offered her help; a year or so later she was sharing the Station Coordinator role with Gordon Fletcher.

As Brisbane slowly woke to the news of 4ZZZ's predicament, David Lennon and Anita Earl were still at Mount Coot-tha, recording and broadcasting further emergency messages. Soon, a makeshift studio was added to the

---

[13] 4ZZZ Emergency Broadcast One. Broadcast on 4ZZZ on December 14, 1988. A copy of this recording is owned by Anita Earl, one of the speakers in the broadcast.

emergency broadcasting kit. Cal Crilly transported equipment up the mountain as soon as he realised what was happening. "We had an eight-track mixing desk, microphone stands, and a bunch of cassettes," he recalls. "I took it all up in my old station wagon. It was basic, but it worked."

Meanwhile, other media started to pick up the eviction as a news item. Former Triple Zed announcer, Tony Biggs, broke the news on his Sydney 2JJJ breakfast show and soon 4ZZZ were conducting live-to-air talkback segments with radio stations in the Southern states from the transmitter site. From a journalistic perspective, it's a federal offence to interfere with the broadcasting of a radio station and the UQ Student Union had done just this, breaching section 124 A1 of the *Australian Broadcasting Act*. This was news!

* * *

4ZZZ's emergency broadcasts prompted a swift and passionate response from the station's supporters. Despite it being university holidays, by 10:00am over 300 allies, listeners, and station workers had gathered at the station. According to Stefan Armbruster, one minute he was sitting outside the station thinking "what will we do, what's going to happen to us?" and the next "hundreds of people" started to arrive. As Mike Brown remembers it, "We thought no one was listening, but when the station was under threat, people came out of the woodwork". Greg Fryer agrees. "That solidarity was something else. All these different groups, punks, unionists, feminists, they all came together. It was 'touch one, touch all' in action."

Kathy Pope was a 22-year listener, with a friend who volunteered as a 4ZZZ announcer. Her reason for joining the protest is representative of many who turned up that day. "Triple Z was our radio station, our music, our world," she says. "Our whole share house in Indooroopilly was in shock and despair at this news. We felt we needed to do something." As Kathy wasn't working or studying that day, she headed straight to the university, keen to show support.

A photo on the front page of *The Courier Mail*. taken on the day of the eviction, shows the outside of 4ZZZ's offices plastered with signs of protest: "Fascists Out"; "Keep alive independent music"; and the rather clever, "Victorian Values". A moustached security guard (ironically wearing a brown uniform shirt) glares at the camera in the forefront of the shot, setting an ominous tone. News reports from the time describe an angry group, chanting phrases such as "National Party Off Campus" and "Free Speech Now". "No-one was banging on windows," says Stefan Armbruster, "although the brown shirts [Student Union Executive members and security guards] were looking pretty nervous".

Around 10:30am Victoria Brazil issued a press statement that gave little explanation as to why the action had been taken against 4ZZZ.[14] Meanwhile Zed workers and supporters met outside the locked station to discuss possible

---

[14] J. Cheverton, 'Union Control Out of Control'. Semper Floreat February 89, no 1, 1989, p. 4.

next moves, and shortly after, a dozen or so protestors pushed their way into a corridor outside Brazil's office. As described in *Semper Floreat*:

> The supporters, interested in discovering why the raid had occurred, decided to move to the President's office and demand an explanation. Victoria Brazil refused to speak to them and locked herself in an office to talk only to the press.[15]

What happened next is unclear. Either 200 to 300 protestors were locked outside by police officers before they too could gain access to the Student Union headquarters,[16] or the 4ZZZ supporters were the ones in control and barricaded Victoria in her office.[17] Regardless, this was the beginning of an extended occupation of the Union premises, motivated by a variety of student concerns with the TBA-controlled Executive that extended well beyond its plans for Triple Zed.

Somehow, in the early afternoon amongst all the chaos, 4ZZZ regained control of its studios. Again, the exact mechanics of how this happened are shrouded in mystery, with wildly differing accounts appearing in various publications over the years, as well as in my own conversations with people there at the time. 4ZZZ journalist Brendan Greenhill says a solicitor for the Student Legal Service gave advice that the cliché of 'possession being 9/10th of the law' held weight,[18] inspiring thoughts of re-occupation. Security was also spread thin while protestors targeted the Student Union president, and with only one guard stationed at 4ZZZ, Mike Brown says the decision was made to "storm the place". While most protestors drew attention to the front of the building, others entered through the back—an unofficial entrance used when the after-hours buzzer wasn't successful in catching anyone's attention. Brendan described it as "crawling inside a small opening". Others recall an unlocked entrance that 'outsiders' weren't aware of. Regardless, 4ZZZ supporters successfully entered the building while a larger group of protestors created a diversion. "All the shit was still happening at the front," says Mike. "They didn't know we were in." A sliding door was quickly unlocked and everyone else ran in, until the 4ZZZ supporters were "packed like sardines".[19]

Next on the agenda was getting the studio back on air—not easily achieved as the Student Union Executives had cut power to the building. 4ZZZ had access to an emergency back-up transformer, however as Greg Fryer remembers, the generator batteries were flat.

---

[15] J. Cheverton, 'Union Control Out of Control', p. 4.

[16] W, Watson. 'Anger at closure of 4ZZZ.', *Sun Brisbane*, 14 December 1988.Evicted staff seize studio, *The Courier Mail*,15/12/88 p. 1.

[17] F. Orr and C. Wockner, 'Evicted staff seize studio', *The Courier Mail*, 15 December 1988, p. 1.

[18] G. Williams, *Generation Zed: No Other Radio Like This*, Brisbane, Kingswood Press, 2000, p. 34.

[19] Williams, *Generation Zed: No Other Radio Like This*, p. 34.

This sparky from the ETU [Electrical Trades Union] comes up and says, 'What's wrong, comrade?'. I told him the batteries were dead, and he says, 'Get me some car batteries!'. People started ripping them out of their cars and passing them in. He jerry-rigged it together. It worked!

Once power was restored, Greg made a triumphant return to the airwaves, kicking off with The Who's *Won't Get Fooled Again*, the first song 4ZZZ broadcast back in December of 1975. Mike Brown is astounded his friend had the presence of mind to make that choice. "I am still in total awe that you thought of playing that song, my brother," he told Greg during our interview. "I wouldn't have even thought about it, but you fucking did!" The Student Union Executive wasn't as impressed. Victoria Brazil told *The Courier Mail* later that day, "it's unfortunate they are still broadcasting, ... they are seeing it in a less-than reasonable light".[20]

Kathy Pope was one of the supporters who ended up inside the studios after 4ZZZ wrestled back control of the station. She was warned the occupation could wind up lasting "all day and all night," determined as the station was to keep control of the property. Kathy and her friend made the snap decision to squeeze through a door that was being locked to prevent the police coming in. "I remember looking at the filthy carpet on the floor," she admits, "thinking, 'I'm not sleeping on that, we're off'".

About 60 supporters did end up staying at the station that night.[21] According to Allan Herriman, there were concerns the Student Union might re-attempt to take back the station, so it was decided "we should have Zed-friendly people occupying the place 24 hours a day". And so began "the best (and longest) party" Allan ever attended.[22]

The occupation would last for three weeks or so, attracting community support from across the city. Rohan Wilton, a volunteer who occasionally helped at reception and with odd jobs around the studios, was laid up with his leg in plaster at the time. Unable to do much else, he decided to join the sit-in. "I remember the community support growing beyond anyone's expectations," he says. "We laughed and had fun without the threat of security and cops, who in those days were not allowed to carry guns on campus." Small local businesses lined up to offer support; nearby restaurant Kookaburra donated box loads of their signature one-metre diameter pizzas, and the Hare Krishnas set up a stall to also provide free food. According to Rohan even announcers from commercial radio station 4MMM "shouted out support on the airwaves".

With 4ZZZ still broadcasting, regular staff such as 4ZZZ journalist Donna Baines needed to find ways to work amidst the occupation. "I was there a lot, but

---

[20] A. Biggs. 'A dawn raid ended the rebel ZZZ era', *The Courier Mail*, 15 December 1988, p. 9.

[21] F. Orr and C. Wockner, 'Evicted staff seize studio', *The Courier Mail*, 15 December 1988. p. 1.

[22] G. Williams, *Generation Zed: No Other Radio Like This*, Brisbane, Kingswood Press, 2000, p. 33.

I don't think I stayed there all night," she says. For others, the station became both a workplace and a living space. Stefan Armbruster pretty much moved in. "I lived at the station ... once it happened," he describes. "I just didn't go back home. It was great fun." For a few weeks, 4ZZZ was filled with a mix of people serving different purposes. According to Donna, some were "still working and trying to solve the problems" while others ensured 4ZZZ wasn't re-evicted. She says Studio Three, an empty room where bands would play live-to-airs, was a favoured spot, often filled with sleeping bodies while others worked around them. The record library also doubled as a bedroom. As Anita Greenhill remembers:

> Right at the back, they had bricked in an old piano ... it was sort of vacant space. So, everybody put down their sleeping bags and they'd come in and out ... then in the daytime, having to figure out and negotiate all the deeds and contracts and deal with the police ... it was very intense. It was busy, but important because if people hadn't stayed at that stage, we would have been kicked out way earlier.

On the first evening of the occupation, 4ZZZ managed to broadcast a snap mini-radiothon which raised over $3000. Some listeners offered $100 to hear their favourite song played; the most memorable donation of the evening, however, came from a worker at the 'Touch of Class' massage parlour who, while donating $50, said, "Don't worry loves. We're the last massage parlour in Brisbane and they tried to close us down last week".[23] Leader of the Queensland opposition government, Wayne Goss, was also quick to support the station. In an interview with 4ZZZ he told listeners the attitude of the Student Union was a blatant political move: "I am urging all young people to support Triple Zed in this rather absurd and ridiculous battle with the union ... You'd better send me a subscription form."[24] He also offered the services of his law firm, Goss, Downey and Carne. A year later, Wayne Goss was Queensland's new Premier, heading the first Labor party to win a state election in over 32 years.

Brisbane's pride in 4ZZZ was reignited by the threat of its closure. The overwhelming support for the at-risk station underscored its continuing relevance to the community. According to volunteer Alex Wightman, the community response really brought home "how broad the support and appeal of Triple Zed was, to a really diverse range of people [who felt Zed] was worth defending to the point of actually occupying". This was greatly welcomed by those who'd been holding the station together over the past year. "The morale internally was so fucked we just assumed that the same [feeling] was out there as well," explains David Lennon. "You felt that no one was listening, but you know, when push comes to shove ... " The shock of 4ZZZ being overrun by a conservative Student Union was enough to invigorate its audiences into action. David Lennon also joined the occupation, which he admits "was pretty much a fancy word for a party". For David, it was an opportunity to rest from

---

[23] 4ZZZ. 'Solidarity'. *Radio Times*. Dec88/Jan89, p. 10.
[24] 4ZZZ. 'Solidarity'. p. 10.

the relentless slog of trying to keep 4ZZZ afloat over the past year. "Suddenly we were no longer short of volunteers, or donations for that matter," he says.

> I quietly stepped out of the limelight and enjoyed a well-deserved break … The following three weeks were the best three weeks of my life. I lived the dream of sex, drugs and rock and roll for that short but blissful part of my life.[25]

* * *

Why did The Better Alternative party feel so strongly that 4ZZZ should be removed from campus? Victoria Brazil—now a Professor of Emergency Medicine at Bond University—declined my request for an interview saying the topic was not relevant to her current work. Back in 1988, Victoria Brazil explained to *The Sun Brisbane*, "I'm not sorry we've done it. Other Students' Union administrations have had problems with them for years and conveniently ignored it".[26] *The Sun* also reported Union claims that the station was both a fire and health risk, "because of accumulated material inside the office,"[27] while Victoria Brazil told another news outlet 4ZZZ "created a poor image of students".[28] In a letter to *The Gold Coast Bulletin* a month after the eviction, Victoria Brazil defended her actions saying 4ZZZ was a community station rather than student-focused, with little connection to the university population. She stated that the space was also needed to provide other "important student services"[29] including childcare facilities.

Financial concerns were, however, the most consistent and prominent reason argued by the Student Union Executive, especially as time passed. According to Victoria Brazil, the time had come "for an end to the interests of a very small group of student politicians being subsidised by all students".[30] Brazil also outlined her motivations in her first President's Report for *Semper Floreat*, the UQ student magazine, arguing that students were funding the station to an unreasonable degree.

> Apart from the initial loan of $250,000 there is a yearly contribution of $15,000 to $18,000 from Student Union fees. Further, the space currently occupied by the radio station is worth $51,000 a year in rent (external estimate). Added to the potential interest on the loan, cleaning and maintenance costs, the total cost to students is well in excess of $100,000 each year.[31]

---

[25] Taken with permission from a Facebook post authored by David Lennon on December 13, 2015.
[26] W. Watson. 'Anger at closure of 4ZZZ'. The *Sun Brisbane* 14 December 1988, p. 5.
[27] W. Watson, 'Anger at closure of 4ZZZ', p. 5.
[28] A. Lawler and D. Lock. 'Triple Dead', *Planet*, vol 9 no 1, 1989, p. 5.
[29] V. Brazil. Letter to the editor, *Gold Coast Bulletin*, 9 January 1989, p. 8.
[30] V. Brazil. Letter to the editor, p. 8.
[31] V. Brazil, 'President's Report', *Semper Floreat*, no. 1, February 1989, p. 25.

4ZZZ challenged this, saying the $100,000 figure was misleading. When first established, the Student Union gave the station $250,000 to set up the studios. By order of the University, this was recorded as a loan rather than a donation, "but interest would never be charged, and repayments were never to be made".[32] According to 4ZZZ, the real debt between the station and the Union was in the form of a mortgage debenture of $63,000, which appeared to have been all but written off. Cleaning and maintenance costs were taken from the Union's annual allocation of funding to the station—monies not considered a handout, but rather "part of fee-for-service contracts".[33] 4ZZZ also pointed out that it provided educational value by training students in media skills. Any Union funds spent on 4ZZZ were, in the station's view, an investment in student opportunities and independent media. In a detailed analysis of Union spending, *Semper Floreat* estimated the contribution to 4ZZZ worked out at "less than $1 per student each year".[34]

Not surprisingly *Semper* was also a target of The Better Alternative's Union Executive. Under the editorship of gay rights activist Jeff Cheverton, *Semper* had written about allegations of electoral fraud and impropriety that had dogged the 1988 union election, reportedly the first time such accusations had ever clouded a UQ Union vote.[35] *Semper* had also obtained documents showing the TBA-led Executive's plan to lease the profitable Refectory to an outside firm, essentially removing it from student control. Notably, according to *Semper*, this privatisation agenda had never been mentioned during TBA's election campaign, and many students felt it was being imposed without mandate or consultation.[36]

The new Union Executive cut funding to *Semper* in early 1989. Student Union funds traditionally financed the newspaper, as it was considered a core student service. However, under Brazil, the Executive sought to financially starve the paper. This was a classic tactic of political control, limiting the resources available to opposition voices while ensuring pro-Union narratives dominated. Beyond cutting its budget, TBA attempted to control the paper's editorial stance by interfering with its editorial board appointments. As 4ZZZ noted:

> The attacks on *Semper* and 4ZZZ are linked, part of a plan to silence any criticisms of their actions ... It has already been announced that they intend to abolish the Gays and Lesbians Collective on campus, the Aboriginal and Torres Strait Islanders Committee, and the Women's Rights Area.[37]

---

[32] J. Cheverton, 'Union Control Out of Control', *Semper Floreat*, no. 1, February 1989, p. 4.
[33] P. Butler & N. Douglas, 'Zed: Never silent, never silenced'. *Radio Times*. Dec88/Jan89, p. 5.
[34] Cheverton, 'Union Control Out of Control', p. 4.
[35] 'Editorial', *Semper Floreat*, edition 8, November 1988, p. 2.
[36] 'Editorial', *Semper Floreat*, p. 2.
[37] Anon, 'Semper under fire: The media attack sequel'. *Radio Times*. Dec88/Jan89, p. 9.

Not all Student Union Representatives supported the actions being taken by the TBA-led Executive.[38] Questions were also being asked about the legal advice given to the Student Union prior to the early morning raid. Some evidence suggests the Executive were told 4ZZZ had a legitimate sub-licence on the premises they had occupied for 13 years, and as such, an immediate eviction would be both unreasonable and considered trespass. However, Victoria Brazil's solicitors also suggested, "it was doubtful 4ZZZ had the resources to test the case in the Supreme Court,"[39] which may have been taken as a green light to execute the eviction notice.

While the occupation at the Student Union building started in response to 4ZZZ's eviction, it soon evolved into a broader sit-in against the TBA-led Executive. Students physically occupied the Union complex for an extended period in 1989, regularly making headline news. In defiance of the elected officials, protesters essentially took over operations of the Union facilities during this time. It would take nearly six months for the University of Queensland's administration to resolve the conflict.

* * *

When a meeting was finally arranged to discuss the stand-off at 4ZZZ, some members of the Union Executive walked out.[40] They then issued a second eviction notice, that gave 4ZZZ four weeks' notice to leave by January 19th, 1989. 4ZZZ strongly objected to the timeframe; a spokesperson told *The Courier Mail* that station staff weren't opposed to moving off campus, but it would take at least three months "to set up a basic station"[41] elsewhere. The UQ Student Union made it clear that police would be called if 4ZZZ had not vacated by the eviction date, and in a separate news article Cameron Spenceley cited the *Vagrants and Gaming Act*, saying "we don't want violence but the union is prepared to stick by what it believes in."[42] The station's response was that staff were prepared to be arrested if they were not ready to leave the premises on time.[43]

4ZZZ kept listeners up to date with developments via its "Fruit and Nut" segment, broadcast twice a day, 9:00am and 6:00pm. Fundraising was still a major priority as the station frantically began searching for a new home. When it became clear this wouldn't happen as quickly as needed, a public meeting was held to discuss the future of the 4ZZZ. Nearly 400 people

---

[38] F. Orr and C. Wockner, 'Evicted staff seize studio', *Courier Mail*, 15 December 1988, p. 1.

[39] F. Orr and C. Wockner, 'Evicted staff seize studio', p. 1.

[40] J. Cheverton, 'Union Control Out of Control', *Semper Floreat*, no. 1, February 1989, p. 5.

[41] P. Whittaker, '4ZZZ gets 4 weeks to leave uni', *The Courier Mail*, 23 December 1988, p. 11.

[42] Anon. 'Radio 4ZZZ looking to stay on air from off campus site', *The Courier Mail*, 28 December 1988. p. 4.

[43] Anon. 'Radio 4ZZZ looking to stay on air from off campus site', *The Courier Mail*, 28 December 1988, p. 4.

Fig. 4.2 Photo of 4ZZZ studio, University of Queensland, St Lucia, taken by Andrew Dent; 1989

attended, and a plan was hatched to resist the eviction.[44] Hundreds of supporters slept at the station on the night of January 19th, however, the Student Union didn't call in police or security as threatened. A few days later, solicitors from both parties negotiated an exit plan for the station. As David Lennon recalls, "it was the actual university administration that finally said enough was enough, which was fair enough in retrospect". 4ZZZ was given a much-needed six-month reprieve, and station staff agreed to vacate by July 8th, 1989 (Fig. 4.2).

Many key people from this period of 4ZZZ's history believe it all turned out for the best. Andrew Bartlett recalls intense discussion at Collective meetings even before the early morning raid, "about the benefits of moving off campus to break [the] student radio stereotype and better connect with the wider community". "It was always assumed we couldn't afford it," he says, "but we were forced off and had to find a way". David Lennon believes "Victoria Brazil did Triple Zed the biggest favour," galvanising the community and "bringing everyone back together". Cal Crilly agrees:

> If Victoria Brazil hadn't done that, Triple Zed might have just faded away. Instead, it became stronger because people realised how much it mattered … They could have just waited a while … Triple Zed would have just gotten too broke to run. But instead, they tried to take it by force.

4ZZZ was not out of the woods yet. The station may have been given six months to move but this did not ease the logistical challenge of rehousing an entire broadcasting operation. Triple Zed was still mostly operated by volunteers and the station had lost its main benefactor. The next few years would prove the most challenging yet (Fig. 4.2).

---

[44] J. Cheverton, 'Union Control Out of Control', *Semper Floreat*, no. 1, February 1989, p. 5.

CHAPTER 5

Shelter(s) from the Storm

Hollis[1] had done tougher climbs. Back in school, they'd ridden marathons every weekend, burning through endless asphalt. But those rides had ended with oranges and the occasional medal. This one finished at a banger of an old caravan, perched on top of Mount Coot-tha and plugged straight into the transmitter like some kind of pirate outpost.

They did this three times a week, hauling a bag of records, weaving through the dark bushland. The climb was brutal—2.6-km with some sections steep enough to make the quads scream. When it wasn't raining, it wasn't too grim. Hollis reflected on the extra shifts they'd had to take since 4ZZZ set up its temporary broadcast studio on the mountain, to keep the station on air during the move from the university. Many of the other volunteers didn't have cars and few were willing to tackle the mountain by bike.

Hollis rolled to a stop as they approached the ageing caravan. The previous announcer, eyes hollow from the nightshift, was already heading for their car, a muttered "Hey" the only farewell before they sped off down the mountain. That wasn't a great sign. Usually, if the overnight shift had gone well, there'd be some banter. Maybe even an exchange of records. This silence? Suspicious.

Inside, the caravan was a shrine to organised chaos. A tangled mess of cables, stacks of vinyl, newspapers pinned to the walls, handwritten playlists dangling from pushpins. Outside the window, the first rays of sunrise painted Brisbane in soft gold. It was a beautiful location with thick bushland surrounding the caravan. The birds chattered in the morning light and the city lay stretched below.

---

[1] Not a real person. This story combines a collection of anecdotes from Zed folk who broadcasted from the Mt Coot-tha caravan site in 1989.

Hollis dropped their bag, flipped through the records, and picked something long—the extended mix of the Sisters of Mercy song, *The Corrosion*[2]—something that would give them a few minutes to sit back, stretch, and enjoy the dawn. The familiar crackle of vinyl filled the caravan. They stepped outside for a breath of fresh air. Instead, they were assaulted with a stench. Not just the usual caravan funk. Something worse. Something … fresh.

Hollis turned their head, eyes drifting downward, and there it was. A steaming pile of human excrement. An unapologetic turd, sitting in the dirt just metres from the caravan steps. Hollis pinched the bridge of their nose in equal parts disgust and frustration. Not again! The sign was right there! A laminated plea, taped to the caravan door in block capitals:

LOOKING FOR THE LOO?
DO NOT SHIT JUST OUTSIDE THE CARAVAN.
IT'S DISGUSTING AND UNHEALTHY.
PUT ON AN ALBUM SIDE, GO FOR A NICE LONG WALK, AND SHIT ON BONDY,[3] NOT ZZZ. THANK YOU.

And yet, here they were. Face to face with the early morning crime scene.

Hollis didn't even need to investigate. The graveyard announcers were infamous for this. Too scared of the dark to go deep into the trees, too lazy to take a proper walk, they just squatted near the door. The opening choral chant of *My Corrosion* washed over the mountain top—an almost religious wall of voices drenched in reverb—as Hollis stepped back inside the caravan, pointedly ignoring the problem until it became someone else's. Or at least until they'd had their morning spliff. Hollis wondered how long it would take for Triple Zed to move into its new home and hoped that there would be good plumbing.

* * *

For the most part, 4ZZZ enjoyed a healthy 'childhood', if you'll forgive me thinking of it as a living entity. During its first thirteen years, the station lived in the warm embrace of the Student Union Complex at the St Lucia campus of the University of Queensland, in the basement of an extension to the Refectory building. This complex, designed by architect Stephen Trotter in the 1960s, was a modernist arrangement of interlinked brick and concrete structures centred around a popular outdoor courtyard called the Forum.[4] The Union building itself was a two-story pavilion enveloped by concrete breezeblock

---

[2] Number 7 in the 1988 4ZZZ Hot 100, as broadcast on 1st January 1989.

[3] These are the words of the sign taped to the inside of the caravan door. 'Bondy' refers to Alan Bond, a media mogul and multi-millionaire who owned Channel 9 at the time (who also had a transmitter on Mt Coot-tha).

[4] J. Harris, 'Push to save UQ Union Complex, hub of Queensland democracy', *Architecture, au*, Australian Institute of Architects, 2019, https://architectureau.com/articles/push-to-save-uq-union-complex-hub-of-queensland-democracy/ (accessed 14 December 2024).

screens and latticework panels, an award-winning design element that provided shade and visual flair.[5] Immediately adjacent was the Schonell Theatre, and together these facilities formed a vibrant student hub for social and political life. As early-'80s Station Coordinator, Danielle Bond describes "Triple Zed was in the basement, *Semper* was nearby, the cinema was across the way, and the theatre was below the cinema ... It was this creative hub".

Anita Earl arrived at 4ZZZ in the latter half of the 1980s and loved the St Lucia studios. "[They] had a lingering sense of Gough Whitlam era Australia where left leaning social enterprise [was] the celebrated norm," she says. David Lennon shares the sentiment. "Living in Queensland back then meant living with a constant feeling of guarded dread. The 4ZZZ studios at the Uni were a refuge from that," he says. There's a lot of nostalgia for Triple Zed's original home. As Anita Earl describes, "the tech room had a distinct smell of stale bong water in the carpet and a light whiff of mouldy concrete". It was the only home 4ZZZ had known, and the Zed folk loved it. But it was time to leave the nest. Here's where we left off from our last chapter; it's mid-January 1989 and a teenaged Triple Zed has agreed to leave home within six months.

4ZZZ started its search for a new place to live soon after the original eviction attempt. "We were fundraising to try and buy a building or get a deposit right from the beginning," says Anita Greenhill. In late December, 4ZZZ's promotions coordinator Amanda Curtis told *The Courier Mail* that the station planned to buy a house within a 10-km radius of the Mt Coot-tha transmitter site.[6] This wasn't an unreasonable goal. In the first few weeks following the early morning eviction raid, over $30,000 had been raised via support from listeners, sympathetic businesses, media, and other organisations.[7]

4ZZZ workers exploited as many fundraising avenues as they could imagine. For example, a new t-shirt design was added to its merchandise collection, a framed copy of which hangs proudly above the current Station Manager's desk. It was based on a drawing by political cartoonist, Sean Leahy, published in *The Courier Mail* as part of its coverage of the eviction. Well-known for his scathing visual critiques of the Bjelke-Petersen government, Sean was even threatened with a defamation claim by the (former) Premier during his fall from grace.

The cartoon (Fig. 5.1) depicts two announcers sitting at a radio panel emblazoned with a 4ZZZ logo. They watch in horror, as a row of truncheon-wielding Bjelke-Petersen clones run into the building. Sean had a trademark look for the ex-Premier (who was still synonymous with Queensland conservative politics despite no longer leading the National Party). "I used to draw [Joh] with the [German] stormtrooper outfit and the cross-banana armbands," he explains. "I'm happy to say I contributed to ... this perception of who he

---

[5] Harris, 'Push to save UQ Union Complex, hub of Queensland democracy'.

[6] 'Radio 4ZZZ looking to stay on air from off campus site', *The Courier Mail*, 28 December 1988, p. 5.

[7] A. Lawler and D. Lock. 'Triple Dead', *Planet*, vol 9 no 1, 1989, p. 5.

Fig. 5.1 Cartoon by Sean Leahy depicting the attempted eviction of 4ZZZ from the St Lucia studios; 1988

was." The banana design clearly resembles a swastika which was a compromise from the first draft of the artist's caricature of Bjelke-Petersen. "I originally drew a swastika on Joh, and it didn't make it to publication," Sean says.

As Sean describes the 4ZZZ eviction cartoon:

> [The announcers] have their hands up in the air as the stormtroopers come in through the door to the Triple Zed studios … And I've got Miss Brazil leading, which is basically Joh in drag … And one of the Triple Zed announcers is saying, "we interrupt this broadcast to pause for a military coup".

4ZZZ gained permission to use the cartoon on a shirt and added the tagline "4ZZZ survives the 14th of December 1988". More than 200 sold in just a few days.

Sean Leahy's cartoon set in motion a myth that continues to circulate, nearly 40 years later. Mark Solway and Darren Tyers were the announcers on air when the dawn raid was enacted. While the cartoon depicts Mark with his short dark hair, the second announcer is a spitting image of Zedder, Stefan Armbruster. But in his own words, "I wasn't on air when the brown shirts came to the door". If you were paying attention in Chap. 4, Stefan was peacefully asleep, racing to the station after his mum woke him with the news. Not long after he arrived, Stefan had his photo taken with Mark outside Triple Zed for a story published in the *Daily Sun*,[8]. Standing next to Mark, hands on hips, with untamed curls and John Lennon-style sunglasses, Stefan was mistaken by Sean as one of the on-air announcers. "I based [the cartoon] on the newspaper article," the cartoonist laughs. "You know, I made the mistake of thinking it's in the newspaper, it must be true!"

---

[8] L. McKay. 'Raiders switch of 4ZZZ, *Daily Sun* 14 December 1988, p. 3.

An unmistakable likeness of Stefan as one of the on-air announcers when 4ZZZ was evicted is now immortalised, both in print and on the t-shirt design.

4ZZZ even made the cheeky attempt to have one last Market Day on the UQ campus. On February 20th, 1989, Station Coordinator Gordon Fletcher wrote to the University Registrar, requesting permission. Nine months earlier, the same Registrar had knocked back a similar appeal citing a range of breaches. Despite Gordon's plea that "fundraising activities such as these ... take on new importance,"[9] it only took the University official four days to refuse the request. 4ZZZ's 1989 Radiothon fundraiser theme was aptly named "A Street Kid Named Zed" with one promotional image showing a dejected transistor radio sitting on a gutter curb with a cloth sack tied to a stick (known as a bindle) over its shoulder. A song was even recorded by The Friends of Triple Zed, called *We want bananas, not brazil nuts*. Its catchy simplistic tune still sticks in my mind:

> We want bananas, we want bananas, we want our radio station back.
> Four Triple-zil nuts, Four Triple-zil nuts, we want our radio station back.

The most notable fundraiser was organised with Sydney's Radio Skid Row, where some former Zed announcers were involved. There was plenty of overlap between the 4ZZZ and Skid Row communities, as both were radical stations fighting for survival in the increasingly commercialised radio landscape of the late 1980s. More to the point, Skid Row had also been kicked out of its Sydney University home and so the two stations organised a benefit concert at the Paddington RSL Club in Sydney, on April 7th, 1989 (Fig. 5.2).

According to Liz Willis, the event collected approximately $10,000, a sum that was almost unachievable for a grassroots community radio fundraiser. "It was just outrageous," says Liz. "So much money at the time from just one night, seemed unbelievable." She retains a vivid memory of ex Zedder Larry Ponting "carrying literally *bags* of money away from the door to safety!". Billed as a 'Public Radio Party', the gig was headlined by Painters and Dockers, a Melbourne band known for their raucous live shows and politically charged lyrics. The love between 4ZZZ and 'the Dockers' was mutual. "We were only too happy to support ZZZ and Radio Skid Row as they were the stations bold enough to play our songs on air," frontman Paulie Stewart says. "It's a great point of honour in the band that our only Number One song on the charts was when our tune *Die Yuppie Die* topped the [Hot 100] list[10] at ZZZ." Docker's trumpeter, Davey Pace, remembers the show vividly, especially because Sydney was considered "a hard market to crack".

---

[9] G. Fletcher, 'Request for Market Day' [Letter to University of Queensland Registrar], 20 February 1989, 4ZZZ archives, Brisbane, Qld.

[10] 1987 4ZZZ Hot 100 as broadcast on 1st January 1988.

Fig. 5.2 Poster for a Joint Effort concert held in Sydney to raise funds for 4ZZZ and Radio Skid Row, designed by Matt Mawson; 1989

> I remember the crowd slam dancing to … our opening number. One guy was lifted into the air above the audience and passed towards and onto the stage. He ran over to Steig, our guitar player, kissed him on the cheek, and then dived back into the crowd. We knew immediately it would be a special night.

The rest of the lineup included Brisbane's Ups and Downs, Sydney-based outfits The Sparklers, Tall Tales and True, and Falling Joys as well as '4ZZZ band', The Black Assassins, who by then had members based in both cities. Former Zed announcer and Black Assassin's drummer, Tony Biggs was a DJ with 2JJJ at the time; as well as playing with the band he also "kept the ball rolling as the master of ceremonies".[11] Everyone performed for free, making it a true grassroots fundraiser. "We didn't pay anyone a cent," says Liz Willis. "I love them to death because of what they did that night."

* * *

Buoyed by the overwhelming financial support in the immediate aftermath of its eviction, 4ZZZ had a few options to consider. Ideally, station workers wanted to buy their own premises, but Triple Zed had patchy financial records and no credit rating. There was little evidence of the long-term financial capacity needed to guarantee that it could meet mortgage payments—unsurprising given 4ZZZ hadn't had a formal rent agreement with the University of Queensland. As Anita Greenhill explains, "we didn't have enough money and assets as a station".

Anita recalls "weeks of looking at endless properties". Sharing a space wasn't practical, although offers were made. "Certain community groups would say, 'you could have this space' but it was pointless, there wasn't enough room," she says. "We knew we'd have to move the entire radio station, the whole record library, plus all of the studio equipment and everything else". Renting was another option, but, as Stefan Armbruster says, "a lot of people didn't want us'". He recalls joining Station Coordinator Gordon Fletcher, who negotiated much of the househunting. "We used to look at houses and buildings all over [town]," Stefan says. "We didn't know what we were doing really, we were just thinking 'shit we need to move'—well I didn't know what I was doing, Gordon might have!"

Over time, the urgency of 4ZZZ's situation began to lose its impact on both volunteers and listeners. After all, the station was still on-air, so the emergency had been averted, right? "There wasn't enough energy, and we didn't have enough money," Anita Greenhill says. Maintaining morale within the station was also challenging. According to Anita, the intense workload, combined with financial strain and future uncertainty, led to burnout among many volunteers. "There was lots of partying and events being organised ... but the burnout was intense," she says. "We were also writing defense letters for swearing on the station and trying to maintain [our university] degrees." As the date to move drew closer, the station was forced to get organised. A small group of Zed folk, some of whom were at the station unpaid but pretty much fulltime, agreed on a location—a rental office at the Manchester Unity Building at 621 Coronation Drive, Toowong. "It was a weird space, but it was long-term enough. All the walls were moveable, so we had thoughts about how we could lay it out," Anita Greenhill says. "It was still close to the uni, right over the road from the ABC [which] ... was still quite supportive ... these things [were] quite positive."

There was never going to be a reconciliation between Triple Zed and the UQ Student Union. In Zed's mind, the university had relinquished responsibility of the station and abandoned it to find a new home. Perhaps bolstered by

---

[11] J. Coomber, 'Concert shows support for public radio', 1989, date and page unknown, cited in G. Williams, *Generation Zed: No other radio like this*, Kingswood Press, 2000, p. 35.

knowing independence was just around the corner, 4ZZZ held an eviction party at the St Lucia site on the eve of its departure. "One of the best parties I've ever been to in my entire life was the eviction party we threw for ourselves at the old studios underneath the Rec Building," says Anita Earl. "We were taking sledgehammers to Studio Three and smashing double brick walls". "All I can say is that everyone celebrated. Everyone laughed and cried in the realisation that we were leaving,"[12] Anita Greenhill adds.

While he empathises with people's frustration, David Lennon says he wasn't very comfortable with the "wanton vandalism and destruction [the St Lucia premises] suffered" in the weeks leading up to Triple Zed's final departure. This wasn't motivated by concern for Student Union property but rather a feeling that it was disrespectful to the institution of 4ZZZ, and the memories held by many who made the station what it was. "We were just silly to leave the sledgehammer leaning against the wall after the windows were removed," David says. "What was originally two window sized holes in the wall, grew daily ... I'm just glad they stopped before knocking down what was holding the ceiling up."

Both Anitas woke the morning after the eviction party to police at their doors, asking about the property damage. "Some of us had to go down to the station and explain what was going on ... how did the holes get in the wall and what was stolen," Anita Greenhill says. A front-page story in *The Courier Mail*[13] included a photo of Victoria Brazil peering through a large hole in a double-brick wall. The article cited the Student Union President's accusation that "hundreds of thousands of dollars of damage was done"[14] including smashed windows, wrecked plumbing and "ripped out electrical wiring, leaving several wires dangling from ceilings and walls".[15] A 4ZZZ representative, Charlie Scandrett, denied the claims saying the station was required to remove "the interior walls, windows, fixtures and fittings ... [as the premises were] a clear open space when we took it over 15 years ago".[16] Charlie added "electrical wiring had been isolated, and exterior windows had not been smashed". Victoria Brazil did not disguise her relief that 4ZZZ had finally moved.

> They were never good housekeepers and were not the kind of people who behaved at the best of times, but this inexcusable wanton destruction is criminal ... I'm glad they have gone.[17]

---

[12] G. Williams, *Generation Zed: No other radio like this*, Kingswood Press, 2000, p. 34.

[13] S. Killen, '4ZZZ supporters hit', *The Courier Mail*, 11 July 1989, p. 1.

[14] Killen, '4ZZZ supporters hit', p. 1.

[15] Killen, '4ZZZ supporters hit', p. 1.

[16] Killen, '4ZZZ supporters hit', p. 1.

[17] Killen, '4ZZZ supporters hit', p. 1.

Brazil and the rest of the UQ Student Executive resigned two days later.[18]

* * *

Opposition to the conservative Student Union Executive had coalesced into an organised movement. Early in 1989, a broad coalition called Students for a Democratic Union (SDU) formed.[19] This ad-hoc group included independent leftists, members of socialist groups, and Labor Party-affiliated students—essentially, all those who opposed the Brazil-led Union. The SDU's core argument was that the TBA Executive had lost the trust of students, and its actions—which included evicting 4ZZZ and interfering with the student magazine, *Semper Floreate*—violated the democratic spirit of the Student Union. They also pointed to unresolved allegations of ballot fraud in the election.

The SDU gathered a petition to call a referendum that if won would indicate a vote of no-confidence; its aim was to dismiss the current Union Executive and trigger fresh student elections. In April 1989, the SDU submitted the petition, reportedly meeting the required number of student signatures. Initially, the Student Union tried to stonewall this effort, rejecting the petition for a referendum on technical grounds[20] and circulating propaganda asserting the "referendum [was] a fraud".[21]

Despite these maneuvers, pressure from student activists grew. The referendum was scheduled for May 1989, at which UQ students overwhelmingly voted "YES" in favor of initiating a new election. The exact figures were not widely published, but the mandate was clear enough that it could not be ignored. Faced with the combined verdict of the student body and months of protests, Victoria Brazil eventually stepped down as Union President in mid-1989. *Semper* celebrated in its July edition with a back-page graphic depicting a stereotypical witch, wearing a 'Joh for PM' badge, riding a broomstick accompanied by the text "Ding Dong, The Witch is Dead".[22]

July 1989 proved a month of significant change in Brisbane. 4ZZZ moved from its home of 13 years, and The Better Alternative party lost control of the UQ Student Union after only six months in office. On a broader scale, *The Fitzgerald Report* was also released that month. Its scathing suite of findings led to criminal charges against several officials, including a former Police Commissioner, and triggered sweeping political reforms. The fallout from

---

[18] S. Killen, 'Brazil, Executive quit; Blame uni executive', The Courier Mail, 15 July 1989, p. 5.

[19] Students for a Democratic Union, "Setting the record straight" [leaflet,] *Students for a Democratic Union Ephemera*, Fryer Library Collection, 1989, p1.

[20] Union executive's letter to Vice Chancellor Brian Wilson calling for rejection of SDU petition for referendum, 17 Apr 1989, p1.

[21] Anonymous, "Referendum a fraud"—Union electoral officer's circular attempting to discredit referendum, signed Bill McKinley. (n.d.), Students for a Democratic Union Ephemera, Fryer Library Collection,1989, p1.

[22] *Semper Floreat*, July, no. 5, 1989, p. 41.

the inquiry ended the National Party's decades-long dominance—a turning point in Queensland's political history

* * *

4ZZZ moved to 621 Coronation Drive, Toowong on July 11th, 1989. This was a significant shift, physically and emotionally exhausting for everyone involved. Once at 'Coro Drive' (as it became known), 4ZZZ had to rebuild the station from the ground up. This involved constructing new broadcast facilities, setting up office space, and rebranding itself as an off-campus radio station. "It was tough," David Lennon admits. "We had to rebuild everything—new studios, new equipment—but it also meant we could finally be independent of UQ politics". According to Anita Greenhill, "there was a lot of trial and error … we had to figure out where everything would go, how to soundproof things, and how to get the best sound possible".

While all this was going on, 4ZZZ still had to stay on the air, 24/7. License regulations required it, but more to the point, a radio station doesn't amount to much if it doesn't have an on-air presence. To keep broadcasting during the move, 4ZZZ shifted its studios to the Mt Coot-tha transmitter site. Just as they did on the morning of the failed eviction attempt, the station would once again broadcast directly through the transmitter, albeit with a little more infrastructure in place. During the preparations to leave St Lucia, a caravan had been acquired and parked behind the station, according to David Lennon. "The techs [Allan Herriman, Andrew Dent and others] were fitting it out with the old Studio Two mixer and everything else necessary for a broadcast van," he says. "[Allan] was tech genius," adds Stefan Armbruster. "I'm sure he had some sort of magic touch, because of the things he kept on air … that just shouldn't have really functioned anymore!"

The caravan "was an old banger," in Stefan's words. "We dragged it up to … the Mt Coot-tha tower in the bush," he says, "which was really hard work because there's no road, just an old, washed-out dirt track; we had to drag it in there and get it up on the blocks". It was parked right next to 4ZZZ's transmitter hut in the middle of the bush; "the best kept secret in Brisbane until the studios were built," in the words of David Lennon (Fig. 5.3). For nearly six months, announcers like the fictitious Hollis broadcast from the caravan, in the middle of the forest without a toilet and rarely a phone line. A simple enough solution, but "the antithesis of public access,"[23] says Gordon Fletcher.

Despite its remote location, quite a few announcers say they loved broadcasting from Mount Coot-tha; the peace and tranquility a welcomed reprieve from the stress of relocating or just life in the city. "It was so romantic to be broadcasting from a mountain top … though I would claim [to the listeners] we were orbiting 150 km above earth," says one. Irena Luckus also "loved

---

[23] G. Williams, *Generation Zed: No other radio like this*. Kingswood Press, 2000, p. 37.

Fig. 5.3 Photo of 4ZZZ's caravan studio, Mt Coot-tha, taken by David Lennon; 1989

doing the graveyards from [that] spot. It [was] like we were 'Major Tom'". Greg Fryer used to hold the microphone out of the window "to capture the magpies and other birds," when he was talking on air.

Unsurprisingly, the remote location wasn't for everyone, and as David Lennon points out, it could be a "very vulnerable scenario, especially at night. Especially for women". Gordon Fletcher notes that "announcers were dropping like flies and/or simply refusing to do shifts".[24] Stefan Armbruster agrees, adding that volunteers often needed transport up and down the mountain. There was also a growing disconnect between those who spent most of their time at Mt Coot-tha and those in the city getting the station premises ready, "working back-room stuff," to steal Stefan's phrase.

* * *

Back down at Coro Drive, the premises were slowly starting to resemble the barebones of a community radio station. Limited funds and dwindling volunteers stretched the renovations out further. These delays would no doubt have been escalated by the diminishing enthusiasm amongst station members about the new location. "It wasn't easy," admits Anita Greenhill. "Not everyone wanted to do it. Lots wanted to just keep broadcasting from the tower, but it wasn't possible."

There's consensus that Toowong felt like an awkward and unnatural fit. "It was claustrophobic," says Stefan. "It wasn't our premises, people didn't feel comfortable going there. There were people shooting up and stuff like that in the car park underneath and in the toilets." Volunteer Tom Maginnis didn't like it "from day

---

[24] G. Williams, *Generation Zed: No other radio like this.* Kingswood Press, 2000, p. 37.

one". Even once 4ZZZ was broadcasting full-time from Coro Drive, there were increasing frustrations within the Collective about the space and a general sense that 4ZZZ needed a better location. Tension was growing between the small number of volunteers who were doing the lion's share of the labour. The move placed enormous pressure on everyone involved, many of whom were already exhausted from the eviction battle and were mostly, if not completely, working for free. There was friction between different factions at the station, particularly over the re-introduction of paid roles versus maintaining an entirely volunteer-driven model. There were times that Coro Drive was a genuinely toxic workplace.

Bitter personal and professional rivalries played out in the background. Things got ugly at times and key people left. Volunteer Guy Ferguson describes one Coordinator "just disappeared without saying anything to anybody". Anita Earl's resignation was a little more dramatic.

> I did my last breakfast shift, played all the noisy annoying music I cared to play, no warnings or anything, and then ... hung [my resignation letter] with a knife into an ox heart, over the Station Coordinator's desk, so when she got into work there was this animal heart with blood dripping on to her desk.

Stefan Armbruster also decided it was time to leave. "Things got quite messy ... it was a really rough time ... maybe that's just because the deeper I got involved, the more factious it was becoming," he says. "But don't get me wrong. It was amazing what was achieved at that place because we stayed, we survived. We survived to fight another day."

Drug use was also prevalent. However, from researching this book I've learned there has always been drug use at 4ZZZ, accompanied by Zed folk arguing about whether or not it constituted a problem. I've come to realise that sometimes drug use is of no consequence; at other times it creates deep mistrust; sometimes there will be "vomit all over the [studio] ground" or a new Station Manager will find a bag of heroin stashed in a filing cabinet; and other times you'll have technician Doug McCallum on your case asking "who's been bonging in the tech room?".

Toowong wasn't always steeped in negativity. Patrick O'Brien joined Triple Zed as an announcer and general volunteer in 1989. He reckons "once we got settled in there it was a good vibe, like we'd survived being attacked and were still alive to stick it to the squares," he says. "But it was ... a pretty drab environment, the record library was too small and it always felt temporary." Patrick says doing live-to-airs at Coro Drive had an almost 'guerrilla' feel. "It's definitely not what that space was designed for," he adds. "I remember The Hekawis nearly shaking the building to the ground one night!"

It was around this time when yours truly also became a 4ZZZ volunteer. I was in my early twenties and keen to make radio, and for the most part, was oblivious to what had been going on in the background over the past year or so. For fresh arrivals such as myself, there was a lot to be positive about.

I wanted to play local punk music on the radio and learn how to be an activist journalist, and there were people at 4ZZZ encouraging me and teaching these skills. Fellow newbie, Darren J says he appreciated the way Triple Zed conducted its business. "It was run out of love rather than money, he says. "Toowong was laissez-faire, anarchist, and really chaotic, but also inspiring in its freedom."

* * *

Soon after the move, volunteer Guy Ferguson saw an urgent need for someone to take on the bookkeeping. "It became clear [the station was] struggling with the finance side," he explains. "[The Station Coordinators] were getting towards their level of burnout … So, I went from journalism into finance because there was an obvious need for someone." By 1989, Guy had fully transitioned into finance, managing subscriptions, bank balances, and rent payments. As he describes it, 4ZZZ had to negotiate the "big jump from being given money by the union every year … to the complete reversal, now paying 25 grand a month rent and paying for everything". The station scrambled to meet its new financial obligations, constantly seeking new ways to pay the bills.

Technical revenue streams, such as renting transmission space to two-way radio companies were explored and utilised. The station even sold broadcast signal to fast food chain Pizza Hut through a highly lucrative process called multiplexing. Normally, radio stations send one clear signal that people can tune into. Multiplexing allowed 4ZZZ to squeeze an extra signal onto their main broadcast, which wasn't heard by regular listeners but could be picked up with special equipment. This is what was sold to Pizza Hut, who used it to broadcast background music in their stores. According to Guy, this could bring in $80,000–$100,000 per year.

The difficult decision to introduce limited on-air sponsorship was made. As covered in Chap. 3, 4ZZZ's founders proudly declared they wouldn't take this route, but a lot had changed since 1975. According to the station's licence renewal, approved in 1990, strict guidelines were set to only accept "announcements from companies and groups which are not promoted on commercial media; which are Brisbane based; and which are not multinational or Australia-wide".[25] 4ZZZ also advised that "announcements should not be offensive to the listening audience". Exactly what a 4ZZZ audience may take umbrage with would become one of the most contentious debates to ever grace Collective meetings for years to come. 4ZZZ also made money on band tour promotions and larger-scale Market Days became a major revenue source (discussed in Chaps. 7 and 8). However, these could only be sustained every six months or so.

---

[25] Australian Broadcasting Tribunal (1990) Public enquiry file on the renewal of 4ZZZ's broadcasting license, 1988–1990. p. 8. Fryer Library, The University of Queensland.

As 4ZZZ's three-year lease at Coronation Drive neared its end, it was clear the station needed a new home. "The neighbours hated us at Coro," Guy Ferguson recalls. "We damaged the ceiling tiles building the place, so we knew we weren't going to get renewed." It must have felt like déjà vu for the volunteers who had stuck around post-UQ. Buying a property was even less viable than in 1989, so it was time to reassess the rental market. A proposal was also developed by The South Brisbane Community Arts Centre Alliance for the State Government to convert one of its unused properties into a fully resourced multi-arts centre.[26] The alliance, which included organisations such as Rock n Roll Circus, the Brisbane Ethnic Music and Arts Centre, Access Arts, and 4ZZZ, argued the need for a permanent home, however, failed to gain support (despite Wayne Goss being Premier).

One night, a chance discovery helped change the course of the search. Guy Ferguson and 4ZZZ producer Connor were walking around Fortitude Valley, an inner-city suburb just north of the Central Business District, in the early hours one morning when a real estate agent's name caught Guy's attention. "It spoke to me," he says, "I wrote it down, and [later] I rang him." The agent began showing Guy (and others) around various properties, none of which were quite right. Then he mentioned one that wasn't on the books formally but might be available. "He said, 'I've got one place that's not listed ... but they're looking for the right people'," Guy recalls.

That property turned out to be 291 St Pauls Terrace (or 264 Barry Parade depending on which entrance you're using) in Fortitude Valley. It was owned by the Search Foundation, an organisation formed by the Communist Party of Australia to look after its assets as it wound down activities. According to Guy, "the Communist Party ... wanted it to go to a like-minded entity, you know, a like-minded institution". 4ZZZ fit the bill.

---

[26] The South Brisbane Community Arts Centre Alliance, '*A proposal for a South Brisbane community arts centre.*', 1990.

CHAPTER 6

Our House (In the Middle of Two Streets)

Terry had been volunteering at the Toowong office for a while—fully trained as a 4ZZZ announcer and taking a weekly front desk shift. One afternoon as he was finishing his shift, fellow volunteers Guy and Josephine walked in, beaming with excitement. "We just picked up the keys to Barry Parade," they announced, holding them up like a prize. "Wanna come see?"

Without hesitation, Terry jumped in the car, and they headed toward Fortitude Valley. The anticipation was palpable. 4ZZZ had finally found a new location, much closer to the city with plenty of room to expand. As they tried to get inside the building, however, the reality was far from the clean slate they had imagined. The place was full of garbage.

The upstairs door wouldn't even budge, blocked by a mass of discarded junk. They tried another on Barry Parade—jammed. They eventually managed to pry open the car park door, stepping inside to find the station's new home drowning in debris. Rubbish piled in corners, dust thick in the air, an eerie stillness in the neglected space. They couldn't do much that day despite there being so much to clear out.

But as they stood there, gazing over the mess, something shifted. This wasn't just any old building. "This is ours," Terry thought. "Our garbage to clean up. Our station to build". The work ahead was immense, but standing in the rubbish, they felt something even stronger than exhaustion—possibility.

Triple Zed's new home was waiting.

* * *

Affectionately known as Zed Towers, 4ZZZ's current premises already had a rich history before it became home to Brisbane's oldest community radio station.Triple Zed occupies a block of land between 264 Barry Parade and 291

St Pauls Terrace: a modest three-story brick building accessible from both streets. The building was constructed in the early 1930s and was first home to Brisbane Spare Parts, which sold pieces "for all makes of cars and trucks," according to a 1946 advertisement in *Queensland Country Life*.[1] The business was owned by Clarrie Beckingham, a political writer known for his work with the Australian Russian Society.[2] Brisbane Spare Parts closed in the late 1960s and the building changed hands, with Beckingham either gifting or selling to the Communist Party of Australia (CPA), at a discounted price.

For the next thirty years, 291 St Pauls Terrace was the Communist Party of Australia's Brisbane Headquarters and a nerve centre of left-wing activism. The Party's state officials worked from offices on the upper floor, just as the majority of 4ZZZ staff do today. The ground floor hosted The People's Bookshop, a public storefront selling leftist literature and serving as a gathering place for like-minded folks. This is where you'll now find Triple Zed's main entrance and reception, accessed from Barry Parade. In the late 1990s the Solidarity Infoshop, a separate entity to 4ZZZ but closely aligned, was granted unused space by the station, based in the same location.

The CPA's headquarters saw its share of conflict and controversy. The building was under frequent surveillance by Queensland's Special Branch police, and the Bjelke-Petersen government's security forces kept a close watch on "291" as it was known.[3] Former activists recall it as an era of banned books and police raids, and people coming and going from 291 St Pauls Terrace were keenly aware they were being observed by authorities.[4]

In 1972 the CPA building was bombed, one of several right-wing extremist attacks at the height of Australia's Cold War tensions. On the night of April 19 (the day before Hitler's birthday), at least 15 sticks of gelignite were detonated near the steps in what is now the 4ZZZ car park, "causing complete wreckage of the party's ground-floor bookshop and printing room, and extensive damage to an upper floor".[5] Windows across the street were broken, and the blast heard in nearby suburbs. Former 4ZZZ Station Manager Stephen Stockwell (Jnr), says rainwater still pools in the place of the explosion.[6] Seven people were in the building at the time of the blast, attending a meeting. This included CPA member, Ted Riethmuller, who (years later) was interviewed by Stefan Armbruster. "All of a sudden there was a big explosion. I can remember jumping over the table to be with my wife who was on the other side," Ted

---

[1] Anon, 'Classifieds', *Queensland Country Life*, 21 September 1996, p. 14.

[2] C. Healy, 'Clarrie Beckingham, Honoured:1905–1998', *The Queensland Journal of Labour History*, no. 2, 2006, p. 11.

[3] J. Darlington, '264 Barry Parade: A History of the 4ZZZ Building', *Radio Times*, 2012, pp. 6–7.

[4] I. Curr, 'Brisbane's Radical Books', 2009, https://workersbushtelegraph.com.au/2008/07/18/radical-books-in-brisbane/ (accessed 27 March 2025).

[5] Anon, 'C.P.A. hits back against terrorist bomb campaign', *Tribune*, 25th April 1972, p. 3.

[6] S. Stockwell, 'If these walls could talk', *Radio Times*, 2010, pp. 16–17.

says. "The room was filled with smoke. Someone raced down to the other end of the building to open windows only to find there weren't any."[7]

A well-known Brisbane Nazi organiser, whose name I won't dignify, allegedly confessed to the bombing, and was charged by the police for the attack but not convicted. Witnesses testified they sold him gelignite on the day of the bombing (with the prosecution even producing a receipt with his name on it), but according to Ted Riethmuller, the accused was acquitted on a technicality. "The rumours have it that [the man charged] threatened to reveal his contacts with Special Branch if he was sent away," Ted says.

Activities at 291 St Paul's Terrace quietened after that, although the building remained a hangout for left-of-centre types in the '70s and '80s.[8] By the end of the 1980s, the Communist Party of Australia was winding down. Internal shifts and the collapse of Soviet communism led the CPA to disband nationally, although as late as 1990 the Barry Parade address was still advertised as the meeting place for a variety of causes including Australian Aid for Ireland and the Australia/Cuba Friendship Society. When the Party leadership decided to liquidate its assets, 4ZZZ reaped the rewards.

* * *

In July 1992, three years after leaving their UQ home, it was time for 4ZZZ to move again and thankfully this time with no need to set up the caravan at Mount Coot-tha. Instead, a temporary studio transplanted directly from Toowong was set up at the far end of level two, where bands now perform for live-to-air broadcasts. Unfortunately, it lacked soundproofing, which wasn't ideal as the street below was noisy with traffic even in 1992. At the start of its lease Triple Zed also shared the bottom floor with the Queensland Folk Federation, and I remember the jaunty refrain of tin whistles and fiddles bleeding through the floorboards, threatening to overpower our voices on air. Gavin Unsworth was a new volunteer technician at the time. "It took quite a few weeks, if not months before Studio One was ready," he says. "It was a huge relief to move out of the temporary digs … 'When will Studio One be ready?' was a permanent topic at Thursday night Collective meetings."

Once again, 4ZZZ would rely on a great deal of volunteer or underpaid labour and ingenuity to transition to a new location. "Can we erect a statue in honour of the technicians who patiently disconnected and re-connected everything to make multiple relocations possible?" asks past volunteer Brett Walker. "They deserve a medal". Doug McCallum and Ray Jousif played major roles. Doug was the lead technician. He'd been involved at UQ but had taken a hiatus from the station for quite a few years. Ray was an unofficial handyman

---

[7] S. Armbruster, *Radical Times*, interview with Ted Riethmuller [audio recording] for SBS, April 2012, http://radicaltimes.info/HTML/popup107c.html (accessed 12 March 2025).

[8] S. Stockwell, 'If these walls could talk', *Radio Times*, 2010, pp. 16–17.

who also played a pivotal role coordinating 4ZZZ's Market Days (discussed in Chap. 8).

Gavin Unsworth began volunteering a few weeks after Zed moved to Fortitude Valley. By that time the basic structure of the studio floor was already in place. "We were basically building studios like it was the late 1970s," he says. "I'd say a lot of ideas came over from St Lucia and got tweaked or improved." Doug designed and built the original studio from scratch, applying various engineering principles for acoustic design and accessibility. Following advice from a book issued by the British Broadcasting Corporation (BBC), he added features like "anti-carpet" ceiling panels for balanced audio absorption. "Carpet is selective in the audio it absorbs," Doug explains, "so on the opposite side … you put anti-carpet". To ensure the studio had enough room to move freely, Doug would often call on yours truly, heavily pregnant at the time, to test mobility around the new broadcast panel. "You were kind of the largest case scenario," he laughs. I don't remember taking this explanation too kindly at the time!

Setting up the microwave link to connect Zed Towers with Mount Coot-tha was another important job. At Toowong, audio made its way to the transmitter via phone lines because there was no 'line of sight' between the two locations. In a nutshell, there needs to be uninterrupted airspace for an FM broadcast to work clearly. Zed Towers had a similar line-of-sight problem, but the phone line approach was expensive. Triple Zed asked its new neighbours to lease out part of their roof, which they agreed to at a cost, and the microwave equipment was brought out of storage.

Doug and Ray were tasked with setting up the microwave dish on the roof next door. A civil engineering company was commissioned to certify that their intentions to "bolt a piece of metal to the side of the building,"[9] wouldn't damage the building's structural integrity. However, the Wang Building (as it was known back then) wasn't built the way it was laid out in the plans. According to Doug, there was a live power cable in a cavity between two faces of brick, which was hit when Ray drove a metal pipe through a hole in the wall. "Giant explosion, lights went out. It was like the end of the world," Doug describes. "And of course the lift well stopped working. People in the Wang building weren't all that happy." No-one was injured and no real harm done, except to Triple Zed's reputation with its new neighbours.

There's usually an enterprising soul or two at 4ZZZ willing to take a risk if they see an opportunity that can benefit the station. During the Zed Towers renovations, a couple of likely lads got word of an abandoned hospital in St Lucia that was rich with materials perfect to repurpose in the new studios and office space. Across a series of midnight raids the volunteers 'liberated' doors, windows, wood, "you know, whatever we could get," they tell me. One night it seemed almost certain the cops had their number.

---

[9] G. Williams, *Generation Zed: No other radio like this.* Kingswood Press, 2000, p. 42.

I had my wagon full of doors and stuff we'd just looted from the hospital, driving towards the Valley, and there's a cop car right next to us ... I said, 'whatever you do, don't look at them!' It was a bit of a hotted-up car back then and you could see all the stuff just piled up, the windows and doors and stuff, driving around at nighttime ... we were really damn suspicious.

Fortunately, the police moved on, and the renegade recyclers were spared from the repercussions of rehousing government property without permission.

* * *

Not long after the move, an old face appeared at Zed Towers—founding member, Jim Beatson, who quickly recognised that owning, rather than renting, the building was critical to the station's survival. "I knew that many members of the Search Foundation had sons and daughters who were involved in the setting up of Zed," Jim says. One crucial connection was through early 4ZZZ journalist Ray Moynihan, whose father had been State Secretary of the Queensland branch of the CPA, while Ray's mother, Josie, looked after the Search Foundation's assets in Queensland. Jim rang Josie and was put in touch with Eric Aarons, a former fulltime CPA Executive member who had led the establishment of Search and managed its finances.[10] Jim drove to Sydney to meet with Eric and after a lengthy chat about the goings on in Bougainville (from where Jim had recently returned), they got to the point of the visit. "I'm working at Zed and interested in organising the purchase of the building from the Search Foundation. Would you be willing to sell the building?" Jim asked the CPA Executive. Eric simply answered 'Yes'.

To fund the purchase, 4ZZZ took out a loan from the Bank of Queensland. Government support in the form of an Arts grant helped with the deposit. On October 14th, 1993, a representative of the Minister for Arts reported to State Parliament that he'd presented a cheque for $73,300 to 4ZZZ towards costs of purchasing the building. The funding was justified by saying that the station provided a regular outlet to "contemporary music performers in Brisbane".[11] Jeanette Clarkson, who volunteered with the programs *Art and About* and *Art There Somewhere* had close ties with the arts community and spearheaded a large-scale auction which, according to Jim Beatson, raised another $40,000.

A newspaper article in *The Courier Mail* at the time included a photograph of a group of 4ZZZ volunteers proudly standing in front of their new home. 4ZZZ had transitioned from a homeless 13-year-old to having a mortgage at the ripe old age of 18. It was a responsibility the station was ready to tackle. However, News Coordinator Kerryn Henry had a clear message for listeners:

[10] Search Foundation, 'Eric Aarons: 1919–2019', Search Foundation, https://www.search.org.au/eric_aarons (accessed 1 February 2025).

[11] Queensland Parliament, *Queensland Parliamentary Debates [Hansard]*, Brisbane, 19 October 1993, p. 5210.

"[4ZZZ] will be making monthly repayments … and being unfunded we cannot allow our fundraising efforts to drop off".[12] As the old saying goes, there's no rest for the weary. No sooner had 4ZZZ staff secured a permanent home at Zed Towers, than its broadcast site needed attention.

* * *

Firstly, the transmitter was on its way out. It had been nearly twenty years since Triple Zed installed its existing transmitter at Mount Coot-tha (Figs. 6.1 and 6.2). Doug McCallum first became involved with Zed the day the 30-metre tower and transmitter were erected in 1978, after hearing a callout on the radio asking for help with digging holes. "I rode my motorcycle up there and swung pickaxes and shovels," he says, "Even jumped on the rock drill". To set the

Fig. 6.1 Photo of 4ZZZ's first transmitter tower being erected at Mt Coot-tha; photographer unknown; 1978

[12] A. Dawson, 'Station workers buy the building', *The Courier Mail*, 24 September 1993, p. 31.

Fig. 6.2 Cover of *Radio Times* magazine celebrating 4ZZZ's full-power licence; designed by Matt Mawson; August 1978

concrete foundations for the tower, the team had to dig holes slightly bigger than a cubic metre, however, quite often they'd hit rock. "Luckily the station had access to a powder monkey [explosives handler]," Doug says.

> All that was needed was for some silly people to jump around on the end of a rock drill, drill some holes and the powder monkey would put the charges in and blow up the rocks. It was really quite uneventful. He had these blast mats which were put over the holes. When he fired the charges, there was this 'whomp' and the ground shook a bit, a bit of dust rose. That was it.

Doug also says the crane operators hadn't been told the site was on the side of a mountain which created a convoluted and precarious situation to raise the tower, by which time journalists who'd arrived to report on the event had given up and gone home. Now, in 1993, it was the transmitter's turn to give up. "[It had] been dying for a long time,"[13] Gavin Unsworth says. 4ZZZ's signal had probably only been pumping out about 30% capacity for years.

Given 4ZZZ had sunk all its finances into a mortgage, the station bought a home-built transmitter from, as Gavin describes, "somebody with a good reputation". It didn't turn out for the best. Many a time, Triple Zed announcers would find themselves off the air. Larysa Fabok remembers the transmitter going down during a graveyard shift, at 3:00am. "I put a record on and curled up under the … desk for a nap," she says. "I knew that when the transmitter was fixed … someone would ring up to celebrate that we were back [on air]. That is exactly what happened!" Peter Rohweder was 4ZZZ's Finance Officer, moving into voluntary Station Manager duties around this time. He remembers having to "rock up at [Gavin's] house a number of times to pick him up in the morning to go fix the transmitter we'd bought for 8K". "He was the only one that we could get to fix it," Peter adds. "Gavin was a lifeline."

To compound issues, Brisbane City Council (BCC) wanted to see changes made at the transmission site at Mount Coot-tha. 4ZZZ and classical station 4MBS had been operating from the mountain location since the latter was issued a licence in 1979 (supported by Triple Zed, see Chap. 10). They were joined by 96five Family Radio in the early 1980s at which point Council "decided having three separate facilities … was a mess and an eyesore"[14] and encouraged the broadcasters to share a building and tower. According to Gavin, BCC said they would raise the rates per installation as an "incentive" to share facilities.[15]

4MBS Station Manager Gary Thorpe came up with the idea to form Broadcasting Park; a private company to manage shared transmitter assets at Mount Coot-tha, allowing each station to broadcast from the same FM antenna and tower. "There was a Queensland Arts grant available for community infrastructure," explains Gavin. The grant application was successful, and the company was formed with 4MBS, 4ZZZ and Family Radio all having a share with two members each on the Board of Directors. The company was officially registered on June 13th, 1995.[16] Fellow community radio stations 98.9 FM (Triple A Murri Country) and Radio 4EB (Brisbane's multicultural broadcaster) joined the company in the early 2000s.

Gavin has been on Broadcasting Park's Board of Directors since the early days. He says establishing the shared site at Mount Coot-tha was "very tough for 4ZZZ as the first piece of construction involved demolishing the Zed hut and tower". As such, Triple Zed had to broadcast from the Family Radio building with a cable over to a temporary antenna on the 4MBS tower. "We lost height and coverage and were in that position for … a couple of years,

---

[13] G. Williams, *Generation Zed: No other radio like this*, Kingswood Press, 2000, p. 45.

[14] Williams, *Generation Zed: No other radio like this*, p. 45.

[15] Williams, *Generation Zed: No other radio like this*, p. 46.

[16] According to records held by the Australian Securities and Investments Commission.

I think," Gavin says. However, once settled 4ZZZ was finally broadcasting at full power for the first time in 15 years or so.[17]

The initial grant provided funding for a building and a tower but little else, which meant the stations involved had to take on significant loans to sustain the project. Peter Rohweder is Chair of Broadcasting Park and has been since 1998. He estimates 4ZZZ needed at least $90,000 to invest in the company, which placed huge strain on the station, which also needed to meet its mortgage repayments. Despite the outlay, Broadcasting Park has enabled five community radio stations to pool their resources and labour to benefit the sector, and to share the responsibilities of maintaining one of the most vital infrastructure components of their operations. It was cited in the Community Broadcasting Association of Australia's submission to the Federal Government's 2023 *Community Broadcasting Sector Sustainability Review*, as an exemplar of station collaboration "to achieve economies of scale and program efficiency".[18] According to current 4ZZZ technician Ben Ryan, Triple Zed and its Broadcasting Park partners are unique because they maintain the entire broadcast chain of their operations, unlike commercial stations that outsource transmitter operations. 4ZZZ announcer, Branko Cosic, is a Technical Engineer by trade. His love for Broadcasting Park goes so far that his band Tape/Off named one of their albums after the venture, in "homage to 4ZZZ".

On the topic of technical achievements, Zed Towers has borne witness to a mind-blowing array of innovations, for the most part implemented out of the goodness of people's hearts and their passion for community radio and independent media. A whole book could (and should) be dedicated to the work required to build a radio station from scratch, and it pains me to gloss over the details. While the 4ZZZ FM channel still broadcasts via the microwave link atop the roof next door, the station also utilises a complex IT system designed by its own volunteers and part-time staff. Doug McCallum built computers for Triple Zed as early as the 1980s. And while internet connectivity is now a ubiquitous part of life, 4ZZZ had to navigate its way through the introduction of this thing called 'the World Wide Web'. As early as 1993, the station was (somewhat) online. "Originally, we had an intermittent connection that we used sparingly. It dialed up as needed," says Gavin Unsworth. Later the station moved to another internet service provider that allowed for emails to be transferred once a day. According to Gavin, Triple Zed also started livestreaming as early as 1997. "As far as I can tell we were the first radio station in Australia to do that," he says. "World-wide would have been in the low hundreds then too".

---

[17] G. Williams, Generation Zed: No other radio like this. Kingswood Press, 2000, p. 46.

[18] Community Broadcasting Association of Australia, *Community Broadcasting Sustainability Review Submission: regarding the sustainability of the community broadcasting sector, including funding, administration and regulation for the Community Broadcasting Program and Indigenous Broadcasting and Media Program*, https://www.infrastructure.gov.au/sites/default/files/documents/cbssr-cbaa.pdf (accessed 12 March 2025).

Most of the features of the 4ZZZ studio have been built by Zed folk. The tech team have designed their own software that allows listeners to communicate with announcers directly via a text-line and connects a security camera at the after-hours entrance to the studio computer so the person on-air can see who is ringing the bell and allow them access remotely. There's even a light in the studio that immediately flashes when someone pays a subscription, accompanied with a message letting the announcer know their name, so they can thank them on-air. As former Station Manager Stephen Stockwell (Jnr) explains:

> We've got our own systems in place ... so we're really well insulated from a service taking something away from us ... The creativity and the ability to problem-solve - it's one of the really inspiring things about being around Triple Zed.

These features are even more impressive when you realise they are built from the ground up by Triple Zed itself. The Queensland Music Awards (QMA) have been paying attention. Zed's Digital Pigeonhole, an internal database designed by Patrick King that allows announcers to plan their shows remotely, won the 2022 QMA for Innovation

* * *

Owning your own home gives you the freedom to decorate, and in 2010 4ZZZ decided to celebrate its 35th birthday by giving Zed Towers a full-frontal makeover. 'Paint the Town Zed' was a campaign to leverage the iconic nature of Zed Towers and make 4ZZZ more visible. The project was initiated by the station management team of Michelle Brown, Giordana Caputo and Stacey Coleman. The remnants of an old sign for Brisbane Spare Parts were still visible on the front façade of Zed Towers and the team decided that this space could serve as a massive canvas for public art. "We were really keen to do something a bit different to try and put Triple Zed back on the radar," Michelle Brown says.

Funding was secured through an Arts Queensland grant and to make the mural a true community-driven project, 4ZZZ held a design competition. It was a challenge to ensure the winning artist had the capability to execute a mural of this scale and the team needed to filter through applicants based on feasibility as much as aesthetics. While the mural was an exciting project, it also carried significant risks. The financial investment, public visibility, and potential safety hazards made it one of the most consequential projects the team had undertaken. "It was a massive risk," says Giordana. "If it bombed or if we made the wrong decision, it was, you know, going to be really bad!"

Brad Eastman, aka Beastman, won the contract. "When I saw the final mock-up, I thought ... it's going to be iconic," Giordana says. Beastman was relatively unknown outside Sydney's street art scene at the time, but his distinctive geometric, vibrant style resonated with 4ZZZ's branding. "Beastman sort of just popped up everywhere [after the Zed Tower mural]," says Stacey. "He became pretty much world-known, so he was really thankful to us, because I think him having done a building like that really launched his career." The process took over a week, with Beastman and his team using a cherry picker to paint the façade. Stacey recalls the experience of watching the mural come to life. "I remember when it got to the third floor, seeing the guys there in the cherry picker outside the window," she says. "They have to do the messy outline kind of thing first for the whole thing, so it looked a bit ridiculous at first." Stacey brought her mum to see the mural's progress and in an unexpected gesture, Beastman gave them a ride to the top floor in the cherry picker to get a closer view (Fig. 6.3).

As the design took shape, it transformed from rough outlines into the vivid mural that still adorns Zed Towers. The Barry Parade entrance certainly catches the eye, with its neon signage and brightly painted entrance, resplendent in

Fig. 6.3 Photo of Zed Towers front facade, Fortitude Valley, during revamp by artist Beastman, taken by Julian Schmitt; 2010

shades of blue, green, and black. This is despite the growing number of high-rises slowly dominating the landscape. "It definitely made an impact," adds Michelle, and "really helped the station get out there … Yeah, you can't miss Triple Zed now. I love it" (Fig. 6.4).

There have been other important improvements at the station. In 2009, Michelle led an initiative to make 4ZZZ more environmentally sustainable. This was a conscious push to reduce the station's carbon footprint and to align Triple Zed with progressive environmental values. People attracted to 4ZZZ are generally affiliated with the goal of being as environmentally responsible as possible, with *Eco Radio* and its predecessor *The Peace and Environment Show* being among the longest running programs at the station. It was also a financial decision, as the station was always looking for ways to cut operational costs, especially electricity. One of the most tangible and impactful changes was the installation of solar panels. The system was designed so that excess power could

Fig. 6.4 Photo of Zed Towers front facade, Fortitude Valley, post-revamp, by artist Beastman, taken by Julian Schmitt; 2010

be fed back into the grid, although Michelle points out this is a rarity "because running a station does take up so much power". To complement the solar panels, 4ZZZ undertook energy audits to assess where they were wasting power and how to improve efficiency. These audits examined everything from lighting, office equipment and broadcasting technology to identify where savings could be made.

* * *

Homeownership also brings with it the responsibility of repairs, and over the past thirty odd years, Zed Towers has needed a lot of tender loving care. Despite a strict 'no drinks in the studio policy,' 4ZZZ technicians have been faced with a sodden broadcast desk on more than one occasion. "The tech people at Triple Zed are just geniuses, right?" asks former Station Manager Stephen Stockwell (Jnr). Stephen says he arrived at the station one morning to present the news show *Brisbane Line* to find someone had spilt wine all over the desk. Before he knew it, the tech team had him relocated to use an old broadcast panel that was quickly assembled as a temporary fix. Stephen recalls Ben Ryan sitting in the hallway, soldering to rebuild the ruined desk. "It's a dark art," he says.

> I don't understand how it works. I'm just leaving them to it … 14 hours after the whole thing fell apart, [Ben had] rebuilt it. And we were back on air [in the main studio].

There were also times when it seemed Zed Towers itself might not stand the test of time. Oh, if those walls could talk! I listened to them once, after producer and announcer Alex Oliver accosted me as I arrived, telling me I should tap on a door frame and put my ear up against it. The building sounded like it was alive, and not metaphorically. A termite infestation was threatening to destroy 4ZZZ from the inside. "The building might have been falling down, it might not have been safe," Stacey Coleman remembers. A structural check determined which sections of the building needed modifying and the exterminators dealt with the rest.

My shock at hearing the crinkly-crackly crawlings of termites in the walls pales in comparison to the day Jack McDonnell arrived at the station to find it flooded. Jack is 4ZZZ's Station Manager now, but at the time he was a student journalist volunteering with the morning news headlines. It was March 2017, and ex-tropical cyclone Debbie had produced a massive rain low over Brisbane for a few days. "I came down to the bottom floor early one morning … and there was around one inch of water downstairs." Jack started moving things and found a broom. "I rolled up the jeans and started cleaning," he says, "pushing water towards the door". The damage would cause on-going problems so that, according to Grace Pashley, by the time she became Station Manager later that year, the station needed to raise $30,000 to deal with rising damp on the bottom floor and apply waterproofing paint. "It was just really mouldy and yuck, and needed to be dried out," Grace says.

You may have noticed a few mentions of stairs in this chapter. Zed Towers has three levels, one of which can only be accessed via a staircase. There are also small steps to the studio floor (level two) which, even with a portable ramp, make it difficult to enter in a wheelchair. The studio doors are also near impossible to navigate in a chair or with crutches without assistance. "I wish we could make the building more accessible," says current Volunteer Coordinator, Salty Otton. "I know if I won the lottery that's where the majority of my money would be going." In 2024 a small advance was made to improve the reception level, with the installation of 'Deanna's Door', an electronic sliding door with automatic sensors and a large entry/exit button. Deanna is an announcer at 4ZZZ who uses a wheelchair and has programmed over 150 episodes of the graveyard show *Randomizzzed* on 4ZZZ. According to Zed's Accessibility Coordinator Owen Sadler, the door is worth around $15,000, funded by donors organised by Deanna and her partner Paul, who is connected in the construction industry.

* * *

There's a chance that 4ZZZ isn't the only resident at Zed Towers. While I've never experienced it myself, late-night announcers have long mentioned peculiar goings on at the station. Announcers Judy Jetson and Jay Bones both say they've heard chairs rolling around on the top floor in the early hours, while Joe Hogar spent one night turning off the same light while being the only one in the building, which—understandably—"really freaked [him] out". "Flashing and dimming lights, footsteps overhead, and shadows lurking on the staircase" have all been reported at the station, says paranormal investigator Dr Gemma Regan (aka Nyx Fullmoon).

Josh Guinan has been involved with Triple Zed for over twenty years. One night in the mid-2000s he was doing a graveyard shift with fellow announcer Gemma Snowdon and they were the only ones in the building. "While we were talking on air, we heard the front door into Studio One slam," Josh says. Rather than dismissing the incident as imagination or paranoia, Josh decided to check the station's audio logs to see if the sound had been picked up. What he found assured them it wasn't just in their heads. "It came up there too," Josh confirms. "That was the night I started believing in ghosts," Gemma Snowdon says. "I don't remember checking the audio logs but do remember seeing someone walk upstairs but when I went up there was no one there!"

Josh also remembers being told about the 4ZZZ ghost as part of his announcer training with Alan 'Schleke' Roberts which would be enough to give anyone the creeps considering new broadcasters usually started with a graveyard shift at that time. Schleke says one night he came downstairs and there was a young man laying asleep amongst some boxes. Not wanting to deal with the stranger alone, he went and got the Station Manager. "When we returned, there was nobody there," Schleke says. "The on-air announcer who was looking through the fishtank window said nobody walked past. The door outside was locked and there was no other way out."

In 2012, Gemma Regan's Paranormal Scientific Investigations (PSI) group was invited by Alex Downs from *Eco Radio* to investigate Zed Towers, after they had attended one of PSI's public ghost hunts. Gemma holds a PhD in Biological Anthropology and a Genetics degree and says she enjoys "utilising [her] scientific background to research supernatural phenomena and so leapt at the thrilling opportunity".

> We spent an eerie night with Infrared cameras, multiple voice recorders and the Ouija board trying to capture evidence of a ghost, all while the diligent announcers were hidden in Studio One entertaining the 4ZZZ night owls over the airwaves ... A midnight seance invoked the usual knocks and bangs, and an orb and a strange mist were captured [on camera] in the storeroom ...

Alex Oliver invited the PSI team onto his show *The Frog and Peach*, to discuss the ghost hunt. Feedback was so positive Gemma became a regular guest, known as Dr Ray-Gun which led to her own show *The Witching Hour*; first in a graveyard slot and then from 10:00pm, where it has now been for 12 years. Gemma says she has experienced many paranormal experiences during her show including seeing an announcer who has since passed sitting in the adjacent studio before they "disappeared before [her] eyes".

The same year, *Tranzmission* host Charlie Woods had their own encounter with what they believe was the 4ZZZ ghost. Working on a database system with technician Patrick King, Charlie kept seeing something out of the corner of their eye, on the stairs. "It kept distracting me, but I tried to focus on the database stuff we were working on," they say. "Suddenly the radio that's downstairs just turned on full blast. I was like 'okay, hello, I get that you really like this song'". Charlie later shared their experience with fellow volunteer Kel, who immediately knew the exact spot Charlie noticed the distraction. It turns out Kel had seen it there "a bunch of times as well". Whether or not you believe in ghosts, the stories at 4ZZZ are enough to make some uneasy about taking on a graveyard shift by themselves. However, don't be too quick to assume what you're experiencing is paranormal. Community Engagement Coordinator Liz Witt did, and "then Ben Ryan crawled out of the ceiling!".

Let's hope any ethereal cohabitors are willing to share the premises for a long time to come. It took nearly 26 years but 4ZZZ has paid off the Zed Towers loan. Grace Pashley had the pleasure of announcing to the 4ZZZ community that it owns the building with no strings attached, during her time as Station Manager. "Every Annual General Meeting, [volunteer] Joe Hogar would ask, 'Have we paid off the building?'," Grace says. "And in 2019, the answer was finally 'yes' ... It felt like a moment of collective victory for everyone who had supported the station over the years."

PART II

Music Runs Through Our Veins

CHAPTER 7

More Than Just a Radio Station

High above Brisbane city, nestled against a fledgling skyline, there once stood a building with a reputation more magical than bricks and mortar could convey. Each evening, its 18-metre-high curved archway was lit against the night, a beacon of yellow, blue, and white fluorescence. When it first opened in 1940, the venue had its own cable-car railway to ferry guests up the steep hill.[1] By 1947 it was renamed Cloudland Ballroom. With its art deco curves, grand façade, and sweeping interior, Cloudland wasn't just a place to dance; it was an experience.

Inside, the marvels continued, especially beneath the dancers' feet. Its sprung floor, modelled after California's famed La Monica Ballroom, was a marvel of design. Built on a suspension of metal coil springs and made of polished spotted gum timber,[2] the floor almost seemed to breathe with movement. It had just the right bounce—not too soft, not too stiff—and made dancers feel like they were floating on air. With cushioned steps, partners could move in unison, their bodies buoyed. It was one of the finest dance floors in the Southern Hemisphere.[3]

My mum, Pam Anderson, still remembers the first time she stepped onto that floor in 1963. She had just moved to Brisbane from Rockhampton in Central Queensland, where dances were held in modest church halls and YMCA gyms, chairs stacked against the walls to make room to move. Cloudland in comparison was irresistible. "Right from when you walked through the huge arch entrance, it was overwhelming," she recalls. "And the

---

[1] J. G. Lergessner. *Cloudland: Queen of the dancehalls*, Brisbane, Boolarong Press, 2013.

[2] Museum of Brisbane, 'MoB Sunday Stories: Cloudland Ballroom', *Museum of Brisbane*, Brisbane, QLD, https://www.museumofbrisbane.com.au/mob-sunday-stories-cloudland-ballroom/ (accessed 25 November 2024).

[3] Lergessner. *Cloudland: Queen of the dancehalls*.

© The Author(s), under exclusive license to Springer Nature Switzerland AG 2025
H. Anderson, *People Powered Radio*,
https://doi.org/10.1007/978-3-032-05689-4_7

cushioned floor was a dream to dance on". Pam remembers the alcoves, too—quiet corners along the edge of the vast dancefloor, where young women sat waiting, hopeful of a dance.

Like its floor, Cloudland was never static—it moved with the times. Less than two decades after Pam's nights of gypsy taps and waltzes, the same floor would tremble under the weight of five thousand punk rockers. In 1982 The Clash stormed the ballroom, Joe Strummer railing against apathy and referring to Brisbane as "Pigsville"[4] as the sprung floor amplified every pogoing stomp. Cloudland had adapted—transforming from elegant ballroom to rock cathedral. For nearly three years 4ZZZ had been booking fundraisers concerts at the venue, mostly under the Joint Effort moniker.

Frontman of Brisbane punk band Razar, Marty Burke, remembers the feeling of approaching Cloudland in the late '70s, both as an audience member and a performer. "You'd look up on top of Bowen Hills," he says, "and you'd see the eggshell-shaped effigy up on the hill. It was exciting right from then". For Marty, performing at a Cloudland Joint Effort was a milestone to be proud of. "I used to hear my mum and dad talking about the Cloudland Ballroom," he says, "because my father was a singer, and my mum a piano player". When he told them his band would be playing there, something shifted. "My dad looked at me and said, 'You're really getting somewhere,' because even he knew that Cloudland was something special to play". Marty pauses, his voice catching. "I didn't have the heart to tell him it was a punk night!"

Cloudland was that kind of place—a rare space where generations, genres, and dreams collided. It held the laughter of beauty queens, the shouts of rockstars, the whispered hopes of young dancers in waiting. But the Bjelke-Petersen government cared little for such cultural pursuits. The Clash concert would be the last for 4ZZZ. Liquor licensing regulators shut the venue down and soon after Cloudland was demolished illegally, under the cover of night, to make way for an apartment complex.[5]

* * *

The 4ZZZ founders always intended to include live music as part of the station's ecosystem. In its earliest promotions, the radio station was advertised as being "beyond radio". A flyer inserted into the inaugural edition of *Radio Times* promised the following:

> … 4ZZ-FM will also be establishing regular dance circuits to provide good entertainment around Brisbane. They will take the form of mid-monthly

---

[4] J. Walker. 'Clash's brutal rock wows fans', *The Courier Mail*, 22 February 1982, p. unknown, http://blackmarketclash.co.uk/, (accessed 25 November 2024).

[5] J. Hinchliffe. 'Brisbane has got its house back': inside two grand heritage restorations in a famously pro-development city', *The Guardian*, 21 July 2024, https://www.theguardian.com/australia-news/article/2024/jul/21/queensland-heritage-house-restorations-newstead-house-lamb-house, (accessed 30 August 2024).

suburban dances, plus monster multi-entertainment specials on the last Sunday of each month. The specials will be held in the Union Complex at the University, and will combine rock, films, folk, food, poetry, theatre and lots of dancing.

While some 'suburban dances' were held, Triple Zed was more successful in upholding its promise of on-campus entertainment, especially in the form of live music. The 4ZZZ promotions department became a driving force that put Brisbane on the map for touring artists, both from elsewhere in Australia and overseas. This clearly benefited the local music scene but was also a substantial and welcomed money-generator for the station.

To stay as independent as possible and remain distinct from its commercial counterparts, 4ZZZ's early policy was one of not accepting sponsorship. Subscription fees could only raise so much money however, especially when the station was operating on a low-power licence with a geographically limited audience. Founding members John Stanwell and Jim Beatson already knew the success of the FOCO Club and HARPO, initiatives from the '60s and '70s that successfully tapped into live entertainment to raise funds. "FOCO was set up primarily as a vehicle to try to radicalise young people," says John. The venue also booked bands and theatre nights, poetry readings and similar arts events, as well as fostering an outlet for political speech and activism. According to John, most importantly "[FOCO] taught the progressives and the left that we could actually make money out of putting on quality activities". John became heavily involved with the FOCO Club's successor, HARPO, where he developed a suite of skills that proved very useful at Triple Zed. "HARPO put on incredible shows ... we had nothing, we were nothing, we were just a bunch of people in a room, and we brought bands up from Melbourne," John says. "Once you had that confidence you could do almost anything."

And so, the Joint Effort was born. The collaboration at the heart of the 'Joint' in the name was between 4ZZZ and Brisbane music. According to John Stanwell, the core concept was "to build an important relationship with the local music scene". This took me by surprise, having often wondered about the origin of the title. 4ZZZ is now so synonymous with local music that it hadn't crossed my mind that this hadn't always been the case. Joint Efforts were 4ZZZ's first attempts to establish those connections. That and to make a lot of money! "The dope reference was a side benefit," John adds. "It quickly led to the coda used in marketing—'you'd be a dope to miss it'."

The first Joint Efforts were held in 1976 during Orientation Week, at the University of Queensland Student Union Complex. 'Joint Effort No. 1' (Friday, 20th February) featured The Carol Lloyd Band (former member of Railroad Gin), Bob Hudson, Quasar, Moonlite, and The Booze Blues & Boogie Band. On Saturday, Quasar and Moonlite returned, joined by Crossfire, and Marga to complete the lineup for 'Joint Effort No. 2'. Admission for each was $2.00.

The Joint Effort events became one of 4ZZZ's defining initiatives during its formative years. Brisbane's live music infrastructure was limited at the time.

There were no large-scale rock or alternative venues, meaning Joint Efforts quickly filled an important gap. "They were fantastic events, and they were well regarded," early volunteer Margot Foster says, adding that "everybody went!". Fellow volunteer Gordon Curtis agrees. "There was such an energy to the night," he says. "The bands brought it, the crowd fed off it, and the whole place felt alive".

The bands were paid but the primary concern was to raise funds for the station. This meant Triple Zed staff and volunteers ran the whole show, taking money at the door, selling food and operating the bar. The scale of the volunteer effort was remarkable, and John Stanwell credits the passion of the people involved for the events' successes. "It was really all about the energy and vision of the volunteers who believed in what we were doing," he says. Margot Foster agrees. "Everybody chipped in ... We did the bars. We did the doors. ... everybody had jobs to do ... It was the focus of your life." According to Tony Biggs, it was a rite of passage to volunteer. "When I started, you couldn't get on air until you'd done volunteering at the Joint Efforts or around the station," he says. "When the Joint Efforts were at the University Refec, you were doing the door, sweeping up, cleaning up after the gig." As Jim Beatson explains, "the way you made a lot of money was to serve beer".[6] The UQ Student Union was already licenced, which 4ZZZ could leverage off, "never having to calculate quantities for or pre-buy alcohol, which was a killer," says John Stanwell. According to Gordon Curtis, "selling beer tickets was chaotic but fun". "You'd spend the whole night running around, making sure everyone had what they needed ... and sometimes I drank a little too much of the beer," he laughs.

At first, 4ZZZ also provided their own security at the venues. "Nobody ever got in for free," John says, but not for want of trying. Prospective freeloaders would even look for ways to get in via the roof. "OH&S people would have a fit," says John, "if they had the slightest idea that unpaid, untrained, unregistered people climbed up what was effectively a four-storey building at some points". Acting as a bouncer wasn't one of Margot Foster's favourite tasks but not for a reason you might suspect. "I remember being terrified of the huge possums on the roof," she admits. Margot would need to "scout around," keeping an eye out for people trying to get in but says "it was the possums that frightened me the most".

Despite 4ZZZ's financial survival being Joint Effort's primary motivator, Gordon Curtis maintains they weren't just about raising money. "It was about creating a space where people could come together and feel like they were part of something," he says. John Stanwell doesn't recall explicit conversations about the strategic outcomes of Joint Efforts. Rather, the entrepreneurs considered "what's the best way to make them good and attractive and maximise

[6] A. Ettling, 'Triple Zed's Joint Efforts: Beer, bands and breaking the news', in A Ettling & I. McIntyre (eds), *Knocking the top off: A people's history of alcohol in Australia*, Coffs Harbour, Interventions Inc, 2023, p. 371.

the income?". Through that, John says, they "unearthed all those other things ... we created spaces for local and visiting bands to perform". "These spaces became more than just venues—they were places where people felt like part of a community."

It wasn't long before 4ZZZ was attracting interstate bands—and then international ones. Margot Foster describes the station's promotional events as a "passing parade of who was fantastic at the time". Local bands, such as Razar and The Survivors, benefited from the opportunity to support higher profile artists. One of Razar's first gigs was a Joint Effort on March 13th, 1978, at the UQ Union Complex, supporting Wasted Days and The Survivors.[7] "That's how we got a lot of exposure," says Marty from Razar, adding "we were lucky". John Willsteed says his band Zero was also afforded some great opportunities through the Joint Effort gigs of the early '80s. "Triple Z was very generous with Zero," he says, adding they supported international visitors such as The Cure and Echo and the Bunnymen.

While John Stanwell was Promotions Coordinator at the station (1975–1977), he believed the Student Union Complex was too attractive to consider other venues for Joint Efforts. It had a set of large-scale and adjoining venues, suitable for a range of different sized gigs and 4ZZZ were treated favorably by the Union. John says it was also beneficial that the university campus generally received a "blind eye" treatment from the police. 4ZZZ did, however, put on other music promotions, mostly organising deals for touring shows, which grew as external promoters became aware of 4ZZZ's power. "This was of course all around 'alternative/niche' musicians," John says. "We went fairly slowly to these things outside the 'formula that worked [i.e. Joint Efforts]".

* * *

David Darling started volunteering at 4ZZZ in February 1978 after moving north from Melbourne. "I got involved in the station because the only people I knew in Brisbane worked at Triple Zed," he says. His friend Peter Williamson was a staff member in the Promotions department and the two decided to branch out from the university campus and investigate organising pub gigs. "Brisbane never really had the rock pub scene traditionally," John Stanwell says. "The venues were more concert halls or coffee shop type places." David knew the "pub rock thing had been going for a year or two in Melbourne," and saw potential for a Southeast Queensland market. For bands like Melbourne's Hunters and Collectors, Queensland was the new frontier. Says frontman Mark Seymour, "early on, we just worked our way up the East Coast very gradually and then dipped our toes in Brisbane. That was a big step".

Peter Williamson found a partner in tour promoter, Harvey Lister who "used to do the big stuff in Brisbane," David says. One afternoon he and

---

[7] T. Murphy, 'Poster advertising The Joint Effort held on Friday 31 March 1978', Jim Goodwin music poster collection. State Library of Queensland.

Peter found themselves at The Queen's Hotel in the Central Business District and couldn't help but notice it had a stage and a beer garden (sporting a kitsch collection of fake palm trees). A deal was arranged and 4ZZZ soundproofed the garden. Melbourne icons Skyhooks played Triple Zed's first gig at The Queen's Hotel, on Wednesday May 24th, 1978, to a crowd of 800 people.[8] Brisbane band The Survivors supported the Skyhooks show. "We used to play a lot for 4ZZZ," says The Survivors' drummer, Bruce Anthon. "It was kind of like a scene without realising it at the time." Bruce sees a clear through-line between those early gigs and 4ZZZ's contemporary reputation as a bastion of local music support, suggesting "[It] just kept bubbling away and then morphed into 50 years of [bands playing for 4ZZZ]".

Between the work involved in Joint Efforts and a blossoming pub scene, 4ZZZ needed to hire a second Promotions Coordinator. "Somehow I ended up with a job," David Darling says, although he downgraded in pay from his previous fulltime position with a screen-printing company. The shift to pub gigs allowed 4ZZZ to expand its audience while ensuring a steady revenue stream from ticket and alcohol sales. The station expanded its network of venues to the Gold Coast, with the Surfair Hotel becoming Triple Zed's out of town venue, hosting touring acts such as Cold Chisel and Mi-Sex.[9] 4ZZZ also started booking bands in the outer bayside suburbs, including the Cleveland Sands Hotel which was advertised as "among the first hotels in Brisbane to provide live rock music for its patrons".[10] Ian Davies remembers playing the Sands with his band Toy Watches, "regulars on the 4ZZZ music circuit in Brisbane," he says. Through these ventures 4ZZZ provided much of Southeast Queensland with a constant flow of alternative music.

* * *

As the pub gig scene grew, tensions arose between different music subcultures, particularly the punk scene and other audiences. David and the 4ZZZ team responded by developing a dual-venue model, running The Queens Hotel for larger, more mainstream acts, and The Exchange Hotel for local punk bands, providing each with their own dedicated space. "It kept the punks from going to The Queens, so they had their own venue up the street," says David. "We used to put 200 or 300 people in the Exchange on a Friday night [and] put 1,000 people in The Queens." However, by March 1979, The Queens Hotel had its temporary licence revoked. There had been noise complaints, and the Queensland Licensing Commission weren't prepared to negotiate.[11] The venues

---

[8] A. Ettling, 'Triple Zed's Joint Efforts: Beer, bands and breaking the news', in A Ettling & I. McIntyre (eds), *Knocking the top off: A people's history of alcohol in Australia*, Coffs Harbour, Interventions Inc, 2023, p. 371.

[9] 4ZZZ, '4ZZZ Presents' *Radio Times*, September 1979.

[10] 'Promotion for Entertainment', *Wynnum-Redlands Herald*, 21 February 1979, p. 30.

[11] 'Pub concerts must move on', *Sunday Sun*, 15 April 1979, p. 14.

were also heavily targeted by police, as were many others throughout the '70s and '80s. Marty Burke from Razar recalls it was a regular occurrence to find undercover police in their audiences. "We used to take great offense," Marty says.

> And I still think it's crazy that a young band of guys ... [are] playing a gig and in comes the police, gradually, in the form of undercover sort of guys. They'd have one or two people walking around and they were definitely not our crowd. And you'd think, 'who's that?'. Next minute someone would get arrested for swearing.

Razar would later release their song *Task Force (Undercover Cops)*, a firm favourite on the Triple Zed airwaves.

Plenty of 4ZZZ staff and volunteers also report being harassed by the police, particularly during Joh Bjelke Petersen's premiership. There are countless stories of 'special attention' from the constabulary, including constant roadside checks, drug raids, and threatening remarks at press conferences and protest rallies. According to announcer Tony Biggs, displaying a 4ZZZ sticker on your car was enough to get pulled over. "Everyone that was ever on payroll ... or that was on air in a volunteer sense, all got raided," he says. "All of us. And the cops would tell us, 'we know what you're doing down there, and we hear it'." Founding Zedder Sue Horton believes most of the people who'd been involved with Triple Zed, would have had Special Branch files on them. "If you went to a demonstration, members of the Special Branch would say hello to you by name," Sue says. "I was a middle-class girl from Corinda, you know. ... For a while there it was incomprehensible."

When licensing issues and noise complaints forced 4ZZZ to leave both The Queens Hotel and The Exchange, the station turned to other venues like The New York and The National Hotel, continuing to have "a profound impact on Brisbane's music scene," according to Zed volunteer and sound engineer Mark Louttit. The Triple Zed promotions team also sought out the Cloudland Ballroom, a larger venue that could accommodate thousands of attendees. David Darling describes how this transition occurred almost accidentally. "We just came up with the idea of going up and seeing the old guy up at Cloudland," he says. It paid off and the ballroom soon became the main venue for 4ZZZ's larger events. The first show was held on May 18th, 1979, headlined by one of Australia's "most important songwriters,"[12] Richard Clapton. According to David, Joint Efforts were starting to lose their sheen with University authorities, who had refused to approve some gigs. "Richard Clapton was meant to be at the Uni," says David. "We'd signed contracts, so we had to find somewhere to put it."

---

[12] I. McFarlane, 'Hello Tiger!', *Rhythms Magazine*, Issue 325, September-October 2024, (https://www.thirdstonepress.com.au/archive-3-blog/2024/11/10/richard-clapton-hello-tiger, (accessed 7 April 2025).

The ballroom floor at Cloudland added an extra element of magic to the venue. 4ZZZ volunteer Dan Flannery vividly recalls the venue's bouncing floor where "you didn't have to move to dance; the floor threw you into the air". Announcer Michael Finucan has similar memories. "The Clash at Cloudland was supreme," he says. "With the sprung dance floor, you were just catapulted into the air along with everybody else who was pogoing." "You'd see roadies hanging off the PA [public address system], just trying to hold it down," DJ Tony Biggs adds. "In fact, I'm pretty sure it came down during an Angels gig once." This isn't surprising given that show drew the largest crowd The Angels had performed to in an indoor venue, with 3200 people in attendance.[13] Volunteer Margot Foster remembers the venue fondly. "My god, that sprung floor. It was just heaving," she describes. "I feel really lucky to have been there at that time when music was going through such a revolution."

The success of Cloudland gigs, like 4ZZZ's other venues, relied heavily on volunteer contributions to keep costs manageable. Volunteers staffed the bar, managed entry, and helped with set-up and pack-down. Anne Jones was Station Co-ordinator in 1982 and was actively involved in working the door at Cloudland and handling the finances. In a time before electronic transactions, the sheer amount of physical cash that had to be counted and secured at the end of the night was mind-boggling. "Thousands of people were going to Cloudland and there we were at the end of the night, just with bags of cash, soaked in beer," Anne recalls. In the later 1980s, Finance Coordinator Stephen Davies remembers similar procedures.

> We would go down to a backroom ... chuck all the money on the table - beer-soaked five-dollar notes - and then we'd have to count it with the band management and divvy it up.

4ZZZ volunteer Mark Louttit remembers XTC, Dr Feelgood, and Ian Dury & the Blockheads as some of the top touring bands to play at Cloudland. There were also plenty of Australian tours. Midnight Oil drummer, Rob Hirst says "the fearless folks at radio 4ZZZ" were the band's greatest allies in the late '70s/early '80s. "During the worst dark days of Joh [Bjelke-Petersen] ... 4ZZZ was a lonely, guiding light for our band and for so many others, both local and interstate." The benefits flowed both ways. "When we had big-name bands like Midnight Oil," volunteer Gordon Curtis says, "the turnout was incredible, and so were the profits". Cloudland made such an impression on Midnight Oil that their song, *Dreamworld* laments the destruction of it and other Queensland heritage-listed areas.[14]

Despite its success, the Cloudland era wasn't without challenges. Licensing issues, noise complaints, and government interference were persistent obstacles. Nearby residents, including judges and other influential figures, lodged

---

[13] 4ZZZ, '4ZZZ Presents', *Radio Times*, September 1979, p. 1.

[14] Midnight Oil, 'Dreamworld', Diesel and Dust, Sprint/Columbia, 1987.

repeated complaints about noise levels. "The noise complaints across the river ... They wielded a lot of power with the Petersen government," says David Darling. Another issue was the congregation of people outside the venue after concerts, which also drew complaints from locals. Anne Jones recalls that "the trouble wasn't the gig itself," but rather "people hanging around afterwards," adding that one complainant said they found a couple fornicating in their front yard!

These post-gig gatherings sometimes drew the inevitable unwanted attention from the police, who weren't too shy to also target the bands. Prior to Sydney shock rock outfit, Jimmy and the Boys playing a Christmas Eve Joint Effort at Cloudland in 1979, the *Sunday Sun* reported that singer Ignatius Jones intended to burn an effigy of baby Jesus on stage. Police arrived at the concert early and "just before [the band] came on, burly plainclothes police took up vantage points around the front of the stage, ready to pounce".[15] Ignatius came on stage, appropriately dressed as Santa Claus, and threw assorted gifts to the audience. "He then blasted *Sunday Sun* [for false reporting], the police and Joh Bjelke-Petersen."[16] No babies were burned. Police went backstage after the show and questioned the band about the story in the newspaper, which Ignatius denied.

Despite efforts to soundproof the space and comply with regulations, the State Government eventually pulled the venue's temporary bar licence, citing alcohol violations. As David Darling puts it, "[Cloudland] did everything they could to keep going for us ... but they just ran out of options". This effectively brought an end to 4ZZZ's iconic run of gigs there. On November 7th, 1982, Cloudland Ballroom was demolished in a controversial overnight operation by the Deen Brothers demolition company. Despite its listing with the National Trust and significant public opposition, the building was razed without official permits, sparking widespread outrage.[17]

In the early 1980s, David and Peter Williamson left 4ZZZ to start their own gig promotion business. However, they continued to work closely with the station, one of their most notable collaborations being the Dead Kennedys gigs in 1982, which saw Brisbane band The Black Assassins reform as a support act, and the Dead Kennedys drummer DH Peligro arrested after one show "for drinking on the street and being black".[18]

* * *

[15] B.Hurst, Cloudland and Beyond, Radio Times, Jan/Feb, 1980 p. 5.

[16] Hurst, 'Cloudland and Beyond', p. 5.

[17] J. Hinchliffe. 'Brisbane has got its house back': inside two grand heritage restorations in a famously pro-development city', *The Guardian*, 21 July 2024, https://www.theguardian.com/australia-news/article/2024/jul/21/queensland-heritage-house-restorations-newstead-house-lamb-house, (accessed 30 August 2024).

[18] The Black Assassins. 'Gigs 1981–2007', The Black Assassins, http://www.blackassassins.net/Gigs.html, (accessed 31 August 2024).

The University of Queensland became increasingly resistant to 4ZZZ holding large-scale gigs on campus as of the 1980s, evidenced in correspondence held in their archives. For example, the Fire Brigade were required to attend two fires at a Joint Effort held in April 1980. A security report from the time claims the Brigade were hampered by a large crowd, "many of them dressed in weird clothing and heavy makeup,"[19] who subjected the fire fighters to "abuse and foul language".[20] Record was also made of students being attacked on the way home from the Joint Effort to their college accommodation. At the time, Student Union President, Eugene O'Sullivan, defended 4ZZZ fundraisers, claiming much of the disruptive behaviour was "neither a new occurrence on campus, nor confined solely to 4ZZZ functions".[21] The UQ Union also denied claims that most punters at the gigs were not university students. In solidarity with the radio station, a motion passed at a meeting of Union Council in June to "continue to allow 4ZZZ to hold Joint Efforts because they provided a good form of entertainment for Union members and are a major source of 4ZZZ's revenue".[22] In August 1981, the University Vice Chancellor overrode this decision and cancelled a 4ZZZ function with four days' notice, saying an application to sell alcohol had not been received. This followed a previous complaint that the station had sold liquor without a permit in February of the same year.[23]

University administration softened their stance early in 1982, although not for long. In September, Joint Efforts were banned on campus for the rest of the year, "thanks to some efficient vandalism,"[24] as UQ student magazine, *Semper Floreat* reports. According to university administration, when British post-punk outfit The Fall played a Joint Effort on Friday August 13th, over $2000 worth of damage occurred across the campus, including 27 smashed glass louvres (in the Architecture, Music & Planning Building) and a broken boomgate. A car belonging to a Triple Zed patron was also broken into and pushed into the university's lake. The *Semper* article mentioned a civil engineering student function on campus the same night and suggested 4ZZZ and its supporters were scapegoats: "it hardly seems fair that Joint Effort goers must sacrifice their fun for the antics of a few vandals—be they punks or engineers".[25] Unfortunately, 4ZZZ's case wasn't helped by reports of "punks sighted" in the areas where the damage occurred; in fact, the Student Union had already

[19] 'Letter from University Security to University Registrar' [letter to University Registrar], 17 April 1980, The University of Queensland Archives, Brisbane, QLD.

[20] 'Letter from University Security to University Registrar', 17 April 1980.

[21] 'Letter from the UQ Student Union President to University Vice Chancellor' [letter to University Vice Chancellor], 10 June 1980, The University of Queensland Archives, Brisbane, QLD.

[22] 'Letter from the UQ Student Union President to University Vice Chancellor', 10 June 1980.

[23] 'Letter from University Registrar to UQ Student Union Secretary' [Letter to UQ Student Union secretary], 19 August 1981, The University of Queensland Archives, Brisbane, QLD.

[24] S. Dempsey, 'Joint Efforts Extinguished'. *Semper Floreat*, no. 8, 13 September 1982, p. 9.

[25] S. Dempsey, 'Joint Efforts Extinguished'. *Semper Floreat*, no. 8, 13 September 1982, p. 9.

introduced a policy to ban punk bands from playing at the university. Station workers must have been somewhat concerned to lose such a lucrative opportunity, but Station Coordinator Anne Jones told *Semper* that 4ZZZ "should survive,"[26] as the station had just created a new hire to focus on fundraising.

Damning as they are, I can't help but feel a little cynicism when I read the police and security reports cited above. I've seen similar documents from the 1990s that describe 4ZZZ 'incidences' very differently to my own experiences of them and been baffled more than once by police accounts of Market Days that completely contradict what I witnessed (see Chap. 9). Given 4ZZZ's reputation with 'the authorities' in the 1980s, and the police harassment reported by 4ZZZ workers at the time, it's not unreasonable to suspect some bias against the station and a conflation of problems at Triple Zed events.

Mark Seymour from Hunters and Collectors has fond memories of the 4ZZZ audience, far removed from those described in the University of Queensland's security reports. Early in their career, they were scheduled to play a Triple Zed gig at the Refectory, but their equipment truck was delayed. Most of the punters were already at the venue, waiting for the band to perform, when the gear finally arrived. "We backed the truck up to a door to the side of the stage and made an announcement," Mark says: "We've got to set up now in front of you now".

> And people started helping … literally pulled the gear out of the truck. And it was a big PA, you know, big, all that old school technology … the tonnage was ludicrous. And just all these kids helped us do it, you know. … Yeah, I thought that was really quite special.

Post-Cloudland, 4ZZZ would run a string of other venues, including Amyl's Nightspace (from 1983 at the National Hotel). Ian Davies from Brisbane band The Colours remembers playing the opening weekend of Amyl's, supporting The Go-Betweens. "Bands such as Real Life, Little Heroes … Hoodoo Gurus and the Laughing Clowns played the venue," Ian says, "however, one of the biggest gigs … at Amyl's was Iggy Pop, The New Christs and Outer Limits". Plagued by licensing issues and the fickle nature of the entertainment industry, Triple Zed's search for a stable venue was never resolved although there were plenty explored over the years, including Sensoria (above the Op Shop in George Street, 1985) and the Crystal Club (Dooleys Hotel, 1987) as well as regular gigs at the Aussie Nash, South Leagues Club, and the Alliance Hotel. Deb Strutt worked in Promotions from 1982 to 1987 and says it sometimes felt like "decades of gig after gig after gig". Joint Efforts continued to go ahead, sometimes at UQ, but also East Leagues and other venues capable of accommodating 2000 or so punters. Notable acts during this time included Nick Cave and the Bad Seeds, Screamin' Jay Hawkins, and Jesus and Mary Chain. "It was a mammoth, massive, amazing time," remarks Deb. "It's incredible looking back at who we put on" (Fig. 7.1).

---

[26] Dempsey, 'Joint Efforts Extinguished', p. 9.

Fig. 7.1 Poster for 4ZZZ Octobanana celebrations, designed by Sally Hart; 1985

There's a letter in The University of Queensland Archives that made me snort with laughter when I read it, which wasn't a good look in the sandstone sanctuary of the university's Fryer Library. It is a memorandum to the University Vice Chancellor from the Acting Registrar, dated April 16th, 1986, which aims to set the former's mind at ease regarding an upcoming concert. It speaks to the deteriorating relationship between university and radio station. 4ZZZ had advertised a concert at the UQ Refectory for which they had not sought permission. "This morning I spoke to the organiser, Debra Strutt, who is new to the job," the letter explains, "and who seems to have been unaware of the need to get permission for such events".

The concert has been advertised with the starting time of 7:30pm and a closing time of 12 midnight. The band is a middle-of-the-road one, called The Saints which, according to Miss Strutt will not attract a punk audience.²⁷

The Rough Guide to Punk describes The Saints' first record *I'm Stranded* as "almost certainly the best punk album to come out of Australia".²⁸

* * *

Once 4ZZZ had settled at Toowong, it continued to offer promotional deals for touring bands (Seattle grunge pioneers, Mudhoney, at East Leagues Club in 1990 were a highlight for yours truly). The station had many more bills to pay now it lived outside the cocoon of the UQ Student Union. The 4ZZZ Market Day—originally a small fete that coincided with Radiothon—expanded across the 1990s, so much so that Chap. 8 is dedicated to the venture. A few attempts were made to start up regular venues but nothing operated directly by 4ZZZ lasted for very long. However, there have been some notable fundraisers, many of which have saved the station in times of desperation (mostly caused by ageing transmitters). The following are but a few.

'Dub Day Afternoon' was a successful annual fundraiser for 4ZZZ, sparked by Phillip Hill, aka Basmati, who had lived in countries where reggae and dancehall were either mainstream or had strong subcultures. Upon arriving in Brisbane, he was surprised by the lack of venues for such music, and by the minimal airtime the genres received on 4ZZZ, aside from DJ No MC (Patrick Whitman)'s programming. Basmati was friends with 4ZZZ announcers Victor Huml and Alan 'Schleke' Roberts, and the trio convinced the station to try a reggae-themed event for which Schleke coined the name 'Dub Day Afternoon'. "I wanted it to be authentic," Basmati explains, "which is why it had that mix of live music styles that Australians are familiar with, and Jamaican sound-system DJ/MC styles as well". After that first Dub Day Afternoon, Basmati took on the event himself.

At its peak 'Dub Day Afternoon' raised $10,000 a year for the station. During the first, an enterprising (and obviously unauthorised) ally of 4ZZZ organised a "green" raffle to raise extra money. Rumour has it that a lot of people bought tickets but, according to a 4ZZZ volunteer "the venture didn't go down too well with the venue, and they had a word never to do it again". In 2007, 'Dub Day Afternoon' coincided with the federal election and Basmati remembers "a buzz in the air as the results came in, announced by various acts throughout the night". When it was revealed that standing (conservative) Prime Minister John Howard had lost his seat, the audience erupted in cheers.

---

²⁷ Acting Registrar, 'Memorandum to University of Queensland Vice Chancellor' [Letter to University of Queensland Vice Chancellor], 16 April 1986, The University of Queensland Archives, Brisbane, QLD.

²⁸ A. Spicer, *The Rough Guide to Punk*. Toronto, Rough Guides, p. 276.

Fig. 7.2 Poster for the 4ZZZ event 'Dub Day Afternoon', designed by Basmati; 2012

Basmati says he loved organising 'Dub Day Afternoon'. "It enabled me to showcase reggae music in an authentic Jamaican style," he says. "Not just to a niche reggae fan crowd but to people more broadly in Brisbane … raising dollars for Zed at the same time." 'Dub Day Afternoon' ran until 2012. "The 10th anniversary of the event was a good time to call it a day," Basmati says. "The workload … was enormous and other parts of my life took higher priorities." (Fig. 7.2)

Basmati also lent a hand to 'Brain Banana', a series of multi-room events at The Jubilee Hotel in Fortitude Valley, co-coordinated with Zed volunteers Sam Kretschman (aka DJ SLK) and Justin Law. In 2006 4ZZZ was again in desperate need of money. The building was at risk of going into receivership so members of the Triple Zed Board approached the team to help. Sam had an already established relationship with The Jubilee through a previous set of highly successful electronica fundraisers called 'Ekkythump', while Justin had worked on the massive 2002

7 MORE THAN JUST A RADIO STATION   111

Fig. 7.3 Poster for the 4ZZZ event 'Brain Banana', designed by Sam Kretschman and Benjamin Constantine; 2008

'Bananangeddon' Market Day and was an experienced booker of punk shows. "We teamed up, put on a three-stage event, Punk, Electro and Reggae, and it was a huge success," Justin says. The name 'Brain Banana' came from Sam.

> The phrase 'It's got me by the BRAIN BANANA' was … a weird *Ren and Stimpy*-esque statement that my friends and I would say when something was very hard to do or contemplate … We thought it was a good name to attract the weirdos, and we certainly did – 1100 of them.

A cast of 4ZZZ volunteers pitched in, helping on the door, managing stages and selling merchandise, reminiscent of Joint Effort days (Fig. 7.3).

'Brain Banana' was held on the Queen's Birthday long weekend every year until 2010. Starting in the early evening, the diverse array of music on offer was enough to impress even the most discerning of tastes. As the night wore on, many punters (including me) would venture into 'the other' rooms to have their brains expanded by new genres and bands. The DIY nature of all three music scenes quickly proved there was more that united than divided them. 'Brain Banana' shows featured a mixture of mostly local outfits, including Zed volunteer artists Samedi Sound System and Nam Shub of Enki, and the occasional touring artist such as Front End Loader, Combat Wombat, and Firehouse. Like 'Dub Day Afternoon', they raised tens of thousands of dollars for the station and revitalised connections between 4ZZZ and underground live music scenes. Collaborating with the Jubilee Hotel also led to Justin meeting his partner Lizzy—their son Harrison shares a birthday with 4ZZZ.

* * *

'Rumble Rock' was another memorable fundraiser, bringing together music and 'professional' wrestling on six occasions between 2009 and 2016. These were initially organised by Hoops and Loki of the 4ZZZ show, *Riff Patrol*. "When I moved to Brisbane, all the wrestling shows were family-friendly events," says Hoops. "I wanted something a bit crazier." Loki was friends with a lot of local wrestlers, so they floated the idea with them and with Triple Zed. Hoops says people at the station were very sceptical about the first show, especially after he "insisted on flying [grappler] Joey Russell Jnr up from Melbourne and advertising midget wrestling". Sponsorship Manager Stacey Coleman got involved after the first and says 'Rumble Rock' is the event she was most proud of during her time at the station. "They were always really successful, and coordinating them was really fun," she says. "I just thought it was amazing to marry the two—rock 'n' roll and wrestling." (Fig. 7.4)

'Rumble Rock' holds a special place in my heart with my son, Kelso Kahoniz, being one of the wrestlers involved. For the show in 2011, he was a heel (villain) who hated 4ZZZ because of the neglect he'd experienced as the child of a Triple Zed volunteer. In a promotional interview with *Kids with Class Kicking Arse* he bemoaned being hungry and begging me to come home and make him a sandwich, to which I'd replied, "I'm sorry but I have to volunteer! You'll need to take care of yourself". In 2012, Regurgitator headlined the band lineup although the show may be most remembered for "the infamous 'flying dildo' incident," as Hoops describes it. "One wrestler threw a sex toy into the crowd and hit an audience member right in the face, cutting her across the nose." Fortunately, she took it in her stride and Hoops and Loki won the 2012 4ZZZ 'Biggest Volunteer-Organised Fundraiser' award for their efforts. However, Hoops says his main memory of 'Rumble Rock' "will always be watching Kelso dive from the balcony at The Arena [in 2013] … and thinking 'this is the best show Brisbane has ever seen'".

Early 4ZZZ Promoter David Darling returned to 4ZZZ in the 2000s, joining the Board of Directors and helping to revive *Radio Times*. He even organised a few more fundraising gigs for the station and helped Stacey

7 MORE THAN JUST A RADIO STATION   113

Fig. 7.4 Poster for the 4ZZZ event 'Rumble Rock', designed by Nyssa Elliott; 2012

Coleman with the last of the Rumble Rock shows. "The costs now!" David exclaims, "I had nowhere near the insurance payments [in the '70/'80s] and all that crap that you've got now". Despite the challenges, David still believes in maintaining a strong events strategy as part of 4ZZZ's operations.

Volunteer-powered Joint Efforts also resurface on occasion. In 2003, a series of events called the 'Banana Buffet' saw 30 shows held over 30 days, finishing with a Joint Effort concert. "'Banana Buffett' was about using live music to plug particular shows on 4ZZZ—that's why there were so many gigs, one for each show," explains co-coordinator Lucas Moore. For example, *Queer Radio* held the fabulously titled 'Whatever Floats Your Boat Cruise'. The Joint Effort gig served up by the Banana Buffet team featured a suite of local and interstate bands, including Sydney hip hop group, The Herd. The outfit were booked before they were well-known,

Fig. 7.5 Poster for the 4ZZZ event 'Return of the Joint Effort', designed by Nathan Smith; 2014

but by the time the gig came around they had really gained some traction. "The Herd headlined the front bar stage [of The Jubilee Hotel] which was meant to be around 150 capacity," co-organiser Justin says. "We crammed well over 300 people in there. There was over 1000 people at the event across the three stages. It was an absolute cracker." The last Joint Efforts were most likely held in 2014 and 2015 when Brisbane promotions outfit Punkfest, (run by Cathy Kerlin and Zed announcer Chris Converse) presented 'Return of the Joint Effort' in conjunction with 4ZZZ. According to Chris, both were sold-out shows with the likes of Zed favourites Painters and Dockers, Cosmic Psychos and Hoodoo Gurus, "along with a star-studded cast of local bands." (Fig. 7.5)

* * *

4ZZZ's car park can accommodate only two cars—four if you don't mind being parked in. Yet when it comes time for a Triple Zed car park gig, the space turns into an outdoor Tardis. "You'd be surprised how many people can fit into the car park," says Ilana (Ili) Tulloch, who used to help organise car park shows in the latter part of the 2000s. Before then, 4ZZZ would sometimes use the basement floor to put on house gigs. The most famous of these would no doubt be with Canadian punk band Propagandhi in 1997. The set was broadcast live-to-air and afterwards the band recorded a couple of promotional spots for the station, one of which can be heard on their album, *Where Quantity Is Job #1*. "I remember us being at the soundboard trying to make them, and we were all laughing and laughing," says Propagandhi's bassist, Todd 'The Rod' Kowalski. Unfortunately, Todd doesn't remember the actual gig as clearly.

Once 4ZZZ started utilising the basement space, house gigs moved to the car park where they've been revitalised more than once, motivated especially by *The Punk Show*. Host Josh Murphy says his favourite so far is the *Bloom* album launch for Lismore band Masochist, in early 2022. "Car park shows had died off for a few years, so I was stoked to help bring them back," Josh says.

> To be able to present such an important band to people without the barrier of entry fees, or licensing or any of the shit that can make live music hard for people was, in my mind, exactly what *The Punk Show* and 4ZZZ in general should always be about.

4ZZZ car park gigs have a different focus to other events discussed in this chapter; rather than existing primarily as a means of raising money for the station, they offer an opportunity for the station to connect with communities on a low-key DIY level. Community engagement activities such as First Nations and Youth Week Open Days also utilise the car park, and performances are sometimes broadcast live-to-air. In 2024, 4ZZZ's prison request program *Locked In* hosted a car park gig as a form of outreach for listeners who weren't behind bars. *Locked* In has a strong hip hop following so they collaborated with fellow Zed program *Pass the Aux* and asked a formerly incarcerated artist Noddy No Mask if he'd like to be involved. "Not only did he play it, but he also organised the whole line-up," *Locked In* coordinator CJ says. "The day was beautiful. All the family came."

4ZZZ's sojourns into live music promotion are nothing if not predictable. With the rapid gentrification of Fortitude Valley there has been a growing number of residential high-rise buildings popping up around Zed Towers, and with that a corresponding number of noise complaints. "At the moment [car park gigs] are at a standstill again because of whinging yuppies," Josh says, "but I remain hopeful we'll resurrect them … again".

CHAPTER 8

Market Dazed

The 1992 'Promised Land' Market Day was coming to an end. Nearly 3000 people[1] had attended the 4ZZZ fundraiser held at Captain Burke Park on Saturday March 14th. It was an ambitious affair featuring 13 artists across two stages: the largest lineup showcased by Triple Zed so far. And the risk had been worth it.

With the last light gone, the air buzzed with spent energy and beer breath. The crowd pressed in close to the stage, shoulder to shoulder, waiting for the headlining act. 4ZZZ volunteer Belinda Sinclair (nee McPherson) was exhausted, running on adrenaline. The Market Day she'd poured months into—every call, flyer, and argument—was down to this. Belinda found her way to the mixing desk and grinned at Paul Curtis, Dreamkillers' manager and co-conspirator in pulling together the day's entertainment. "We were both just over the moon, so happy," she says. "I can't remember what he said to me, but it encapsulated what a wonderful moment it was. We had to stop and pause … it was magic."

Dreamkillers hit the stage like a battering ram as flames burst from the front of the stage, scorching the night air. The crowd exploded. Singer Les prowled like an animal, shirtless and electric, the band's noise thick and punishing. Belinda could feel the sound in her ribs. She saw arms thrown skyward, bodies slamming into each other with joyous abandon, a sea of limbs and sweat lit by orange firelight.

This was it. All the grief from the nay-sayers at 4ZZZ who didn't think it could happen, all the chaos—the collapsing second stage, the screaming mother backstage, the thousand small things she'd fixed with grit and caffeine—none of it mattered now. People were laughing, dancing, yelling, clinging to strangers. It

---

[1] G. Williams, *Generation Zed: No other radio like this*, Kingswood Press, 2000, p. 62.

© The Author(s), under exclusive license to Springer Nature
Switzerland AG 2025
H. Anderson, *People Powered Radio*,
https://doi.org/10.1007/978-3-032-05689-4_8

was mayhem, but it was beautiful. "We did it," Belinda thought. "And look how happy everyone is." The final notes rang out and the crowd roared.

The 'Promised Land' Market Day raised $6,000 for 4ZZZ at a time when it was desperately needed.[2] It established a model that was tested and tinkered with for over a decade, involving hundreds of volunteers and thousands of punters. It was an integral part of keeping the station financially afloat.

* * *

The earliest mention I can find of a 4ZZZ Market Day is in the September 1976 edition of *Radio Times*. "One of the long-term fund-raising ideas dreamed up by the Triple Z finance team is the holding of a huge Fair or Fete," the article states. The original 4ZZZ Market Days didn't feature live music; they were small events held outside the station premises at the University of Queensland during Radiothon to engage with the public, attract subscribers, and build station visibility. The last of these was held in March 1988 (albeit with a few live acts). This chapter focuses on the 4ZZZ Market Day as it is more recently remembered: a Brisbane-centric music festival that, at its peak, attracted 10,000 people and was the station's primary income earner.

In the late 1980s 4ZZZ held a few small Market Days off-campus; the first of these in October 1988 at Albert Park (now the Roma Street Parklands) in the Central Business District of Brisbane, and again in 1989 on the Wests Rugby Union oval in Toowong as part of its 'A street kid named Zed' radiothon (raising money to move from the UQ campus). In 1990 it was held at the Paint Factory, a tin theatre in the inner-city suburb of West End. Market Day moved back to Albert Park in 1990 and 1991, with the lineup growing each year.

By October 1991, 4ZZZ was feeling the pinch of the rental market, having been at Coro Drive in Toowong for over two years. An attempt was made to revamp Market Day, with a move to Captain Burke Park, below the southern end of the Story Bridge in Kangaroo Point. The smaller park allowed the bands and markets to be closer together, creating a more cohesive experience. The venue had a good vibe, and it wasn't long before Zed folk were hatching a plan for something a little bigger.

Belinda Sinclair started volunteering at 4ZZZ in 1989, mostly with the newsroom. She didn't play a major role in organising the first Market Day at Captain Burke Park, but the experience lit a fire. "It was fantastic," she says. "I had this vision of it being bigger," which would have greatly benefited the station as it prepared to relocate again. Volunteer Donald Gunn suggested putting bands on the back of a trailer, an idea Belinda initially dismissed. "That's just mad," she thought. "Where are you going to get one of them? But of course, being Don, he magically pulled the trailer out of somewhere." Music promotor and band manager Paul Curtis also played a crucial role

---

[2] G. Williams, *Generation Zed: No other radio like this*, Kingswood Press, 2000, p. 62.

Fig. 8.1 Poster for 4ZZZ's 'Promised Land' Market Day, designed by Dean McInerney; 1992

helping to secure bands for the bill. Paul would continue his support for many years to come.

The idea was to expand to two stages (the second in a small tent) for continuous live music and hire lights to allow performances into the evening. Thirteen bands graced the 'Promised Land' Market Day stages, many of them staples from previous iterations. There isn't the space to list all the artists that played at Market Days, but you'll find most of them in Garry Williams' magazine, *Generation Zed: No other radio like this*. Chopper Division played 'Promised Land', surviving a collapsing tent and going on to play at least six

Market Days, making them one of the bands to perform at more than most (Blowhard and Dream Poppies also played six each according to statistics recorded by SetList.fm). The event was free, and the drinks were cheap (Fig. 8.1).

There were the inevitable teething problems and cleaning the park afterwards was a nightmare even before the rain set in, but as mentioned at the start of this chapter, $6000 was raised, mostly through alcohol sales. According to Finance Coordinator Guy Ferguson, charging $3 for a can of beer that cost 80 cents, and then selling thousands of them at a music festival was a surefire way to raise revenue. Guy recalls being completely unprepared for the large amounts of cash 4ZZZ was dealing with. "I remember having tens of thousands of dollars cash in someone's car boot and no security guards to move the money," he says. To top it off, Belinda met Lance Sinclair from Brisbane band Noose that day; a few months later, they became a couple. "It's been 32 years," she says.

* * *

Buoyed by the success of the 'Promised Land', 4ZZZ held another Market Day in October 1992, again at Captain Burke Park. By this point, David Lennon had moved into the Promotions Coordinator role, and this was his debut festival event. "It was a steep learning curve," he says, "but [we] got the formula right eventually". The poster for 'Octobanana' promised "comedy, stalls, food, cheap beer and free entry" and a lineup of sixteen bands, including Sydney acts Velvet Hammer and Smudge. "We ran out of beer really quick that time," says David, "and had to run around to get more, but not from our initial preferred supplier because they didn't have enough!".

Musician Heli Puhakka from Gravelrash remembers being nervous about playing her first Market Day. "All I could view in front of me was a 'sea of heads'," she says. "Apparently there were thousands of people at the show". My band Acid World also played; I was six-months pregnant and coordinating the stages. I'd continue to help at Market Days for over ten years.

4ZZZ found its groove and the Brisbane underground found its bi-annual music event. A change of venue back to Albert Park was a mere hiccup, and in March 1993, Triple Zed held its 'Elect-O-Cution' Market Day to coincide with the federal elections. A skate ramp was added to the day's entertainment, the event was still free, and fifteen bands were on the bill. Securing a spot on a Market Day lineup was becoming competitive. As Zed announcer Garry Williams notes, "the competition for a place … could be quite heated, given the opportunity it offered to get your band in front of a large crowd". Don't forget that decisions were still being made through the Collective, which added an extra layer of debate. "There were always bees in bonnets because you could only put so many bands on," says volunteer Bec Moore. "Everyone wanted their best friend's band to play." 'Elect-O-Cution' was Dream Poppies third Market Day, and the band held a sausage sizzle to raise money for their upcoming EP *Don't Go*. "The crowds were always so diverse, and we were proud to be part of the local scene," says guitarist/vocalist Tracey Kick. You Am I also came up from Sydney, still relatively new on the Australian indie scene.

A core team of 4ZZZ workers was starting to form, and pretty much as soon as the dust settled from one Market Day, the next would be up for discussion. Besides booking bands, there were liquor licensing requirements to contend with, semi-trailer stages to arrange, booze to be ordered, stalls to be booked and a myriad of other bureaucratic tasks to complete. This was all coordinated by volunteers. Hundreds more would join on the day to work the bar or wherever else needed attention.

Tobin Lyall was unaware of any of the behind-the-scenes goings-on in early 1993. He'd had a fabulous day at 'Elect-O-Cution' and didn't even mind sleeping in his car at the end of the night after a mischievous friend had let down all its tyres. Dusting off the cobwebs the next morning, he saw Triple Zed volunteers packing down and cleaning up, so decided to pick up rubbish around the park. Tobin soon drew the attention of a volunteer so integral to Market Day at the time that the minutes for a Market Day meeting in 1993 refer to him as Ray 'the buck stops here' Jousif. Possibly suspicious of Tobin's motivations, Ray asked him what he was up to. Before he knew it, Tobin was packing down tents and signing up to volunteer at the next event. He'd stay involved for years. Ask Tobin for his best advice for running a Market Day and he'll most likely reply, "you can get a lot done with the promise of a carton of beer"!

* * *

'Zed World' Market Day was held at Albert Park in October 1993 with an expanded lineup of 19 bands, including Dead Flowers from New Zealand, and 4ZZZ's first outdoor dance event, coined the 'The Dance Out'. Volunteer Jane Grigg had returned from the United Kingdom where she was enamoured with the outdoor daytime dance experience of the Notting Hill Carnival. "Brisbane's weather was better than London's so of course I wanted to add a dance stage to Market Day," she says. Jane involved as many of the 4ZZZ 'dance DJs' as possible, including Peter Mogg of *Crucial Cuts* and the *Queer Radio* crew. "We had fun playing funk, rap, house, techno, hardcore, jazz, swingbeat, disco, soul, roots, reggae, dub and many in between things," she says, "to an appreciative and/or baffled bunch who wandered over the hill".

According to Garry Williams, 'Zed World' set "new records ... in beer and t-shirts sold and the most subscriptions in a day".[3] However, it also attracted a large group of 'neo-nazi' skinheads which, according to Garry was foreshadowed. "There were rumours beforehand of [them] coming to ... cause

---

[3] G. Williams, *Generation Zed: No other radio like this*, Kingswood Press, 2000, p. 65.

trouble. After all, when you don't have a fence, anyone can come."[4] Volunteer Alex Wightman was wearing a sundress with his Doc Martens that day, MC'ing the main stage; nothing out of the ordinary for Alex or a Triple Zed crowd. "It was a hot day," he says. "Soon a bunch of skinheads got really, really aggressive towards me." Fortunately, there were plenty of Triple Zed supporters nearby who didn't have any patience for the neo-nazis or their close-minded opinions. "A whole bunch of people I didn't know, who were in the audience, just basically shut them down," Alex explains. "It was amazing." Some of the bands also contended with the skinhead contingency, who eventually got the message they weren't welcome. "That was the night [the band] Fat taught the skinheads how to dance," comments volunteer, Brentyn 'Rollo' Rollason.[5]

'Zed-O-Vision' Market Day in March 1994 included four stages and over 40 acts—still at Albert Park and still free of charge. The poster advertised a skate ramp, over 80 market stalls, a Chai tent (featuring world and blues music), fire breathing, and stilt walking. Jo Bowditch from Sydney melodic-punk band, Blitz Babies says she'll never forget this first Market Day they played. "[4ZZZ] made us Sydneysiders welcome," she says. "I had never played a show that big. The audience was amazing as were all the people who helped us".

4ZZZ volunteer Wave Beach was a regular member of the Market Day crew. "I wouldn't be rostered, but I would do bits to help out," he says. Wave is fondly remembered for continuing the tradition of Alex Wightman's Market Day fashion choices. "I saw Alex one year at an Albert Park one in a real lacy kind of dressy thing, so that got me inspired," Wave says. From that point on, he began his Market Day scouring the stalls for an extravagant outfit. "They were like no other market you would see anywhere, all the 'Zeddy' types with their different wares … I'd pick up a dress on the day." Wave's outfits were always a treat. "One of the highlights … was always seeing what frock [Wave] Beach was going to be rockin'!" adds volunteer Donna Williamson.

'Zed-o-vision' was even more successful from a financial perspective. Guy Ferguson (who'd been involved in Market Days before the 'Promised Land' days) remembers seeing the figures grow each iteration, "up to $50,000 in just a few Market Days". "It was just amazing how finances turned around in just a year or two," he says. However, the Brisbane City Council was not happy with Triple Zed's post-Market Day clean-up efforts. Founding member Jim Beatson, now back at 4ZZZ, says he soon discovered "we couldn't use Brisbane City Council property anymore because [Lord Mayor Jim] Soorley had banned Triple Zed". According to Jim, "there was so much broken glass because people were bringing in mountains of booze … Soorley got really pissed off and said, 'right, that's it, we've had a gutful'". Jim arranged a meeting with Council, at which the Lord Mayor explained that not only was

---

[4] G. Williams, *Generation Zed: No other radio like this*, p. 62.

[5] Rollo passed in 2019, and I didn't have a chance to interview him for this book. This, and other quotes from him are taken from public social media posts.

the physical aftermath of Market Days a problem, but 4ZZZ had also publicly encouraged listeners to harass his office. "He said his staff got literally dozens of phone calls from people … using foul language," Jim says. After many assurances, promises and apologies from Jim the situation was smoothed over. 4ZZZ didn't have permission to return to Albert Park but could plan a Market Day for October under a strict list of conditions, outlined in a *Radio Times* article:

> 4ZZZ [is] required to provide security, fencing, staffing and professional cleaning to the tune of thousands of dollars. This basically means the end of 'free' Market days by the unfortunate look of things but don't get too worried, it's not going to cost the earth.

4ZZZ finally secured Musgrave Park, West End as its venue less than three weeks before the next Market Day was scheduled. Musgrave Park is a central meeting place for urban First Nations people in Southeast Queensland. According to Brisbane Aboriginal elder, Paddy Jerome, the park survived as the last special gathering area for neighbouring clans as white expansion progressed across the city.[6] In its contemporary setting, Musgrave Park is "a site of protest marches, arts markets, sports festivals, NAIDOC[7] Family Fun Day and memorials".[8] According to Market Day minutes, Kirstyn Lindsay was nominated to liaise with the Murri community and "write an invitation, welcoming them to participate". It was decided that any First Nations people would not be charged an entry fee, recognising the radio station was temporarily occupying their space.

The 'West End Of The World' Market Day went ahead on October 29th, 1994. It carried a $5 cover price, with subscribers still allowed free entry. By this stage, volunteer Peter Rohweder had joined the Market Day organising team. He says that after much deliberation at Collective meetings about the ethics of charging an entry fee, it was agreed that "the majority of people going … weren't subscribers. So, fair enough, they should pay". The line-up was slightly pared back with 27 artists on the bill. Rain hampered the first few hours but by the evening, according to Garry Williams, "it was starting to feel like a real Market Day, with Fur, Budd, Blowhard, Sound Surgery and Misery getting the crowd jumping around … and stage diving".[9] Bands at the 'heavier' end

---

[6] R. Kidd, (2000) 'Aboriginal history of the Princess Alexandra hospital site', http://www.linksdisk.com/roskidd/general/g2.htm, (accessed 27 June 2024).

[7] NAIDOC stands for National Aborigines and Islanders Day Observance Committee. It's a week-long celebration, held annually in July, that recognizes the history, culture, and achievements of Aboriginal and Torres Strait Islander peoples in Australia.

[8] C. Go-Sam, 'Fabricating Blackness: Aboriginal identity constructs in the production and authorisation of architecture'. *Society of Architectural Historians, Australia and New Zealand (SAHANZ) Annual Conference*, Brisbane, Australia, 7–10 July 2011, https://espace.library.uq.edu.au/view/UQ:245276, (accessed 4 June 2024).

[9] G. Williams, *Generation Zed: No other radio like this*, Kingswood Press, 2000, p. 66.

of the musical spectrum featured prominently at Market Days and "stage diving was becoming a reflex Pavlovian action"[10] much of the time. At 'West End of the World', a punter named Rod West hit his head stage diving. He died not long after.

Rod West and Tony Puhakka had known each other since childhood and grew up hanging around the local BMX track and skate park. Rod was a few years older, lived out at Burbank, a semi-rural area, and had a "country" background. Tony says Rod wasn't deeply involved in the local music scene; he liked bands like Metallica and AC/DC, but Tony introduced him to punk and hardcore music which he loved. Tony's sister Heli plays heavier-styled music herself—you might recognise her name from elsewhere in this chapter.

Rod came to Market Day because of his friendship with Tony and others, not because he was part of the regular gig-going crowd. "Rod loved to party," Tony says. "He was always up for anything. That's why I suppose he was like 'let's do it, let's go'!" Tony describes himself as "a crazy-arse stage diver," at the time. "You know, it's just what we did. We were all jumping off the stage and stuff, so [Rod] gave it a go."

The friends separated at some point, and later at a party, someone mentioned that Rod had hit his head while stage diving and wasn't doing well. Initially, they thought he'd be okay, but the next day, the seriousness of the injury became clear. Eventually, doctors turned off the life support machines after determining there was no recovery possible. Tony says Rod's parents never expressed strong anger or blame toward Triple Zed, describing them as "good country people". In the aftermath, Tony and his friends gathered for an informal wake that lasted a week. "I think about Rodney all the time," Tony says.

* * *

There wasn't much to celebrate after 'West End of the World'. While the event made its usual profits, Brisbane City Council didn't want Triple Zed to return to Musgrave Park and after Rod's death, enthusiasm for another was dampened. But 4ZZZ had grown reliant on the regular cash-injection that came from Market Days, and it was facing some serious financial difficulties. It was around this time that 4ZZZ's transmitter was rapidly deteriorating and Broadcasting Park was being established, not to mention 4ZZZ had monthly mortgage payments to uphold.

The station had some success with a Ladysmith Black Mambazo[11] tour organised by Promotions Coordinator Jason Kinniburgh, and 4ZZZ's *WorldBeat* world music program had a strong following, presented by perfumer Jonathon Midgley (the best smelling 4ZZZ volunteer to walk the earth). The station decided to capitalise on this growing market and hold a different

---

[10] G. Williams, *Generation Zed: No other radio like this*, p. 65.

[11] Of Paul Simon's *Graceland* fame.

style of musical event, called 'Transglobal'. The idea was to piggyback off the relatively new WOMADelaide world music festival in Adelaide, now an internationally renowned event. 4ZZZ would fly the major artists to Brisbane the following weekend for a second festival. While this was being organised, the idea for taking Market Day back to the University of Queensland was raised. According to Peter Rohweder, the consensus was, "we're kicked out of Albert Park, kicked out of Musgrave Park, with nowhere else to go ... we can do a deal with UQ, make Market Day happen there".

The Student Union agreed and the 'Zed-O-Matique' Market Day was held at UQ on February 18th, 1995. 'Zed-O-Matique' was still free for Zed subscribers and $5 for others, and there were 40-odd artists on the bill. Originally destined for the Great Court in the heart of UQ's campus, the space was considered too small for the 10,000 punters expected to attend. A newly built multi-storey car park which hadn't yet opened to the public became the most viable location, after other options like playing fields were denied due to noise restrictions. Hydraulic lifts were needed to move bands and equipment up and down. Volunteer, Terry O'Connor says at one stage he had to run the lift drunk and untrained, after the designated operator left unexpectedly. "There were so many reasons why I should not have been in control of that hydraulic lift," Terry laughs.

Despite the litany of complaints from organisers, there was still a lot of excitement for punters and performers alike. Local artist Tylea played in a café side-stage and says she was "really, really excited to be playing". "I felt like it was a great spot to observe people from the small stage—a very relaxed vibe." The car park stages were a completely different atmosphere, which Kellie Lloyd from Screamfeeder says was "memorable". "It felt like you were on some bad acid in the middle of [an] industrial nightmare," she says. "It was really fun, but it was just so loud, and it was just such a weird place to have a show."

To cap it off, Peter Rohweder says 'Zed-O-Matique' didn't generate a significant profit for the station, "because we didn't have control of the bar". "I don't know what money we made," he says, "but we didn't make much at all". This placed even more importance on 'Transglobal' being a success, but that was not to be. February was unseasonably wet, and heavy rain was predicted to interrupt the world music festival, scheduled to be held at a large outdoor area. It was moved to a smaller indoor piazza, "and then of course, people just didn't buy tickets," Peter says. "I don't know whether the market research was right or not, but essentially the ticket price was too expensive". The performers still needed to be paid, and according to Peter, 4ZZZ ended up $90,000 poorer as a result.

To manage the debt, bookkeeper Jason Pfingst organised to pay everyone back in installments. As Peter describes, "we put it to all the promoters, 'you can take us to court and get no money because we don't have any money, or we'll slowly pay you over time'". Most of the promoters agreed, although some weren't pleased. A single-word response came from the management agency of one prominent Australian band. Delivered through the fax machine it simply read, "cunt". "They were owed 10 grand, and we couldn't pay them—they were not happy," Peter says.

* * *

4ZZZ is nothing but resilient. Musgrave Park was somehow secured for an April Market Day, this time named 'Zed Beat'. The station employed Tracy Green, a former Station Coordinator who'd worked on earlier Market Days, and pulled the whole event together in six weeks. The poster advertised forty bands across four stages and 100 market stalls. Further thought was given to the advantages of having a gate entrance where people could subscribe on the day to take advantage of free entry and discounted drinks tickets. Much of the responsibility for organising the front entrance fell on the shoulders of Subscriptions Coordinator, Maisy O'Keefe.

The Zed Beat line-up was a mix of newer arrivals on the scene and regular favourites. Powderfinger played their one and only Market Day and Dreamkillers returned as a surefire crowd puller. This was Thomas Rowen's first Market Day—that's my husband! We didn't know each other then, and he also didn't know the band Snappahead. "Who is that guy singing the *Theme from the Muppets* in a dress?" Thomas thought. "It was amazing!" The guy was Andy Peachey, aka Andy Snappa/Chopper, and Thomas would play in bands with him for the next thirty years (and counting). A fledgling Frenzal Rhomb also came up from Sydney, having released only one album at the time. "4ZZZ was our 'in' into Brisbane," says vocalist Jay Whalley.

> We were doing ok in Sydney but not really anywhere else ... I can remember ... meeting some really passionate and supportive people that really facilitated us being able to tour Queensland in front of more than eight people ... At some point everything got set on fire. It seemed on brand.

Not quite everything was set on fire, but a few punters did decide to combat the cool evening by setting cardboard boxes alight. Some were hard to contain and volunteer Donna Williamson "lost an eyebrow"[12] in the process. While Market Days were proving a great success, they were starting to attract an audience that didn't listen to—or care about—4ZZZ. There were fights and word got out afterwards of a sexual assault. The core team of Market Day organisers found it difficult to justify organising another, despite 'Zed Beat' paying off a substantial portion of the 'Transglobal' debt.

After a six-month break, 4ZZZ went ahead with 'Zed Rox' at The Roxy[13] on the weekend of October 28th and 29th 1995, to coincide with the venue's 10th anniversary. It wasn't intended as a Market Day and it was held inside a

---

[12] G. Williams, *Generation Zed: No other radio like this*, Kingswood Press, 2000, p. 67.

[13] The Roxy later became The Arena.

nightclub with a 2,000-person capacity.[14] According to Terry O'Conner the decision was made to add the words 'Market Day' to the poster "because people were going to call it one anyway".[15] There were 27 bands booked across the two days, the second of which was billed as 'Zed Pop Rox'. Entrance was still $5 or free for subscribers. Given the relatively small capacity of The Roxy, its adjoining side street was closed to accommodate a second stage and the stalls. Theoretically, "there would be no work for the station, just a few Zedders to do the door,"[16] Terry explains.

After a mix-up over who was responsible for organising the street closure, Brisbane City Council decided to shut down the outdoor component at 6:00pm on the first day instead of at 10:00pm as advertised. Terry says 4ZZZ got word of the early closure only an hour or so prior, which gave him just enough time to arrange for stallholders to pack up before the police arrived. "Typically, we'd never had that many problems with police [at Market Days]," says Peter. "But there was a reason the Coalition Against Police Violence was located out of Triple Zed." *The Sunday Mail* reported that "up to 40 police were called in to quell the trouble after a market day and street dance party turned ugly".[17] An unnamed witness cited in the article said, "the police just waded in" as the "crowd was milling round at the end of the markets". "I haven't seen the police act like this since 1984 … this is like when Joh was in power,"[18] the witness said.

According to news reports around 20 people were arrested, including Donna Williamson who'd been working as a 4ZZZ volunteer at the event. She approached a group of police to explain the street event wasn't scheduled for closure yet, and after a somewhat heated exchange was grabbed by an officer as she walked away. I saw the whole incident playing out in slow motion, as one of my best friends was thrown into the back of a paddy wagon. Donna passed her bag to me, which was filled with Coalition against Police Violence flyers, calling for me to distribute them. A quarter-page photo of Donna being led away by police was the lead image of *The Sunday Mail's* reportage,[19] her body language screaming, "Are you serious right now?".

Sunday's festivities were shut down after only a few hours, this time due to claims of a liquor licensing breach. Food was supposed to be served but police had closed the food vendor the previous day, citing health regulations. "'Zed Rox' did not make a lot of money," sighs Peter Rohweder. The emotional and physical toll on staff and volunteers was also tangible. "We'd just been doing

---

[14] Anon, 'Triffid: Brisbane To Have New Live Venue', *Scenestr*, Brisbane, QLD, 15 July 2014, https://scenestr.com.au/music/triffid-brisbane-to-have-new-live-venue, (accessed 4 June 2024).

[15] G. Williams, *Generation Zed: No other radio like this*, Kingswood Press, 2000, p. 68.

[16] G. Williams, *Generation Zed: No other radio like this*, p. 68.

[17] 'Police arrest 20 as street party sours', *The Sunday Mail*, 29 October 1995, p. 3.

[18] 'Police arrest 20 as street party sours', p. 3.

[19] 'Police arrest 20 as street party sours', p. 3.

too many big events," says Terry O'Connor. "It wasn't healthy at all ... The station's purpose was to be a radio station, not a promotions company."

* * *

4ZZZ caught a break in 1996 when they met a Zed-friendly Brisbane City Council (BCC) employee who was willing to act as a go-between. "He was an American that had been to festivals [back home], you know, a bit of an old hippie [who recognised Market Day] was good for youth culture," Peter says. Unfortunately, I can't find records of his name, but 4ZZZ's BCC guardian angel investigated past Market Days and determined other festivals received just as many complaints which hadn't been escalated to the extent of those organised by Triple Zed. According to Peter, "he seemed to think that we just had to manage the noise complaints and said, 'if you go ahead and follow the rules, then that's fine'". Sometimes the rules were hard to follow. Annie Winter remembers Liquor Licensing being particularly difficult to navigate. "One time licensing said we were only going to be allowed to serve half nips of alcohol," which contravened the *Liquor Act 1992*. "It felt like they were actually stitching [us] up to make us do something illegal so they could come and shut the whole thing down on the day."

'Zed-O-Mitter' Market Day saw a return to Musgrave Park on March 23rd, 1996 with thirty bands on the main stages and a Doof Tent (dubbed the Garden of Earthly Delights) with a separate line-up of electronic acts. "It was a very punk and folky event," describes Peter. This echoed the broader makeup of 4ZZZ at the time, with Promotions Coordinator, Christine Goebel connected with the local folk scene. I remember this Market Day as one of my favourites; the 4ZZZ 'vibe' felt restored. This may have been the first that volunteer Darren Marston worked at. He was 16 years old when he started at Triple Zed and says that, from driving beer-laden utes around the park to dismantling marquees in the rain, every moment was a learning experience steeped in shared purpose. "I have nothing but fond memories of the whole experience," Darren says, even when it rained so badly his feet peeled "from wearing wet boots for three days".

The 'Zed-O-Mitter' energy was felt early in the day when Scrumfeeder, fully embracing their (rugby league) football-inspired name, took to the stage around 2:00pm. "We were front of house, left stage [with a] beautiful big field of crowd," says vocalist/bassist JJ Speedball. A photo of the gig graces the insert of Scrumfeeder's debut EP, *Guts for Garters.*

> We had a [foot]ball for the 'kick-off' ... walked on, [guitarist] Mungus and me in our Souths Jerseys, [drummer] Brett in his Parramatta Jersey, and I kicked the ball straight off the first song ... When we played our final chord, the football that I kicked out into the crowd of thousands came back to the stage—and I walked off with it. Amazing.

Touring band Nancy Vandal also had a blast. "In Sydney, the punk scene at the time was more about getting your head punched in by someone for wearing the wrong band t-shirt," says guitarist/vocalist Mike 'Fox' Foxall. "Being embraced by the Brissie [4ZZZ] crew was a legit thrill and a window into what a scene could/should be. Unpretentious, fun, a bit weird and collective minded." The night finished with The Toothfaeries, a local acoustic folk/pop dance band described in a *Time Off Magazine* review as being "on the next 'big Brisbane thing' [list]".[20] It was a deliberate decision to winddown with The Toothfaeries, who had the whole crowd dancing rather than moshing. I remember stage managing that night alongside volunteer and artist Gaye Higgs, with big smiles on our faces as we watched thousands of grooving happy punters from behind the stage.

The police arrived on cue at the end of the night and cleared the park "with completely undue haste, herding people like cattle through the one exit".[21] Volunteer Donald Gunn remembers my response more clearly than I do. "There were all these punks and skinheads gathering, facing up against the police," he says. "You strolled up to them saying, 'We've had a great day here, let's not give them what they want'—the best case of crowd control I'd ever seen." Despite this, 'Zed-O-Mitter' marked a return to successful Market Days of old.

Perhaps lulled into a false sense of security, 4ZZZ began plans for 'Cybernana' Market Day in October. Volunteer announcer and graphic artist Will Serantak had already produced a drawing of a futuristic banana character, that included the phrase, 'Cybernana'. This made a great impression on Peter Rohweder. "There was no more debate, you know, the next Market Day was going to be 'Cybernana'," he says. "Will had already drawn the character, 'you've done the poster, it's on the drinks fridge', so it was easy, and then the lineup just came together real easy." Perhaps it was all coming together a little too easily. After an uneventful and enjoyable day, 'Cybernana' was forcibly shut down by more than 60 police. Chapter 9 provides the details.

* * *

Not to be beaten, especially by the Queensland Police Service, 4ZZZ was determined to hold a Market Day in 1997. "Once again, we're back to the drawing board," Peter Rohweder says. "Council was against us again in a big way, State Government was against us, politicians saying 'I don't want this on my watch', all that stuff." Zed volunteers targeted the annual May (Labour) Day rally to gather thousands of signatures of support from a demographic that strongly represented the constituency of the Labor government, who were in power at the time. Albert Park was secured as the venue under the caveat that

---

[20] L. English, L. Denison, E. Dick and A. Stafford. '4ZZZ Market Day', *Time Off Magazine*, 27 March 1996, p. 23.

[21] G. Williams, *Generation Zed: No other radio like this*, Kingswood Press, 2000, p. 70.

Triple Zed hired a professional consultant (which added another $12,500 to the budget).

'Zed Bubble' Market Day was held on October 18th, 1997. It was still free for Triple Zed subscribers although there was a price increase to $10 for others. The poster advertised 37 artists across two stages, the Doof tent and an 'Ethno Super Lounge'. According to *The Courier Mail*, "fifteen special duty police officers and private security were employed for the concert compared with only three officers last year".[22] Despite needing 5,000 payers to break even (meeting minutes noted "8–10,000 punters will be comfy"), it all went without a hitch. Even the hired consultant was impressed, according to Peter, commenting "it's just not my scene ... but you can see that you've got ... five to ten thousand people here that are just really having a great time".

An outside broadcast van simulcast the proceedings for three hours in the afternoon and a Kidzone area was introduced. Former 4ZZZ volunteer Greg Fryer, who was now living down south enjoying a successful acting career, was very happy for his band Lee Harvey and the Oswalds to be booked for 'Zed Bubble'. "Nothing to this day will ever beat that," he says. "It was the shit, man. We played on the Triple Zed Market Day and got in number 19 on the [1996] Hot 100. It was all my dreams come true."

4ZZZ introduced a unique strategy to assist the mostly younger crew of organisers in dealing with Brisbane City Council and other authorities. It didn't seem to register at the time, but most of the main volunteers were under the age of 25. As Peter Rohweder explains, "we felt like these guys are treating us like a bunch of kids, you know ... let's see if we can get some older people involved". Peter's father—an avid coin collector—helped with counting the money while Annie Winter and Darren Marston's mothers volunteered in police liaison. "We set that area up right beside the Doof Tent," laughs Darren. "The mums had techno music pumping all night long." Annie's mother was full of questions such as 'why are the cops hassling people for having purple hair?'. "She was most offended," Annie adds.

4ZZZ settled on running Market Days once a year. Volunteers like Annie Winter, Donna Williamson and Kirstyn Lindsay moved away from Brisbane yet still returned each year to help. "That was quite amazing," says Peter. "They moved themselves back to just focus on getting another market day happening each year". "You'd get to see all your old friends," Donna explains. "It was almost traumatic for me to leave Triple Zed and move [away] and I still miss it." Others, such as Peter, Ray Jousif and Tobin Lyall, would take a week or more away from their paid employment to work on Market Day preparations. "I'd see the dedication of people there," says Ray, "and I thought, if I could make it easier for them, to keep the place going, then I would".

By 1998, Peter Rohweder was employed at 4ZZZ, filling the role of Station Manager and, by default, Market Day coordinator. 'Zedification' Market Day

---

[22] M. McKenna, 'CJC reports on concert clash', *The Courier Mail*, 19 October 1997, page unknown (taken from a clipping in the author's personal collection).

on October 17th was again at Albert Park, with 60-plus bands on the bill and the price still $10 for non-subscribers. The increased number of performers was in part due to the Doof Tent, which had grown "from a small side tent to a full production with a huge sound system and proper world-renowned underground DJs," according to Phill Thomson, a 4ZZZ volunteer who also performed as Nam Shub of Enki. "It was the sort of place that just heaved all day and night—no standing around—full tilt vibes with a crowd that just wanted to lose it on the dance floor!" he says.

> I remember playing alongside a who's who of proper underground Oz techno ... and I was just so chuffed to be involved. Zed was like your mother's arms cradling this fledgling musical movement.

4ZZZ also branched out and organised a full video and audio livestream. A dedicated website was set up with live audio from multiple stages, and live video from the main stage with volunteer Chris Holland taking care of much of the footage. The video was postage-stamp sized, playing at about four frames per second, according to technician Gavin Unsworth, but still "a huge undertaking and very complicated technically". Don't forget this was 1998. "I think it was the first streamed event," Peter Rohweder adds. "We think we might have beat Lollapalooza or something like that by a month. We streamed to one person because bandwidth was very minimal at the time," he says with a laugh. David Lennon—still volunteering at the station—badly broke his leg falling off a ladder setting up cables for the livestream. "When the ambulance took me to the Royal Brisbane Hospital's Admissions and Emergency Ward, guess who was the Head Registrar on duty?" David asks. The answer is Victoria Brazil, the UQ Student Union President who led the attempted eviction of 4ZZZ in 1988. "Life is one big irony," David adds.

The following year's Market Day, called 'Day of the Living Zed' was held at Albert Park on October 23rd, 1999. "Everything went smoothly," confirms Peter Rohweder. The set-up was very similar to 'Zedification' with a slight increase in price, however still free to subscribers. More than 10,000 people attended. While Market Days were permanently ingrained in the Brisbane music calendar, this didn't make them any less special for bands to play. Seja Vogel from Sekiden says it was "a real badge of honour". "I remember it being a big crowd and that being really exciting as we were just getting started as a band," she says. "It was also cool that it wasn't just our usual indie kids in the audience, it was also older punk dudes and fairies and hippies," Seja says, "which I think represents what was special about Market Days". "It really brought every corner of the 4ZZZ community together and everyone was having a lovely time without judgement."

Not long after 'Day of the Living Zed', Albert Park was approved for development, soon to become the Roma Street Parklands. Davies Park in West End was secured, but with a new venue came additional costs and the budget for Market Day was almost unmanageable. 'Return of the Living Zed' was held on October 7th, 2000, following the familiar format. I broke my wrist at the start of the day when I fell from the back of an ice truck; fortunately, Terry O'Connor stepped in to take over my Stage Coordinator duties. Later in the evening I needed to return to the hospital to have my cast loosened, and as I sat waiting to be treated, I heard a young man explaining his injuries to a nurse in the cubical next to me. "I was jumping over a fence trying to get into a music festival," he says. I was so angry I couldn't help but yell a little abuse his way!

'Return of the Living Zed' was successful from an audience perspective, but at the end of the day, it barely broke even. It's unclear why—ticket prices for non-subscribers (now $20) may have been considered too steep or perhaps the change in venue kept punters away. What was clear was the sheer amount of work needed to pull together a Market Day, combined with the financial outlay and risk involved, made it too difficult for a volunteer-run community radio station to sustain. "We were spending $100,000 to make $105,000," Terry says. "You don't risk the station's money to make five grand, it makes no sense. But we loved them so much. It was very hard to kick the habit."

It would be two years before another Market Day was organised. Peter Rohweder was now working full-time managing Brisbane's multicultural community radio station 4EB. A new Station Manager, Dominique Haslan secured a State Government grant, allowing Zed to employ 15 people full time for 18 weeks for marketing, promotions and event management purposes, under the Breaking the Unemployment Cycles Community Jobs Plan Scheme. As "the largest community-based training project undertaken by an Australian community radio station,"[23] it mostly comprised people who already volunteered at the station. According to Peter "[Market Days] couldn't be done with volunteer labour at this point". The budget was about $250,000.

'Bananageddon' Market Day was held at Davies Park on October 26th, 2002 (Fig. 8.2). It featured six stages, skateboarding demonstrations, a film festival, and over 60 artists, and was the first to charge 4ZZZ subscribers an entrance fee ($10 which included a drink ticket). Touring bands on the bill included Spiderbait, Ed Kuepper (formerly of The Saints) and The Celibate Rifles. I had the pleasure of stage managing the All-Stars Tattoo Tent, sponsored by a local tattoo company of the same name. For the most part, this involved hanging onto the tent's centre pole, grinning at my co-workers as we held the thing in place amid the chaos of the crowd. Tamara Bell remembers playing in the tent with her band Gazoonga Attack. "I was going to Market Days since I was 16 and never thought I'd be ... one of that gang, so I was so proud," she says. "My dad had come to see us for the first time and may have had quite a shock," Tamara adds. "People were climbing up the pole in the middle of the tent, some girl pashed me from behind somehow....my poor dad, I always hoped he didn't see that."

---

[23] K. Torpy, 'Meet Market, Triple Z's annual bash bypasses the mainstream', *The Courier Mail*, 21 Oct 2002, p. 12.

Fig. 8.2 Poster for 4ZZZ's 'Bananageddon' Market Day, designed by Adrian from Rinzen; 2002

'Bananageddon' was a complete success, raising around $50,000 for the station. However, Triple Zed recognised the success was closely tied to the Community Jobs Plan Scheme and didn't push its luck with another until 2005.

* * *

4ZZZ's last two Market Days were held at the RNA Showgrounds, neither with a special name. The first, on December 17th, 2005, celebrated Triple Zed's 30th birthday with the likes of David McCormack and the Polaroids, Resin Dogs and Ed Kuepper returning for a second time. Set across a series of pavilions in the Showgrounds, Market Day had a different 'feel' but still was considered an important event to perform at, especially for newer bands. John Mercer says "it was a massive deal" for his band Dick Nasty to play their one and only Market Day. It was also the first he'd attended that he hadn't worked at, "so it was rad to walk around and not be responsible for front gate or have to do a bar shift". "I remember the whole thing buzzing," adds band mate Lucas Moore. "There hadn't been a market day for a few years, and everyone was stoked to be there … the crowd was big, and the sound was good." In a throwback to previous Market Days, volunteer Geoff Wilson witnessed an incident of police violence that escalated into a court case. He was called as a witness in court to testify and provided evidence that challenged the police's version of events, especially their justification for the arrest. "It always felt like [police] were looking for trouble rather than trying to keep things safe," Geoff says.

In 2006, 4ZZZ held its last Market Day to date, again at the RNA Showgrounds on October 21st, with over 50 international, interstate and local bands. Former staff member, Stacey Coleman played in Butcher Birds that day but remembers the other acts much more clearly. "One of my favourite New Zealand bands Batrider played so I had a good dance to them," she says. Butcher Birds' bassist, Jo Nilson, recalls thinking how unusually nice everyone working there was, compared to other festivals she'd attended. "It made me really realise what I'd missed out on by not being able to go to prior ones," she says. Volunteer Josh Guinan agrees. He was working the bar for most of the day which gave him a clear view of the festival's atmosphere, as he observed both the performances and the crowd's energy. "There was such a clash of all different styles of people, genres of music and just a really good vibe," he says.

The night ended with more unwelcomed interference from the police and, the two RNA Showground Market Days raised less than $4,000, combined. Events such as 'Brain Banana' and 'Dub Day Afternoon' (discussed in Chap. 7) were much more successful fundraisers involving a lot less financial risk. The 4ZZZ Market Day was finally considered unviable. "It got to the point where the effort involved for the return just wasn't worth it," Geoff Wilson says. "It was sad to see them fade out, but things had to change to keep the station going."

There are so many unsung heroes whose names are missing here. Market Days brought together volunteers, bands, artists and the broader Brisbane community, creating a shared experience that left a lasting impression on many. For those involved in organising the festival, it was intense but—for the most part—incredibly rewarding. "I've never known so many people come together for a common cause in such a positive way," says Tobin Lyall, "I've never known such camaraderie". Alex Wightman agrees, saying "the whole Triple Zed community came out to pitch in together, in one way or another".

Recently, a few of the 4ZZZ Market Day crew gathered on a Zoom call to collectively jog each other's memories in preparation for me to write this chapter. It had been a while between drinks for a few of us, but it wasn't long before the anecdotes were flowing, accompanied by a good dose of laughter. It reminded me of one of the most cherished rituals of Market Day, which came after the music had stopped and the crowds had gone home: the debrief. As exhausted volunteers gathered in tents or around the back of trucks, they shared stories from different corners of the event. This is when we'd sometimes discover for the first time what had gone wrong, what had gone wonderfully, or what had been hilariously bizarre. "Just sitting in the tent with everyone being able to really relax and chill out and have a bit of a party ourselves," Donna describes, "sharing some war stories from the day". After the Zoom meeting was closed, my phone pinged to indicate a message from Donna. "That was awesome," she wrote. "Made me realise how much I miss all these folks." For me, those friendships were by far the strongest outcome of the legendary 4ZZZ Market Days.

CHAPTER 9

The Police Riot Formerly Known As 'Cybernana' Market Day

"Fuck the police! Fuck the police!" Torrential rain dampens the battle cry until I'm among the sheltering crowd. The concrete beneath the South Brisbane railway bridge creates acoustics that amplify the chant. "This can't be good," I think, but the police aren't taking the bait and simply continue to herd the soggy mob towards the Vulture Street train station, away from the mayhem of inner-city Musgrave Park.

Only an hour earlier the mostly younger crowd had been enjoying the 4ZZZ 1996 'Cybernana' Market Day. Many fans had been dancing to Brisbane punk-ska stalwarts, Blowhard, while others waited at an alternate stage anticipating the (now) platinum-record selling Melbourne trio, Something for Kate. I had been volunteering as the primary stage coordinator, and it had already been a long day when an unseasonable and unpredicted super-cell storm took everyone by surprise, drenching the partying masses.

Also caught in the downpour was the mass of police who had seemingly appeared out of thin air and begun to forcibly clear the park. I'm not entirely sure why I decided to follow them as they marched patrons away from the venue, although I suspect it was motivated by a duty of care and fear for people's welfare.

There was good reason for my concern; I had witnessed the bleeding head of a station co-worker who'd been struck by police in the chaos, and I had also fretted over the safety of a young man who'd been handcuffed to a chain link fence while lightning cut across the sky.

In hindsight, I was also most likely in shock.

* * *

The 'Cybernana' Market Day was held on Saturday October 19th, 1996, at Musgrave Park in West End. The fourth Market Day at this venue, by many accounts it was a highly anticipated event (Fig. 9.1). As described by one patron:

> Attendance was essential if you were a 4ZZZfm listener and all the alternative music makers and lovers from the whole town turned up to mix it up together and celebrate being different in this conformist city … It was the '90s, we were cyberkids.

There was nothing out of the ordinary in its lead-up and the regular crew of volunteers was in place. Efforts had been made to develop a sound working relationship between the radio station and officers from the local West End police station and meetings had been held to run through tactical issues such as

Fig. 9.1 Poster for 4ZZZ's 'Cybernana' Market Day, designed by Will Serantak; 1996

controlling under-age drinking, arrangements for selling alcohol, logistics such as stage and stall location, as well as start and finishing times.

The station obtained the usual 'General Purpose' permit under the *Liquor Act 1992* from the Department of Tourism, Small Business and Industry, which allowed the operation of a bar within a marquee, with the whole of Musgrave Park fenced off as the designated drinking area. As a further condition of the permit, 30 security guards were hired to patrol the event in its entirety, alongside two uniformed police officers between 11:00am and 11:00pm (the designated finishing time) with an additional uniformed officer from 7:00pm.

Across the course of the event an estimated 8000 people attended to experience a line-up of over 30 live acts, a Doof Tent and nearly 70 food and market stalls. 4ZZZ subscribers (and folks from the local Murri community) were exempt from paying the nominal $5 entrance fee. While alcohol sales always contributed a major component of the profits raised at Market Days, during the daytime it was common to see families (often with small children) enjoying the music and markets. Brisbane's underground scene is just as prone to making babies as the rest of society and 4ZZZ accommodated this with an 'all-ages' policy and child-appropriate entertainment, including, on this occasion, a jumping castle. My three-year-old son was in attendance with his father, as was my eldest niece, a seven-week-old baby Brennah attending her very first concert with her parents. Fortunately, both extensions of the family decided to head home during daylight hours, the responsibilities of parenthood providing a welcomed escape from the later chaos.

According to a gig review in weekly street press, *Rave Magazine*, 'Cybernana' was "just another Market Day—a fun-filled day of great music, weird people and warm beer".[1] Musical drawcards included hip-hop fusion act, Elevation and metal lords, Misery, alongside various touring artists, including indie slack rockers from Perth, Diolene. Brisbane success-story Screamfeeder, at the peak of popularity on the heels of their album, *Kitten Licks*, were also secretly added to the line-up, simply billed as "Mystery Band".[2] Honourable mentions went to The Subteraneans—a clear favourite, with more than one gig review noting their incorporation of an Indian sitar into a guitar-rock genre, and Dogmachine, who, according to Zed reviewer Garry Williams, "played the set of the day with one member banging and sawing bits of metal, sending spectacular plumes of sparks into the audience".[3]

Performers enjoyed themselves as much as the crowd. Shane Schiavone, guitarist for Brisbane crust-punks, Dregs of Humanity, was excited to play.

---

[1] R. Coburn, "'Cybernana'— 4ZZZ Market Day review', *Rave Magazine*, issue 259 (Oct 30— Nov 5, 1996), p. 27.

[2] Screamfeeder played an album launch gig a few weeks earlier. 4ZZZ agreed to withhold that the band was on the Market Day lineup until after their album launch, to not discourage people to attend.

[3] G. Williams, *Generation Zed: No other radio like this*, Kingswood Press, 2000, p. 70.

"I thought it was the best thing ever," he says. "I was waiting years to get on a Market Day." Kicking off early at 1:00pm, even as one of the first bands on the bill the energy was high.

> It was daylight and it was great. There were all these young kids at the front, and they had this corrugated flooring right at the front. I could hear they were bouncing ... all these kids were having a great time.

Similarly taken by their audience's enthusiasm was Wishing Chair's vocalist/guitarist Stacey Coleman (who would later work for 4ZZZ). "I was really surprised when we started playing how well the crowd reacted ... we had a huge crowd and dudes up the front were even moshing and stuff." The local pop band had secured first-place in 1995's 4ZZZ Hot 100 chart and were playing a little later in the day than Stacey had expected. "It was the best gig of the year," as far as she was concerned, despite nearly being hit by an empty spirit bottle, which should not have been in anyone's possession.

> I heard this whoosh past my head. I look back and see this 750[ml] empty bourbon bottle hit the drummer's kick drum. But it was sort of a thing back then, if you remember, that people would throw things at you when they liked you, you know, out of excitement ... but it wasn't animosity ... And I think I remember saying, 'if you're going to throw a bottle up here, make sure it's full'.

* * *

Nobody is claiming that, among the thousands of festivalgoers, no-one engaged in illegal behaviour. Alcohol had clearly been smuggled into the event, but even after her near-miss with flying contraband, Stacey Coleman is adamant she "didn't sense anything bad at all, ever". Drug-taking was also part and parcel of festival culture of the time, and it only takes a quick scan of social media comments relating to 'Cybernana' to see marijuana and LSD were two popular drugs of choice, particularly a type of acid named Red Dragon. As Screamfeeder bassist/vocalist, Kellie Lloyd, admits, "I know a lot of people were walking around on acid and having a fun time or whatever, but as all market days ... it was just really chilled out".

4ZZZ's liquor permit required the presence of a small number of police officers to work the festival, and there had been some arrests in the earlier part of the day. Newspaper accounts vary; while there were a few arrests for possession and use of drugs, under-age drinking and disorderly behaviour, exact numbers are unclear. Nearly 40 people were charged with the relatively innocuous charge of 'indecent manner', more commonly known as 'urinating in public'. Dregs of Humanity's Shane Schiavone remembers a Zed volunteer "coming up to me and saying not to pee on the trees because the police are really cracking down on that, which I was a bit surprised about". As 4ZZZ volunteer announcer, Rollo, (who also performed with *Blowhard* on the day) astutely commented at the time, if people "peeing against the fence at a State of Origin[4] football game were treated in the same manner there would be apprehensions made in the hundreds". Legend has it that magistrate Di Fingleton agreed, throwing several of these cases out of court and berating police for wasting the court's time. Unfortunately, after so many years she can neither confirm nor deny this claim, though agrees this sounds like something she would have done.[5]

* * *

After speaking with countless musicians, stallholders, festivalgoers and 4ZZZ volunteers, the resounding majority confirm my own memory that 'Cybernana' was rolling along nicely—a successful, mostly trouble-free affair, with the only incident officially recorded by security being a self-inflicted injury to a sword swallower. However, by late afternoon, operations were not going so smoothly for Triple Zed's Security/Police Liaison Officer, Terry O'Connor. After months of planning with local police, Terry was suddenly challenged with a change in police command and point of contact for the event.

In the lead-up to the October event, Sergeant John Vincent and Constable Mark Simpson from the West End Police Station were the officers liaising with 4ZZZ. Sgt Vincent, who'd worked previous Market Days, had already flagged he would be taking leave on the actual day. Constable Simpson was to be Field Commander in charge, rostered to attend 'Cybernana' on special duty for the whole event. According to Terry, he tried to check in with Constable Simpson just after 4:00pm, as they hadn't seen or spoken to each other for an hour or so.

> As I approached [him], there was a larger number of police officers than weren't actually supposed to be there, and as soon as he saw me coming, he quickly came and spoke to me before I got close to the other police officers ... [Simpson] informed me he'd been removed from his position as the senior officer on duty. He identified to me the officer who was now in charge of things, an officer who I'd never met before, who'd never been to any of the meetings, who had no idea of things, and that officer informed me that basically that I should go away, that he had a job to do and talking to me wasn't part of his job.

That officer was Sergeant John McFaul, described in later police documentation as Overall Field Commander.

---

[4] The State of Origin is an annual best-of-three rugby league series between the Queensland Maroons and the New South Wales Blues, and one of Australia's premier sporting events.

[5] It's not surprising this small event in a long career has slipped through the cracks, given Fingleton would later be appointed as the first female Chief Magistrate in Queensland, then jailed for intimidation of a witness, and finally pardoned by the High Court of Australia.

Police are on record saying this change in command had been pre-planned, and that 4ZZZ were aware of this.[6] To this day, the station disagrees. Terry is adamant he did not meet, or know of, Sergeant McFaul until around 4:00pm on the day, and this is supported by his notes from the event. Despite this changing of the guard, Terry continued to communicate with Simpson, trying to ascertain why the Constable was no longer in charge, and why there were more police at the park than arranged. "At the time I honestly believed that he couldn't tell me anything because he didn't know anything, and my opinion hasn't really changed since," says Terry. "I still think he was completely in the dark about what was going on, and why these guys had replaced him." From that point, Terry says, constructive communication between the station and the police became "non-existent".

* * *

Anthony was relatively new to 4ZZZ in 1996; he'd finished his volunteer shift around the same time Terry O'Connor was navigating the changing police chain of command. "I was having a great day," he recalls, still sounding a little confused when recounting the events. It was around dusk, when he noticed police cars lining up around the park. "I vividly remember just one cop car and then another one behind it, and then another one behind it, until the whole park was just surrounded by police cars," Anthony says. "It was a bit sort of scary when you see that happen. I hadn't seen any trouble." He wasn't alone in this observation. There has been extensive testimony that police gathered near Musgrave Park in the later part of the afternoon and early evening. Queensland Council for Civil Liberties Vice-President, Terry O'Gorman told *The Courier Mail*[7] police had the Public Safety Response Team (or PSRT, more commonly known as riot police) on standby before any alleged troubles began at the event. Multiple patrons and 4ZZZ representatives, including Market Day Coordinator, Peter Rohweder, say they saw the PSRT unloading shields, batons, and helmets near the park in Russell Street around 7:00pm. This was also confirmed by an independent witness at a nearby auto shop, who later spoke to non-4ZZZ journalist John Birmingham in an article for *Rolling Stone Magazine*.

4ZZZ staff (and others) were perplexed and concerned to see police gathering around the outskirts of the park as the sun began to set—a key moment of the day that is disputed by the police. In an early newspaper report[8], police claim they responded to a brawl and then increased their presence to deal with an 'ensuing riot'. No-one from 4ZZZ called for police assistance at the event or recalls an altercation that required police reinforcements. There had been

---

[6] Criminal Justice Commission, *Police Behaviour at a 4ZZZ Market Day Function: Investigation report*, December 1997.

[7] M. Robbins, Police accused in concert raid', *The Courier Mail*, 21 October 1996, p. 3.

[8] M. Robbins, Police accused in concert raid', p. 3.

sightings of at least one argument, witnessed by Terry O'Conner and others, one of whom told a journalist she saw an argument between two men and a woman in "the waning hours of the afternoon". Around six or seven police appeared "out of nowhere".

> They immediately put this guy on the ground when he'd done nothing. His girlfriend was getting hysterical. A huge crowd was gathering. The police came out of nowhere and whipped up a frenzy.[9]

The testimonies of musicians from various bands that performed in the afternoon and evening share memories of seeing mounted police surrounding and entering the park between 7:00 and 8:00pm. Corroborated by set-lists and stage maps, their versions of events are compelling, yet sharply contrast the Queensland Police Service's narrative. Stacey Coleman stuck around after her set with The Wishing Chair. She'd enjoyed local bands Turtlebox and Webster, and was waiting for Something for Kate, when the sky began to darken. As "black clouds came over," she remembers "looking around and seeing [police] horses just around the perimeter". Screamfeeder's Kellie Lloyd, having quickly packed up the band's equipment in the realisation that a fierce storm was about to hit, was leaving at around this same time.

> *Something for Kate* might have been setting up and sound checking ... And then as my partner and I started to drive out, there were police on horseback coming in the way we were going out and it was like, 'whoa, this is becoming really full on. Why are the cops here on horses?'.

As the storm front advanced, lightning crackled across the sky, illuminating dark clouds with brilliant flashes of green. Thunder rumbled in the distance, growing louder and more frequent as the storm drew nearer and the wind picked up, sending debris swirling through the air. Kellie—an avid storm watcher—could see it building as Screamfeeder were performing. "You know when a storm comes you feel that sort of change in the air," she says, "like it gets staticky, it gets tense, like you know something's going to happen". The full brunt of the storm struck around 8.20pm, unleashing torrential rain that fell in sheets, obscuring visibility and flooding parts of the park within minutes.

Police reports first estimated between 5000 to 7000 people were at the festival when the storm hit, however this was significantly reduced to 3000 in. later documentation. 4ZZZ records estimate about 2000 people remained. Like Kellie, a good proportion of the crowd could see heavy rainfall was imminent, and there were only a couple of hours left before the scheduled close time. Market Day Coordinator, Peter Rohweder suspects many weren't keen to be caught in an evening thunderstorm of that magnitude and departed for drier pastures.

---

[9] Molony in J. Birmingham 'It's Raining Cops', *Rolling Stone Magazine*, Issue 533 (March 1996), pp. 38–40.

As the rain engulfed the festival, 4ZZZ staff decided to temporarily close off the electricity to tills and stages to prevent electrocution, fully intending to restore power and restart the bands once it was safe to do so. With live music at a standstill, police numbers growing, and the storm intensifying, Stacey Coleman decided to leave the park. Walking towards home, she looked back to see "this sort of dark, chaotic mess going on". Nikola Shaw was playing trumpet with Brisbane band Blowhard, when the power was cut. She and her bandmates could see what she described as "mayhem at the gates," and in an effort to keep the crowd pre-occupied, the brass section (who didn't need electrical amplification) launched into cheerful ditties such as *How Much is That Doggy in the Window* and *El Cumbanchereo* while the band's singer Rollo tried to warn people about the growing police numbers.

* * *

With much of the ground very quickly turning to sludge, some people were covering themselves in mud, throwing handfuls at each other. Others turned puddles into playgrounds. Patron Steve Johnston was one, looking to kill a bit of time until the storm passed. "Obviously with the blackout, there's no more bands so the natural progression was to get another beer," says Steve, "not thinking that if there's no power [for the bands], there'd be no power at the beer tent".

> Then we were just milling around, talking and then, obviously, massive puddles! We just started a water fight, there was a group of us in a circle, there might have been eight of us, just amusing ourselves basically.

Not everyone was happy to cavort in the rain and mud. A 17-year-old patron, Jeff Hahn, remembers people crammed into what shelter they could find. To him, "everything was pretty low key at this stage, people were singing and carrying on and being pretty patient waiting for the rain to pass". Also playing the waiting game was volunteer Daniel Endicott, his stint at the bar interrupted by the storm. As he remembers it, the bar was laid out along the edge of the tent, meaning there was no overhang for the waiting crowds to avoid the sudden downpour. When the rain came, people pushed quite unsuccessfully against the tables to try and keep dry. Daniel's summation from where he stood is that the crowds weren't angry, boisterous or violent. Steve Johnston agrees. "Once we realised ... the bar tent wasn't open, nobody was jumping the fence trying to steal beers," he says. "We thought we'd go to another bar ... maybe we would have been allowed in, probably a bit sodden and looked a bit worse for wear!"

Steve wouldn't get to try his luck in another, drier drinking establishment. As previously mentioned, he and his friends were "carrying on a bit," playing in the puddles, when he noticed someone dressed in blue, heading towards them. He eventually realised it was a police officer, who walked "right into the circle of the water fight" as his friend unknowingly continued to kick and splash with his back to the officer. Figuring he was already probably going to be arrested, Steve reciprocated. "[The police officer] got involved in a water fight that he probably wasn't invited to," Steve says. "He could have just kicked some water back and gone, 'right, get out, you little scallywags' and left us to our own devices." But he didn't. Steve was grabbed and, as he describes it, "frog marched towards the paddy wagons" by two policemen, when there was a stumble and all three fell into another puddle. "That's when everything sort of went quiet," he says.

> I couldn't hear because they would hold my head underneath the water. I don't know how long it was, it wasn't just for a second, it was for a little while, while they got themselves composed and decided when they were going to get up and I couldn't breathe, I was ... completely underwater.

Steve spent the "next hour or so" in a police van, as it was slowly filled with other hapless arrestees. According to numbers drawn from news accounts, in less than two hours, over 60 officers including mounted police, Public Response Safety Team officers and military police, swept through and cleared the park. Between 60 and 90 people were arrested (72 by 4ZZZ's records), on charges including 'riotous manner', 'assaulting police' and 'abusive or obscene language' alongside lesser offences earlier in the day, most of which were for urinating in public.[10] The Queensland Police Service (QPS) account of events claimed officers felt they had no choice but to take the actions they did because of violence "erupting all around them and the possibility that the situation might get completely out of control".[11] They claimed that excessive violence was used on them, with many police officers fearing for their own safety and that of their colleagues.

Witnesses do report seeing violence perpetrated towards police, however, the consensus is this was in self-defence or after being antagonised. Steve Johnston saw a small crowd's attitude turn against the police during his arrest after he was held underwater, surmising that "behaviour breeds behaviour". "I think the crowd seeing the police do that got them [thinking] 'you're an asshole ... what are you doing?'" Steve comments. "Anyway, it did escalate from there; then everyone was kicking water [at the police]." It is also not disputed that projectiles were thrown at police and horses. "Cans being thrown at the cops was one of the few things that was actually true, that [police] claimed to happen," admits Terry. "I was with the cops when the beer cans got thrown at them, their embellishment being that people had pissed in the beer cans first". Some patrons say they were frustrated; many had been at the previous two Market Days which had both been 'interrupted' by police as they

---

[10] *'Cybernana' Riot Day [CD]*, Brisbane, 4ZZZ, 2000.

[11] Criminal Justice Commission, Police Behavior at a 4ZZZ Market Day Function: Report of an Investigation, 1997.

wound down. Some were exasperated by what they saw as continued harassment of supporters of 4ZZZ and the alternative scene in Brisbane. Police claim the above-described behavior was dominant, and therefore responsible for any perceived forcefulness on the side of the police, however, witnesses describe a quite different picture.

Patron testimonies show them fearing for their safety, seeing and/or experiencing indiscriminate violence at the hands of police as they forcibly cleared the park. Volunteer Anthony describes "just absolute panic" with people and police running everywhere, while another witness saw "hundreds of people screaming and running towards us … being chased by mounted police". Patron Jeff Hahn remembers police patrolling between the marquees and "making their presence felt," and while outnumbered, seemed in Jeff's opinion intent on agitating the crowd. When he saw what looked like riot police bearing down "in formation," he grabbed a friend by the hand and they "legged it" through the park towards a nearby railway station.

> It was like an action sequence in a movie, people getting slammed all over the place I just picked a spot and ran to it with my friend while in front of me, behind me, in my peripherals, I could see and hear panicked people getting hurt or taken down.

The police formation Jeff refers to was described in one newspaper account as "shoulder-to-shoulder with batons drawn and facing the crowd," much of which was sheltering under trestles and makeshift tents until moved "through a narrow entrance to the parkway where they had to run a police gauntlet". 4ZZZ journalist, Kirstyn Lindsay describes a similar procedure. "The way that they moved everyone from corner to corner and then brought this line forward to move everyone out", she says, "it just was unsafe".

Kelly Smith, who had worked the market day stall, 'Hippy Kidz', for most of the day, saw people running in all directions as police moved through. She describes one young woman who, running out of the park, tripped and fell into a pothole full of water—"and [a] cop on [a] horse went straight over her". Another attendee, Sarah remembers everything happening very quickly: "I was surrounded by police with batons, shields, on foot and horseback. So scary! We ran!". She says she still has no idea why the police acted the way they did. Even more confused at the time was one 4ZZZ volunteer who'd taken an acid trip after their shift and hid behind the bar area during the whole incident, watching what looked like "cyborgs coming in with the shields". Another 16-year-old volunteer was left barefoot and bloodied (albeit not her own), unable to catch public transport home. "I lost my shoes being pushed out onto Russell St," she says. "I tried to get on a bus … but the driver wouldn't let me on because I had no shoes on, and my shirt had blood on it." Before being removed from Musgrave Park, she had helped an older Murri man, who was bleeding from his leg. He said he'd been pushed into the fence after getting too close to a police horse. It is likely the man was at Musgrave Park due to cultural and community connections rather than to attend the event.

Somehow amongst the chaos, the Doof Tent—a haven for electronic music lovers—was protected from the rain and therefore still with power and in full party mode. Doof Tent coordinator Annie Winter, alongside performers and "doofers" inside the tent, was oblivious to the tensions of the outside world. The first Annie knew of police clearing the park was when Terry O'Connor, and Bar Coordinator Donna Williamson arrived with a small crew of volunteers, asking her to turn the music off and urge everyone to leave for their own safety. While some of the 4ZZZ workers stood across the entrance, trying to delay the police line, Annie—ever the quick thinker—opened the back of the tent and shoved "lots of fake fur leg warmer clad doofers out that way," to relieve the congestion caused by the police line entering the tent. "One woman turned, freaking out and asked me 'WHY?'," remembers Annie, "I told her I had no idea, and just to get out". Another patron remembers chatting at the Doof Tent, when people started running towards them, "blokes limping, girls crying. We asked what was happening and they just pointed. Within a minute we were running from a line of cops who were beating stragglers". Terry says that after failing to clear the Doof tent before the police line swept through, he "pretty much went into shock" and doesn't remember much more of the evening. For Donna, this moment clearly cements her belief that police were not interested in clearing the park for anyone's safety or wellbeing.

Long-term volunteer, Alex Wightman, found himself at the front of a panicking crowd. Pushed to the front gates, he ran into a Civil Liberty Union lawyer he knew from political protests. The lawyer gave him a Legal Observer vest, a brightly coloured tool of the trade that identifies those who wear them as qualified to support and report, usually in protest situations. Alex then found himself in the impromptu role of trying to calm those who had been cleared out of the park, triaging who was in trouble from who wasn't. Alex says the vest gave him relative immunity from the police:

> Being able to drag people that were injured out and get them out onto the pavement where they could be dealt with by other people ... There were young children there who were getting separated from parents, there were people falling over and getting stood on, there were people coming out with significant head injuries that could only have been caused by baton charges.

Alex also took details of people that wanted to make police complaints, finding that the legal observer vest attracted people to approach him with their stories. "People would come up to you and tell 'I'm like this because I got hit by the police' and I'd take down their name and address." This would be invaluable for 4ZZZ in the aftermath of the event, collecting statements to support a formal complaint against the police.

Not all 4ZZZ staff were as safe, with a few caught up in the melee. Chris McLean was 4ZZZ's volunteer Administration Coordinator and had been working the bar on the day. When the storm hit, he first took shelter in an abandoned tent but then noticed what he describes as "squads of police" heading for the front gate. Realising something was wrong he ran to see if he could help. As a staff member (and identified as such) he went to the front of the crowd. Chris says he was confronted by riot police two deep, stretching the width of the field, with mounted police behind them.

> The next thing I heard was the beating of batons against riot shields. I received a punch to my left jaw. When I turned to see where it came from, I received another hit to my head. Then the mounted police charged at full speed into the crowd, I saw at least two people trampled underfoot before I fell back.

As Chris managed to make his way to the main bar area where 4ZZZ staff were congregating, his nose was bleeding, he had a cut on the side of his face and at least one tooth had broken through his lip. Chris remembers me "shooing coppers away" as we all tried to take stock of what was happening. Announcer and stage manager, Jason M was lucky to escape with minor injuries after being kicked by a skittish police horse. He was talking to a mounted police officer at the time, and in the process of trying to get out of the way of a crowd being pushed towards him, ducked under the animal and was accidentally clipped.

Most baffling of all was the arrival of military police to assist their civilian counterparts. In Australia, military police have no powers over civilians—records in the Weekly Hansard report from 1995 show then Minister for Defence, Senator Robert Ray, confirming this to be the case, "with very few and specifically niche exceptions".[12] Not since the raid of a hippy commune in Far North Queensland in 1976 had the Australian military been employed in a civilian operation (see Chap. 13).[13] In the week following 'Cybernana', Lieutenant Colonel John Weiland confirmed that five military police from the '16 Military Police Platoon' were conducting a joint patrol in a neighbouring area as part of Exercise SUMAN WARRIOR, which involved some 300 foreign troops on leave in the Brisbane area. They responded to a call for assistance over the police radio calling for reinforcements at Musgrave Park. Lt Col Weiland said the MPs assisted in the dispersal of the crowd, and at no time did they "touch anybody, manhandle, arrest or wrestle any people to the ground".[14] However, a 4ZZZ journalist Jon Baird[15] told *The Courier Mail*

---

[12] Queensland Parliament, *Queensland Parliamentary Debates [Hansard]*, Brisbane, 21 March 1995, p. 1848.

[13] M. Hele, 'Military police accused over festival brawl', *The Courier Mail*, 21 October 1996, p. 2.

[14] M. Hele, 'Military police accused over festival brawl', *The Courier Mail*, 21 October 1996, p. 2.

[15] Jon Baird passed in 2018, and I didn't have a chance to interview him for this book. This, and other quotes from him are taken from newspaper accounts.

he saw a military policeman pin one man to the ground and apply handcuffs, as other civilian police struggled to restrain him.[16] Volunteer Anthony says the arrival of military police was "surreal". "How did this event require army attendants to control it?" he asks. "I still have no understanding of exactly what happened that day."

On a lighter note, volunteer Tony Browne and a friend found refuge at the back of the bar tent, after witnessing Market Day Coordinator Peter Rohweder pleading with police that shutting down the bar would cause more problems than it would solve. A police officer gave an order to dispose of crate-loads of pre-poured drinks that were laid out ready for service but then walked away. Rather than tip them all out, the enterprising volunteers "downed as many as they could". With a laugh Tony tells me, "I got a taste for Bourbon that day and a grandstand view in a private box of the chaos happening outside the tent". "It was my first time volunteering for the zeds," he says. "What a first impression! It really got me hooked after that." Tony went on to become a 4ZZZ Board Director and only stopped volunteering there in 2015 (Fig. 9.1).

* * *

Finally, after about two hours, the police had all left and Musgrave Park fell quiet. Zed folk who'd managed to avoid being caught up in the park clearance gathered at the main bar area. Everyone was mentally and physically exhausted, and the grounds were a sodden mess, badly torn up during the police operation. According to Peter Rohweder, "it was just too much of an effort to clean that night, with half the team". It was time for 4ZZZ to take stock of the damage and, as Donna Williamson describes, "lick our wounds". Drinks were served and the de-brief began.

Before long, some of us would head to the 4ZZZ studios leaving Peter and a small crew to stay at the park. Overnight security was not part of the station's budget, so sleeping onsite was routine. Usually, most folks would set up camp under the beer tent, but the soggy conditions made this very uncomfortable. Peter Rohweder remembers, "you had to get off the ground," so he set his sleeping bag on a trestle table—"it was very uncomfortable sleeping". Unsurprisingly, the combination of environment and residual adrenalin meant nobody got much rest. 4ZZZ volunteer Kirstyn Lindsay also stayed at the park which, in hindsight she says, "was crazy, because all this violence had gone down, there was no sleep really happening". "We were just thinking, 'what was that?'"

Meanwhile, those who'd been arrested, including Steve Johnston, whose 'water fight' had resulted in a charge of 'riotous behaviour', were held at the Brisbane City Watchhouse. According to Steve about "60 of us" were crammed "for hours and hours," with standing room only in the main holding

---

[16] C. Dore, 'Army to Answer over riot control', *The Australian*, 21 October 1996, p. 5.

cell. He says spirits were quite high, despite the lack of liberty, although the police weren't allowing people to use the bathroom.

> Obviously people had been drinking beer, and they're just takin a leak through the bars ... It was hilarious. There was no aggro ... That's what I loved about Four Triple Zed and the punk scene in Brisbane ... You'd never see any drama. ... And same with the lock up, same sort of people, just in the same situation. Yeah, 'it'll be over soon, they'll let us out'.

Not everyone at the Watchhouse was appreciating the lighter side of the situation. One Market Day performer says that "because the cops were just going through willy-nilly ... people were taking all of their drugs, so they didn't have anything on them". A couple of people she knew ended up being arrested, "and they were tripping, spent the night in the Brisbane Watchhouse, like, not dealing".

Journalist Brendan Greenhill was back at the radio station in the early hours of Sunday, rostered to host the graveyard shift. In discussions with other Triple Zedders, he decided to play music and forgo speaking about the evening's events. Brendan says no one knew what to say. "I remember the first track we played was The Clash's *White Riot,* which I thought was quite appropriate, then we randomly picked songs that were sort of hinting away," Brendan says. "There wasn't a voice spoken for about four hours on the radio." Volunteers at the park remember sitting "dejected" behind the bar, listening to this playlist of anti-police songs. "We all assumed it was going to be the last Market Day ever," volunteer Ben Pennings says.

With still no sleep in sight for the core 4ZZZ team, a community announcement was quickly put together by production whiz Mikey Roberts and Donna Williamson. The announcement begins with audio of a police scanner exchange calling officers to meet at the main oval to start clearing the park, recorded by Brendan before his recorder malfunctioned in the wet conditions. Backed by militant punk-rock music, Donna—who would later play a key role in arranging legal representation for people arrested at the park—reads out a statement sprinkled with trademark dark humour, and clearly laying out 4ZZZ's position:

> Approaching our 21st year in radio, to mark our coming of age, the Queensland Police Force threw a party. Prematurely closing the event, police deployed riot police with helmets, batons and shields, horses and dog teams.
> If you were arrested, beaten by police, or witness to Queensland's own unique brand of community policing you need to call 4ZZZ on 32521555 right now and talk to members of our special Zed Task Force.
> If you were injured, you need to obtain medical reports as soon as possible. And witnesses and victims should record, in writing or on tape, details of everything they saw or experienced.
> Scenes of riot police indiscriminately beating anyone in their path and mounted police charging into crowds is no longer witnessed from the safety of your own

lounge room relayed around the world via satellite. It's in your face and coming at you live.
Police deny use of excessive force. This cannot go unchallenged. If you're prepared to join with others in the fight for justice, call 4ZZZ on 32521555 for information.
At least we won't beat it out of you.

The announcement was scheduled for heavy rotation and first played around 6:00am. From that point, the phones seemed to ring continuously, for at least the first few days. Volunteers took actual book-loads of messages. Most calls were from people who had been hurt and/or arrested, witnessed police violence, or just wanted to know what had happened (as they'd left before the storm). Notably, parents were also contacting the station, outraged at the way their teenage children had been treated by police. One volunteer, Michelle Vlatkovic remembers a father who "was really ticked off" because what his daughter had witnessed "totally annihilated any idea she had the police were there to help". Sam Kretschmann, in the audience on the day, received a concerned call from her father, who'd seen it "on the TV news and wanted to know what was going on". Sam says he was "appalled" to hear of "cops on horseback and the military beating up kids in the rain".

* * *

Sam was also one of many who responded to 4ZZZ's call for assistance, which was the beginnings of her long and ongoing involvement with the station. She went to the studios on the Monday (21st October) to see what she could do to help:

> The station atmosphere was a thing to behold. The phones were running hot, subscriptions and support from the public were pouring in and everyone was worried about the punters. How could the station help them? Some of them were still in the lock up, and others were nursing sore heads and broken limbs.

In addition to phone calls from people affected by the 'riot', as it was now commonly being referred to, 4ZZZ also received a plethora of support and advice from a wide range of political and cultural organisations, including other radio stations and media outlets. An unknown, enterprising ally at the local ABC Radio newsroom forwarded all its communications from the QPS, once 4ZZZ realised it had been taken off their media mailing list. Media Monitors[17] compiled lists of news coverage for the station, a vital resource for keeping track of police and government versions of events.

While he sees the funny side of it now, Terry O'Connor found himself the recipient of a less-than-supportive phone call on the Tuesday after the event, from Brisbane Lord Mayor, Jim Soorley. 4ZZZ still hadn't finished cleaning

---

[17] Australia's largest (at the time) press clipping and broadcast monitoring service.

and loading out of Musgrave Park, mostly due to the soggy conditions. Heavy load vehicles would have torn up the grass even more and there wasn't much to be done until conditions dried out. So far as Terry was aware, this had been communicated to the relevant Brisbane City Council department, and to begin, Terry thought it was a prank call.

> What I got was 'get that shit out of the park, clean that fucking park up today,' and I'm like 'what the hell?,' ... I said, 'I'm sorry, who are you?,' and he ... made it very clear that he really was who he was and then reiterated to 'clean that shit up'. And he hung up.

Soorley's phone call was the first the station knew of complaints from residents of the Musgrave Park area. A quick call to Brisbane City Council confirmed they had received no complaints besides ones from the police themselves and the neighbouring Greek Orthodox Church. It was no secret the church and its adjacent Greek Club was strongly and vocally opposed to 4ZZZ holding events in Musgrave Park.

In response, Donna and Subscriptions Coordinator, Maisy O'Keefe immediately sent a fax to the Lord Mayor, signed on behalf of the Triple Zed Collective, which made clear the station "did not appreciate the manner" in which he spoke to "Mr. O'Connor," and the language used did not "befit a man of [his] station". The formal yet subtly cheeky missive pointed out that the station had not received any complaints about the park before the Lord Mayor's phone call, emphasised the stressful conditions faced by 4ZZZ volunteers, "operating on little or no sleep" and called for kinder treatment. Terry can't help but laugh when sharing that Brisbane City Council's response was along the lines of "they thought that sort of language was part and parcel for 4ZZZ, so didn't think there would be any chance of being offended".

* * *

Managing media coverage of the 'riot' became a full-time job for allocated 4ZZZ volunteers, who were mostly more experienced journalists such as Jon Baird. He had his work cut out for him as not much had changed to diversify Queensland mainstream news since the station was established 21 years earlier. Initial TV and newspaper coverage referred to a "bloody brawl' and a "youth riot" and connected the event to previous troubles between 4ZZZ and authorities. Much of the news media published QPS facts and figures without question, and this was especially the case for arrests and attendance numbers which were regularly conflated. Even when accurate, arrest numbers lacked context and failed to clarify that over half the arrests were for urinating in public rather than riotous, violent or abusive behaviour.

Police Union President, Gary Wilkinson, used the sympathetic ear of *The Courier Mail* to put pressure on the State Government to ban 4ZZZ Market Days indefinitely, saying the station's fundraising events regularly degenerated into "drunken anarchy". Sgt Wilkinson blamed "a combination of alcohol, drugs and the type of music," suggesting that 4ZZZ supporters who attend Market Days "cannot act like ordinary, civilized persons". The newspaper regularly cited the Police Union President verbatim, including unsubstantiated claims that a police horse was stabbed in the chest with a broken beer bottle, stole officers' watches, and tried to steal their guns. Terry O'Connor was present at a meeting where police revealed a cache of items they claimed were confiscated from 'rioters'.

> [They] pulled out their bag of weapons, which included an extraordinarily rusty screwdriver, which looked like it had been sitting in the grass at Musgrave Park for about five years, a sharps bin, a very rusty nail file ... and a couple of other implements, none of which most people would actually think 'oh look, that's a weapon'.

Most questionable was the allegation[18] that members of the crowd tried to set fire to a police car. How this was remotely possible in the torrential rain was not questioned by *The Courier Mail's* Chief Police Reporter. 4ZZZ questioned the timing of the accusations in a media release, saying, "It's strange that these allegations are made a week after the event, and even stranger that they come 24 hours after a formal complaint has been lodged".[19] Triple Zed also raised the fact that there had been no charges laid for any of these clearly criminal acts.

The 'media war' on 4ZZZ did have its benefits, galvanising more support than the radio station had seen in years, which was reminiscent of the 1988 eviction attempt. According to Jon Baird, there was a "sixfold increase"[20] in membership subscriptions in the immediate aftermath of the incident, with many past workers and supporters also coming out of the woodwork to lend a hand. Jon cheekily suggested to a 'gossip style' column in *The Courier Mail* that 4ZZZ were considering adding the Police Union president to their Christmas card list as they "couldn't have bought this kind of publicity for $1 million".[21]

In an unexpected twist, Police Minister Russell Cooper contradicted the Police Union's stand against 4ZZZ. Terry O'Connor and Peter Rohweder both recall Minister Cooper being supportive and respectful at a meeting between senior police and 4ZZZ workers, to debrief with the Minister. According to Terry, "after the police officers had their rant ... I began to speak in response and the cops interrupted me a couple of times".

---

[18] R. Callinan, 'Police union urges 4ZZZ events ban', *The Courier Mail*, 26 October 1996, p. 11.

[19] 4ZZZ, *Police Union claims border on metaphysical [media release]* undated.

[20] Anon 1996, ZZZ thanks police, *The Courier Mail*, 29 October 1996, Letters to the Editor, p. 14.

[21] Anon 1996, ZZZ thanks police, *The Courier Mail*, 29 October 1996, Letters to the Editor, p. 14.

And then Russell Cooper told him to shut up and let me speak. I thought that was very cool … The Minister of Police has just told a cop to shut up and let me speak. What planet am I on?

Soon after, Minister Cooper came out publicly in support for 4ZZZ's Market Days. Not only did he reject Police Union calls to ban the fundraiser but went on record to say he would attend the next one. While that didn't eventuate, it was very unexpected for a leading figure in the conservative State Government of the time to tell media it was wrong to "stigmatise" a specific group of people and that 72 arrests in a crowd of 6000 people[22] made for a "pretty small percentage".

* * *

On Thursday October 24th, five days after the event, Brendan Greenhill and I nervously hand-delivered a letter of complaint to the Criminal Justice Commission offices. The decision to do so was not taken lightly. The CJC had a reputation for whitewashing allegations of police violence and some Zed volunteers had experienced this first-hand. Activists and civil rights organisations in Brisbane often referred to the CJC as "police investigating police"—indeed part of its remit was to work alongside law enforcement to investigate organised and major crime. Regardless, this was the only formal avenue of redress available to the radio station and, despite the time and energy invested in compiling the complaint, there was little expectation that anything of substance would come of it.

Addressed to Chief Complaints Officer, Michael Barnes, the letter listed three main grievances—excessive use of force by members of the QPS, the "complete disregard" by police for the pre-arranged agreement between police and 4ZZZ, and the unwillingness of police to liaise with official 4ZZZ representatives on the night. 4ZZZ also asked the CJC to consider the events of the night within a broader context:

> 4ZZZ feels that it is vital that any inquiry does not simply break the night's events down into a series of isolated independent incidents, but view them in an overall context, including police harassment at other recent 4ZZZ events.

The station forwarded 17 additional statements from individuals who had been at the event and the CJC received yet another six direct complaints about police conduct on the night. It would take over a year for the CJC to report back with its findings. Meanwhile, the formal complaint was not the end of 4ZZZ's advocacy work in response to police behaviour at 'Cybernana'. Over 70 people still faced court from arrests at the event, and the station was

---

[22] 6000 was the attendance cited by Russell Cooper in the news article. Numbers vary across publications, however, 4ZZZ recorded approximately 8000 in attendance overall, and estimate 2000 still on site when the storm halted proceedings.

committed to supporting as many of these people as possible. After all, they were listeners of the station, or at minimum, supporters of local live music, and therefore part of the 4ZZZ community. Free legal representation was arranged for the majority with the support of high-profile and well-regarded defence lawyer Terry Fisher and Vice-President of the Queensland Council for Civil Liberties, Terry O'Gorman. 4ZZZ made every effort to have someone attend the court cases, with Donna Williamson taking on the lion's share of this work supported by myself and 4ZZZ Chair, Fiona P.

Attending court was an eye-opening experience. We heard testimony from arresting officers that not only directly contradicted events we had witnessed but also changed over the course of the day. Most notably, an officer gave testimony in one court that he was certain of the time, because he remembers checking his watch; later he claimed in a different hearing that his watch was stolen, before the time he mentioned in his earlier testimony. Our minds boggled! For Fiona, it was the overt misogyny in the way male and female defendants facing an 'indecent manner' charge were treated that made an impression.

> It was a four-minute hearing for a bloke who did it, and it took 45 minutes when it was a woman. It was just sickening, you know? They both pissed behind a tree and the girl had a boyfriend holding a towel around so nobody could see, but it was almost degrading, the way she was treated by this Magistrate. It was just outrageous.

* * *

On December 17th, 1997, the CJC finally handed down its report. The delay in finalising the inquiry was attributed to its complexity and scope alongside difficulties locating several complainants who had submitted written statements. This was compounded by the time dedicated to a concurrent inquiry (ironically into the future role, structure, powers and operations of the CJC) as well as budget cuts that reduced the Commission's investigative capacity. The report, *Police Behaviour at a 4ZZZ Market Day Function*, found "evidence cannot establish wrongdoing on the part of any particular police officer" and did not recommend action against any person involved in the incident. Not one of 4ZZZ's complaints was upheld.

CJC Chairperson Frank Clair praised the QPS for "the way it reviewed the incident with other stakeholders shortly after the 4ZZZ function to establish arrangements to minimise the dangers that incidents of this nature pose".[23] This refers to a debrief held at an inner-city police station in the week after

---

[23] Criminal Justice Commission, *No Title* [media release], 17 December 1997.

'Cybernana', with representatives of the QPS, the Australian Defence Force (ADF), CAP Security, the Brisbane City Council, the Liquor Licensing Division, and the St John Ambulance service. Conspicuously absent from this conversation was a delegate from 4ZZZ, who had not been invited. A list of recommendations from this meeting were accepted and endorsed by the CJC in its report. Frustratingly, some of these recommendations mirrored procedures already followed by 4ZZZ, such as nominating a police liaison officer. The CJC appeared unaware—or disinterested—that Terry O'Connor had worked this role at numerous Market Days over the years. On a more positive note, the CJC put forward suggestions to "ensure that persons arrested at such functions are not detained for extended periods in unsuitable conditions"—a response to the unreasonable lengths of time some arrestees, such as Steve Johnston, were detained in police vans, before relocating to the City Watchhouse.

The ADF also conducted a formal internal investigation into military police involvement during the 'disturbance', which concluded that accusations made against the military police were unsubstantiated. This is contradictory to what witnesses told the CJC, the media and 4ZZZ. Despite finding no wrongdoing, the ADF recommended joint MP-Queensland Police patrols be ceased immediately.[24] The CJC reported it was satisfied that the involvement of military police was fully considered, and the findings are in accordance with its own conclusions.

Needless to say, 4ZZZ was disappointed but not surprised at the outcome of the complaint. The Criminal Justice Commission's findings aligned completely with the police and military accusations, disregarding all allegations of police violence made by 4ZZZ and other witnesses. Looking back, Brendan Greenhill wonders whether the investigation would have happened in the same manner in 2024. With the ubiquitous nature of smart phone cameras, "in this day and age there may have been footage," he says.

* * *

In the aftermath, there was no shortage of theories circulating about the 'Cybernana Police Riot'. Most support the narrative that it was planned as payback for 4ZZZ's long-standing and on-going reporting on police abuses and malpractice. As 4ZZZ wrote in its 1997 *Radio Times*:

> The conspiracy theorists out there have suggested that our constant troubles with the police are not coincidental – but if we annoy them so much that they have to bust up our fundraising with truncheons then we must be doing something right.[25]

---

[24] This information was provided to the Australian Anti-Bases Campaign Coalition in a letter from Senior Advisor to the Minister for Defence, Peter Jennings.

[25] 4zzz. "Introduction"—Summer 96/97 *Radio Times*, p. 2.

Many agree. One supporter recalls "lots of old [Zed] heads reminding traumatised young punters that, this is just what happens in Queensland under a conservative government". Volunteer Daniel Endicott is scathing in his critique of police, saying "they weren't there to keep the peace or help lost children. They were called in to roll the Zeds". While Admin Coordinator Chris McLean doesn't think the actions were premeditated, he does suspect they were "part of ongoing, long-term animosity. The chance arose, things got out of hand".

Some take the idea of payback a step further and claim 'Cybernana' was a pre-arranged training exercise. That Brisbane was host to more than 500 police from 54 countries at the 27th International Police Association Conference,[26] two days after the Market Day, does not quieten such suspicions. Annie Winter recalls a caller to 4ZZZ's *Talkback Show*, saying his brother-in-law was police, and that the riot was "planned in advance as a training exercise as the terrain was flat, everyone was fenced in". The anonymous whistleblower said it was "common knowledge within the department that it would be happening, regardless of if there was a riot to prevent or not". A 4ZZZ volunteer, who later spent ten years working with the police in an administrative role, believes this could be true. He says changes in the political climate in Queensland post-Fitzgerald Inquiry, meant that by 1996 most police didn't have training for crowd control under protest type conditions (referred to as 'Shield Wars'). According to this source, 'Cybernana' was seen as an opportunity to hold a training exercise, especially while the military police were in town. "There's no way that was put together at short notice," he says.

If anything, the events at 'Cybernana' and its aftermath only strengthened 4ZZZ's resolve to hold another Market Day. It took a year, but as you've already read, 'Zed Bubble' Market Day went off without a hitch.

---

[26] Queensland Police Service, *Brisbane to host International Police Association Conference* [media release], 9 October 1996.

CHAPTER 10

Our Core Business Is Community Radio

It's inevitable that some musicians and bands won't have positive experiences with 4ZZZ. The announcers are all volunteers; human beings with their own musical tastes and personal politics, uncompelled to showcase any specific band or song. To be frank, there's too much music out there to be bothered with tunes that don't resonate. Ideally, the diversity of volunteers counteracts individual taste. But on rare occasions artists may find themselves banging their heads against the wall in the quest for recognition. Some will take drastic action.

'Evil' Dick Richards currently plays in the internationally acclaimed rock 'n' roll band, HITS, alongside Stacey Coleman, who was part of the 4ZZZ management team in the early 2010s. On nine different occasions, his bands have placed Top Ten or above in the 4ZZZ Hot 100. It's hard to imagine that in the late 1990s he was issued a lifetime ban by 4ZZZ for a stunt pulled out of frustration that his latest band offering Strutter wasn't being played on the station.

Strutter set out—in Dick's words—to be "the dirtiest, meanest, most offensive band Brisbane had ever seen". And they succeeded. Pretty soon they were blacklisted almost everywhere. "It wasn't just music we were making. It was inebriated chaos," Dick says. Strutter "destroyed as many gigs" as they played good ones and often ended up in fisticuffs with other Brisbane band members. "We were no angels, and we brought a lot of backlash onto ourselves," Dick admits. "When I look back, I'm not exactly proud of these moments. But we were the band 'we wanted to see'. That was our mission statement."

4ZZZ didn't want a bar of Strutter, even though their album *Motherfuckers from the Bowels of Hell* received rave reviews from *Kerrang* (UK), *Maximum Rock n Roll* (USA) and others. Earache Records even contacted them about a European tour with controversial act, *The Dwarves*. Angry that 4ZZZ refused

© The Author(s), under exclusive license to Springer Nature Switzerland AG 2025
H. Anderson, *People Powered Radio*,
https://doi.org/10.1007/978-3-032-05689-4_10

to play their music, even on *The Punk Show*, Dick and band member Graham Don devised a plan to force their way onto the station. Hopped up "on a cocktail of vodka, spliff and some MDMA" they arrived at 4ZZZ under the pretence of having an interview. Once inside, they locked the host in the record library and hijacked the broadcast for a couple of hours. They played their own records, mocked other bands, and antagonised 4ZZZ live on air. "All this time, this poor fella was banging on the door asking to be let out, so after a while we relented and let him sit on the floor," Dick says. "He actually interjected and said we were quite good ... should have our own show!" The siege ended when a crowd of angry station members arrived to eject them. Consequently, both Dick and Don received lifetime bans from 4ZZZ, Dick nearly lost his job at Rocking Horse Records, and the volunteer announcer was fired, which Dick says he "always felt bad about as it wasn't his fault at all". As for the ban, it lasted about seven years. According to Dick, when another of his bands, The Aampirellas, was nominated 'Album of the Week' on Triple J, "it was kinda hard to ignore me and my somewhat matured level of 'agitation'!"

* * *

There's been one element missing from all this talk of music in Section Two, and that is what 4ZZZ does more than anything else: plays songs on the radio. Audio is dynamic and personal, which means describing a radio station's 'sounds' requires more than just words. The stories of Triple Zed's coming of age, of its events and its politics are much more tangible. You really need to listen to understand the place of music within the station's ecosystem. Fortunately, there are many ways to tune in to 4ZZZ. Besides the traditional FM frequency at 102.1 you can listen live online; you can also tune into Zed Digital, a second channel hosted on the digital spectrum (and live-streamed) with almost completely different content. There's the opportunity to listen to older shows on-demand, as well as some podcasting. Besides the latter,[1] music is an integral part of whatever you'll hear on 4ZZZ, including its news and information-based programs. And what a glorious hodgepodge of tunes it provides!

It was always the intention for Triple Zed to be a music-based station. Indeed, "Stereo Rock" was an original tagline. A flyer from 1975, promoting the station's launch, asks:

> Are you tired of hearing ... the same boring singles, the same on every station? ... [4ZZZ] will be playing mainly LP [long play] music – the records which make up 75% of the sales, yet which receive little or no airplay.[2]

---

[1] Due to the type of licence 4ZZZ operates under.
[2] 4ZZZ, *4ZZZFM 105.7 MHz* [leaflet], 4ZZZ, 1975.

As 4ZZZ founding member Sue Horton explains, "in terms of the music, that was a real opportunity ... to play music that was on albums and wasn't Top 40". This was particularly exciting with the station broadcasting via an FM signal with "a clear high quality stereo signal, unlike the muddy sound of existing radio".[3] The seeds of 4ZZZ may have been sown out of frustration with the mainstream media's coverage of social justice issues, but the original members also identified a need for more diverse musical choices.

According to Alan Knight, "the ABC was inward-looking and played crap music ... Australian rock music was not being played anywhere and commercial radio was playing the same rubbish it plays now". 4ZZZ wanted to be different, says Stephen Stockwell (Snr), "not just playing the same old Top 40 rubbish you could get anywhere else". Jim Beatson agrees. "We were making sure that we weren't just replicating what you'd hear on commercial radio. We wanted people to be exposed to different kinds of music."

The first edition of *Radio Times* discussed the station's music policy (or lack thereof). "A discussion of the Music policy of 4ZZ—FM is not easy because we like to think we don't have one,"[4] the article begins.

> It has been mentioned many times that 4ZZ-FM is just another "rock station" and we have to admit that as a station primarily directed at young people our programs will be often drawn from the contemporary scene. It should be emphasised however that this is not the only type of music being played and that our attitude to good, neglected rock music is no different from our attitude to good, neglected jazz, classical, folk, traditional and country music.[5]

The 'Programme Notes' for the December 1975 schedule mentioned *Jazz on Record*, *Nothin' but the Blues*, *Country* and *Classical Music* as specialised music shows.

Jazz and blues have stood the test of time. *Nothin' But the Blues* is most likely the longest running show on 4ZZZ, with former broadcaster Mark 'The Colonel' Doherty hosting for roughly forty years. *The Jazz Show* has also been on the air almost continuously, presented for decades by Sid Bromley, who established the Brisbane Swing Club in 1941. It was always a pleasure to have a beer with Sid at the 4ZZZ Announcer Meetings in the late 1990s, when he would have been nudging a spritely 80 years of age. Rod Ferguson was another longtime jazz host, father to Guy Ferguson who played a crucial role in locating the premises at Zed Towers.

Country music fell out of favour with 4ZZZ until Murri broadcasters started their own show in the mid '80s, and even then, there was resistance. "That was a whole other level of music controversy," remarks announcer and Promotions Coordinator Jane Grigg. However, with the growth of alternative country in

---

[3] 4ZZZ, 'Music', *Radio Times*, December 1975, p. 1.
[4] 4ZZZ, 'Music', p5.
[5] 4ZZZ, 'Music', p5.

popular culture, you'll now hear the twangs of country music on the station, including during *Rhinestone Cowgirl*, hosted by Triple Zed's Volunteer Coordinator, Salty Otton. "I can find a country song for anyone," Salty says. "One of the best compliments I've ever gotten is 'I didn't think I liked country until listening to your show'."

The *Classical Music* show would directly support Brisbane's aspiring fine music station, 4MBS, in securing its own licence. 4ZZZ offered the four-hour slot on Sunday mornings for the classical music group to air programs, acquire broadcast skills, and build an audience.[6] This growing support was crucial for 4MBS's licence bid—it demonstrated to regulators there was a volunteer and listener base ready for a dedicated classical station. 4MBS went to air on March 1st, 1979, and it would be the beginning of a long relationship between the two radio stations, despite their vastly different target audiences. 4MBS Station Manager, Gary Thorpe has been involved since the start. "There was an extraordinary sense of camaraderie," he says, "and I'm thrilled to say that still exists".[7]

4ZZZ originally decided on 'strip programming' for most of its broadcasting schedule. This meant there were few specialised programs (known as 'block programs'), especially during the day. Rather, a roster of regular announcers played music interspersed with bite-sized pieces of spoken word programming including news packages, announcements, specials and the like. The idea was that an average listener would tune in to 4ZZZ all day rather than for specific shows of interest, and the content would be varied enough to hold their attention. Gay Walsh was first to host the morning show. In her memoir *Free Radical*, she says strip programming was "a successful format; and because commercial radio was truly terrible in those days, we successfully won the ratings war, especially from the youth audience".[8] Helen Hambling also hosted a week-day program until early 1977. "It was mostly about … playing the music of the time," she says, "but I always thought that we were there for a purpose". The goal was to create an accessible, engaging station where music and information were blended rather than separated into strict categories.

From day one, 4ZZZ has been "a home for music outside mainstream radio taste"[9] and that tradition carries on strong. Tune in and you might catch Brisbane indie bands on *Brighten the Corners*, or fierce feminist rock on *Megaherzzz*. There are programs for lovers of folk (*Goldilocks Folk*), electronic music fans (*Electric Crush*), and so much more. Listen for long enough and you'll be sure to discover your new favourite band!

* * *

[6] 4MBS, "30 years of 4MBS 1979–2009", *Classic FM Program Guide*, February 2009, pp. 8–9.

[7] G. Thorpe. 'Interview with Heather Anderson [radio], 4ZZZ, March 18, 2022.

[8] G. Walsh, *Free Radical: A Memoir*, London, Austin Macauley Publishers. 2021, p. 164.

[9] 4ZZZ, *4ZZZ Radio—Submission Community Broadcasting Sector Sustainability Review*, https://www.infrastructure.gov.au/sites/default/files/documents/cbssr-4zzz.pdf, (accessed 9 February 2024).

Robert Forster started listening to 4ZZZ as a first-year University of Queensland student. Later he would go on to form The Go-Betweens, one of Brisbane's most internationally renowned bands (the city went so far as to name a bridge after them). He remembers perching his transistor radio on the windowsill to get reception, such was the weakness of the signal for those who lived in Brisbane's gully suburbs. "They were playing music that no one in Brisbane was playing ... the commercial stations weren't playing anything like it," he says. Robert was a fan of the announcer, Bill Riner, "a fairly wildly eclectic American guy".

> Those early announcers were definitely people from the early '70s, so ... to my recollection, it was more like a West Coast American FM station from that era, you know ... there was a lot of Jackson Brown ... they'd play Side Three of Led Zeppelin's [album] *Physical Graffiti* - the whole side - ... and Bill Riner fit it perfectly ... with great musical taste.

Alan Knight was one announcer who didn't care about trends or tastes—of the station or its audience. For his *Saturday Night Request Show*, he adopted an abrasive on-air persona named Dwayne Flicque,[10] deliberately constructed to satirise the tone of commercial radio. "One of the things I hated about commercial public radio was the treacly announcers," Alan says. Michael Finucan acted as "the request show sidekick ... answering the phones and running the records to Dwayne" during his early days as a volunteer in 1976. He says Flicque was "an erudite and acerbic on-air personality". "I would describe it as a Barry Humphreys-esque style," Michael adds.

> There was a really strong subculture of theatrical performative stuff going on in Brisbane at the time and various Triple Zed people were part of that. So, I think Alan had a little attachment to that and he was an amazing performer. The character was fantastic.

According to Alan, "Dwayne was particularly caustic about hippies and people who had bad taste in music". What music did Dwayne Flicque approve of? "Oh, *Sympathy For The Devil*," his alter ego replies. "That was it, pretty much!"

It wouldn't be long before punk rock would make its mark on 4ZZZ. Seminal Brisbane punk band, The Saints, released their debut album, *I'm Stranded*, in 1977 but they'd been playing around Brisbane for a few years, mostly at their own house and hall parties. "The music changed within that first decade of Triple Zed from being primarily about album-style music that hadn't been played on radio before, to punk stuff," says Sue Horton who went to school with the original Saints lineup. Robert Forster agrees. "Punk came, and [4ZZZ] virtually changed overnight, ... it just suddenly flipped, and it was very much a younger generation". "We were all listening to punk, right?" asks The Go-Between's drummer Lindy Morrison, who was playing in a band called

---

[10] Also spelt as Flick and Fleecque in different editions of *Radio Times*.

Zero, with 4ZZZ volunteer Irena Luckus in the late '70s. Michael Finucan suggests that punk was picked up quickly at the station because, even though Brisbane "seemed like a backwater," it was "the perfect crucible for what was happening with youth culture at the time". "There were a lot of disaffected people who really were losing interest in the overblown, standard rock output," he adds, "so I think the time was right for things to change … it was rapid in that people were ready to have something different, and something different appeared".

Michael Finucan took over the Breakfast shift in May 1977 and became a very popular announcer who helped define the station's sound of the time. For many, he represented the heart of Triple Zed's music ethos. "Michael Finucan changed my life," says Carole Quinn (who started at the station in 1986). "He was so funny, and he played the best music [like] Siouxsie and the Banshees and Buzzcocks." Another future announcer Victor Huml shares a similar memory. "Our little crew worshipped Michael Finucan," he says.

> I used to listen to him before getting on the bus for high school. He played all these amazing bands I had never heard of like … Talking Heads, The Specials, The Psychedelic Furs … His sarcastic readings of *Courier Mail* articles had us in stitches. We all wanted to be as cool and funny as him.

Michael credits other 4ZZZ announcers such as Stuart Matchett, Ross Crighton, Judy Crighton and Ashleigh Merritt for developing his own musical expertise. While he was already "music obsessive" before joining the station, he says that when he got to Triple Zed he was immersed amongst others who were not only playing music Michael listened to at home but also "other stuff that I hadn't heard of, which was fantastic".

According to announcer Tony Biggs, there was a bit of a split between the older and newer folk at Zed, but punk soon became the ethos of the place. "Of course, punk will be played here," he says. "It annoys people!" Not everyone embraced the genre, with the station "still caught between playing Steely Dan and punk," according to Lindy Morrison. "There were some really hip presenters yet then there was still your old school." Jan Bewes presented a music program on Sunday nights, but her musical selections sometimes didn't align with what the station wanted. "They kept threatening to sack me," she says with a laugh, "because I didn't play Triple Zed type music, I didn't play the Sex Pistols". However, as the '80s rolled in, punk and its derivative forms found a comfortable foothold on the airwaves of 4ZZZ. The Sex Pistols' *Anarchy in UK* topped the 1980 Hot 100, then ranked number two in '82 and '83.

* * *

4ZZZ's approach to music has always been deeply tied to its identity as a radical, community-driven station. The decisions about what music to play, or exclude, reflected the broader cultural and political dynamics at play within the station. Don't forget that programming decisions were made at the weekly Collective meetings and, as a growing diversity of musical tastes developed within volunteers and staff, so did the heated discussions. For as long as there was a Collective in place, there were arguments about what music was and wasn't acceptable. Geoff Wood, an announcer from 1981 to 1988, says one way of managing this was through the weekly review of the 'Hot Bin', which Geoff describes as a milk crate of recent records "deemed worthy of high rotation on the station". "Needless to say," adds Geoff, "these meetings could be smooth or acrimonious, brief or lengthy, depending on the records and announcers involved".

At its peak in the late 1970s, and during the '80s, disco was a lightning rod for debate at Triple Zed. Many Collective members dismissed it as too commercial, mainstream, or lacking the rebellious edge associated with punk and post-punk music. Local band, Razar's *Stamp out Disco* was much more likely to be featured than anything by KC and the Sunshine Band. However, the disdain for disco mirrored broader cultural prejudices at the time; it was heavily tied to LGBTQ + communities and communities of colour. By rejecting disco, the station inadvertently excluded music from these marginalised groups. Electronic music also faced resistance from 4ZZZ's more 'rock-oriented' culture and it was often women announcers forging the path for genres that didn't follow the generic guitars-bass-drums formula. Jane Grigg started at Triple Zed in 1983 and has been involved on and off ever since. While she was "into the punk stuff, new wave, rock and bluesy stuff," Jane also played a significant role in seeing dance and electronic music introduced into Triple Zed's regular programming and having Zed announcers DJ at Zed gigs. Even in the '90s, Phill Thomson (better known as artist Nam Shub of Enki) says it was hard to propose an electronic show "because most of the Zed hierarchy did not like dance music, and they couldn't differentiate between the commercial rave music and underground sounds".

Heavy metal also faced similar, if not stricter, scrutiny, with some Collective members viewing it as overly aggressive or out of sync with the station's core ethos. There was precedent for this—when Stephen Stockwell (Snr) was Program Director in 1980/81 he had to sack some "heavy metal enthusiasts who couldn't resist being sexist arseholes on their second show". In the mid-'80s, the station was again debating whether to allow a 'hardcore' metal-genre program. Mid '80s Finance Coordinator Liz Armstrong remembers arguments at several consecutive Collective meetings, "really trying to put a stop on this thrash metal". These days she says they "had no right to do that now that [she] looks back on it". The genre would later find a home on the station in the mid-1990s as *Hell Metal*, hosted by Judy and Rachel, two of the most knowledgeable experts to ever curate heavy metal music at the station. Despite the constant conflict over the merits and deficits of an array of musical styles (which also included rap and hip hop), once the dust had settled 4ZZZ would often become an early champion of emerging genres.

In the early 2000s, 4ZZZ experimented with the idea of a Programming Committee in response to dissatisfaction with on-air sound. Michael Crook was a volunteer at the time, working in both Front Desk and Announcing Coordinator roles during his tenure. "There were a lot of people ... at the station who had very strong views about what Triple Zed listeners did like and didn't like," he says, but when Michael asked how they knew this, the response was "well, it's just obvious". Less confident, Michael took on the task of surveying attendees at two Market Days and an annual Radiothon.

> We just collected a whole lot of listener habits. When they listened, what other stations they listened to, why they listened, those sorts of things and got some very interesting data out of it ... A lot of people were shocked that [respondents] listened to more commercial radio ... we weren't the only radio station they were listening to.

In response, Michael proposed an overhaul of programming. This wasn't the first time audience surveys had shown a disconnect between station and audience, although little had been done to actively address the concerns. "A lot of people got really, really angry with me," he says, but his work led to the formation of a new Programming Committee that "ended up changing a lot of things in a lot of the formats". Michael says he personally favoured 'strip' over 'block' programming but acknowledges the latter allows for more diverse community participation. The key was to include plenty of music regardless of the type of radio show being produced.

A few years later, long-time volunteer Josh Guinan found himself a member of the Programming Committee. He remembers one Station Manager proposing to turn specific timeslots into commercial-friendly programs. The goal was, according to Josh, to brand those as "our advertising slots, commercial radio style, and then the rest would be what Triple Zed should be". The Programming Committee strongly opposed this shift, rejecting the proposal outright, and with the backlash so strong, the Station Manager didn't stay much longer at the station.

Programming decisions at 4ZZZ are now made by the Programming Coordinator in collaboration with the Station Manager who, along with two nominated members of the Board of Directors comprise a Programming Sub-Committee. According to current Programming Coordinator, Ian Powne, the committee's focus is on strategic planning "as opposed to getting into the minutia". There's also a Program Review Team which, says Ian, works to encourage "self-reflection for announcers, building confidence, [and] maintaining accountability".

* * *

In 2025, most music at 4ZZZ is stored on a digital file-server library along with news items, promotional spots and live recordings. Announcers access this digital music library from computers in the studio and most artists and labels digitally submit their products to the station. Previously, 4ZZZ's Record Library was the place to find music. Thousands of albums, singles and later, CDs, slowly built up over the decades; categorised as either Local, Australian or Overseas, and a Hot Bin for new releases so that announcers could stay abreast of the latest offerings. At Zed Towers, the library sits adjacent to Studio One and still contains an impressive, although depleted, physical collection which is slowly being digitalised thanks largely to volunteer Kate, who spends hours every week archiving its contents.

Back in the mid-1970s, 4ZZZ's founding members set out to establish a record library rather than be the "captive of volunteers with a large record collection," as John Stanwell describes it. "This meant the station had to use its meagre resources to buy the records that announcers played," a difficult though not contentious decision, "since the free records that the record companies offered ... were mostly rubbish". John says local import record shops were supportive, charging cost price and even gifting records when they were confident that 4ZZZ airplay would lead to sales. This reciprocal relationship would prove to be lasting. Bruce Anthon managed Rocking Horse Records in the late '70s and early '80s, when the store usually donated two new albums a week. A cluster of independent record stores in the city did the same, in part to boost their own sales and visibility within the music scene. Bruce (who also drummed for The Survivors) says import record stores were especially valuable, as they supplied music not yet part of the mainstream which was exactly the music 4ZZZ wanted to play.

Stephen Stockwell (Snr) remembers Bill Riner showing him the ropes for picking up records. "We would go to Rocking Horse Records ... [then] Skinny's," he says, where "Tony Biggs would give us two records that he thought would improve our sound". This introduced Tony to 4ZZZ announcers and eventually led to his involvement with the station and the formation of band, The Black Assassins (with Stephen Stockwell and other Triple Zed alumni). Former announcers who moved overseas would also keep 4ZZZ in mind. Michael Finucan would often receive music from Judy and Ross Crighton after they moved to London and secured jobs at the prestigious Rough Trade Records. "They used to send me singles all the time," he says. "They were probably songs that Triple Zed was the first place to ever play them to air because there weren't many radio stations that were programming like that." According to Michael, record companies also realised that it was in their interest to send music to 4ZZZ.

> Suddenly these punk bands were selling quite reasonable numbers and [the labels] sure as hell knew that ... the commercial stations were not playing those records. So how were people hearing them? They worked out they were

hearing them on Triple Zed and they suddenly started giving us a lot more records and being very kind to us in their reptilian way.

Jane Grigg, who hosted the *New Import Releases Show*, also recalls the generosity of the alternative local record stores in the early '80s, including Kent Records. "We'd go there usually the day of our shift and borrow a bunch of records," she says, adding Kent also usually donated a record or two.

By the 1990s, it was common for one or two Zed folk to volunteer as Music Coordinators, facilitating the collection of new tunes and managing other aspects of the music side of operations. This included my 'little' brother, Scott Anderson, who would often send me fantastic interview opportunities. Most memorable was the time he woke me early one Sunday morning to ask, "How quickly can you get to the studios?". Alice Cooper was scheduled to call and Rachel and Judy from *Hell Metal* were accidentally locked inside their deadbolted apartment. I'm not sure anyone else at 4ZZZ was aware of my obsession with the Prince of Darkness since seeing him on *The Muppet Show* as a kid!

Kylie G's time in the mid '90s was deeply intertwined with her love of music, especially once she was in the Music Coordinator role. "It felt like Christmas every day," she says. "Pretty much everyone who was a Music Coordinator became really good friends with the people who worked at Shock Records," says Kylie. "We'd often go and stay with them when we were coming down to Melbourne." Kylie's successor Robin Steward took the initiative to contact international labels directly, with independents like Doctor Strange and Empty Records regularly posting material from overseas. Robin also implemented a playlist system to track what was broadcast and provide evidence to overseas record companies of the music getting played so he could "write off and say, 'Send me your CDs!'". In the late 1990s, Wave Beach decided to increase the diversity of 4ZZZ's collection, rather than focusing on rock genres, which already had strong support: "That stuff was looking after itself ... they sent it anyway," he says. "So, I went and found world music labels, jazz, underground electronic."

Each Music Coordinator played their own unique role in growing the station's musical collection, making the 4ZZZ's Record Library a treasure-trove for music-obsessed announcers. "The music education was in the library," says Tony Biggs. "Just idly rummaging through the record library and pulling out Parliament Funkadelic and Johnny Guitar Watson and ... proper reggae, you know, ... that was the joyous education." Twenty years later, Lorena Cappellone experienced her own love affair with the Triple Zed music collection. According to Lorena, exploring the Record Library "was like being a kid in a candy shop". "I lived in that frickin' record library," she says.

* * *

The music played on 4ZZZ is curated by the announcers. There's no expectation to play any specific songs, artists or albums but it's not quite a free-for-all. Announcers have an on-air commitment to meet a set of quotas: 40% Australian music, well above the 25% required by the Community Radio Broadcasting Codes of Practice[11]; 30% local music[12]; 50% female content[13]; 30% new releases (from the last 4 months) and 5% First Nations artists.

These have changed since I first started at Zed in 1991. There was no quota for the inclusion of First Nations music and the others sat at 30%, with local music a little lower. Female content was determined by whoever was singing. This annoyed me no end because it dismissed the women who played instruments or worked in production roles. However, I'm still grateful to promotions coordinator Deb Strutt who lobbied for "a 10% must-play women's voices quota" in the 1980s. "Much to our amazement it went through," Deb says. To support the initiative, she created a comprehensive list of all women artists in 4ZZZ's record library to make it easier for announcers to comply. Gradually the definition of 'women's music' expanded to include material that involved anyone who identifies as a woman playing any role in its production.

The latest significant changes to music quotas were implemented during Grace Pashley's period as Station Manager, not long after she took the job in 2017. "It's probably my formative fight," she says. "I was pretty naive to the backlash that could come about implementing what I thought had broader agreement." Some announcers and other Zed folk were concerned there had not been enough consultation, and that they wouldn't have time to implement the changes. The resistance was mostly against the 50% female music quota amidst concerns that, for some specialist programs, this would be tokenistic with the same few artists on repeat. A 'compromise period' was established that allowed people to transition to the new expectations.

According to current Programming Coordinator, Ian Powne, 4ZZZ announcers now exceed their quota in most areas, although women's music can still come in slightly under the mark, averaging 45.5% in 2024. Ian is surprised the female music quota isn't quite met, "considering some of our most played artists fall under this category, and a majority of announcers on 102.1fm (where the data is extracted from) are non-male". 4ZZZ does not have problems playing Australian and local music. And while the First Nations music quota was introduced as 'aspirational', most announcers quickly embraced the opportunity to increase their knowledge of Indigenous Australian artists. As Grace explains, "if you're in one of the Drive or Breakfast slots and you have three hours to fill, you should really be trying to

---

[11] Community Broadcasting Association of Australia, 'Community Broadcasting: Codes of Practice', *Community Broadcasting Association of Australia*, Sydney, QLD, Community Broadcasting Association of Australia, 2018 (accessed 6 September 2024).

[12] Southeast Queensland region.

[13] That is, with women, including trans women, involved in the production.

find some First Nations bands to play". The gamble paid off. "Every single year we hit the mark," Grace says. "Some years [First Nations music] was sitting up around 15%."

In 2018, the Federal Minister for Communications and the Arts called an inquiry into the Australian music industry to investigate "factors contributing to the growth and sustainability of the Australian music industry".[14] Grace was invited to join representatives from the Community Broadcasting Association of Australia to speak to the inquiry about 4ZZZ's approach to music quotas. The Commonwealth Government's *Report on the inquiry into the Australian music industry* noted that 4ZZZ's Australian music airplay was averaging 60% (at the time). The report credited community radio as "integral to the growth and sustainability of the Australian music industry," saying "there is a strong and growing demand for the locally focused and diverse content offered by [the sector]".[15] Even within the community broadcasting sector, 4ZZZ stands out. Craig Tigwell from Melbourne band Tina & The Hams says they received far more support from the Zeds than they did from their own local community radio. Although this exposure didn't necessarily lead to greater sales or bigger audiences, Craig believes it "did pave the way for [them] being playlisted for a while at other stations, but the support was never to the extent that we received from 4ZZZ". Mike 'Fox' Foxall from Sydney's Nancy Vandal agrees.

> Back when Nancy Vandal was in its infancy 4ZZZ was our first and strongest ongoing supporter. They gave us our first bit of community airplay, helped organise our first interstate shows and 4ZZZ Market Day was the first festival we ever played. The thrill of heading up to Brisbane and the shot in the arm of an actual radio station playing our music cannot be underestimated.

Ian Powne coordinates most of the training for new 4ZZZ announcers and says the quotas don't stir much of a reaction during the sessions, as there is "a general acceptance they're in line with the station's values". In 2024, the station played nearly 55% Australian music and almost 32% local offerings. Just over 39% of songs were new releases and 8.2% represented First Nations music, demonstrating that most announcers are comfortably finding a diverse range of artists to feature on their programs. Grace agrees. "It's become a cultural thing," she says.

* * *

---

[14] Commonwealth of Australia, 'Report on the inquiry into the Australian music industry', Commonwealth of Australia, Canberra, ACT, Tabled: 2 April 2019, https://www.aph.gov.au/Parliamentary_Business/Committees/House/Communications/Australianmusicindustry/Report (accessed 26 March 2025).

[15] Commonwealth of Australia, 'Report on the inquiry into the Australian music industry', p110.

While announcers are expected to work within the guidelines of music quotas, there is still a lot of autonomy when it comes to the music they choose to play. Station Policy states:

> 4ZZZ will not impose rigid censorship decisions on programming material, but we will strive to ensure announcers act in accordance with station values, policies and charter, as well as the CBAA Code of Practice.[16]

It also recognises that "situations of conflict between certain aspects of 4ZZZ's charter may arise, particularly with respect to censorship and racism, sexism, homophobia". Challenges sometimes emerge when songs or artists are played that others consider hateful or hurtful towards sections of the 4ZZZ community, especially those whose voices are already marginalised.

The freedom afforded to 4ZZZ announcers to program their radio shows has, on occasion, seen the station in the crosshairs of federal government authorities. Broadcasting law in Australia is regulated primarily by the *Broadcasting Services Act 1992* and enforced by the Australian Communications and Media Authority (ACMA) (previously by the Australian Broadcasting Tribunal [ABT]). When it comes to obscenity, offensive language, and swearing—which Triple Zed will usually find itself in trouble for—the law has evolved significantly, moving from strict prohibitions to a more contextual approach that allows for greater freedom in certain circumstances. In the early 1980s, 4ZZZ played a role in fostering these leniencies.

4ZZZ's licence needs to be renewed regularly; currently this means every five years but in the early days of Triple Zed this was usually every three. The station successfully renewed its first licence, upgrading to full power in 1978.[17] However, by the time it came to renew again in 1981, the Australian Broadcasting Tribunal, had received a substantial number of complaints about the material 4ZZZ put to air. These complaints often related to offensive language and controversial music. According to volunteer Gordon Curtis, in the early days the station was "constantly under threat of losing the license because people didn't like what we were saying or playing".

Rona Joyner was one such person. A prominent Queensland conservative activist during the 1970s and 1980s, Joyner was renowned for her campaigns against materials and educational programs she deemed inappropriate or immoral. She founded two organisations: the Society to Outlaw Pornography (STOP) and the Campaign Against Regressive Education (CARE).[18] Her activism significantly influenced Queensland's educational and moral landscape

---

[16] 4ZZZ, 'Station Policy 1.5', 4ZZZ, 2025, p. 14 https://jeff.4zzz.org.au/sites/default/files/media/4ZZZ%20Station%20Policy%201.5.pdf, (accessed 26 Feb 2025).

[17] G. Williams, *Generation Zed: No other radio like this*, Kingswood Press, 2000, p. 18.

[18] J. Gerrard and H. Proctor, "For the love of God: how pornography and an explicit reading list turned Rona Joyner into a conservative activist", August 16 2021, https://blog.aare.edu.au/for-the-love-of-god-how-pornography-and-an-explicit-reading-list-turned-rona-joyner-into-a-conservative-activist/, (accessed 26 March 2025).

during that era and STOP consistently monitored 4ZZZ and complained to the ABT whenever they heard an 'obscenity'.[19] STOP used organised letter-writing campaigns to bombard the Tribunal with complaints which was a tactic that exaggerated the scale of the public outrage.

One of the first songs to put 4ZZZ under the ABT spotlight was Marianne Faithfull's *Why D'Ya Do It*, from her 1979 album *Broken English*. The song was known for its explicit sexual language and, in Australia, Festival Records refused to release the album until *Why D'Ya Do It* was removed. However, the ban didn't extend to import copies, which is how 4ZZZ came to access the song. Not surprisingly, announcers at 4ZZZ have a rebellious attitude toward censorship, often responding to restrictions by intentionally pushing boundaries. As Gordon Curtis says, "if you tell someone at Triple Zed, they can't use the word 'fuck' on air, guess what's going to happen?".

The Australian Broadcasting Tribunal Annual Report (1980–81) states that 4ZZZ was reported to the ABT for "possible contravention of section 118 of the *Broadcasting and Television Act 1942* ... which prohibits the broadcast of material which is blasphemous, indecent or obscene".[20] After investigation, the Tribunal gave Triple Zed the benefit of the doubt "but warned the station of the need to exercise care with certain types of broadcasts and that the Minister for Communications had been advised of the matter".[21]

Later in 1981, U.S. band Dead Kennedys released the single *Too Drunk to Fuck*. Anne Jones was hosting a Saturday afternoon shift, when news came through that all copies of the single had been impounded from a record shop at the Gold Coast. According to Anne, "I just said on the radio that word had come through that the Dead Kennedys single had been seized and that this was a terrible thing for free speech". She was aware of the controversy surrounding the song, so rather than playing it, she chose to air another Dead Kennedys track, *California Über Alles*. However, the very mention of the offending title on air was enough to trigger outrage. "The right-wingers who used to listen to 4ZZZ," as Anne describes them, had heard it and complained.

Other songs, such as Millie Jackson's *Fuck U Symphony*, Sex Pistols' *Friggin in the Riggin* and spoken word tracks from Derek and Clive, had already been reported to the ABT so when it came time for 4ZZZ to renew its licence again, station staff prepared for a serious battle. An inquiry was held in Brisbane on December 18th, 1981.[22] According to announcer Andy Nehl, a team from Zed accompanied by a solicitor argued that the ABT had to consider a range of factors, including audience, intent, whether a warning had been given, artistic

---

[19] G. Williams, *Generation Zed: No other radio like this*, Kingswood Press, 2000, p. 18.

[20] Commonwealth of Australia, *The Australian Broadcasting Tribunal Annual Report (1980–81)*, Commonwealth of Australia, Canberra, ACT, 1981, p. 27.

[21] Commonwealth of Australia, *The Australian Broadcasting Tribunal Annual Report (1980–81)*, p. 27.

[22] Commonwealth of Australia, *The Australian Broadcasting Tribunal Annual Report (1980–81)*, p. 25.

merit and accepted community standards. "We basically changed the law of the whole country when that Tribunal handed down its decision the next year," Andy says. The station got its "knuckles rapped [and its] licence shortened from three years to two".[23]

You'd think the staff who defended 4ZZZ's licence so passionately to the ABT would have gone on to be a little more cautious about their on-air decisions, but not so for Andy Nehl. One afternoon in 1982 while Andy was on air, the station's then Promotions Coordinator, "the late Dave Cooke," came into the studio excited with a copy of the new 12-inch of *The Litanies of Satan* by Diamanda Galas. He suggested to Andy "it was pretty full on" and suggested he should barricade the studio door.

> I [introduced] the song and let *Litanies of Satan* rip. It took about 10 to 15 seconds before then Station Coordinator, Anne Jones [and] a heap of other Zed staff, were trying to get in, ... yelling at me through the window to get it off air. But Cookie held firm at the door. The song became a bit more accessible around 45 seconds into it and after a minute or two the crowd outside studio dissipated when they realised there was nothing they could do.

The full track of *The Litanies of Satan* goes for about 17 minutes. Andy says he played about six to give the listeners a good taste, followed by "something really poppy and accessible".

4ZZZ's broadcast licence was never seriously threatened again, mostly due to the loosening of expectations of what was and wasn't considered obscene. However, staff still needed to defend the musical choices of 4ZZZ announcers at various times. Nyx Westerman remembers being heavily involved in protecting the station during their time in the role as Station Coordinator between 1985 and 1987. "There's a long tradition ... of doing that," they say. "There's actually this repository of beautiful arguments about freedom of speech, the vernacular, the connection in audiences." The letters often took on an academic and legal tone, incorporating philosophical justifications for free speech, as well as discussions on the role of community radio in reflecting real-world language and culture. "Even regulatory bodies were a bit sick of having to put out those fires by that point," Nyx admits. On a lighter note, announcer Patrick O'Brien remembers finishing a shift with *Constipation Blues* by Screamin' Jay Hawkins and soon after being visited in reception by a mother and her daughter. The mother said her daughter had made her put Triple Zed on the car radio and just as they did, they heard a song about constipation. "I thought they were going to go off on one about vulgarity on the radio," Patrick says. "Instead, they wanted to know what it was because it was the ... father's birthday and they reckoned he'd love it ... All radio should be like that, right?".

---

[23] G. Williams, *Generation Zed: No other radio like this*, p. 22.

4ZZZ failed a defence circa 2000, when announcer Jamie Hume pushed the limits by playing two extremely sexually explicit songs back-to-back during a morning timeslot. While he did give a 'language and concept' warning in advance, a listener with children in the car chose to keep the radio on and was shocked to hear Susie Bright's *Circus Whore* followed by Thug's *Fuck Your Dad*. ACMA ruled the songs Jamie played should not be broadcast again, and he was removed from his time slot. In response, station management instituted a policy restricting extremely explicit content to the hours between 6:00pm and 6:00am. Jamie suspects the listener had been actively looking for something offensive to complain about. Despite the controversy, he reflects on the incident with some amusement, especially when comparing past censorship standards to modern radio content. Jamie notes that explicit songs, such as Lily Allen's *It's Not Fair* which discusses impotence and premature ejaculation, were later played on mainstream radio without issue. He's also made guest appearances at announcer training sessions to talk about the incident, saying "do things for a laugh, but be careful".

Most recently 4ZZZ was referred to ACMA in 2024, accused of broadcasting anti-Israel music and commentary. The Queensland Jewish Board of Deputies complained after a segment on the show *Exit Stage Zed* featured songs by three different pro-Palestinian artists. *Sky News* reported that the Jewish group described the lyrics and comments as "provocative, rabble-rousing, historically inaccurate and highly offensive". 4ZZZ Chair Ruth Gardner rejected the group's interpretation of the content saying, "it would be inconsistent with 4ZZZ's policy and aims in supporting diverse, minority and Indigenous voices and communities, to intervene to censor the programming choices in question". The complaint was escalated to ACMA, who decided there was no breach of the Community Radio Broadcasting Codes of Practice.

* * *

4ZZZ made a commitment to local artists in the first edition of *Radio Times* in 1975. "4ZZ-FM will give support to Australian bands in general and local bands in particular,"[24] the article reads. This support has emerged in different ways, primarily through airplay, interview opportunities, gig bookings, promotion and some opportunities to record. Support for Brisbane music has oscillated over the decades, sometimes favouring certain genres, and often buoyed by individual announcers passionate about homegrown talent. For example, Mick Medew from Brisbane band Screaming Tribesman credits announcers like Andy Nehl and Tony Biggs for playing their song *Igloo* on high rotation in 1983/84. "It was referred to as the 'Friday night song' at the station, although it would be played at any hour of the day," he says.

---

[24] 4ZZZ, 'Music', *Radio Times*, December 1975, p. 1.

4ZZZ '80s announcer Geoff Wood says whenever the station committed to playing local music, it in turn encouraged artists to start recording and releasing their own. "The formats and quality of the recordings did vary wildly," he says. "I recall playing recordings on air that were on 2 track 1/4 inch reel-to-reel tapes, vinyl singles, EPs and albums, most self-funded and self-released". Some bands were able to record their material in the 4ZZZ studios, often performing tracks live-to-air that would then be stored on tape cartridges (known as carts), mostly used to play community announcements, jingles and the like. If an announcer was ever stuck for something to play, they could always quickly insert a cart into the cart machine, and it would be ready to go.

As Andrew Bartlett points out, some of these demo versions became "Triple Zed hits". Choo Dikka Dikka's *Cyclone Hits Expo* was one—a song wishing bad fortunes on the Expo 88 World Fair that brought gentrification to the area now known as Southbank. "I don't think it was ever actually released properly as a song," Andrew says, "but just built that iconic nature purely by … Triple Zed airplay". This was also the case for Kev Carmody's early recordings (see Chap. 12) and The Parameter's, *Pig City*, which became Brisbane's antiauthoritarian anthem of the era. When Tony Kneipp wrote *Pig City*, he wanted to record it at 4ZZZ using their eight-track tape deck. However, the rest of the recording space was a shambles. According to Tony, "to make space, a staircase had been ripped out, leaving a pile of bricks and rubble, a huge steel girder and a gaping hole in the ceiling".[25] He was able to strike a deal to use the eight-track if he built in the ceiling, with 4ZZZ paying for the materials. "I remember a whole team of people moving that bloody great girder with the aid of a block and tackle," he says. The work took a few months, but *Pig City* was mixed down and ready for airplay on 4ZZZ just a few days before the 1983 Queensland elections.

4ZZZ has also operated as a quasi-record label, sporadically releasing compilation albums, CDs and cassettes. With so much local music accumulating in the 4ZZZ collection, it seemed only logical. One of the first compilations, *Queensland in Quarantine: A compilation of diseased music* (1984) wasn't technically a Triple Zed production but was so closely associated with the station it deserves a mention. An independent production spearheaded by 4ZZZ announcer Linda Wallace, the cassette featured Brisbane bands interspersed with political news clips from the stations' newsroom, sourced by Zed journalist Harley Stumm. "It was thrashed [on the radio]," Harley says, "and it was obviously very Triple Zed aligned".

Two years later, 4ZZZ released its first vinyl offering, *State of Emergence* (Fig. 10.1). According to Promotions Coordinator of the time Deb Strutt, the album was a collection of "politicised local bands who had all written songs or put themselves on the line by doing gigs that were openly in … criticism of the powers that be". Some of the tracks were recorded at

---

[25] T. Kneipp, 'The recording of Pig City', *A Records Brisbane*, March 17 2010, https://arecordsbrisbane.wordpress.com/2010/03/, (accessed 1 February 2025).

Fig. 10.1 Album cover for 4ZZZ compilation 'State of Emergence', designed by Cora Lansdell; 1986

a concert held by 4ZZZ at the UQ Refectory while others, such as the Mop and the Dropouts song, *Brisbane Blacks*, were re-releases of independent singles. The back cover featured a Matt Mawson cartoon of Joh Bjelke-Petersen reeling dramatically from a transistor radio, repelled by the sounds of 4ZZZ.

So far as I can tell, it would be over ten years before Triple Zed released another compilation, the first of a series on Zed Hed Recordings. A double-CD collection of Hot 100 songs from the 1996 countdown called *4ZzZ's Hot 100* marked twenty years of the chart which had Triple J's solicitors all fired up for the briefest of moments (more on that in Chap. 11). This was quickly followed by two compilation CDs that were the brainchild of Brentyn 'Rollo' Rollason. *Lots of Brisbane Punk Bands* (1998) and *Heapz of Brisbane Punk Bands* (2000) captured the eclectic and flourishing local punk scene of the era.

That same year, 4ZZZ volunteer, musician and filmmaker Chris Holland "stupidly decided to do a double CD of trucking songs," after working with Rollo on the Brisbane punk band compilations. "I was looking to use a broad selection of bands around Australia [and] cold-called a bunch of artists," Chris says. This resulted in some unlikely collaborations, most notably variety entertainer Barry Crocker and garage rockers The Celibate Rifles covering the truckers' anthem, *Six Days on the Road*. The CD even featured an 'improvised piece' by my son and a couple of friends (billed as Killer Keller, Callum and

Jack) sporting the imaginative song title, *Trucks*. When the final product, *Get Trucked: 32 Australian Trucking Songs* was launched, Chris asked drummer Fred Noonan to chaperone country singer Nev Nicholls until the gig started "and the two got ridiculously plastered but pulled off a great show". "The album pretty much engulfed my life for that period," Chris says, "but was totally worth it!".

The year 2000 was also 4ZZZ's 25th anniversary. As part of the celebrations, an eclectic group of Zed music lovers curated a collection representative of the station's first quarter-century. *Behind The Banana Curtain: 1975–2000* (*BTBC*) featured 41 local artists, starting with The Saints and ending with Regurgitator. Ten years later, Triple Zed picked up where *BTBC* left off. *4ZZZ Presents Beyond The Banana Curtain: A compilation of Brisbane bands 2000–2010* featured 23 artists. These two compilations are a local music lovers dream, mapping many of the bands popular on 4ZZZ across 35 years of broadcasting.

Both CDs were launched at birthday party gigs. 'Live Behind the Banana Curtain' was a two-day affair; both gigs had similar lineups, with Sunday for all-ages. The shows featured a cross-section of the artists on the CD including Blowhard and Screamfeeder. Several bands from earlier decades reunited, such as 1980s psychedelic punk outfit Pineapples From The Dawn Of Time and pop icons The Riptides, first active in the late '70s/early 80s'. Terry O'Connor was involved in organising 'Live Behind the Banana Curtain'. His highlight was the reunion of Isis, known for their incredible harmonies and acapella performances. Ten years later, a scaled-down CD launch for *Beyond the Banana Curtain* would mark 4ZZZ's 35th birthday, held at The Zoo with SixFtHick, Monster Zoku Onsomb!, Turnpike, and Nikko.

A few other CDs were released by 4ZZZ in between. The Market Day police riots (covered in Chap. 9) were marked by the double CD release, *Cybernana Riot Day: Whose Riot? The People . . . Or The Police?* (2000). One CD showcases bands from the festival's lineup, while the other features artists who performed in the 'Doof Tent', possibly making this release the first to feature a significant proportion of electronica. This was followed in 2001, by *Gizmo: A 4ZZZ Electronic Compilation*, a free CD funded through the Community Broadcasting Foundation (CBF). The *Gizmo* liner notes explain that 4ZZZ was sent over 90 submissions for consideration in the project. Future Station Manager Michelle Brown was one of the artists whose submission made it onto the CD, under the artist name Zmx performing, as she describes, "digital game boy sounds". *Gizzzmo 2* served as a follow-up in 2003.

Not to be left out, 4ZZZ's *Ska Show* also secured funding from the CBF in 2005 to release *Stop Wondering Now*". The compilation of local reggae, ska and dub bands was free to download from the show's website and included Bertha Control, Kooii and Heavyweight Champion.

* * *

Garry Williams, who joined Triple Zed as a volunteer announcer in 1988, is well respected for his unwavering support of local music. He believes that while some local artists—The Saints, Riptides, Razar, Mystery of Sixes and The Parameters—became staples at 4ZZZ, "no one really focussed on the local scene". His first radio show was a four-hour "all-Brisbane Graveyard shift". In 1992, Garry started to host the *Demo Show*, which mostly played local bands' unreleased recordings. Although he didn't establish the program, he became its main DJ for four years. Garry says cassettes were much cheaper to make than vinyl records, "so anyone could do it"; later, bands could also burn CDs of their recordings. "The point of the *Demo Show* was to act as an open mic for local acts," Garry describes. "You send it in, we'll play it," he says. Later *Demo Show* host Geoff Wilson agrees, saying the show emphasised inclusivity, ensuring even the smallest, most experimental acts had a chance to be heard. Patrick O'Brien agrees. When he was presenting The *Demo Show* in the early '90s, he would receive "an obviously homemade tape" from the same artist every couple of months. "[The music] got consistently weirder and weirder," Patrick says, "like a staring contest where they were challenging me to see how far they could go before I'd stop playing them. This was Zed, though, the weirder the better".

4ZZZ is often still the first media outlet to broadcast the work of up-and-coming independent bands from Brisbane and its surrounding areas. As Lindy Morrison of Zero and The Go-Betweens points out, the station has long provided exposure to local artists who lacked mainstream appeal, enabling "even inexperienced musicians" to find an audience. The Go-Betweens founder, Robert Forster remembers taking the band's first single into the station in 1978. "They started to play it, and really quite heavily," he says. "That was great, because ... it really brought people to shows."

Artists may now be able to upload their songs to music streaming platforms and use social media to promote themselves, but when a song gets played on the radio it means someone else has actively chosen to showcase it. "Community radio ... [is] the place that most bands get their very first airplay," says Kellie Lloyd from Screamfeeder and Deafcult (among others). "Those people who are the volunteers, who are the announcers ... are often the people who go to the gigs and see those bands as well, so it's like this ecosystem, we're all part of that together." Being Jane Lane are a good example. Vocalist, Teigan Le Plastrier, says 4ZZZ was the first station to ever play their music in 2013, "and have continued to support our endeavours ever since". The band had their first live-to-air interview on *The Brown Couch* and were invited to promote their music on *Queer Radio* and *Dykes on Mics*.

Other musicians credit 4ZZZ for extending their musical education. Randall Kempel from Emu Smugglers—whose song *Born and Bred (on Triple Zed)* topped the 2008 Hot 100—says that without the station he "wouldn't have been exposed to half the bands who influenced all of us".

For activist folk singer Phil Monsour, Triple Zed is where he first heard "political or alternative ... sort of music". He also remembers being quite young, walking out of a guitar store and hearing one of his songs playing on a car stereo for the first time. For Dave Tug of the Square Tugs, "the joy of getting played on the radio" was hard to describe, while for Victor Huml from Mouthguard it is still "a real thrill".

I'll leave the final word to Lizzie Cook-Long, who has listened to 4ZZZ since its beginnings. "As teens of the late '70s & early '80s, 4ZZZ was our lone voice of reason in Brisbane during the Bjelke-Petersen years," she says. "The St Lucia studio was the mothership of radical thought and original indie music." Lizzie's band Kathleen Turner Overdrive has graced the 4ZZZ Hot 100 three times, making number 9 in 2024 with *I Want To Believe*. Her love letter to 4ZZZ sums up the feelings of many local independent musicians.

> The first time we heard ourselves announced and played on 4ZZZ was by Billie on *SubNovo*. Was there a sneaky tear and waves of pride at being played on the station that has always stood up for the marginalised and the so-called miscreants? You betcha!!! Thanks heaps 'ratbags since 75', for building community, belonging and safety for the straights, the queers and all things in between.

CHAPTER 11

Community Radio Is Hot Stuff

It's New Year's Day, 1994, and the air is thick with Brisbane's summer heat. 4ZZZ's Hot 100 countdown is about to begin which is as good an excuse as any for a party. Watermelons sweat on the kitchen bench; their flesh partially scooped out to make room for vodka. We carve chunks from the boozy fruit, hoping to stave off the oppressive humidity. I'm the bass player in Acid World, and our album *Children of the Privileged West* has been quite popular on 4ZZZ this past year. If I'm honest I'm hoping—no, expecting—to hear at least one song come up in the countdown.

And then there is Rollo. Larger than life in every way, the frontman of Blowhard and a fellow volunteer at 4ZZZ, my dear old mate and occasional friendly rival. He's as jolly as ever, his infectious laugh shaking the walls whenever someone says something even remotely amusing. Rollo and I have a secret competition in place—who can get more songs in, who can climb higher on the chart? But really, it's all in fun. We both know that no matter what, local music wins.

The countdown starts rolling. At number 75, the jazzy refrain from Blowhard's *Fat Juicy Cop* fills the room. Rollo throws his arms up in triumph. Shortly after, Acid World has its first nod with *Exiting the Womb*. One after another, more Acid World songs make their way up the list—36, 35, 32. Yes! Then it's Blowhard's turn again—a song at 30, then 28. Acid World climbs to 13 with *21st Century*, a track I don't even expect to hear. The Top Ten ticks by until, Acid World again at number three with *Children,* which starts with the gurgles of baby Keller, a tiny piece of my heart forever recorded.

Blowhard strikes back at number two with the now-iconic *V8 Rock n Roll*. Rollo howls—half in victory, half in disbelief. We were both in the top three. Surely, we'd taken it all. Then the announcer reveals the number one song: *Cannonball* by The Breeders. Not even a local band!

© The Author(s), under exclusive license to Springer Nature Switzerland AG 2025
H. Anderson, *People Powered Radio*,
https://doi.org/10.1007/978-3-032-05689-4_11

Rollo and I lock eyes and burst into laughter. He thrusts out his hand, and without hesitation, I grab it. In the middle of that sticky summer evening, as *Cannonball* blasts, we swing each other around, spinning in circles, laughing and dancing to the song that has bested us both.

That was Rollo—always up for a dance, always up for a laugh.

He's been gone since 2019, a heart attack stealing him just before a Blowhard gig. But his voice, his presence, and the shared memories of his unwavering passion for music, family and friends—those things haven't left. They never will. I miss him all the time.

* * *

A reliable way to understand the breadth of music played on 4ZZZ is to peruse its Hot 100 lists. Since New Year's Day in 1977 4ZZZ has almost always

Fig. 11.1 Poster for 4ZZZ's Hot 100, designed by Josh Murphy; 2021

broadcast the results of this annual music poll. While its parameters have changed over the years, it has consistently represented the songs most popular with listeners; originally selected from an infinite pool of songs and now slightly more curated.

In its current form, the Hot 100 represents songs released the year prior.[1] 4ZZZ provides a shortlist on December 1st although voters can nominate other songs released during the eligible timeframe. Artists are limited to three songs and while anyone can participate online, a subscriber's vote carries twice the weight. While this might sound a little convoluted, the criteria ensures that for the most part, 4ZZZ's Hot 100 represents the most popular music as played on the radio station over the past year, as opposed to listeners' broader suite of favourite songs (Fig. 11.1).

In June 1976, the idea for a Hot 100 was raised in *Radio Times*. "What we're trying to do is put together a representative list of the all-time favourites amongst Triple Zed listeners ... giving someone the opportunity to win five great albums".[2] Founding member Stephen Stockwell (Snr) won the grand prize by picking the most songs in the countdown. He'd previously been involved with the UQ Media Committee, but by 1975 was not active within the station. Stephen says if the competition was rigged, he didn't really benefit. '[I] got a bunch of records that no-one else wanted," he says. "They were really crappy records that they wouldn't play on the radio station." *Good Vibrations* by the Beach Boys took out the top spot that year.

The next Hot 100 didn't happen until 1980. According to announcer Andy Nehl, not long after he started at the station, he saw reference to the 1976 Hot 100 in *Radio Times*. "I thought it would be fun to resurrect it and see how the listeners' taste in music had changed," he says. With the blessing of the Collective, Andy ran the 1980 Hot 100 and the change was stark, with Sex Pistols at both Numbers One and Three. Local and Australian music now dominates the countdown with punk music still making strong appearances each year.

* * *

Up until the early 1990s, 4ZZZ was the sole voice of alternative music and countercultural ideas on the Brisbane airwaves. When the ABC's Sydney-based youth radio station Triple J expanded nationally, it had a significant cultural impact and brought independent music to a broader audience. Its arrival in Brisbane in 1990 was a challenge for Triple Zed. Fully funded by the federal government, Triple J had access to resources, infrastructure, and promotion that far outstripped that of a grassroots volunteer-run community station. As Zedder Stefan Armbruster explains, "It was hard to compete with something

---

[1] Between November 1st of the previous year and October 31st of the year of the Hot 100.

[2] 4ZZZ, "Hot 100", *Radio Times*, June 1976.

that had such massive resources ... they had all the money and the polish". When Triple J announced its own Hot 100 countdown in 1989, 4ZZZ was not happy.

The story is detailed in an episode of 4ZZZ's podcast history series, *From A to Triple Zed*. Andy Nehl was now manager of Triple J. He was approached by Laurie Zion, an ABC trainee from Melbourne with an idea for a Top 100 chart, inspired by similar polls in *Rolling Stone Magazine* and the *Billboard 100*. According to Andy "I replied something to the effect of 'funny you should mention that ... we did that at 4ZZZ, and it worked really well'," giving Laurie the green light. Andy recommended Laurie call it the Hot 100, "as Hot sounds a lot better than Top". It should be remembered that Andy was instrumental in revitalising 4ZZZ's countdown in 1980, and Triple J were not yet broadcasting in Brisbane. "Not much consideration went into using the name Hot 100 beyond my quick off the top of my head response," he says. "It probably would have been better if I'd thought more about it before telling Lawrie to call it the Hot 100, but what's done is done."

The following year, Triple J's national expansion reached Brisbane. According to Stefan Armbruster, "[Triple J] posed all these other existential threats to us, and then on top of everything else ... now they're doing a Hot 100. But that's ours!".[3] Anita Greenhill was Station Coordinator at the time. "I wrote a letter and threatened them that this was our intellectual property, that they needed to not use 'Hot 100', or they needed to acknowledge [4ZZZ]." There were meetings, and the lawyers got involved, but according to Anita, "we couldn't get them to back down, they knew they were bigger".[4]

According to 4ZZZ, a compromise was struck. Triple J would change the name of their chart to the Hottest 100. Andy Nehl maintains that "given the 'Hot 100' name was 4ZZZ's baby, I decided we needed to change [it] before the next one in 1991". Regardless, both stations continue the tradition today with different names, played on different days. My adult son, who grew up with 4ZZZ a significant part of his life, is a much bigger fan of the Triple J Hottest 100—one of my most serious failings as a parent!

I can clearly hold a grudge, yet institutional memory must not be as strong at Triple J. In 1997, 4ZZZ decided to release a double-CD compilation—simply called *4ZzZ's Hot 100*—to mark 20 years of the countdown. Triple J immediately threatened legal action. Zed volunteer Terry O'Connor was liaising with Shock Records to coordinate the CD's release.

> We got a fax ... Not actually from Triple J but from their lawyers ... essentially it was a cease-and-desist letter ... saying that 'the Hot 100 CD infringes on Triple J's product – their Hottest 100 CD – it's too close in name and in content and it was too easy for the public to confuse the two'.

---

[3] 'How Triple J Stole the Hottest 100 (well ... kind of)', *From A to Triple Zed* [podcast], 4ZZZ, 12 February 2021,(accessed 9 June 2024).

[4] 4ZZZ,'How Triple J Stole the Hottest 100 (well ... kind of)'.

Terry says the legal action was quickly resolved. "We simply pointed out to them that … Triple Zed had allowed them to use Hottest 100 when they started broadcasting in Queensland," he says. According to Terry, once reminded of the situation, it wasn't long before Triple J's legal team "basically went 'oh yeah, that's right, sorry!'."

* * *

A Brisbane band first won the Hot 100 in 1984. Andrew Bartlett was working at the station at the time, and rather than cast a vote himself, he was tasked with tie-breaking responsibilities. If songs had the same number of votes, Andrew would decide which would rank higher. When it came to the top two spots, local band President's XI's *Summer Vacation* was tied with The Cure. "I cast my vote," Andrew says. "Number two was The Cure with *Primary*." Despite the slightly shady circumstances, it was rewarding to see a local band finally cracking the top five rankings, let alone number one.

According to *Radio Times*,[5] the 1986 Hot 100 was the most diverse at the time; 3500 different songs were voted for, out of which 21 Brisbane bands made the cut, with five in the Top Ten. This included Ups and Downs, I am Vertical (Andrew Bartlett's band) and the Parameters with their cult-classic *Pig City*, recorded at 4ZZZ. *Pig City* still holds the record for most times a song has appeared in the Hot 100 (nine), an honour that under the current rules can't be surpassed. Local music has grown to dominate the Hot 100, making the countdown "hyperlocal," to steal Andrew Bartlett's words. An astonishing 81% of songs in the 2024 countdown came from artists based in Southeast Queensland. With this level of localism comes occasional accusations of rigging and favouritism, but also a lot of pride, especially for grassroots and independent artists who most likely will only ever be recognised by the 4ZZZ audience.

One of Brisbane's most successful exports Screamfeeder have placed in the Hot 100 a staggering twenty times (between 1992 and 2024), reaching Top Five on three occasions. Bassist/vocalist Kellie Lloyd is now a 4ZZZ announcer. While she agrees "it's hugely important that local bands are celebrated in this way," Kellie notes the station receives its fair share of criticism because the high-placing local bands are often not that well known outside of a certain niche or genre within Brisbane. "So that's a … bit of a strange one," she says, "but I think everyone appreciates the fact that we—the local bands—are taken seriously". Andrew Bartlett believes 4ZZZ's role in promoting lesser-known local artists through the Hot 100 is vital. "Some bands that chart in the Hot 100 will be forgotten in five years," he says, "but that doesn't matter. They'll always have that moment". Announcer and Being Jane Lane vocalist Teigan Le Plastrier is a little more pragmatic. "The Hot 100 is an interesting subject … good and bad for upcoming bands," she reflects, saying the voting system can be tricky and may leave people feeling disheartened by results. "On the flip side

---

[5] 4ZZZ, "Hot 100", *Radio Times*, January 1987.

it can be really encouraging," Teigan adds. Being Jane Lane have made the chart six times, twice cracking the Top Ten. "I think overall it's a bit of fun for local bands and the community to have some friendly competition, and a fun event to cap the year off."

Dave Tug has been playing in Brisbane bands for forty years. His current band Square Tugs won the 2022 and 2023 chart but says his "bigger joys" come from seeing other, often younger or marginalised, bands succeed. "Making The Hot 100 tells them 'We admire you, whether you are trans, gay, non-binary—we follow you and are moved by your music'," Dave says, adding "I'm actually tearing up right now typing this". Experienced musicians can also find their own Hot 100 placing quite sentimental. In 2024, Mick Medew and Ursula placed third with their self-described "gimmick" song *Punk Grandma*. "It's where I am in my life ... Grandkids and music," says Ursula, who's played in bands since the early '80s. "It was a very emotional experience," she adds. "I feel very fortunate and humbled that I still have a voice and when I have something to say, people can hear it thanks to 4ZZZ!".

Pop-punk band Flangipanis have won the Hot 100 five times, including a hat-trick between 2015 and 2017. They've ranked every year between 2015 and 2023, a testimony to their prolific back catalogue and longevity as a band. Flangipanis' guitarist, Josh Murphy has volunteered at 4ZZZ in some shape or form since 2009 and currently co-hosts *The Punk Show*. He says he's seen the value of the Hot 100 Listening Party grow. "When we first won (2013) it felt like a bit more of a niche event, there was no official party ... and it didn't seem to be followed ... particularly widely." The band would organise their own parties or have the countdown playing in the background at a gig or pub. "We celebrated our first number one sitting in the dark in the 4ZZZ car park because the [nearby] bar had closed and we didn't know where else to go," he laughs. Josh says the Flangipanis' success in the Hot 100 has been a mixed blessing.

> The immediate feeling that a bunch of people from your community have bothered to vote for you, remembered your song ... affirm[s] all your hard work. The flip side is that ... people talk about it like it's somehow a magic key to success or better shows ... but the rise and plateau of 'Flange' should really put that idea to bed. It looks good in a bio, it's a fun boast, but no-one has ever booked us 'because' of the Hot 100.

PART III

Without Community There Is No Soul

CHAPTER 12

A Kaleidoscope of Communities

Just in case you've forgotten, 4ZZZ is a *community* radio station and a broad range of communities have been represented at Triple Zed over the past half-century. There have been programs in solidarity with Trade Unions, Latin-American resistance and the Irish Republican Army; a kids' show and one for lovers of movies. Current Programming Coordinator Ian Powne says there's been a lot of growth in the "non-music focused content" of 4ZZZ over the past few years, resulting in "many wonderful shows that increase our community representation". These include *Workers' Power* (worker rights), *The Home Show* (housing precarity/accommodation) and *ARTache* (visual arts). Beyond its on-air programming, 4ZZZ has operated countless community development projects to engage pretty much any group that has struggled to find a voice in the mainstream media. I could fill a chapter merely listing the communities with which 4ZZZ engages and has engaged.

Instead, I will focus on the origin stories of three of these—First Nations, LGBTIQ + and women—all of which have long and robust histories at the station and maintain relevance to this day. It pains me to neglect other Triple Zed shows and radio personalities (did someone say volume two?); as such I'll also touch on two more recent stories that capture the 'Zed-geist': a sporting event that puts Triple Zed 'out there' in the local community, and an accessibility program that encourages people to 'come in'. It's a bit of a kaleidoscope, just like the station itself.

* * *

There has been a feminist program on 4ZZZ since the station was just a month old. *Through the Looking Glass (TTLG)* is first mentioned in the January 1976 edition of *Radio Times*—an hour-long show broadcast on Saturdays from 5:00 to 6:00pm. It's described as:

> an experimental feminist-oriented program which aims to discuss prevailing attitudes and expectations of importance to women ... to break down the concept of the authoritative 'disc jockey', the all-knowing figure behind the microphone.[1]

Early members included Fiona McLeod and "a few friends, in particular Jane Evans, Alison Hunter and Julie Goodall". Fiona says *TTLG* was designed "by women for everyone listening to Triple Zed. But we only played women's music. And tried to get as many women's—feminist—stories that we could".

TTLG was developed as a panacea to the dominance of male voices on the radio, including the 4ZZZ airwaves. In its early years, station staff and volunteers were often at loggerheads over community access, indicative of a wider conflict about on-air sound and the station's core objectives. Complaints described a predominantly male-driven "homogenised Stereo Rock"[2] format. "If you are supposed to be an alternative station what is wrong with alternative songs, women's songs ... ?,"[3] a listener wrote in 1976. A year later, the Brisbane Women's Media Collective published an article in Australian academic journal *Hecate* which offered a scathing critique of the station's treatment of feminist voices: "Over time, women were gradually forced out of their position of para-equality on the station until, at the present time, they are little more than fringe dwellers on its periphery".[4]

Fiona McLeod held a paid position as Administration Coordinator alongside her *TTLG* duties. She says she never felt feminism was negatively received at Triple Zed. This was a common response from the women staff and volunteers of the late 1970s I've spoken to. Founding member Helen Hambling says she felt safe and "certainly didn't feel ... discriminated against". However, she also notes 4ZZZ may have looked different from outside.

> I was a young feminist ... All of the men certainly espoused an understanding of feminism, whether they really did or not is another matter. But, you know, it was the dominant philosophy there ... In retrospect, I think we were not great at making the place inclusive. And that was by accident ... We all had such a strong bond from the intensity of the time ... We thought 'we'll just invite people to come, and they'll come' ... What I know now is there are a whole lot of things you need to do—not just be nice—but actually make people feel empowered to participate.

---

[1] 4ZZZ. 'Through the Looking Glass', *Radio Times*, January and February, 1976, p. 7.

[2] Brisbane Women's Media Group. 'TRIPLE Z: 'maintaining credibility' or, did homogenised radio turn sour?'. *Hecate*, vol 3 issue 1, 1977, pp. 108–114.

[3] C. Mann. 'Letter to the Editor', *Radio Times*, October, 1976, p. 6.

[4] Brisbane Women's Media Group, 'TRIPLE Z: 'maintaining credibility' or, did homogenised radio turn sour?', pp. 108–114.

This became part of *TTLG*'s mission, to involve more women in the program and the station. The topics covered could easily appear on 4ZZZ's feminist program today: "women's arts. ... sexuality, sport, child abuse, abortion [then illegal in Queensland] and contraception, children's literature [and] Queensland school systems".[5] According to Fiona McLeod, one of the show's most significant achievements was winning the 1979 Australian FM Radio Award for Best Community Service Program, for *TTLG's* Mothers' Day special; described as "an attempt to portray the realities of being a mother ... not the gilt edged, sugar coated image Mothers' Day usually projects".[6] Fiona says it was controversial for its time, and included talk on abortion as a legitimate option for an unwanted pregnancy. "I never did hear why the judges ... thought it was prize-winning," Fiona says. "But it was a really good program with ... really good research about services in Brisbane for women."

Fiona continued to volunteer with *TTLG* after she ceased employment at 4ZZZ in 1979 but it's unclear when the show finally wound-up, due to a gap in published program guides. What we do know is that in 1983, journalist Amanda Collinge joined Triple Zed and quickly recognised the need for a women-specific program. Amanda felt that 4ZZZ, like Triple J where she'd worked for many years, "was closely aligned to rock 'n' roll and the music industry" with an on-air gender imbalance that reflected broader trends in the sector.

A group of women, including Amanda Collinge, Liz Willis and Deb Strutt established a new women's collective which Liz says she quickly named *Megahers*. Training was an important component for attracting new volunteers: "Do you want to come and join the women's radio collective? We'll teach you how to use super scopes and record on tape", read the promotions. Gabrielle O'Ryan was recruited on "the Regatta Hotel's verandah ... approached by a radio feminist with a handful of pamphlets".[7] She joined up immediately. In an autobiographical short story, Gabrielle describes sitting around in a circle at *Megahers*' first meeting, drinking black and tans "in an attempt at feminising beer guzzling".[8]

> In a warm embrace we learnt how to edit tape, mix music and words, cue records and move from one good idea to an even better one ... A man from the newsroom taught us how to edit out coughs and ums in the middle of words. We decided that the mistakes were moments of resistance, and we could leave them in.

Megahers impacted the station more broadly. "[It] wasn't just a show—it was a movement within the station," Deb Strutt says (Fig. 12.1). "The [4ZZZ] Collective became more and more embracing of feminist politics and this was reflected in the on-air sound". For example, Station Coordinator and *Megahers*

---

[5] Jane, Fiona, Julie, Allison, 'Through the Looking Glass', *Radio Times*, February 1979, p. 11.

[6] Jane, Fiona, Julie, Allison. 'Through the Looking Glass', p. 11.

[7] G. O'Ryan, 'Oh bondage: Up yours!', *Continuum: Journal of Media & Cultural Studies*, vol 6 issue 1, 1992, p. 120.

[8] G. O'Ryan, 'Oh bondage: Up yours!', p. 121.

Fig. 12.1 Poster for 4ZZZ show *Megaherz*, designed by Nyx (Nancy) Westerman; 1985

member Nyx Westerman helped organise rape crisis workshops at the station. There were concerns about sexual violence and harassment on the University of Queensland campus and Nyx says 4ZZZ was uniquely positioned to offer support. "We thought about it, we talked about it ... we're open 24 hours a day. We can be a port of call," they explain. Furthermore, as a 24-hour station, 4ZZZ was almost always staffed and it was important to ensure the space was safe for everyone.

The station liaised with Women's House, a local rape crisis centre, to deliver the workshop series. Their efforts were not universally welcomed, with some male staff and volunteers reacting defensively to the idea. But volunteer Geoff Airo-Farulla believes the initiative was "groundbreaking because it ... [required 4ZZZ folk] to engage in difficult but necessary conversations about gender, power, and violence".

I presented *Megaherz*[9] from 1993 to circa 1997. The show was on during my 'child-free' time of the week on a Sunday afternoon. I shared hosting duties

---

[9] Spelling has changed over time, most recently to Megaherzzz.

with several different women, but most often with my good friend Kirstyn Lindsay. "*Megaherz* opened the doors for me," Kirstyn says. "I don't know if I would have survived if I hadn't got involved in 4ZZZ. It opened a world that I would not have known of." We were in our early-to-mid-twenties, discovering the excitement of anarcho-feminism and the delights of being angry young women. *Megaherz* was where we learned about intersectional politics, of abolition as an antidote to the pitfalls of reform. "[It] was … an opportunity to say, 'stuff it, I'm here and you're not going to shut me up'," Kirstyn adds. "I finally was at a point in my life where I could be politically active … and I had a platform to agitate." Emboldened by the women we'd encountered and learned from through the program, a group of us marched topless at a Reclaim the Night rally in 1994, brightly painted by Vicki, singer of local hardcore punk band Zooerastia. "It was about learning to be OK with body image," Kirstyn explains. A photo from that night shows beaming faces, breasts encased in acrylic sunflowers and bold lines traced across scars.

The *Megaherzzz* Collective is alive and strong today, anchored by Denise Gibbons, Sarah and Sisi. Denise says getting involved with the show has "ignited [her] feminism again" and enabled her "to meet other like-minded people". The program's promotional blurb on the 4ZZZ website describes the current iteration of *Megaherzzz* as "an intersectional feminist program [that amplifies] various marginalised communities".

Complementing *Megaherzzz* is a newer addition to the 4ZZZ schedule, *Tranzmission*, "a show born out of necessity, perfect timing and a whole lot of courage".[10] Feminism may have long held a space at the station, but for transgender folks in 2021 there was definite room for improvement. Early in the year, not long after Stephen Stockwell (Jnr) took over the Station Manager position, "a long-running program broadcast some unsavoury TERF (Trans Exclusionary Radical Feminist) rhetoric"[11] in a speech recorded at a recent rally. In an attempt to address the harm caused to trans volunteers and listeners, Stephen approached Ezarco Dos Santos, who was Executive Producer of gaming show, *Zed Games* at the time. "He asked me if I'd like to do a 5-part miniseries interviewing different experts … about trans people," Ez writes in a *Radio Times* article. Once he started researching, Ez knew the series needed to be more than a temporary broadcast—"it needed to be during a high listenership spot, and it needed to be by trans people and for trans people,"[12] he says. Soon after, Ez met Charlie, a new volunteer who proved a perfect choice of co-host. *Tranzmission* first broadcast on June 7, 2022, and is still on the air today.

* * *

---

[10] E. Dos Santos, 'Tranzmission: An origin story', *Radio Times*, 2022. p. 3.

[11] Dos Santos, 'Tranzmission: An origin story', p. 3.

[12] E. Dos Santos, 'Tranzmission: An origin story', *Radio Times*, 2022. p. 4.

Queer broadcasting has also been front and centre of 4ZZZ since day one—literally, with John Woods speaking the first words uttered on the station. Openly queer woman, Gay Walsh hosted the first morning program from December 1975, and in a few short months managed to "suffer the opprobrium of the Christian Right"[13] after playing interviews with sex workers and offering a prize for listeners to send in their most humorous 'sin stories'. In the early days there was also Lauren McKinnon's Gay & Lesbian Radio Collective to ensure queer stories were included in the strip programming favoured at that time.

When 4ZZZ transitioned to include specialised 'block' programs in its schedule, a queer-focused show quickly secured a spot. *Gay Rave* was established by Zed producer and announcer Gary Summerville and first aired in March 1985. The program was described as "non-sexist ... open not only to gay men, but lesbians as well [which] ... brought good feedback from the public".[14] Initially airing on Thursdays at 5.30pm, *Gay Rave* was scheduled immediately after what was simply titled *The Gay Radio News*.

A Letter to the Editor in the October 1985 *Radio Times* underscores the significance of queer programming during this period. In response to a listener's disapproval of the *Gay Radio News* segment, Robert M (a very satisfied subscriber) reminded readers that 4ZZZ served more than just fans of alternative music—it was also a platform for marginalised communities. His letter was prominently marked with hand-drawn arrows by the *Radio Times* editorial team, illustrating their efforts to highlight voices that advocated inclusion.

In September 1986, *Gay Rave* evolved into the more widely remembered *Gay Waves*, maintaining its Thursday evening timeslot. Not to be confused with a similarly named program on Sydney's 2SER, *Gay Waves* was launched by the Gay Wave Collective, which originally included Nils Van Der Beek, Ingrid Tall and Deb Strutt. The show set out to explore "topics and news of interest to both lesbians and gay men,"[15] and over the years, it featured a rotating cast of hosts, most notably Toye De Wilde, who became the first transgender candidate to run for the Queensland Legislative Assembly during the 1987 Merthyr by-election.

In 1990, longtime volunteer Gai Lemon joined the *Gay Waves* team. She was the only woman in the regular lineup at the time, encouraged to participate by friends already involved in the show. Gai says she fell in love with both *Gay Waves* and 4ZZZ immediately. "There's something about radio ... how organic it is,' she says. This was particularly the case in the '90s when, according to Gai, "there was so much happening in the queer space trying to support people and help them through what were fundamentally quite difficult times". During the height of the AIDS crisis, and shortly after the World Health Organisation removed homosexuality from its International Classification of

---

[13] G. Walsh, *Free Radical: A memoir*, Austin Macauley Publishers, London, 2021, p. 167.

[14] Anon. 'Gay Rave'. *Radio Times*, May 1985, p. 2.

[15] N. Van Der Beek, 'Gay Waves', *Radio Times*, September 1986, p. 6.

Diseases, queer broadcasting provided crucial support—particularly for those grappling privately with their identities. "If somebody came into the room while you're listening, you could just flick the switch over and be listening to ... [commercial Brisbane station] 4KQ, or whatever," Gai notes. "I think it made it very safe. It was unlike having a book or printed matter in your house, which was evidence of your so-called 'deviancy'."

In September 1992, *Gay Waves* was restructured into *Queer Radio* and *The Lesbian Show*. This decision to change both the format and title came amid a growing commitment by contributors to gay and lesbian politics, particularly around the evolving notion of a broader queer community.[16] These programs aired on Wednesdays from 6:00 to 9:00pm, with *The Lesbian Show* occupying every third week and *Queer Radio* the other two. John Frame joined 4ZZZ around this time and would go on to volunteer with *Queer Radio* for 15 years or so. He describes the supportive nature of the show as being "like the presenters are holding your hand in real time". By late 1996, *The Lesbian Show* underwent a name change following a listener's suggestion. As Gai Lemon recalls, "this was pre-Internet, pre-email ... so we used to get handwritten letters from fans". One opened with the greeting, 'Dear Dykes on Mykes'. Gai said to her co-announcer Deb, "Oh my god, that's our name!". "We just took it and ran with it," she adds.

In 1999, 4ZZZ participated in the Sydney Gay and Lesbian Mardi Gras Parade for the first time. John Frame described the event as "a great profile-raiser for the station as ... a significant part of Australia's gay and lesbian media". A team of eight delegates, including John, represented the station at the parade, distributing 'Assorted Family' biscuits to onlookers and receiving enthusiastic support from "more than a few Zed Heads".[17] Hearing 700,000 people "cheering and screaming ... is an experience that can't be equalled," John remarks. "People say being proud to be gay is nothing but being proud to be honest—I think that's really quite important."

In August 2002, *Dykes on Mykes* and *Queer Radio* were allocated individual timeslots. Each program was granted a two-hour weekly slot, following significant lobbying, not necessarily to separate the shows, but to gain more airtime. The shows remain a core part of 4ZZZ's programming, with *Dykes on Mykes* syndicating on Joy FM in Melbourne, Australia's only LGBTQI+ community radio station. Long-standing co-hosts Ruth Gardner and Kate Mackie have been involved with *Dykes on Mykes* since approximately 2008 and 2013 respectively. Ruth is also 4ZZZ's Chairperson of the Board of Directors. Blair Martin has coordinated *Queer Radio* for at least 13 years, having volunteered at the station more broadly for over twenty. In 2010 he won the Brisbane Pride Festival Queen's Birthday Community Awards for Entertainer of the Year. Blair has reported for Queer Radio from the

---

[16] G. Lemon, 'Queer Radio', *Radio Times*. March 1993, p. 5.

[17] J. Frame. 'Queer Radio', *Radio Times*, February/March 2000, p. 5.

Eurovision Song Contest—"the world's biggest musical celebration of creativity and by association queerness and pride"—on five occasions. "It was a wild ride that will always be amongst my highlights," Blair says. He describes Queer Radio "as a medium for communication and sharing joy, standing against oppression, and making the world a brighter, more colourful, and queerer space".

* * *

During its first week of broadcasting, 4ZZZ featured an interview with Guwamu[18] activist Cheryl Buchanan, who had just returned from the Cairns Land Rights Conference in Far North Queensland. An article in the inaugural edition of *Radio Times* promoted the interview and wrote about the importance of land rights.

> It is essential now that we all recognise the continuing moral, spiritual and economic significance of land to the [A]boriginal people and how vital the solution of this issue is to future race relations in Australia.[19]

While First Nations issues were a regular topic of 4ZZZ's news and current affairs coverage from its beginnings, representation within the station wasn't as prominent. Nicola Joseph noticed this when she moved up from Sydney to take a position in the newsroom in 1980. "One of the real shortcomings for Triple Zed was its … relationship with minority communities, especially the Indigenous one," Nicola says. "4ZZZ was only ever putting Indigenous people on one side of the mic."[20] This began to change by the time of the 1982 Commonwealth Games land rights protests with which 4ZZZ became closely involved (discussed in Chap. 13).

Warinkil Aunty Glenice Croft is a Woppaburra[21] elder who became heavily involved with 4ZZZ soon after the Commonwealth Games protests. "The Four Triple Zed mob … they reached out to us in community," she says, "and luckily we had Ross Watson there". Uncle Ross[22] was a respected activist, editor of *Black Nation Newspaper* and coordinator of the Black Protest Committee which led the actions against the Commonwealth Games. 4ZZZ

---

[18] The Guwamu/Kooma are an Australian First Nations group whose country lies in what is now south-west Queensland (https://aiatsis.gov.au/austlang/language/d33; https://aiatsis.gov.au/explore/map-indigenous-australia).

[19] Anon, 'Land Rights'. *Radio Times*, December 1975, p. 8.

[20] Unpublished transcript of interview with Nicola Joseph by 4ZZZ volunteer, Scott Mercer, recorded in 2020 for the *A to Triple Zed* podcast series.

[21] The Woppaburra people are the traditional owners of the Keppel Island Group, approximately 15 km off the coast of Yeppoon, near Rockhampton in central Queensland (https://woppaburra.com.au/).

[22] Uncle Ross Watson passed away in 2013. I was unable to interview him for this book but had the great privilege of working alongside him at 4ZZZ for a short while.

journalist Louise Butt (and others) had reached out to Ross, encouraging him to get involved with the station. "Four Triple Zed must have approached Ross about ten times," Warinkil Aunty Glenice says.

> And in the end, he thought, 'yes, this is going to be good for the community. This is something we really need. You know, we have to have our voices heard'. And he always spoke up for justice.

Warinkil Aunty Glenice joined Uncle Ross at the station. She brought along her kids, and with Alfie Shillingsworth, Hedley Johnson, Ricky Pascoe and a few others, became a mainstay of First Nations broadcasting at Triple Zed. Warinkil Aunty Glenice's daughter, Shellah M Ballesteros was a teenager at the time. "What I remember is, the older people and elders knew there was a need for a lot of stuff to be done," Shellah says. "We weren't trying to be radicals. We were trying to conserve [culture]." Greg Fryer—already volunteering at Zed—also got involved with Murri programming; an important milestone for a young man who'd grown up part of the Stolen Generation. "Culturally, I didn't know anything ... and I suppose that sort of attracted me to Triple Zed initially," Greg says.

> My first contact with community was *Murri Radio*, and it was the beginning of my journey coming home. I might not have landed where I am now in my life without that happening ... With Triple Zed, whether you're a Blackfella, Stolen Gen, or you think differently, you're queer, whatever basket you come from, it was that nice place of comfort.

According to an article written by Ross Watson in *Queensland Review*, the official radio show, *Murri Hour* first went to air in July 1984. As the name suggests, it broadcast for one hour per week (originally pre-recorded for a Sunday timeslot) but slowly increased in length over the years. *Murri Hour* was the first program in Brisbane to regularly broadcast Indigenous music and perspectives and, most importantly, says Warinkil Aunty Glenice, adhered to strong cultural values both in the materials broadcast and the ways it went about creating radio (Fig. 12.2). As Ross describes:

> Prisoner and community requests had a strong unifying effect. Bonds were strengthened and formed with unions and other groups and individuals opposing the corrupt and racist government. Activities included community reporting and messages, as well as participation in street marches, meetings and protest action.[23]

Shellah remembers working alongside 4ZZZ producer David Lennon to record musician Kev Carmody performing *Thou Shalt Not Steal* during *Murri Hour*. David—who Shellah speaks highly of as a hands-on trainer—worked out a way to create a stereo sound by having both producers stopping and starting

---

[23] R. Watson, 'Murri Hour'. *Queensland Review*, volume 14, Issue 1, January 2007, p. 49.

Fig. 12.2 T-Shirt artwork for 4ZZZ show 'Murri Time', designed by Shellah M Ballesteros; 1983

reel-to-reel recorders in synch with one another. "The sound of the songs was so deadly,[24]" she says. Now one of Kev Carmody's most famous tunes, *Thou Shalt Not Steal* wasn't officially released until 1988. The album version is a different recording, and the lyrics are slightly different which always catches me off-guard when I hear the more recent version.

The benefits of *Murri Hour* flowed both ways. Non-Indigenous staff and volunteers learned about First Nations issues and culture. "That was the start of my education in Indigenous politics," says announcer Tony Biggs. Journalist Donna Baines and announcer Stefan Armbruster both say they treasured time spent learning from the *Murri Hour* team. "Every Monday I'd get to hang out with Glenice Croft … and the crew. I met Aboriginal people and spent time with Aboriginal people," Stefan says. "As a white, economic migrant from Germany … it was just something completely new." Donna says she learned a lot working alongside Warinkil Aunty Glenice. "She was inspirational to me … a strong single mum working and doing what she needed to do."

---

[24] 'Deadly' is an Aboriginal English word that translates to 'excellent' or 'great'.

The broader 4ZZZ community, however, had mixed reactions to the growth of *Murri Hour*, which contrary to its name expanded to eight hours in its second year and then 18 hours per week by the 1990s. Volunteer Geoff Airo-Farulla believes this growth was vital, particularly in a city like Brisbane where tensions between Aboriginal communities and authorities were high. "I thought that was fantastic because it really provided a launching pad for something much bigger," he says. "The station's commitment to giving airtime to the Indigenous community was one of the things I was most proud of during my time there." *Murri Hour* proved "a bit of a culture shock" for some at Triple Zed, according to Louise Butt. Announcer Liz Willis agrees, noting tension within the mostly white University-educated Collective. "It was ... so controversial," she says. "They're playing country music; they're talking about football ... people were not liking it."

Murri Hour also challenged the 4ZZZ Collective's ideas about what was considered 'good radio', forcing them (and the audience) to reconsider conventional norms such as acceptable speech patterns and pacing. Other members of the Collective were impatient with volunteers who didn't follow best practice for handling media and recording gear. "People were working on the *Murri Hour* who probably hadn't had access to a lot of equipment before", says one volunteer. "People were losing their minds over records being misplaced!"

Tom Maginnis got involved at 4ZZZ in 1987 and is described by his Zed peers as a staunch advocate for the Murri community at Collective meetings. "A lot of the acrimony towards the Murris was just straight-out racism," he says. One of the earliest Collective meetings he attended at 4ZZZ quickly descended into a heated debate about First Nations participation at the station. "There was this huge debate about vandalism being caused by Murri kids," Tom recalls.

> That was the time when tagging was just coming in, you know. And so, the older people didn't like it and, the younger people didn't care ... It was just tagging ... something that comes from Black American communities ... Politically, I was closer to the Aboriginal people and their goals and aspirations than I was to people who were concerned about the decor and graffiti and stuff.

Announcer Julia Tresidder experienced similar frustration over complaints about graffiti on record covers, which she felt were trivial in the broader context of supporting First Nations broadcasting. Tom says these types of disagreements split the Collective. "Half the room went, 'that's vandalism'. And the other half went, 'no, that's political speech'." Allies of the *Murri Hour* worked behind the scenes to educate 4ZZZ's mostly white staff and volunteers. Collective members were invited to attend decolonisation workshops that, according to Tom, were "a life changer". "We had responsibilities as non-Indigenous people to educate ourselves," he says. "We'd tell our own stories of our dealings with Indigenous people and then discuss how we frame those relationships," Tom explains, "and then talked about whether that was racist or not, or fair or not".

By late 1987, with Australia's Bicentenary approaching, 4ZZZ faced a major decision: How should the station handle the 200th anniversary of British colonisation?

For First Nations communities, January 26th, 1988, was not a day of celebration but a day of mourning marking invasion, dispossession, and resistance. Tom Maginnis says Ross Watson and Tiga Bayles (Ross's nephew, who ran Radio Redfern in Sydney) developed an ambitious plan to link up multiple community radio stations across the country and co-deliver a national Invasion Day broadcast. The stations included 4ZZZ, Radio Redfern and the Central Australian Aboriginal Media Association (Alice Springs) with the goal to create a live broadcast through which First Nations broadcasters across the country could share stories and protest the Bicentenary.

Tom handled the technical logistics. "My job was to get onto Telecom and push ahead to have landlines plugged into the desks ... so the broadcast could be synchronised, going live to air." The broadcast was a major success and most likely one of the first live radio syndications of its kind in Australia. Tom says there was a real excitement to the seamless live crossovers. However, the initiative nearly led to financial disaster when Telecom later attempted to charge 4ZZZ an exorbitant amount of money for the landline connection. Tom boldly bluffed his way out of the bill. "They said, 'You guys owe us', I think it was $5 000, 'for the network hookup on Australia Day'," he explains. "I lost [my temper] and said, 'Get out! You can't charge Aboriginal people that ... they were the first people here!" That was the last 4ZZZ heard of the charges, which was a relief given it was 1988 and Triple Zed was in deep financial trouble. Nevertheless, it refused to advertise a Bicentennial Ball being held at the Queensland Institute of Technology, despite its Student Union contributing a substantial amount of money to the station's annual budget.[25]

Following the Bicentennial, the *Murri Hour* continued to grow. By October 1989, the 'hour' ran from 5:00am to 8:00pm on Mondays plus an extra five hours on Saturdays from 7:00am. "I think it's important that people realise how community organisations played a big part in Murri radio," Warinkil Aunty Glenice says. "They were always there, and they helped us ... we had lots of volunteers." Shellah was Production Manager, training all the new arrivals, while Warinkil Aunty Glenice worked as a journalist. According to Shellah:

> The Brisbane Black Community and the Original First Nations' *Murri Hour* Mob[26] always had a Cultural Awareness about their voices without losing our way

---

[25] Queensland Parliament, *Queensland Parliamentary Debates [Hansard]*, Brisbane, 30 August 1988, p. 210.

[26] 'Mob' is a colloquial term identifying a group of First Nations people associated with a particular place or country. Mob can represent family groups or a wider Aboriginal community group (see https://deadlystory.com/page/tools/aboriginal-cultural-support-planning/cultural-planning—frequently-asked-questions).

of speaking to our audience. We interviewed across the broad cultures, [but] our main reason was to reach out to our Mobs, to realise we are still here, and we are warrior survivors."

As time went on it became clear the Murri broadcasters needed more airtime. To expand, they formed the Brisbane Indigenous Media Association (BIMA). "That way, we would have a governing body ... so we could apply for funding," Shellah explains. "Uncle Rossie was still there. He was right there," she says. "Uncle Rossie was always there as a motivator, kept us on track, and he always had his finger on the tab of what was happening in the community."

Through BIMA, Uncle Ross, Warinkil Aunty Glenice, Shellah and the rest of the *Murri Hour* team successfully applied for their own community radio licence in 1991 and established 4AAA Murri Country 98.1fm, which continues broadcasting today. "If we hadn't been at 4ZZZ, if we hadn't learned all the ... goings-on, we wouldn't have been able to do that," Warinkil Aunty Glenice says. "It's important to keep reminding people how much [4ZZZ] has done for our community," adds Shellah. "It's part of my mother and Uncle Ross, myself and all the other people originally there; that's part of our legacy."

BIMA's association with 4ZZZ is best encapsulated by a faux par made by Neville Bonner AO, the first Aboriginal Australian to become a member of the Parliament of Australia. At a launch event for 4AAA, the usually unflappable public speaker outlined the station's origins as the *Murri Hour* on 4ZZZ. "We've had a tremendously wonderful relationship with the staff and management of Triple Zed," Mr. Bonner said, "and I do here now want to say a very sincere thank you to them for their help, their encouragement over the past few years". "Welcome all," the white-haired dignitary continued.

> Tune in. I beg you, tune in. As from this moment onwards, tune in to Aboriginal Radio 4-Triple-Z. Oh, I beg your pardon. See how it is? We were so accustomed to being with 4ZZZ for so long that even I can make a slip like that.

* * *

4AAA's gain turned out to be 4ZZZ's loss for quite some time, as almost all the First Nations broadcasters moved across to Murri Country Radio. It would be nearly twenty years before Triple Zed showcased a First Nations program again; *Indigi-Briz* first appeared in 4ZZZ's 2011 Program Guide, hosted by Gumbaynggirr[27] man Leon Petrou. This was followed by *SoulJah Sistars* in 2017

---

[27] Gumbaynggir/Gumbainggir lands stretch from the Clarence River down to the Nambucca River on the mid-north coast of New South Wales (Australian Indigenous HealthInfoNet; https://aiatsis.gov.au/explore/map-indigenous-australia).

and, since then, a growing number of other programs including *The Custodian* and *Raparations* on ZedDigital and *Culture Vultures* (now on 102.1fm).

Expanding First Nations engagement at 4ZZZ became a significant part of Grace Pashley's term as Station Manager (2017–2021). Grace wanted to increase participation beyond just a few dedicated programs, so First Nations broadcasters could be involved across all aspects of the station, whether that's music, journalism, training, or technical roles. "We'd say, '4ZZZ supports First Nations communities. We've always been here for First Nations voices'," Grace says. "But by the time I was there, I was asking, 'What does that actually mean in 2017?'."

Around this time *Indigi-Briz* was expanding, with a core group of First Nations broadcasters, including Gamilaroi[28]/Croatian descendant Michelle Vlatkovic (who had previously been involved with 4ZZZ in the '90s) and Tabatha Saunders, a Bidjara woman with ancestral ties to the Badtjala and the Kokumberri (Gulf) people.[29] Tabatha says that ever since she started making her own "mixed cassette tapes" in the early 80's, she has wanted to work in radio. "Nearly a whole life-time and several careers later I am finally living my 'dreaming' as a story-teller with the guidance of my powerful ancestors," she says, "and being gifted with the responsibility of sharing my love of music and story-telling with others and the power that brings to all within our community". Tabatha and Michelle established *SoulJah Sistars* in June 2017, described on its social media as "radio by Aboriginal women and accomplices, presenting voices that move them". In a creative non-fiction piece published in *Overlander*, Michelle describes their relationship.

> Tabatha, my Bidjara Sistar, has wisdom curls, though she is the younger of us two. Tab is in her mid-forties, a single mum with three kids. She sings and is studying Aboriginal health. We share similar interests: music, culture and politics. There is repetition in our family stories: love and care, state intervention, dislocation and all the things they talk about on the news, repeated over and over again in government reports and never comprehensively addressed.[30]

In addition to new programming, the First Nations broadcasting team worked with Grace Pashley on long-term structural improvements to ensure that First Nations participation was ongoing and not just tied to specific events. One of the biggest policy changes was to introduce free subscriptions for First Nations volunteers for the first 12 months of their involvement with the station, as part

---

[28] Gamilaroi/Kamilaroi lands extend from New South Wales to southern Queensland, forming one of the four largest Indigenous nations in Australia. (https://aiatsis.gov.au/explore/map-indigenous-australia).

[29] The Bidjara people are of south-western Queensland while Badtjala country covers K'gari (Fraser Island) and a small area of the nearby mainland in southern Queensland. (https://aiatsis.gov.au/explore/map-indigenous-australia).

[30] M. Vlatkovic, 'Every Saturday at one: on 4ZZZ's SoulJah Sistars'. *Overlander Literary Journal*, 30 October 2017, https://overland.org.au/2017/10/every-saturday-at-one-on-4zzzs-souljah-sistars/, (accessed 4 October 2024).

of its 'Pay the Rent' strategy which is now embedded in Station Policy. "We had to change the constitution so First Nations people could become members without payment and still get voting rights," Grace explains. The goal was to remove financial barriers that might discourage participation, making sure First Nations people still had a voice in station governance, and to recognise that 4ZZZ occupies unceded land.

4ZZZ also developed 'Pass the Mic' in conjunction with the Community Media Training Organisation; a specialised training program for First Nations broadcasters which is now into its fifth year. Delivered in partnership with 4AAA, 'Pass the Mic' not only trains First Nations people in radio broadcasting skills but ensures delivery is led by Indigenous trainers (with Tabatha Saunders and Celeste McIntosh taking on most of that work) and encourages broader participation beyond First Nations-specific programs. "It's a proud moment when you see mob overcome their fears and shame and become amazing content producers and broadcasters," Tabatha says.

> To share my knowledge and experience in radio broadcasting with mob is something I will never tire of because ... we need to lift each other up. The smiles mob bring when they overcome some very personal hurdles and realise they have the talent and the commitment to themselves and their communities, gives all of us confidence to keep going as Black media broadcasters in Meanjin.[31]

Tessa Bobir completed the 'Pass the Mic' training in 2022 and went on to present *The Custodian* as well as co-host *SoulJah Sisters*. She had never heard of 4ZZZ when she caught the end of an interview with Leon from Indigi-Briz on her car radio. "He was talking with some other Blackfullas, and they were talking about some really in-depth stuff, and I was like wow, to have this on the radio!" Tessa says. "I couldn't believe I was hearing Blackfullas yarn about spirituality the way that they just did. I felt like this is what I'd been looking for."

According to Tabatha, since 2017, First Nations people have become increasingly engaged with 4ZZZ not only as volunteers, but as guests and supporters. The station introduced First Nations Open Days as another means of engagement with the 2024 event featuring local artists Eleea, Say True God? and J4H Z3N, the current host of *Indig-Briz*. Coverage at rallies and similar events has also improved, particularly since the station purchased an outside broadcast kit that allows announcers to walk in protest marches and report live as they do so.

As mentioned previously, Invasion Day (otherwise referred to as Australia Day in mainstream colonial culture) is a contested National Holiday. Explaining the significance of this, Tabatha says:

> Not only do we have the weight of our ancestors' pain and suffering on our shoulders but as First Nations broadcasters we also have the incredibly mammoth responsibility of reporting the rally with truth and integrity.

---

[31] Meanjin is a traditional name for the place now known as Brisbane (see https://www.turrbal.com.au/our-story).

The Invasion Day rally broadcasts are fully supported by 4ZZZ, says Tabatha, "with unwavering support for all the technical and organisational aspects of the day, by many who volunteer ... knowing the grief and trauma it inflicts on First Nations people". She credits Justine Reilly (a former *Zedlines* presenter) in particular, for being "a committed non-First Nations ally since *SoulJah Sistars* began" who repeatedly offers to be in-studio for support during the entire Invasion Day broadcast. "It's a tough day," Tabatha adds, "but when that day is through, I feel blessed to belong to such a welcoming and safe family".

* * *

This may draw a long bow to connect the following section, but it's a lesser-known fact that in 2001, 4AAA and 4ZZZ were rivals on the cricket pitch. As part of the Brisbane Band Cricket Association, 4AAA's team 'The Warriors' took out the Grand Final that year. I never imagined that sport would be a topic I associated with community radio *or* community engagement, but neither would I imagine I'd learn to play Australian Rules football at the age of 54, all in the name of supporting my favourite radio station and promoting social inclusion through sport.

The Reclink Community Cup is an annual charity Australian Rules football (AFL) match that brings together musicians and media professionals to raise funds for Reclink Australia, an organisation that provides sport and recreation programs for disadvantaged communities. It began in Melbourne in 1993 as a social footy match and fundraiser for the Sacred Heart Mission. Over the years the event expanded beyond Melbourne, eventually reaching Brisbane in 2016. Founder Jason 'Evo' Evans played a key role in bringing the event to 4ZZZ's (and his own) hometown. He pulled together an organising committee by reaching out to local community groups and media. This is where 4ZZZ comes in, when Michelle Brown was Station Manager. "We were very keen on getting the different community radio stations together [for the media team] ... but were never able to get other players besides Zedders and a few from the ABC," she says. To represent the musicians and set up some friendly competition, Evo approached Zedder Michelle Padovan, who was now working at Q-Music, Queensland's music industry development body:

> [Evo] told me later that it was his ploy ... because I used to work with Michelle [Brown] at Triple Zed - if he got in both of our ears and inspired us that we'd be like, 'yes, let's do it'.

It worked, and despite representing rival teams, Michelle Padovan and Michelle Brown both received the Foster McLennan Award at the first Brisbane Cup for their contributions for getting the new chapter up and running.

Evo named the musicians' side 'The Rocking Horses' after Brisbane's long-running independent import record store and the media side 'The Brisbane Lines', a clever nod to 4ZZZ's flagship news and current affairs show and

Queensland's WWII history (Chap. 13) while riffing off the official Queensland AFL team's name, 'Brisbane Lions'. Former Station Manager, Stephen Stockwell (Jnr) reflects fondly on his experience with the Reclink Community Cup in Brisbane, participating as both an organiser and player for 'The Brisbane Lines'. Stephen says the Cup helped reconnect Triple Zed "back into parts of the music industry we had drifted away from". He describes training sessions and the game as times when musicians and media folks can come together without transactional expectations, just to have fun. "They just want to have a good time running around," Stephen says.

Evo sees the Community Cup as more than a match—it's a way to bring together artists and broadcasters, a good proportion of whom may have never played team sports. "I like calling [it] giving sport a good name," he says; a claim I can attest to. Before joining 'The Brisbane Lines' in 2023, I had never played a game of AFL. Anthony 'The Accountant' Rutherford from 4ZZZ's sports show, *Ballzzz in the Air*, convinced me it didn't matter and I'm glad I listened. The main attraction for me is embedded in the 'Spirit of the Community Cup' which decrees that everyone should play "with inclusivity, fun and safety in mind".[32] "We inherited a ready-made model that promoted all of these aspects," says Michelle Padovan. The Cup is an all-gender game that adjusts regular AFL rules to ensure cis men[33] are positioned so that they can't dominate. Players are encouraged to be "conscious of their ability, size, [and] experience" and to use their skills to involve less-confident players in the game. Plus, there are no tackles! "Remember," the rule book states, "you're there for the entertainment factor—to have fun and run amok; not to pretend you're a real footy player or be focussed on winning".[34]

Game day is a buzz—when you're playing you hardly notice the thousand-odd people, repping their team colours with every scarf and shirt sold raising funds for Reclink's programs. A flat-bed truck acts as a stage with the muso's providing half-time entertainment and media supplying commentators— Danika E from *Kids with Class Kicking Arse* and her co-host Chris Converse (also of *Ballzzz in the Air*). Danika started at 4ZZZ when she was a 16-year-old high school work experience student. I co-opted her into the Youth Show, allegedly saying something along the lines of "You! You're a youth. Wanna do a radio show?". We've been friends ever since and I didn't miss the shock in her voice when I took a mark during my first Reclink game. "Doctor Ando has actually caught the ball!" could be very clearly heard on the field.

Players represent a range of genders, ages and abilities, including one with Early-onset Parkinson's. 4ZZZ Volunteer coordinator, Salty Otton reminds everyone at the start of each training session that she can't risk a knock to the

---

[32] Reclink Community Cup, 'Game Rules' https://communitycup.com.au/gamerules, (accessed April 4, 2025).

[33] Men identified as such since birth.

[34] Reclink Community Cup, 'Game Rules', https://communitycup.com.au/gamerules, (accessed April 4, 2025).

head and then gets stuck into the game. In terms of inclusion, the Community Cup is kicking plenty of goals—almost as many as the current (three-times in a row) champions, the mighty Brisbane Lines.

* * *

In the same ways that Reclink leverages sport to promote social inclusion and accessible sports, 4ZZZ has spent the past ten years improving its capacity to cater for people living with disabilities. 4ZZZ's first disability rights program, *Only Human* began in 2015. It was established as part of the 'Ability Radio Project' airing on Zed Digital. *Only Human* became a live show on 4ZZZ's FM station in 2016 and is now on both platforms. It is broadcast by a diverse team of producers with varied abilities, including people living with blindness and autism, and "provides opportunities for experience in a live studio environment without the commitment or skills needed to run a weekly show".[35]

Only Human was created by 4ZZZ producer Kim Stewart, who is also a social worker and trainer with the Community Media Training Organisation. Kim was an early station advocate for people with a disability at 4ZZZ and has been instrumental in fostering media participation through outreach, training, and inclusive radio programming. Guests on *Only Human* have explored radical critiques of institutional harm, from First Nations suicide prevention models to exclusionary policies of the National Disability Investment Scheme (NDIS). According to host Belle Behan, "for people with trauma such as ours, storytelling, like radio interviews or facilitated discussions, can help people access healing, justice and community".[36] Belle says that working on *Only Human* has allowed her "to connect deeply with the disabled community and to tell [their] own stories in their fullest; joys, struggles and [everything] in between".

Meanwhile, 4ZZZ's *Strategic Plan 2021–2024* identified accessibility as a key focus area and the station has since developed a strategy and action plan, collectively called 'Accessible Zed', to improve inclusion for people with disabilities over the long term. While 4ZZZ has made strides in amplifying the voices of women, LGBTQI+ communities and First Nations Australians, Accessibility Coordinator Owen Sadler says connecting with people with disabilities has posed more of a challenge. Supported by Volunteering Queensland grants, 'Accessible Zed' funded a Disability Coordinator (Salty Otton), an accessible announcer training course (led by Ben Snaith), and policy development by Owen. An Accessibility Reference Group, including people with lived experience, was also established. The results have been promising. According to Owen,

---

[35] K. Stewart, C. Spurgeon, and N. Edwards, 'Media participation by people with disability and the relevance of Australian community broadcasting in the digital era', *3CMedia*, vol 9, 2019, p. 55.

[36] K. Stewart, & A. Behan, 'Critical disability theory: A framework for inclusive community radio in Australia'. In K. Saxton (ed.). *Social Work for the Real World* [Manuscript in preparation] Routledge. 2025.

over 60 people living with disabilities were introduced to 4ZZZ through 'Accessible Zed', and many have gone on to contribute to station programming.

Zed Towers remains a major obstacle as it spans three levels with no accessible internal connections. Some initial improvements have been made, including the installation of an automatic sliding door at reception and a rudimentary portable ramp for the studio floor entrance, however, retrofitting for full accessibility is costly. For many who can't physically access the studios, remote broadcasting is another option. As Owen Sadler says, "people do not need to physically be at Barry Parade to be part of the 4ZZZ community". The need for remote accessibility became more than a disability issue during the COVID-19 lockdowns of 2020 and 2021, when the majority of 4ZZZ announcers needed to work from home. Leveraging off the innovations developed by Triple Zed's tech team to enable remote broadcasting during COVID, *IncubatorZZZ* was developed as a spin-off of *Only Human*; a ZedDigital program that allows contributors to work remotely on pre-recorded segments. *IncubatorZZZ* was specifically designed to accommodate people who are immunocompromised, mobility-impaired, or neurodivergent, and enables contributors to engage with the station who can't access Zed Towers or otherwise need flexible participation (such as those with fluctuating health).

As Kim Stewart and Bella Behan point out, while "community media can be strongly differentiated from commercial media as being more open to difference, it is still not immune from societal ableist norms and attitudes".[37] 4ZZZ is far from perfect but its accessibility initiatives are a step in the right direction. Listening to people with lived experience, finding funding for initiatives, and shifting cultural expectations are key to making 4ZZZ more accessible, and more just, for everyone.

---

[37] K. Stewart, & A. Behan, 'Critical disability theory: A framework for inclusive community radio in Australia'. In K. Saxton (ed.). *Social Work for the Real World* [Manuscript in preparation] Routledge. 2025.

CHAPTER 13

Where Your News Isn't Limited

The streets of Brisbane pulsed with protest. It was 1982 and the Commonwealth Games were underway, an international celebration of athleticism shadowed by the grim reality of First Nations injustice in Queensland. Musgrave Park had become a temporary village of resistance.

Amanda Collinge, then a young journalist with pink hair and a Superscope recorder slung over her shoulder, had travelled up from Sydney, sent by the Public Broadcasting Association of Australia (PBAA) to document the unfolding resistance. 4ZZZ's Louise Butt and Kerry O'Rourke were already in the thick of it, broadcasting updates and forging ties with community leaders.

Despite Premier Joh Bjelke-Petersen's declaration of a State of Emergency, which effectively made public assembly illegal, protesters gathered undeterred. The crowd that surged down the street that day wasn't supposed to exist. No permit had been granted, but as Uncle Ross Watson said before the march began, "We don't need a permit to exist on our own land".

Amanda had her press pass ready. She waved it at the line of officers in blue. It didn't matter. Media or not, she and Louise were shoved into the back of a paddy wagon with a group of protestors, their equipment confiscated.

That afternoon, in the close concrete of the Brisbane Watchhouse, Amanda met Aunty Maureen Watson, a well-respected Murri woman recognised as a "tireless educator and campaigner for the rights of her people, gifted and passionate performer … poet, author and playwright".[1] Despite the clang of metal doors and the fear amongst the other women in the cell, Aunty Maureen was unshakable. She told stories rich and lyrical. She spoke of Country, of justice, of survival. Her calm presence turned the cold, crowded cell into

---

[1] Murri School, 'Maureen Watson:1931–2009', *Murri School*, Brisbane, https://kooriweb.org/foley/heroes/biogs/maureen_watson.html, (accessed 9 February 2025).

a classroom. Young women, journalists, protestors; they all listened. Amanda, despite everything, felt lucky to be there.

They were bailed the next morning and the charges—flimsy and rushed under hastily passed laws—were dropped. Amanda moved to Brisbane to work fulltime in the 4ZZZ newsroom soon after.

Recently at a public lecture, Aunty Maureen's granddaughter, Mundanara Bayles, mentioned her family's perspective of this event. Her father Tiga Bayles was General Manager of 4AAA for a long time, and before that involved in Radio Redfern. She says "it was 4ZZZ that raised the money [for bail] through the white community in Brisbane".[2] The station put an announcement over the air explaining that police had tripled the bail costs for Aboriginal people to deter them from returning to the protests. According to Mundanara, her family still "talks about that":

> To just remind people that there's a lot of positive things that have happened in this community here in Brisbane, between black and white, that you won't find written anywhere. And to remember those positive stories and to keep sharing those, because I think that's what my Gran would want me to do here tonight.[3]

* * *

News, current affairs and other information-based programs have always had an important place at 4ZZZ. At different times over the past fifty years, the Triple Zed newsroom has been heralded for breaking news, winning awards, training journalists, and providing a platform for lesser heard voices. 4ZZZ's news and current affairs program *The Brisbane Line* has been running since 1976, with many other shows across the years providing a unique perspective on a range of social issues. Bridging them all is a commitment to representing the communities at the heart of these stories. This chapter covers just a handful.

In the first edition of *Radio Times*, 4ZZZ posed the following to its audience:

> Have you noticed how identical and predictable the commercial news services are? Are you disappointed at the way existing news services shirk their responsibilities to the listening public? If so, then the 4ZZ alternative news and information service will offer you, for the first time in Brisbane, news bulletins/information slots/documentaries that delve below the surface, seek out undisclosed facts and supply background information to put the news into a coherent perspective.[4]

For its first ten years or so, 4ZZZ had a fully functional newsroom with two or three paid journalists covering all aspects of news and current affairs including

---

[2] M. Bayles speaking at Streets of Your Town: Mapping Brisbane's street press, public lecture, State Library of Queensland, 28 February 2025.

[3] M. Bayles, *Streets of Your Town: Mapping Brisbane's street press, public lecture*.

[4] 4ZZZ, "News and Information", *Radio Times*, Dec/Jan 1975/6, p. 5.

headlines, updates and more substantial reportage. "We assumed our audience was clearly on the left of politics and younger than average," says Linden Woodward, a 4ZZZ journalist during the late '70s and early '80s. "We looked at drug laws, housing rights, and legal information for renters or people accused of shoplifting,"[5] she says, to give a few examples of the stories that 4ZZZ was covering at the time.

According to founding member Alan Knight, "the mainstream press in Queensland was doing a pretty poor job of reporting what was in the community ... Triple Zed was the only voice of dissent". The 4ZZZ newsroom took pride in this position in the Brisbane mediascape, emerging not just as a radio station but as a bastion of activist journalism and independent media in an oppressive political climate. The first 4ZZZ journalists were conscious of trying to develop a different kind of reporting, "not just taking press releases and repeating them," as founding member Marian Wilkinson makes clear. "We had this idea that we should be going out and talking to people who weren't being heard," she says. "That included Indigenous people ... women, it included people who were on the margins of society. [We] wanted to tell those stories in a way that made people care." In her memoir, *Free Radical*, 4ZZZ's original breakfast announcer Gay Walsh writes about broadcasting first-hand accounts from the invasion of East Timor.

> Indonesian troops invaded East Timor (now Timor-Leste) on 7 December 1975. 4ZZ/Z had started the very next day. I was handed a tape recording that had been obtained via a pirate radio station in Darwin and was asked to play it. I was chilled to the bone and will never ever forget this vivid audio confirmation of the atrocities that occurred on that day.[6]

At the same time, political reportage was also integral to the newsroom. Linden Woodward recalls the station covering "the State Government in a way that no one else did".[7] Its journalists regularly questioned ministers, including Bjelke-Petersen, despite his evasive style. In recent years 4ZZZ returned to political reporting, courtesy of *The Pineapple Rebellion*, airing from 2019 to 2025. Created and hosted by journalist Alexis Pink, the show blended in-depth political analysis with satire and humour. The name—suggested by Zedder and former Senator Andrew Bartlett—was inspired by an obscure 1939 uprising in Queensland. Dubbed the "Pineapple Rebellion," it involved disaffected rural social credit supporters to siege Parliament House. Alexis embraced the name for its blend of political symbolism and Queensland eccentricity. The show focused primarily on Queensland state politics but regularly tackled local

---

[5] S. Mercer, 'Unpublished transcript of interview with Linden Woodward', *A to Triple Zed podcast series*, 4ZZZ, 2020.

[6] G. Walsh, *Free Radical: A memoir*, Austin Macauley Publishers, London, 2021, p. 165.

[7] S. Mercer, 'Unpublished transcript of interview with Linden Woodward', *A to Triple Zed podcast series*, 4ZZZ, 2020.

issues (such as Brisbane City Council appointments) and national or international stories with local implications.

In the News Coordinator role, Alexis also spearheaded election coverage at the station, starting with the 2019 Federal election. Her team created the *4ZZZ Breaks the Election* daily podcast which helped journalism students and volunteers stay informed throughout the campaign, ensuring that on election night they were "able to join in and be involved in the conversation". The coverage mixed analysis of voting trends and legislation with satirical radio plays. As Alexis puts it, "we can play music, we can make fun of people … [and] make election night less boring. Less election-y".

Alexis Pink's experience as the first openly transgender political journalist in Queensland's parliamentary press gallery can't be ignored. She says she often encountered a mixture of curiosity, discomfort, and quiet resistance, though rarely outright hostility. On her first day, despite holding a valid press pass and having the Press Gallery President's number on hand, she was turned away by security who "didn't know what 4ZZZ was," reflecting both institutional unfamiliarity with community media and a subtle scepticism of her presence.

* * *

The 4ZZZ newsroom came to prominence in August 1976, when Zed journalist Steve Gray broke the story of a violent police raid on a remote commune at Cedar Bay in Far North Queensland. While visiting Cairns shortly after the raid, Steve heard rumours of the incident and tracked down a member of the Cedar Bay community who had fled the scene. The man gave a phone interview recounting how a large force of Queensland police assisted by narcotics and customs agents, stormed the beachside settlement, allegedly in search of marijuana.[8] Steve's timely reporting exposed a police operation that might otherwise have remained hidden. His interview sparked public scrutiny of the State Government's law enforcement tactics and prompted wider media attention, including the ABC sending journalist Andrew Olle to investigate. Without 4ZZZ's intervention, the Cedar Bay raid could easily have been buried by distance and silence.

The details revealed were shocking. Homes were torched, food and belongings destroyed, fruit trees slashed, and residents detained without proper charges. Among those caught up in the chaos was Candy Kelly, a 16-year-old who recalls being handcuffed naked to a coconut tree while police laughed nearby. "It was horrifically traumatic," she says. "There were helicopters, a naval launch, police coming through the bush … it was all pretty crazy." Candy was eventually allowed to grab some clothes from her burning hut, witnessing firsthand the destruction. "From having this peaceful existence where you're just living totally in Nirvana … to suddenly being overpowered by the police, it was just a blur after that," she says.

---

[8] B. Wilkie. (2019). Paradise lost: The Cedar Bay raid. *Griffith REVIEW, 65*, 35–42.

4ZZZ's support did not stop at reporting. Candy recalls Triple Zed organising a benefit concert at Albert Park to raise funds for the displaced Cedar Bay residents. "People wanted to meet us, to help," she says. The funds helped cover immediate needs and contributed to the legal fight that followed. 4ZZZ subsequently covered the committal and trial of four police officers charged over the raid, with Steve Gray back in Far North Queensland and operating on a tight budget. "There always seemed to be free public telephones at Cairns Post Office from where I filed my reports," Steve says. "Apparently if you super-glued a coin and dropped it into the slot of the phone it would render it free until it was discovered and removed." A Cairns jury trial eventually dismissed charges against all four policemen.

Nearly fifty years later, Candy has reconnected with 4ZZZ. "It can almost make me cry to see what a beautiful community it is and how it's strengthened over the years," she says. Now a subscriber, Candy says it has been great to rediscover Triple Zed after all those years. "I follow the Rhinestone Cowgirl … and I love the trans show, *Know Idea*, *From the Roots*, *The Jazz Show*; such quality and diverse content," Candy says. "It's such a colourful, vibrant community."

* * *

4ZZZ has always walked a fine line between news production and activism. Early volunteer Margot Foster says she marched for Indigenous land rights, abortion access, and against apartheid, all while documenting these movements for Triple Zed's listeners. "We covered most demonstrations," adds journalist Dan Flannery. For example, the first time a nuclear-powered ship came into Pinkenba Wharf (Brisbane), 4ZZZ were down at the docks. Dan was involved in a motorbike accident on his way back from the protest and ended up in hospital. "But the story got through!" he adds.

On occasion, 4ZZZ journalists approached their craft with the full knowledge they would be arrested, most notably in 1982 during the Brisbane Commonwealth Games. At this time, Queensland still maintained repressive policies through outdated 'Protection Acts', denied Indigenous land claims, and refused to recognise bodies such as the National Aboriginal Conference.[9] First Nations people and their allies saw the international spotlight of the Games as a chance to expose these injustices, despite the government banning street marches. Their actions were part of a broader national push for treaty, sovereignty, and justice for First Nations Australians.[10]

Once the Commonwealth Games arrived, Triple Zed covered the protests extensively and provided practical support. The station held Radiothons to

---

[9] Anti-Discrimination Commission Queensland. 'Aboriginal people in Queensland: a brief human rights history. *Anti-Discrimination Commission Queensland*, https://www.qhrc.qld.gov.au/__data/assets/pdf_file/0013/10606/Aboriginal-timeline-FINAL-updated-25-July-2018.pdf, 2017.

[10] *The whole world is watching* [film], A. King (director), Frontyard Films, 1982.

raise money for bail funds and to support the protesters camped at Musgrave Park. Louise Butt was one of the 4ZZZ reporters who covered the campaign. "Triple Zed was there the whole time through the protests and at Musgrave Park interviewing people," she says. This was also some of Jon Baird's first experiences with journalism, having been invited to volunteer at the station around this time (Fig. 13.1).

According to Dan Flannery a roster was established for Triple Zed journalists that denoted "who would be arrested and what needed covering". Reporting at one of the protests (mentioned in the opening of the chapter), Louise Butt made "a last-minute decision" to give her tape recorder to another journalist, "and then got arrested as well". "I was taken to the Watchhouse with all the other women … at least there would be somebody there who could be a voice … and a witness," she says. When they were bailed "Triple Zed was outside the Watchhouse waiting for reports".

Dan Flannery covered the 1982/3 Franklin River protests in Tasmania, one of Australia's most significant environmental battles. The protests opposed the Tasmanian government's bid to dam the river, a move that activists argued would destroy a pristine wilderness area. "I was down there probably three weeks," Dan says. "I sent back a few reports and … was there when bulldozers came in". He was ultimately arrested and jailed in Queenstown, though the Australian Journalists' Association helped secure his release. Dan believes his

Fig. 13.1 Poster for 4ZZZ Solidarity Drive to support First Nations protests during 1988 Bicenterary, designed by Sally Hart; 1988

reporting captured the spirit and urgency of the protests. "I thought it was Walkley Award material," he says, joking that another nominee won the prestigious award because "some guy down in Adelaide burned his own house down on live TV".

At other times, 4ZZZ journalists were arrested when it wasn't their intention. During the height of the 1985 South-East Queensland Electricity Board [SEQEB] dispute, 4ZZZ journalist Harley Stumm covered the prolonged and heated conflict between the Queensland government and striking electricity workers. The strike, which began over the contracting out of services by SEQEB, sparked mass picketing. Harley was arrested while covering a picket outside the SEQEB depot in Fortitude Valley. "I was just thrown in the back of the paddy wagon," Harley recalls, noting he was detained alongside union leaders and activists. "I'm pretty sure [I felt] a mixture of being really pissed off and angry ... antagonised and kind of proud that I ... put my neck on the line." Harley was arrested under the *Electricity (Continuity of Supply) Act 1985 (Qld)*, with the police accusing him of refusing directions and photographing plainclothes officers. Despite the risks, Harley saw his journalism as part of a broader movement that defined 4ZZZ. "We had these kinds of fantasies that our activism was going to have a big impact and sometimes it did," he reflects. At just 20 years old, Harley was not only reporting but helping to organise initiatives like a 4ZZZ Radiothon to support the strikers.

Journalist Brendan Greenhill was arrested twice while reporting on free speech protests for 4ZZZ. His first occurred in the mid-1980s during the Queen Street Mall protests, which were part of a broader campaign challenging Queensland's restrictive public assembly laws. Brendan was arrested while trying to document the demonstration. Fortunately, he says he had "both a tape recording and good witnesses, and that was enough to beat the charge in court". Brendan's second arrest came in 1993 during another free speech rally in the same location. In that instance, a police officer admitted under cross-examination that Brendan was distracting him and had been arrested for being "annoying". I was in the court that day, reporting on the case for Triple Zed. When his solicitor asked the officer if he'd "also attempt to arrest a fly if it created an annoyance, buzzing around his face," I burst out laughing and had to quickly leave the proceedings to compose myself. Reflecting on that second arrest, Brendan says it "wasn't far from the Joh era ... it was the old school way of doing things—pressure from above to make examples of people".

The tradition of activism journalism continues. In the late '80s the 4ZZZ news team made use of emerging technologies to broadcast live from a protest using a mobile phone, considered an uncommon and controversial device at the time, associated by many at 4ZZZ with corporate culture and yuppie excess. Protesters had occupied a Commonwealth Bank of Australia building to hamper plans to demolish the historic sandstone structure in Brisbane's CBD, which was part of a broader wave of heritage destruction and urban redevelopment that activists opposed. Stefan Armbruster was part of the occupation and covered the event for Triple Zed. "We were so excited, modern technology here we come," Stefan says. With streamers hanging from windows and activists celebrating inside, using a mobile phone the broadcast brought listeners directly into the heart of the protest, which was organised by SQUID (Squatters United in Desire). "It was just a magic moment, Triple Zed being on air [from the bank], you had that feeling that other people were listening," Stefan remembers.

In 2014, 4ZZZ covered the G20 summit in Brisbane—a high-security intergovernmental event that drew widespread protests, particularly over First Nations rights. The *Indigi-Briz*[11] Collective wanted to broadcast live from the protests at Musgrave Park, so 4ZZZ technician Ben Ryan helped orchestrate an outside broadcast. Ben and his team transformed a non-descript car into a covert mobile radio station. "We loaded up a very … generic Mitsubishi Verada," Ben recalls, setting up equipment in the boot so the whole operation could "disappear in a moment's notice if required". With security forces monitoring protest activity closely, this makeshift setup allowed them to avoid detection while the *Indigi-Briz* team reported the protests live from location. Ben describes the venture as "a really, really awesome moment … to make those links, make those connections, make the 'almost too-hards' easy".

Ben Ryan and the *Indi-Briz* crew weren't overreacting in their efforts to keep their mobile broadcasting set-up concealed from authorities. As has been covered throughout this book, the relationship between 4ZZZ and the Queensland Police Service has often been tense. Early '80s Station Coordinator, Danielle Bond says government authorities, especially the Special Branch, closely monitored 4ZZZ's reporting during her time at the station. This was also the experience of journalist Amanda Collinge. "The house I lived in was raided twice. My car was stopped twice when I was driving late at night," she says.

> A Special Branch guy in plain clothes came up to me and said, 'How's life going at [my address at the time] … and how do you manage to survive on that $104 a week?' … Yeah, it was harassment.

4ZZZ were also investigated in relation to the Boggo Road riots of 1983, after the station broadcast clandestine recordings from people incarcerated in the gaol (see Chap. 14). Jon Baird's coverage of the protests won a PBAA Golden Reel award in 1984 for best current affairs program,[12] but it also attracted the attention of the authorities. According to Danielle Bond, because Triple Zed provided a platform for activists, it was frequently accused of being "too political" and of inciting protests rather than just covering them. "There's always that fine line between being journalists and activists," she says, "but any suggestion that we incited anything was complete B–S". Even after the Bjelke-Petersen era, trouble persisted. Kim Stewart says she was targeted by police in the mid 2000s, when covering anti-nuclear protests and activism targeting companies like Barrick

---

[11] A First Nations program on 4ZZZ—see Chap. 12.
[12] 4ZZZ, 'Triple Zed Newz', *Semper Floreate*, no 8, September 10, 1984. p. 4.

Gold. Kim says she was interviewed by Special Branch, who confronted her with personal details in an apparent attempt to intimidate her.

* * *

The Brisbane Line—launched in the station's earliest days—is 4ZZZ's flagship news and current affairs programs. It was first mentioned in *Radio Times* in April 1976:

> For three hours every Sunday afternoon, a jolly and dedicated team is providing comprehensive coverage of the major local and national stories of the week, areas frequently ignored by the rest of the media and the performance of the media in general also comes under our scrutiny.[13]

Over the years it has evolved in format but remains central to 4ZZZ's programming (now simply *Brisbane Line*). It broadcasts for one hour, three times weekly on 102.1fm, with *Brisbane Line Extra* on Zed Digital once a week. Other iterations have included *Beyond Brisbane* (international news), *London Line*, and *Behind the Bamboo Curtain* (news from China). The latter two programs were reports phoned in by Jon Baird, who was living outside of Australia at the time.

The name 'The Brisbane Line' carries layered historic and political meaning. Rooted in World War II, the Brisbane Line was an alleged government plan to abandon northern Australia in the event of a Japanese invasion and concentrate defence south of a notional line near Brisbane.[14] Though a controversial strategy, the term became symbolic of political decisions about who and what gets sacrificed in a crisis. In the 1960s, Brisbane's student radicals repurposed the term as the title of an underground newspaper which they launched in 1968 to challenge the city's media monopoly and conservative government.[15] By naming its news program *The Brisbane Line*, 4ZZZ paid tribute to that earlier dissident publication and signalled a continuity of the newsroom's rebel spirit.

It hasn't always been easy for the Triple Zed newsroom, which since the late 1980s has operated almost exclusively on volunteer labour. Claire Grenet was one of the last of the paid journalists. "We all just shared the workload … morning news bulletins, evening news bulletin, *Brisbane Line* … we used to take it in turns to do breakfast." During the Toowong days and early into 4ZZZ's time at Zed Towers, the newsroom had little infrastructure. When Jim Beatson and Jon Baird both returned to the station in the early 1990s, they worked on rebuilding it. "We brought in journalism students and professionals to run workshops," Jim says. "It was all about making Triple Zed a place where

---

[13] J. Woods, "*The Brisbane Line*", *Radio Times,* April 1976, p. 1.

[14] J. Dedman, The 'Brisbane' line. *Australian Outlook*, vol *22* no 2, 1968, pp. 141–161.

[15] A. Knight, 'Radical media in the deep north: The origins of 4ZZZ-FM'. *Queensland Review*, vol *14* no 1, 2007, pp. 95–105.

real news could happen". Jim also established a relationship with the University of Queensland's journalism department to contribute student-led news bulletins. "These were variable in quality, but consistently competent," comments Jim. "However, their political line was sometimes less than good."

4ZZZ now runs its own news headlines—called *Zedlines*—on the hour during the week, from 8:00 to 11:00am. Each bulletin begins with an introduction (known as a sting) that incorporates music from The Saints' song, *Know Your Product*, and the tagline "*Zedlines*—where your news isn't limited", a not-so-subtle dig at Australia's media landscape that is dominated by the Murdoch-owned company News Limited. Student interns quite often cut their teeth producing the headlines and, according to *Zedlines* Coordinator Mack, many stay on after their formal internship, having found "their community". Current station manager, Jack McDonnell is a case in point. In 2016, he applied for an internship as a 21-year-old journalism student. "I've always been interested in music, and I knew of 4ZZZ," he says, "so it kind of made sense ... that's when it all changed for me, really".

> I show up at 7:00am on a Friday morning [to do *Zedlines*] and who opens the door? Robert Anderson from [radio show] *This!* He goes, 'Hey man, here for *Zedlines*?' and then he plays punk music and he rides off on his motorcycle - this is the coolest person who's ever existed. Of course I'm going to hang out here. This is just the best.

Zedlines were launched in 2006, at a gig at The Rev, which included guest speakers from the 4ZZZ newsroom and bands Kafka, Doch, and The John Citizens. This coincided with 4ZZZ's *Convergent Community Newsroom* (CCN), developed as a response to the rapidly evolving digital media landscape. Designed by Giordana Caputo and Lucas Moore, the project aimed to expand the station's news output beyond traditional broadcasting into multi-platform content creation. Participants were trained in video production, blogging, online writing, and multimedia storytelling, reflecting a forward-thinking approach to citizen journalism. "We [thought] this is what we should be doing, that Zed should be doing this," Giordana explains. "It's not just about the broadcast. We should be getting on all the other channels." The program integrated experienced newsroom volunteers as mentors alongside new recruits, creating a buddy system that emphasised skills development across platforms. Although it ran for only 18 months, the CCN project helped embed digital literacy and multi-platform journalism into the station's culture, at a time when most community broadcasters were still focused solely on radio. Its influence can be seen in the way that Zedlines are now repackaged as multimedia stories on the 4ZZZ news webpage.[16]

Since 2009, 4ZZZ has also included a regular sports show in its schedule, called *Ballzzz in the Air* which broadcasts on Saturdays at 9:00am. This was

---

[16] https://4zzz.org.au/news.

preceded by *SportsLine*, which aired circa 2006. '*Ballzzz*' is a one-hour show that was established by volunteers Jay Beatson and Chris Converse and is now presented by Chris and Anthony 'the Accountant' Rutherford. It takes the approach "that all sport is worthy of a spotlight, and that there are many ways to be involved," according to Anthony. "We want to celebrate all of them," he says. Cricket and football are constant staples of discussion, with 'football' in this context spanning the round-ball game (soccer) as well as the various oval-ball codes, especially rugby league and Australian Rules football.

Women's sport is given as much attention as men's, and results from local fixtures form the backbone of most episodes. *Ballzzz in the Air* doesn't shy away from lesser-known or less-covered sports such as water polo and curling, and organisations like Sporting Wheelies make a regular appearance. "It really is great meeting all kinds of people from all kinds of sport," Chris says. Niche segments such as speedway racing and unique sports stories like the annual Hobby Horse Queensland Championships also pop up, reflecting *Ballzzz in the Air*'s eclectic and inclusive take on the 'world of sports'. "Many measure sport by wins and championships," Anthony says. "We look at passion and enthusiasm."

Regarding national news, 4ZZZ contributes to *The Wire*, a weekday current affairs program, broadcast nationally on the Community Radio Network and CAAMA (Central Australian Aboriginal Media Association) Radio. A consortium of stations, including 4ZZZ and 4EB in Brisbane, 2SER in Sydney, Radio Adelaide and 3ZZZ in Melbourne, collaborate to produce the show. Between 2007 and 2009 I worked as the Brisbane Executive Producer for *The Wire*, supported by some of the brightest emerging journalists I've had the pleasure to work with—Emma Carroll, Gemma Snowdon and Stephen Stockwell (Jnr).

Prior to this, I also collaborated with my good friend Lucas Moore on the youth news and current affairs program *13-23*. The show was funded by the Community Broadcasting Foundation, broadcast on the Community Radio Network, and covered news of relevance to a younger national audience. Lucas was 18 years old when we established the program. "We were delving into some really serious issues about youth incarceration, about racism towards young people, about media stereotypes," he remembers. "[We didn't think] we had to be this kind of journalist or that kind of journalist," Lucas says. "We just asked the questions that we wanted to know the answers to and we weren't afraid to ask people in positions of power to explain the decisions they'd made." In 1999, *13-23* was a finalist in the National Youth Media Awards. We travelled to Sydney for a very posh gala dinner and proceeded to get belligerently drunk after losing to Triple J. I do believe Lucas' first words the next morning went along the lines of, "I think I may have ruined any chance I ever had of getting a job with the ABC!".

* * *

4ZZZ has also had success using journalism as a tool for community and cultural development. One standout initiative from the mid-2000s was the *Milpera Airspace Radio Project*, which brought refugee students from Milpera State High School into contact with the station. Lucas Moore and Giordana Caputo delivered media training at the school and later invited the students into the studio. "We did that project because we … heard a lot of talk about marginalised opinions and voices in [4ZZZ's] mission statement," Lucas says. "One of the most marginalised groups in Australian society was refugees … so we wanted to flip the table … and have young refugees take over the microphone." Giordana adds that, "more than anything, it was just making them feel like there were people out there who cared about them". The Milpera students created personal and powerful radio pieces, including a rap in both English and a Sudanese language, and an account of a young girl's journey from Myanmar to a Thai refugee camp. According to Lucas, "they were making a radio program in a different language in a new country, and they just smashed it".

Indeed, there have been plenty of information-based shows that provide platforms for community engagement through their delivery of news and current affairs content, some of which are discussed in Chap. 12. Linda Rose and Kim Stewart (also from *Only Human*) made a huge contribution in this area, spanning multiple shows, particularly *Eco Radio*, *The Anarchy Show*, and *Radio Democracy*—collectively referred to as Radical Radio with each program having its own focus: environmental activism, anarchism, and social justice respectively. *Eco Radio* continues to broadcast, and the program hosts now organise regular bush regeneration working bees that listeners are encouraged to join.

Kim Stewart frequently reported from protest sites that were underrepresented or ignored by mainstream media. One of her most vivid memories involves a months-long anti-nuclear protest camp. "We were going there almost every day and did a lot of live crosses … People came by who were part of the anti-nuclear movement to talk about it," she says. Likewise, Linda Rose participated in protest coverage and field reporting, most notably from the blockade at Narangba against a food irradiation facility. She also covered national actions like the S11 protests (against meetings of the World Economic Forum) in Melbourne in 2000 and travelled to Pine Gap in 2002 for anti-war protests. "We marched down to the gates … and blockaded the road … and had a dance party all night," Linda recalls. This activism journalism mirrored the work of earlier 4ZZZ newshounds who reported from the Franklin Dam blockades and Commonwealth Games protests in the 1980s.

Linda and Kim's contributions are also part of a much longer tradition of environmental broadcasting at the station. In April 1976, *The Environment Show* was introduced as a weekly segment on Helen Hambling's drivetime program.[17] The *Peace and Environment Show* then emerged as its own show, circa 1989, with announcer Damien Le Goulon who interviewed figures like Bruno Manser, the

---

[17] 4ZZZ, "*The Environment Show*", *Radio Times*, April 1976, p. 6.

Swiss activist campaigning for the preservation of Sarawak's rainforests in Malaysia. The program also produced early coverage of the greenhouse effect, "before it was politicised,"[18] discussing climate science well before it became mainstream. The *Peace and Environment Show* remained a hub for grassroots environmentalism throughout the 1990s. Barry Brown and Angel Kosch carried the torch, covering urban bushland actions like the Highgate Hill gully protests and interviewing scientists and community groups. "It was easy to get guests because I was directly involved in the activism,"[19] Angel says, illustrating how tightly woven the station's journalism was with on-the-ground resistance. Given that mainstream outlets often vilify protesters, independent media coverage is important. As Linda Rose explains, "when you go out and report on protests, you can't be neutral. You have to be on the side of the people fighting for justice".

Today, the legacy of radical programming continues with long-running programs such as *The Paradigm Shift* and *Radio Reversal*. The latter started in 2012 and offers radical political analysis grounded in anti-colonial and abolitionist frameworks. *Radio Reversal* is created by a collective of "mostly settler and migrant voices," according to one producer, and focuses on amplifying local resistance movements and the lived experiences of those most affected by systems of oppression, particularly carceral and colonial violence. The show blends theory with grassroots activism, using field recordings from protests, interviews, and deep conceptual explorations to challenge dominant narratives around policing, incarceration, and state power. *The Paradigm Shift* started in 2009 and is now presented by Andy Paine who describes it as a show about radical politics that "talks to thinkers and activists who are working towards a more equal and sustainable world". Andy has been involved with 4ZZZ since 2013, filing stories for *Brisbane Line* and writing reviews for the *New Releases Show*, before focusing on *The Paradigm Shift*. He says "4ZZZ has been an amazing space, politically" and believes it is vital for social change movements to have such channels "to communicate and articulate" their work. According to Andy, it is "important for independent stations like 4ZZZ to host ideas which do not get an airing on commercial media"; ideas that are "vital to making better communities and society but exist on the margins and do not serve the interests of advertisers".

4ZZZ has faced several threats of defamation and legal action due to its radical and activist programming. In the early 2000s, volunteer Denis Smith covered a controversial article originally published in a university newsletter, humorously discussing "stealing as a student survival tactic". The mainstream media sensationalised the issue, and an edited interview Denis gave to *Today Tonight* implied endorsement of theft. This led to a serious scare when then-Federal Minister Simon Crean threatened legal action against both Denis and 4ZZZ. Although the threat eventually dissipated, Denis says it was emblematic of the risks community radio can face

---

[18] 4ZZZ, '40th Birthday Special', *Eco Radio* [radio], 4ZZZ, 9 December 2015.

[19] '40th Birthday Special', *Eco Radio*.

when tackling controversial topics. At other times, pressure to redact statements has come from mining companies, and from prison guards whose names were mentioned on air by formerly incarcerated announcers. These incidents underscore the precarious position community broadcasters like 4ZZZ occupy, amplifying marginalised voices and activist causes while navigating potential legal minefields without the resources typically available to larger media organisations. Mindful of this, the station contributed a submission to a federal government inquiry into the *Defamation (Model Provisions) and Other Legislation Amendment Bill 2021*. 4ZZZ advised that "for small organisations, a defamation action might be enough to shut them down, if not cripple [their] ability to function"[20] and suggested "provisions for a fairer and more just allocation or assessment of damages, in line with the means of a publisher, would be preferable".[21]

Occasionally, announcers have felt under pressure from 4ZZZ to tow a particular editorial line. In 2000, Adam Scott and John Mercer, hosts of the *Voltron and Charlie Show*, launched a satirical 'Kill the Music' crusade. This was meant as a critique of 'Save the Music', a campaign run by a group of Fortitude Valley venues, that the announcing team felt only represented a narrow slice of the Brisbane music scene. "The fact that the ongoing gentrification of the Valley meant that live music was being threatened by noise complaints from fancy new apartments was objectively terrible," says Adam.

> But we couldn't help but see a certain grim irony there, as the punks and rockers who initially helped turn the Valley from a crime-ridden cesspit into Brisbane's hippest suburb had themselves already been gentrified out by the venues now under pressure.

In response to the criticisms, Adam says 4ZZZ's management convened a meeting and issued a warning against the two announcers, citing concerns about upsetting advertisers and political supporters. Adam and John were informed they weren't to mention the situation on air again, only minutes before their show started. "Rather than acting like a responsible community broadcaster, and supporting freedom of speech, 4ZZZ was acting like a commercial radio station," Adam recalls. Instead of complying, he publicly quit, tearing up his subscriber card on air and walking out of the station. Adam says it felt "heartbreaking" to be put in the position of having to choose his ethics over 4ZZZ.

* * *

---

[20] Legal Affairs and Safety Commission. *Defamation (Model Provisions) and Other Legislation Amendment Bill 2021*: Report No. 9, 57th Parliament. June 2021. Commonwealth of Australia. p. 7.

[21] Legal Affairs and Safety Commission. *Defamation (Model Provisions) and Other Legislation Amendment Bill 2021*: Report No. 9, 57th Parliament. June 2021. Commonwealth of Australia. p. 7.

This chapter could not be considered even partially complete without mention of the ritual of cold-calling the Premier Joh Bjelke-Petersen on the telephone. Jim Beatson describes this as the "almost daily ... interview with Joh himself as he willingly, incoherently and confidently let Triple Zed's listeners into his very strange thinking".[22] "He always came to the phone," Amanda Collinge says. "It was never 'no comment'." If you called the Bjelke-Petersen residency, Joh's wife 'Lady Flo' would usually answer. "She'd put the phone away [from her mouth and call out] 'it's that girl again'," explains Amanda. "And then Joh would get on ... 'Don't you worry about that' ... and just hang up. That would be our morning chat with Joh".

On the topic of Joh, in 1985 announcer Patrick Whitman and his co-hosts staged an audacious on-air prank that mimicked 4ZZZ's news reporting. Teaming up with the Unemployed People's Theatre Group, the crew presented a radio dramatisation that reported on the "hospitalisation and imminent death" of the Premier. The hoax gained traction fast. "Apparently everyone believed it—it was pretty good—and calls starting to come in asking for more [information],"[23] 4ZZZ journalist Harley Stumm told the *Daily Sun* newspaper. So convincing was the broadcast that, according to Patrick, "one of the Premier's advisors ... instructed [him] to go on air immediately and state that it was a hoax". Local TV crews reportedly rushed to the hospital, after which one of the stations made a formal complaint to the Australian Broadcasting Tribunal accusing 4ZZZ of unfair representation of the news. Patrick wrote to the Tribunal defending the stunt as political commentary on the concentration of power in one man's hands. Despite the drama, no sanctions followed.

Having 'grown up' at Triple Zed hearing stories of pranking the Premier, I thought it would be a lark in 1995 to revisit the tradition and try it myself in preparation for 4ZZZ's twenty-year anniversary. Even though the ex-politician had been out of public service for quite some time, he was still very much in the public eye and his home phone number was listed in the telephone directory. Lady Flo answered the phone and very kindly put me on a very frail sounding Bjelke-Petersen.

> Me: Hello, Sir Joh, It's Heather Anderson from 4ZZZ. The radio station is turning twenty years old soon - would you like to send them a birthday message?
> Bjelke-Petersen: That's very kind dear, but it's not my birthday until next month.
> Me: No Sir Joh, *4ZZZ's* birthday, it's tomorrow. Do you remember?

The line went dead. True to form, the former Premier hung up on me!

---

[22] J. Beatson, 'The Importance of Locally-Owned Media', *Radical Times*, 2012, http://radicaltimes.info/PDF/Beatson.pdf, (accessed 14 May 2024).

[23] Anon, 'Airwave rebels survive decade: Irreverent 4ZZZ rocks on', The Daily Sun, 7 Dec 1985, p. 15.

CHAPTER 14

They Can Starve for All I Care

In 2022, 4ZZZ's prison request show, *Locked In*, collaborated with a local musician to produce a song inspired by Paul Kelly's 1996 hit, *How to Make Gravy*. The original song revolves around a heartfelt letter written by a (fictional) incarcerated man to his family just before Christmas. In Australia, *How to Make Gravy* has become synonymous with the holiday season, so much so that the date mentioned at the start of the song, December 21st, has gained widespread recognition on social media as #GravyDay.

According to *Locked In* coordinator CJ, celebrity chef influencers have turned the day into a time to share their gravy recipes, drowning out the social justice conversation which previously took place on Gravy Day. "To help us to take back some of that conversation," she explains, "we wanted to make our own version of the song". To bring this vision to life, CJ gave Jodie Lawlor, the driving force behind the band Flangipanis, a box of several hundred letters written to *Locked In* by incarcerated listeners. Jodie, also a volunteer at 4ZZZ, hosts the show immediately before, and is well-acquainted with *Locked In's* format. Familiar to many of the show's listeners, she used phrases from the letters to compose new lyrics. The reimagined song was called *How to Fly Kites*.[1]

> Hey LIC [*Locked In* Crew], how the fuck are ya?
> I listen to yas every Monday night.
> It's Jodie here, it's my first time flying a kite.
> Thanks for what you do for us krims inside.

---

[1] In prison slang, letters are called "kites" because of their resemblance when attached to a string and passed between cells.

© The Author(s), under exclusive license to Springer Nature Switzerland AG 2025
H. Anderson, *People Powered Radio*,
https://doi.org/10.1007/978-3-032-05689-4_14

Reading six months-worth of correspondence from *Locked In* listeners was a sobering endeavour for Jodie. "I initially thought it would be a fun time, but the experience really opened my eyes to the reality of isolation that comes with incarceration," she says. "The letters also helped me realise how important *Locked In* is ... [with] such a positive impact on the mental and social well-being of very isolated groups of people."

Two of the people name-checked in *How to Fly Kites* have since died in custody. To quote CJ, "their names now hold a permanent place at Number 15 in the 2023 Hot 100".

* * *

4ZZZ has a long history of standing in solidarity with incarcerated people[2] and amplifying their voices. Advocating for the rights of those in prison is challenging given the social stigma that surrounds them. Prisons often lack transparency and external oversight, making it difficult to document and address abuses. The inherent power imbalance between incarcerated people and prison officials, coupled with fears of retaliation, discourages many from speaking out about violations. Furthermore, a significant proportion of people in Australian prisons come from marginalised communities already facing systemic discrimination. Public apathy and a focus on punishment rather than rehabilitation hinder efforts to promote humane treatment and systemic reform. As a result, those affected by the criminal justice system are often disenfranchised. Evan, a formerly incarcerated volunteer at 4ZZZ, says *Locked In* is important "because it humanises incarcerated people". "My education ... until I fled the nest was that prisoners are bad people. You don't talk to them. That was the extent of my education around the legal system," Evan says. "Once I got in there, I found out how dehumanising it is and how small things can make a difference."

During the ultra-conservative Bjelke-Petersen government era, it was unsurprising that the rights of incarcerated individuals were not prioritised on mainstream agendas. The history of H.M. Prison Brisbane, more commonly known as 'Boggo Road Gaol', exemplifies this. Serving as Queensland's primary prison from the 1880s to the 1980s, it was originally a men's facility and a site of executions. A separate women's gaol was set up at the same site in 1903. Records of internal and external protests against the conditions at Boggo road date back to the 1920s. It was in the 1970s, however, that the 'prisoner rights' movement in Brisbane gained significant momentum, with at least three major protests during the decade. The demonstrations, primarily advocating for better food and living conditions, were often suppressed with the use of tear gas. To cite the official Boggo Road Gaol history website:

---

[2] Prison justice advocates (such as the Vera Institute) suggest avoiding terms that make people's incarceration the defining feature of their identities (e.g. prisoner, inmate). I choose to follow this lead, however, have not altered the language of others.

Riots, mass escapes, hunger strikes, drugs, rooftop protests, staff strikes, murders, suicides and bashings became a regular part of the news cycle as the prison became an increasing embarrassment to the Queensland government.[3]

In the early 1980s, 4ZZZ introduced a show called *Inside Information*, produced by the Prisoners Action Group (PAG), an activist organisation committed to supporting the rights of the incarcerated. A handful of 4ZZZ volunteers were members of the PAG, including Geoff Airo-Farulla and journalist Jon Baird, who had done time at Boggo Road Gaol. Fellow Zed journalist Amanda Collinge credits Jon with establishing strong relationships within the prison. "Jon had excellent contacts with the prisoner network," she says. "We were getting a lot of letters and information smuggled out." During this time, PAG also started a series of weekly pickets outside the gaol which were promoted on *Inside Information*. 4ZZZ were providing first hand news on conditions at the jail, countering what Geoff Airo-Farulla refers to as the mainstream media's "managed news" narrative. "Triple Zed really played a critical role in independent news around what was going on there," he says, "because it was able to get some direct sound of things that were happening in the jail".

One priority for the PAG was securing better access to media for people in prison. Authorities claimed newspapers were a fire risk; instead, incarcerated people were allowed to buy transistor radios, which significantly grew *Inside Information*'s audience. Access to these small AM/FM radios became vital in the years of protest that lay ahead.

* * *

The solidarity between incarcerated people and 4ZZZ is clearly visible in a series of events in 1983. Early in the year, the station received two unexpected packages—both paintings—sent from inside Boggo Road. Journalist Louise Butt was recipient of the artworks. "The second one that arrived was of a woman playing chess," Louise says. The painting sat there for quite some time. "I think we had some kind of a message from memory ... to say, 'have you had a look at it more closely?'." Journalist and Promotions Coordinator Stephen Stockwell (Snr) agrees. "The message came through," he says, "'You idiots, look under the cover of the back', so we took the cover off and there was the tape". Between the artwork and the back cover, cassette tape had been flattened and concealed. Once the tape was reassembled, it revealed vivid firsthand accounts from at least six long-termers describing the harsh realities of life inside Boggo Road Prison. "It was a very humbling experience, listening to the

---

[3] Anon. '1970s-80s: The Desperado Decades', *Inside Boggo Road*. Boggo Road Gaol Historical Society, Brisbane, QLD, 19 October 2015, https://www.boggoroadgaol.com.au/2015/10/1970s-80s-desperado-decades.html (Accessed 12 December 2024).

information," Louise says. "The amount of work that had been taken to get [the tape] out and to us ... was incredibly impressive."

According to the recordings, conditions in No.2 Division were appalling. The cells lacked toilets and running water, food was inadequate, and incarcerated people were treated with frequent brutality. Boggo Road was a century behind the rest of Australia. Jon Baird called the tape "sensational".[4] *Inside Information* broadcast the recordings after disguising the voices. This drew significant attention from mainstream media and sparked widespread controversy. While the content of the recordings was shocking, it was the methods by which 4ZZZ had acquired them that particularly angered authorities. The Prisons Department (now Queensland Corrective Services) accused the station of engaging in "clandestine communications" with incarcerated people and threatened criminal charges.[5] Although none were filed, relations between 4ZZZ and the prison system deteriorated. Tensions within Boggo Road Gaol escalated as the year went on.

If the smuggled recordings hadn't already provoked enough ire, events in November 1983 firmly established 4ZZZ as a thorn in the side of Queensland's prison system. A food poisoning outbreak hospitalised over 30 people, triggering outrage over poor conditions and the lack of accountability. A hunger strike was organised in protest. Word of this strike reached 4ZZZ, which broadcast messages of solidarity along with details of a protest planned outside the prison gates. The hunger strike quickly gained momentum, with more than 400 people refusing food over the weekend[6]. As tensions mounted, prison authorities implemented a total lockdown.

The situation escalated at a press conference on November 20th, when the Minister responsible for prisons, Geoff Muntz, stated: "The protesters have been offered food, and if they don't eat it, they can starve for all I care".[7] 4ZZZ journalists broadcast this remark and the impact was immediate. People began rioting, destroying their cells and other property. Fires erupted across the prison, forcing guards to retreat in riot gear and call police reinforcements to secure the perimeter.

During the first night of the riot, journalists and activists from the Prisoners Action Group managed to communicate with some of the protestors. One, fearing retribution, shouted from within. "The screws are outside my cell. They're going to give me a hiding for talking to you. Hey, if they are going to bash me, you can watch!"[8] This chilling statement became the defining soundbite of the Boggo Road Riots.

---

[4] G. Williams, *Generation Zed: No other radio like this*, Brisbane, Kingswood Press, 2000, p. 28.

[5] G. Williams, *Generation Zed: No other radio like this*, p. 28.

[6] 'Starve if you want to, hunger strikers told', *The Courier Mail*, 21st November 1983, p. 1.

[7] G. Williams, *Generation Zed: No other radio like this*, p. 28.

[8] Williams, *Generation Zed: No other radio like this*, p. 28.

Five days later, as prison authorities assured the media that unrest at the prison had been quelled, two incarcerated protestors climbed out onto a window ledge and held an impromptu press conference. Shouting above the noise of helicopters and ground traffic, Don Nowland told journalists and supporters, "you aren't allowed in here, so we've come up here to let you know what's going on".[9] Ever present at such events, Jon Baird asked Don if the protesters had been able to keep in touch with the outside world. "Only through the radio," Don replied, before confirming this meant 4ZZZ: "Subscriber number 12359! Hey, I've had me subscriber card stolen!" he added, before making a statement "on behalf of everyone in here".

> We're here *as* punishment, not *for* punishment. This is what it's come to. You can't do anything by sitting in here and writing letters. They won't listen ... You've gotta make a mark, so they can see all this ... We expect to be treated like humans.[10]

Don Nowland would later volunteer at the station in between periods of incarceration.

The riots caused over $600 000 worth of damage.[11] Over 120 cells were rendered uninhabitable for nearly six months, forcing the Queensland government to launch an inquiry into the prison system. Led by former politician Sir David Longland, the inquiry heard testimonies from a variety of stakeholders, including *Inside Information* and the PAG. Geoff Airo-Farulla believes that 4ZZZ's coverage was pivotal in kickstarting Queensland prison reforms. "Those 83 riots were probably really pivotal in terms of the reform process that kicked off," says Geoff. "Having reporters on the ground and filing reports as things happened really made a difference to how the perception of what was going on there changed." The *Longland Report* concluded that No.2 Division failed to meet the United Nations' minimum standards for prisons. It recommended several reforms, including healthier food, improved visitation systems, and the closure of 'the hole' or 'the pound', which was Boggo Road's underground detention unit, infamous for its inhumane conditions. However, conservatives were still in power in Queensland and reform was hard to put into practice.

* * *

Despite some changes at Boggo Road following the Longland Inquiry, conditions at the gaol not only persisted but, in some cases, appeared to worsen. This deterioration was marked by increasingly determined resistance from inside. 4ZZZ's support and involvement in highlighting these struggles wasn't limited

---

[9] This quote is taken from a radio transcript that is displayed on a wall at 4ZZZ. There is no context provided besides that the document is a transcript from a radio segment broadcast on 4ZZZ.

[10] As per previous footnote

[11] 'More riots if no inquiry, former prisoners warn', *The Courier Mail*, 24 November 1983, p. 3.

to the *Inside Information* program; the station's newsroom also played a crucial role, regularly reporting on the ongoing unrest at the gaol. Journalists were trusted by prison justice activists to accurately represent their voices and, further cementing this relationship, families with loved ones inside would also reach out with their concerns. A 4ZZZ report from the time gives the example of a father who contacted the station after a visit to his two sons incarcerated at Boggo Road. He'd witnessed protesters who were injured but allegedly denied proper medical care.[12]

In December 1986, there was another major protest and riot following a second hunger strike. According to formerly incarcerated Murri musician, Ricky Pascoe, 4ZZZ were always first on the scene to cover such events and this day was no different. From her home in a nearby suburb journalist Claire Grenet saw the prison was on fire and quickly headed to the site. She interviewed a man occupying a roof of the prison, yelling questions from the footpath and later broadcasting the raw exchange.

> Protester: We're ready to come down, but we wanna talk. We don't wanna get belted, we don't wanna get gassed …
> 4ZZZ: How many screws are there?
> Protester: About a hundred … the riot squad's here, the coppers are here
> 4ZZZ: How many prisoners? …
> Protester: 130. They've already got one wing of the yard … There's only 42 left of us here and a half a dozen left in the other wing and they're all getting bashed, tear gassed … the fucking lot.
> 4ZZZ: Did they try and take your radios away from you?
> Protester: They haven't had the chance to take anything yet but, believe me, they'll take them when they get the chance … and they'll smash em.[13]

This tradition of interviewing people behind bars via shouted exchanges would continue for as long as Boggo Road operated. In the early '90s, 4ZZZ volunteer Paul Kempis was contacted by the station because he lived near the gaol and there had been reports of a disturbance. Paul went to check it out, and "heard yelling and banging from the high security area". He yelled out a question and was told that a search was underway, and it was being conducted with violent force. According to Paul, he found out "a prisoner attempted escape when going to court using a fake gun made of soap". "A screw came up to the fence and told me to piss off or join my mates inside and pointed a shotgun at me," Paul adds. "The prisoners … cheered when I said I was from *The Prisoners Show*."

* * *

---

[12] 'Bonus episode: What led to the Boggo Road riots of 1986', *From A to Triple Z* [podcast], 4ZZZ, 20 January 2021, (Accessed 7 June 2024).

[13] 4ZZZ, 'Bonus episode: What led to the Boggo Road riots of 1986'.

It was around the time of the 1986 riots that *The Prisoners' Show* began (also known as *Prisoners' Program* in some 4ZZZ program guides). It's unclear when *Inside Information* ceased, or if it simply morphed into *The Prisoners' Show*. By 1987, it was coordinated by Kate and Barb, who would host for the next four years or so. Both were already busy in the activist community, and in 1987 Barb had served a month at the State Prison for Women at Boggo Road for wilful damage charges related to graffiti. Kate would later run music workshops at the same gaol. In addition to reporting on prison news, requests and messages became a prominent aspect of *The Prisoners' Show*, a tradition that continues today. According to Kate, this was an important element of the program which further cemented relationships between 4ZZZ and people whose lives were impacted by incarceration.

> It just meant so much to people inside, to have their messages read out, to feel connected in some way. To think that there were people outside who cared about them, who were prepared to give them their time of day.

Meanwhile, most of the problems identified in the *Longland Report* five years earlier remained unaddressed, with conditions in parts of Boggo Road Gaol now considered unliveable. On February 13th, 1988 a man known as Spider was shot by a prison guard. Incarcerated protesters once again rioted and staged a hunger strike in what became the most significant of several years of resistance at the gaol. Twelve days into the hunger strike, five incarcerated men climbed to the rooftop of F Wing, where they staged an almost week-long occupation despite the blistering summer sun and heavy rainfall at night[14]. They painted their demands for justice and a public inquiry onto the roof slates, bedsheets and clothing. Ultimately, the men were removed from the building with the assistance of fire crews, but not until Corrections Minister, Russell Cooper, announced an inquiry into the entire prison system in Queensland.

The 1988 Boggo Road rooftop protesters were joined outside by hundreds of supporters—including Barb and Kate; a constant presence keeping vigil on the streets below (Fig. 14.1). "We were sleeping out there for a while … while the blokes were on the roof," says Kate. "We'd record stuff and then scuttle over to Triple Zed and try our hardest to turn it into something that we could play on air." Kate and Barb also used *The Prisoners Show* to air statements from the rooftop protestors about their demands and ongoing actions. Through these they ensured the demands were heard outside the prison walls, putting further pressure on the government and prison authorities and generating public discussion about the conditions inside Boggo Road.

Adding a unique dimension to the 1988 rooftop protests was the involvement of a local punk band who were keen to show their solidarity. The band,

---

[14] *Boggo Road Gaol Riots* [online video], The Feed, Sydney, Australia, SBS, 2019, https://youtu.be/w4Aq1-H2GD0, https://www.youtube.com/watch?v=KZBlJNsRa-o, (Accessed 2 January 2019).

Fig. 14.1 Poster in support of Boggo Road Gaol rooftop protests, produced by 4ZZZ's Prisoners' Show; 1988

called ACT, performed across the road from the prison. I remember seeing television news coverage of the event, recognising the band from gigs I'd been to (having recently moved to Brisbane). I couldn't believe they had made prime time TV, if only for a few seconds. Members of ACT included 4ZZZ volunteers Greg Fryer, Mike Brown, and Cal Crilly, who would later be involved in getting 4ZZZ back on the air after Victoria Brazil's attempted eviction in December that same year (see Chap. 4). According to Mike:

All of us being involved with 4ZZZ meant we all had a link to the prisoners in some way. [As] Front Desk Coordinator ... during *Murri [Hour]* I had to take all the ... requests from folk who wanted to dedicate songs for relatives and loved ones in jail. So, you felt a part of what was going on, I guess.

The band quickly mobilised, with Greg Fryer contacting Uncle Ross Watson from *Murri Radio*, who lived across the road from the prison. "Next thing, we're in his front yard with all the gear," Mike recalls. Through their modest setup, consisting primarily of a single Yamaha amplifier, the band played a mix of originals and covers, including (of course) AC/DC's *Jailbreak*. The sound carried across the street and into the prison yard, where it was met with enthusiastic cheers from the incarcerated audience. "When we stopped playing there was a big roar out of the prison!" Mike says.

Buoyed by their Saturday night success, ACT returned Sunday afternoon and, according to Cal, "probably played for half an hour before any cops or the media ... came in". A recording exists of the interaction between police and Uncle Ross when officers arrived at his property. Although somewhat muffled by the sounds of children playing in the background and the noise of passing cars, Uncle Ross's staunch advocacy for First Nations rights and calm demeanour were evident. In the recording, he is heard asking police to not raise their voices at him while on his property and questioning their interpretation and application of legislation in relation to excessive noise. While an unauthorised gig in the yard of an Aboriginal household in 1980s Brisbane certainly had its risks—for both the musicians and those who lived there—the band felt the benefits outweighed them. According to Mike, "I don't think I was too worried about being arrested. We really weren't doing anything wrong, but I was more worried about them confiscating our gear, however crappy it was".

The 1988 riots became the final tipping point for significant reforms. That same month, prominent businessman Jim Kennedy was commissioned to review Queensland's criminal justice system. The resulting *Kennedy Report* described the state's prison system as outdated, overcrowded, and inhumane. Boggo Road Gaol was deemed unsuitable for modern correctional needs. The report criticised its poor sanitation, ventilation, and lack of rehabilitation programs, as well as the excessive use of solitary confinement, and inadequate healthcare. It also highlighted the systemic overrepresentation of First Nations Australians in the prison population, as well as the lack of training and support for correctional staff.

The *Kennedy Report* became instrumental in driving reforms that eventually led to the phased closure of Boggo Road Gaol. No. 2 Division, which had been at the heart of the unrest, was shut down in 1989. The women's section of the prison remained operational until 2002. Today, the former prison site is home to the Boggo Road Urban Village, with parts of No. 2 Division preserved as a heritage-listed museum and tourist attraction.

* * *

Another significant outcome of prison resistance in 1988 was the formation of the Incarcerated People's Cultural Heritage Aboriginal Corporation (IPCHAC), a groundbreaking initiative led by incarcerated Aboriginal men; President Yudin Dali Ted Watson, Secretary Owen McEvoy, and Treasurer Bejam Denis Walker. Much to the annoyance of prison authorities, IPCHAC was able to leverage federal law to carve out a space for First Nations Australians in prison to organise and advocate for cultural programs. Because IPCHAC was incorporated under the federal *Aboriginal Councils and Associations Act 1976*, members and the executive had certain rights under federal legislation which could not to be impeded or overridden by State law. This included the right to hold meetings. IPCHAC's primary mission was to reconnect incarcerated First Nations people with their culture, land, and families. This work extended beyond the prison walls, creating pathways for cultural, educational, and spiritual engagement.

IPCHAC developed a notable partnership with 4ZZZ. In the summer of 1988–89, Bejam Denis Walker, a prominent Aboriginal activist, artist, and son of renowned poet and activist Oodgeroo Noonuccal, reached out to John Tracey, a volunteer with 4ZZZ's *Non-Indigenous News Show*. Bejam invited John to visit him at Palen Creek Correctional Centre where he was incarcerated, and the two developed a friendship.

In 1989, Bejam invited 4ZZZ to take part in an IPCHAC-led media workshop at Boggo Road Gaol. This event brought together members of the Murri community, media professionals, and academics, to train incarcerated people in media production skills. IPCHAC acquired some basic recording equipment, and John brought it into the prison after a crash course in its use from *Murri Hour* volunteer Greg Fryer. Once inside, incarcerated prison activist Don Green took charge of organising musicians for a spontaneous recording session, producing songs that 4ZZZ would later broadcast.

This collaboration led to the creation of *Yalga Bindi*, a one-hour weekly show broadcast on 4ZZZ, Thursday nights. The program was led by Kuku Yalanji[15] man Qawanji Vincent Brady, IPCHAC's senior cultural tutor, and Secretary Owen McEvoy, with John Tracey acting as the main producer. *Yalga Bindi* became a voice for IPCHAC, mixing what John describes as "heavy raves" on cultural and political topics with shout-outs to families and communities. "I did what they told me," John says, "which was basically to take a tape recorder into Boggo Road and Borallon [Correctional Centre] to IPCHAC meetings and programs, record prisoners, in particular the IPCHAC leadership, and broadcast it". The show ran until mid-1991, at which time John followed Qawanji on a research trip to Cape York, in Queensland's Far North.

IPCHAC's collaboration with 4ZZZ extended beyond radio. The corporation arranged for people to come to the station on day-release from prison. A

---

[15] Kuku Yalanji country spans the rainforest regions of the Daintree Rainforest and the Mossman Gorge region in Far North Queensland (https://aiatsis.gov.au/explore/map-indigenous-australia).

November 1989 letter tabled in Queensland Parliament reports on a visit to 4ZZZ by Don Green and a second incarcerated man. Written by a Security Services officer to the General Manager of Brisbane Correctional Centre, it notes "the escort ran quite smoothly". Interactions between the incarcerated volunteers and 4ZZZ staff are meticulously recorded.

> While at 4ZZZ the prisoners were never unobserved by us, and we accompanied them whenever they had to leave the area. Whenever the prisoners wanted a drink or food, the station staff or the IPCHAC member supplied the prisoners with money.[16]

Additionally, IPCHAC and 4ZZZ organised a handful of concerts inside prisons, featuring local bands friendly to their cause. Again, Don Green played a key role. According to John Tracey, "nobody negotiated with the screws or prison staff, all logistics were organised through Don". At Triple Zed's end, Tom Maginnis was the main point of contact. He had grown up with Bejam Denis Walker and saw the concert as an opportunity for 4ZZZ to better engage with and support people in prison. There had "never been a gig in a jail in Queensland before," Tom says. "But [Premier Wayne] Goss was in, so we thought maybe there's hope."

The first was held at Borallon Training and Correctional Centre and Tom managed to book an appearance by Australian blues legend Phil Manning, best known for his work with the band Chain. It was a logical musical fit, says Tom. "[Phil] thought 'well, this is the blues ... where else do you hear the blues if not in a jail?'." In addition to Phil Manning, the lineup included seven or eight bands and Tom felt "it was a great day" for almost everyone. One band thought it a good idea to smuggle marijuana into the prison. "They stashed pot in the bass speaker and the screws at the jail found it," explains Tom. "So that was just this big nightmare ... I think they arrested the whole band and took them away."

Despite this, 4ZZZ were able to organise a handful more prison gigs in the early 1990s. Blues musician Lil' Fi performed at least two shows at Borallon Correctional Centre and one at Boggo Road Women's Prison. Reflecting on the experience, she says "the gratitude from all the inmates for breaking up the monotony for them, was unforgettable". Zed volunteer Donna Williamson echoes these sentiments having gone along to an IPCHAC-organized event with Alien Virus (which featured Cal and Mike from ACT). "Some of the music, the prisoners were probably thinking, 'What is this?!'" Donna recalls. "But they were just so happy that bands had bothered to come in and play for them, they didn't care."

---

[16] S.R. Coops. 'Re—Escort to 4ZZZ of Prisoners D.R. GREEN and K.J. VIERITZ' [letter to General Manager, Brisbane Correctional Centre], 8 November 1989. Tabled to Queensland Parliament, Brisbane, Queensland, 25th October 1990.

By the early 1990s, both *Inside Information* and *Yalga Bindi* were no more. The *Murri Hour* also ended in 1993 after the establishment of 4AAA. However, Triple Zed's commitment to prison justice persisted through *The Prisoners' Show*, which continued to play requests from incarcerated listeners, share messages from family members and interrogate both Correctional Services and police conduct. While Boggo Road may have been dismantled, the number of prisons in 4ZZZ's broadcast footprint was steadily growing. Specific reforms had improved some aspects of prison operations, but the overarching issues of mass incarceration and the disproportionate representation of First Nations Australians in prison and deaths in custody were (and still are) a painful reality for many whose lives were tangled up in the criminal justice system.

For ten years or so, a suite of 4ZZZ volunteers took responsibility for ensuring there was always someone committed to keeping a prison request show on air. I would occasionally help and remember hosting the show with Donna Williamson and Leah Nunya one night, when we learned a riot had broken out at the Woodford Correctional Centre. Less than a month after its opening, 200 to 300 high- and medium-security protesters "trashed" the prison "over insufficient and poor-quality food, non-smoking rules and operational bungling by prison officers and management".[17] As often was the case, Don Green found a telephone inside the prison. I vividly remember the chaos of that night but not which one of us took the call. According to Donna, "they'd broken into an office, phoned up, and said, 'Quick, start recording'. We played *The Roof is on Fire* by the Bloodhound Gang to go along with it".

* * *

Circa 2000/2001, *The Prisoners' Show* was renamed *Locked In*. However, this was not the first time that name appeared in 4ZZZ's programming. It gets a little confusing, so bear with me! The first iteration of *Locked In* debuted on July 25th, 1994, as a 30-minute news and current affairs program syndicated nationally through COMRADSAT (now the Community Radio Network). The show provided an in-depth look at criminal justice issues and complemented the request-driven format of *The Prisoners' Show*. The inaugural flyer for *Locked In* outlined its mission: "To educate the broader community about prisoner issues, provide a non-violent voice for the expression of prisoner issues, and act as a support system for the incarcerated".[18]

By this time *The Prisoners' Show* prioritised connection—mostly featuring messages and dedications to loved ones. *Locked In* took a more journalistic

---

[17] K. Fredericks. 'Queensland's 'prison time bomb' goes off', *Green Left Weekly*, Issue 269, April 9 1997, https://www.greenleft.org.au/content/queenslands-prison-time-bomb-goes (accessed Jan 1 2025).

[18] 4ZZZ, 'Locked In: A national radio program exploring prison issues and culture' [promotional flyer], August 1994 (accessed from 4ZZZ archives 6 February 2004).

stance, focusing on in-depth stories about criminal justice reform, systemic inequalities, and human rights abuses in the prison system. Its segments included interviews with prominent figures in the prison reform movement, national and international news roundups, and weekly poetry readings,[19] often submitted by people in prisons across the country.

The program's original concept was conceived by Don Nowland, a formerly incarcerated listener who'd been a part of the 1983 Boggo Road protests. Don already contributed to *The Prisoners' Show* but he envisaged a second, harder-hitting investigative program that would bring light to injustices often ignored by mainstream media. Don had a strong vision but he didn't have the skillset to execute his idea. Fortunately, fellow 4ZZZ volunteer Kitty van Vuuren had not long returned from Melbourne, where she had honed her skills in radio program production at university and then at both public and community media outlets. Kitty had a former boyfriend (in the Netherlands) who'd been to jail, so she wasn't bothered by Don's background. "I think Don had been trying to get his project [going] … but wasn't getting anywhere, and I was looking for something 'meaningful' to do," she explains.

> I liked Don, I took the time to listen to his ideas for *Locked In* … I had trained … broadcasters in Melbourne, so I had the skills and knowledge to guide him towards his goal, as well as train a handful of other volunteers … interested in contributing to the project.

Kitty's skills in grant writing secured crucial funding for the team, enabling 4ZZZ to purchase new recording equipment and to offer a small stipend for the program's production.

Don had a very specific goal in mind for the first episode, which he achieved—to interview former Premier, Joh Bjelke-Petersen. By this time, Bjelke-Petersen's political legacy was overshadowed by the findings of the Fitzgerald Inquiry. He was famously tried for perjury in 1991, but the case ended in a hung jury, reportedly due to one juror's strong bias in his favour. Don has left this mortal coil, so I can't ask him why he wanted to speak to a man that had been loathed by so many in alternative and activist circles. Listening back, it is evident Don took the interview seriously and respectfully. Perhaps as a result, Bjelke-Petersen was quite candid in his commentary on the court system:

> I feel sorry, because I had many a time that people have come to me and said to me - when I was Premier – 'can't you help us because Dad's in jail, he shouldn't be there, he never did what they said he did', he'd been verballed or something or other, misconstrued in court, and I cannot get over the terrible system that operates.

---

[19] Poetry was a popular part of *Locked In* and an anthology of incarcerated people's poetry was released by the show in 1998. *Words from the Inside: Locked In Poetry Anthology* was compiled by 4ZZZ volunteers and sponsored by the Queensland Office of Arts and Cultural Development. It contained 19 poems and was distributed free of charge by 4ZZZ.

Unfortunately, Don was not up for committing to a regular weekly schedule. According to Kitty van Vuuren, he suffered from terrible headaches and carried a great deal of unresolved trauma. This no doubt contributed to his periods of incarceration and was exacerbated in turn by the time he spent behind bars. Kitty continued producing *Locked In* for about a year, when journalist Brendan Greenhill took over the reins. Across its lifetime, many 4ZZZ volunteers contributed to the show, including international correspondents such as Jon Baird, who was by this stage in the United Kingdom. When *Locked In* (version one) ceased production *The Prisoners' Show* took on the name.

* * *

I included *Locked In* (version two) as a case study for my PhD research investigating ways that community radio supports prison communities and people of lived prison experience. Because of this, I rejoined the program in 2005 as an 'insider-researcher' but didn't leave once my thesis was complete! My good friend Nicki Clarke had been the main host since 2004 (following a brief stint helping in the late '90s) and for nearly ten years we volunteered our Monday nights with the program. Nicki says she was motivated by her belief that "we are all responsible for the society that we live in". "When I think about the system of retribution and punishment that we are immersed in," she says, "I feel this terrible sadness that can only be countered by doing something to challenge it".[20]

Soon after, formerly incarcerated volunteers started to join us and the *Locked In* team grew, for the first time in years. Charlie joined shortly after his release from prison. During his 13 years in adult incarceration, he'd been a devoted listener and frequent letter-writer to the show. He became a dedicated member of the *Locked In* team as soon as he got out and stayed at 4ZZZ for over 15 years. Speaking early into his tenure, Charlie says he saw it as his responsibility to keep that connection alive for others still on the inside.

> I promised them many years ago that as soon as I got out, I'd be here. I've left a lot of good Chynas [prison friends] inside, and I can't see them anymore … It's just something I've gotta do. Hook, line, and sinker. Otherwise, I'd be letting people down inside.[21]

Charlie wasn't alone. Around the same time, Zim joined the program. He had been involved in the IPCHAC workshops in the late 1980s and was determined to inject more political content into the show. Zim wanted *Locked In* to

---

[20] H. Anderson. 'Raising the civil dead: Prisoners and community radio. Peter Lang Publishers, 2012, p. 120.

[21] Anderson, *Raising the civil dead: Prisoners and community radio*, p. 123.

challenge the prison system head-on and push for reform. "The state of Queensland never let[s] me let go of my criminality, I feel that this is something I can contribute to that doesn't belong to that side,"[22] Zim says. "[4ZZZ] lets me be me, and that's what I like about it. It's part of my life." Soon after, Blue joined the team. He and Zim had served time together twenty years prior and after a chance meeting in the city in 2006, Blue accepted Zim's offer to visit the studios during a program. For him, the show was all about providing camaraderie for the listeners. "It's good doing the show and helping them have a laugh, forgetting about jail for that couple of hours and playing their favourite songs they wanna hear,"[23] Blue says.[24]

The highlights of my time with *Locked In* always fell on Christmas Day, when we would take over the airwaves regardless of what day of the week it was. For several years, we utilised 4ZZZ's talkback system so families could speak directly to their loved ones on the inside. Children on the phone always brought a few tears to the eye (in the studio and in the prisons, according to one letter we received).

> First Daughter: Hello Dad, I love you, I got lots of presents from Santa, I hope that you will be here next year, lots of love, Madison.
> Second Daughter: Hello dad, (whispering) what do I say? Happy Christmas, I love you lots, I hope you come next year, and I got lots of presents, I love you.[25]

When a cheeky listener surprised us by sucking on a water bong with its distinctive bubbling and exhaling sound effects, yelling "having one for you Uncle!," we thought it best to shut down the talkback. *Locked In* still broadcasts on Christmas Day. In 2024 a 16-hour broadcast included recorded messages from family members and a revolving cast of presenters.

Over the years, *Locked In* has lost and gained members, always holding the Monday 6:00 to 8:00pm timeslot where it has been since 2002. At the time of writing, the core crew comprises two formerly incarcerated 4ZZZ volunteers, Em and Evan, and coordinators CJ & Traci, who are responsible for shaping the program, organising events, broadcasts, and building community partnerships. The *Locked In* Crew, as they are generally known, places a strong emphasis on community engagement, building pathways for volunteers whose lives have been impacted by the criminal justice system, to engage with 4ZZZ outside of 'just' *Locked In*.

Em has completed newsroom training and is a presenter on the *Zedlines* team. She is a passionate artist, and this connected her with 4ZZZ as a teenager back in 2008. "I did a lot of spray paint, graffiti and stencil [work] that is still

---

[22] Anderson, *Raising the civil dead: Prisoners and community radio*, p. 124.

[23] Anderson, *Raising the civil dead: Prisoners and community radio*, p. 120.

[24] Blue passed in 2015, after I interviewed him for my PhD research.

[25] H. Anderson. *Raising the civil dead: Prisoners and community radio*. Peter Lang Publishers, 2012, p. 190.

there to this day, out in the car park," Em says. "And that has been a huge part of how I started being involved in Triple Zed." As you enter the studio level of Zed Towers it's hard to miss Em's stencils. An elephant comprised of fingerprint swirls represents being fingerprinted at the watchhouse while an industrious frog with a broom provides a commentary on community service. However, the piece that always catches my attention is a simple stencilled excerpt from 'What is Government', an essay by 19th century anarchist Proudhon.[26]

Evan contributes to Zed Digital as well as *Locked In*. Most recently he worked with CJ to create a series of Graveyard show playlists, curated by incarcerated listeners. This was motivated by a listener who sent in such a long list of requests, the *Locked In* Crew thought it would make for a great standalone program. Evan says he cannot overstate the effect that volunteering has had on his life.

> I've had family turn their back on me. I've lost a lot of friends. But I came into Triple Zed, and they were like, 'yo, you got something you can bring to the table? Don't be an asshole and you're good' ... There was no judgment on my past. It was just my present and what I could bring to the future.

Locked In now holds regular events, such as poetry and spoken word nights, 'prison pen-pal' letter-writing sessions and stencil art workshops. In 2023, a two-month exhibition 'Unlocked' was held at Banshees Bar and Art Space in Ipswich[27] to celebrate 40 years of prison radio on 4ZZZ. The promotion read:

> Through more than 150 drawings, paintings, sketches and scribbles Unlocked will show how art is a tool for connection to culture and community, and one of the only positive forms of self-therapy available to isolated humans. Art saves lives.[28]

A *Locked In* art gallery started to grow inside a stairwell at Zed Towers in 2018. The show has long received artwork accompanying letters with song requests, often on scraps of paper or envelopes. Selected pieces were originally Blu Tacked ad hoc to a stairwell wall, but over time the buildup became overwhelming and began to damage the art. Recognising the emotional and cultural significance of these artworks, CJ—who has a background in art therapy—organised for a permanent exhibition space within the station. The *Locked In* crew repainted the walls, collected frames donated by the 4ZZZ

---

[26] P.-J. Proudhon, *What Is Government? General Idea of the Revolution in the Nineteenth Century*. Translated by Robinson, J. (1923) [1851]. London: Freedom Press.

[27] Ipswich is a small city about 40 km south-west of Brisbane CBD, often considered the outer regions of Brisbane.

[28] Banshees Bar and Art Space. 'Unlocked: 40 Years of Prison Radio on 4ZZZ', Banshees Bar and Art Space, Ipswich, QLD, I https://bansheesbar.com.au/exhibition/unlocked-40-years-of-prison-radio-on-4zzz.(Accessed 1 November 2024).

community and created a permanent gallery. "There's nothing more thrilling than when someone's drawn you something," CJ says.

> I know when someone is making angry pencil strokes and brush strokes that there's something going on inside them that needs to come out ... Now, when somebody sends us a piece of artwork, they know that they're getting a space on that wall.

Prison justice issues are not siloed within *Locked In*. They are discussed on other news and information-based programs, and even more so since a new, conservative State Government was elected on a 'tough on youth crime' platform in 2024. Long-running politics and philosophy talk show, *Radio Reversal*, for example, regularly covers topics like the prison industrial complex and prison abolition. Most recently it produced a series called "Challenging Colonial Copaganda," tracing the origins of colonial policing and prison systems, and the ways people are resisting them. Prison justice is also incorporated into 4ZZZ's *Rights Framework*, a document that outlines the principles that underpin its process "for responding to situations, behaviours and actions impacting on somebody's rights at the Station".[29] This includes to be "non-colonial, non-carceral, non-punitive and resist disposability culture".[30] Lofty aspirations perhaps, but ones that 4ZZZ has proven its commitment to for nearly fifty years.

---

[29] 4ZZZ. 'Rights Framework', *4ZZZ*, Brisbane, QLD https://jeff.4zzz.org.au/sites/default/files/media/4ZZZ%20Rights%20Framework.pdf (Accessed 1 March 2025). 2025, p. 1.

[30] 4ZZZ. 'Rights Framework'. p. 1.

CHAPTER 15

A Living History

The rain was intermittent at first—the petrichor of warm water hitting concrete wafted through the front door at 4ZZZ's reception. By Friday, the warnings were official: 2025's Tropical Cyclone Alfred was churning toward the Southeast Queensland coast, and Brisbane was expected to be directly in its path.

For most people, that meant a run on bottled water and toilet paper. But for the folks at Triple Zed, it meant keeping the station on air. The Triple Zed car park was a hive of activity as volunteers bolted down loose fixtures and tied tarps across areas where the rain might get in. Announcers that lived close to Zed Towers volunteered to cover for those who couldn't travel, and arrangements were made for others to broadcast remotely.

Station Manager Jack McDonnell made the call to stay overnight, just in case something happened to the building. "The roof already leaks in a few places when it rains normally, so if Alfred had hit, who knows," he thought. "If something went wrong, I could at least be on hand to deal with it right away."

Patrick King, Ben Ryan and the techie team weren't taking any chances either. They feared the high winds might knock out 4ZZZ's transmission link to Mount Coot-tha, so they repurposed a redundant underground pathway—a backup route using buried cabling and internet lines. If the signal went dark, it would reroute in seconds. And just in case that failed too? A computer up on the mountain was loaded with a pre-programmed emergency playlist, complete with cyclone-themed tunes and tongue-in-cheek announcements that was ready to kick in after two minutes of silence.

Alfred never eventuated, turning into a tropical low as it hit the mainland and sparing the city from the worst. But Brisbane's weirdest, most beloved radio station proved once again that it would always be there, come rain, hail, or cyclone.

* * *

People Powered Radio is only a partial history. The sheer volume of people involved at the station makes it impossible to tell all its stories. More to the point, 4ZZZ is still operating, creating new narratives every day. I must stop writing at some point, so let's finish with a look at Queensland's oldest community radio station in the year 2025.

In true community radio fashion, 4ZZZ still runs predominantly on people power—a passionate crew of a few staff and hundreds of volunteers. Station Manager Jack McDonnell started out as one of those volunteers years ago and never lost the 4ZZZ spirit. He recalls how he fell in love with the station as a place "where people felt that they could be themselves, that they could hear people like themselves, and feel like they are part of something bigger". That welcoming, come-as-you-are culture is a big reason volunteers stick around (or return after stints elsewhere). Jack's role these days is to steer the overall vision, manage the staff and budget, and make sure 4ZZZ keeps thriving.

Alongside the Station Manager is a small paid staff that helps to coordinate the chaos, some of whom are funded through the Community Broadcasting Foundation. These folks keep the ship steady, but most of 4ZZZ's content and labour is produced by volunteers who give countless hours to the station and its community. Around 160 announcers present shows on 4ZZZ, and then there are journalists, producers, music librarians, receptionists, cleaners, and technicians, to name but a few roles at the station. Many start in one job but end up wearing many hats. "When you're at the station long enough, you end up doing all sorts of things," says Programming Coordinator Ian Powne of his own trajectory. This DIY ethic and cross-training makes for a tight-knit, can-do culture. Everyone pitches in for big events like Radiothon, and when something breaks at 4ZZZ odds are a volunteer knows how to fix it or at least will have a crack at it. In short, people are the lifeblood of 4ZZZ.

This also includes over 160,000 people who tune to 4ZZZ each month.[1] These listeners aren't passive consumers but part of the extended 4ZZZ community. As Accessibility Officer Owen Sadler describes it:

> At the very basic level, anyone can be a Zedder. You are Zedder if you listen to the station, maybe you subscribe, attend Zed-aligned events, support Zed-aligned artists or businesses.

So, who are these Zedders? According to the most recent audience survey,[2] the station attracts a young, educated, and culturally engaged crowd with 52% male-identifying, 42% female-identifying and the remainder gender diverse. About 41% of listeners are aged between 16 and 35 years and a healthy portion

---

[1] 4ZZZ. '4ZZZ Audience Overview' [Internal document supplied to author], 4ZZZ, Brisbane, QLD.

[2] 4ZZZ. '4ZZZ Audience Overview' [Internal document supplied to author], 4ZZZ, Brisbane, QLD.

identify as part of the LGBTQIA+ community (15%) reflecting 4ZZZ's strong connection with Brisbane's queer and alternative subcultures.

What unites this diverse listenership is a love for local content and a deep trust in the station. A whopping 98% of the audience say they strongly relate to 4ZZZ, and 96% strongly trust it. These numbers underscore how unique the station's relationship with its community is. Listeners tune in because 4ZZZ offers something they can't get in mainstream media. Additionally, 72% said they listen for local news and events coverage, 49% for connection to local subcultures, and 44% for arts and cultural programming not heard elsewhere. Whether it's hearing their friend's band on *Right Here, Right Now*, getting the scoop on a protest via *Paradigm Shift*, or just feeling part of Brisbane's creative pulse, people turn to 4ZZZ for its localness and uniqueness. About half of listeners do so via the internet or DAB+ digital radio while the other half still listen old-school on the FM band in their cars or at home.

4ZZZ listeners are subscribing to the radio station more than ever before.[3] In 2023, the station's annual Radiothon exceeded all expectations. By mid-2024 the station hit a historic milestone of over 3200 active subscribers, marking a 6% rise despite a tough economic climate.[4] Seeing consistent monthly growth in subscriptions indicates the station must be doing something right in the eyes (or should that be ears) of its audience. Jack McDonnell attributes this success directly to the content on air. "This is thanks to the great work done by our on-air announcers," he says, "articulating the value of the station, how we connect with communities and why that needs support".[5] In other words, engaging radio begets engaged listeners.

4ZZZ's programming spans just about every genre and interest group imaginable—true to its mission of "amplifying the voices of our local communities". On 102.1fm (and sibling channel Zed Digital), you might hear an eclectic mix of underground punk, soul and techno all in the one show, followed by news on environmental vandalism and a segment spotlighting traditional village cricket in Vanuatu. 4ZZZ deliberately breaks its lineup into a mix of general music shows, specialist genre programs, news and current affairs, and sociocultural shows to ensure there's room on the airwaves for everything from cutting-edge local music to long-form interviews. In 2023, 4ZZZ overhauled its volunteer training modules, which Programming Coordinator Ian Powne credits with boosting the confidence and technical skills of its presenters. That training pipeline is paying off, with a wave of fresh voices in the 18–24 age bracket joining the station over the past year.[6]

* * *

---

[3] 4ZZZ, '4ZZZ Annual Report 2024'. *4ZZZ*, https://jeff.4zzz.org.au/sites/default/files/media/Annual%20Report%202024%20.pdf, (accessed 3rd April 2025).

[4] 4ZZZ, '4ZZZ Annual Report 2024'.

[5] 4ZZZ, '4ZZZ Annual Report 2024'.

[6] 4ZZZ, '4ZZZ Annual Report 2024'.

When the COVID-19 pandemic hit Australia in 2020, 4ZZZ suddenly faced one of its biggest challenges since the attempted eviction of 1988. How could a busy, volunteer-driven radio station, dependent on people coming into a shared studio, continue operating under lockdowns and health restrictions? Like the story that opened this chapter, 4ZZZ's response to COVID involved a Triple Zed-style mix of community spirit and technological ingenuity that not only kept the station on air but made it stronger.

Grace Pashley was Station Manager at the time. "I'm so glad it happened in my third year of managing, not my first," she says. Her immediate response was to limit the number of people at the station, with only one person in each studio at any given time. Community broadcasting was recognised as an essential service in Australia, meaning volunteers could still attend 4ZZZ during lockdowns. This didn't mean that it was feasible for everyone to do so. "We kind of made it opt-in," Grace says, "[saying] if you're immunocompromised or if you have other reasons why this is too much for you at the moment, please just tell us. You're not going to lose your slot".

Within a remarkably short time, Technical Manager Patrick King and the tech team created a 'remote studio' capability so announcers could present shows from their homes. Using a combination of broadcast software and some clever audio routing, 4ZZZ enabled its announcers to access the station's playout system from home. They even solved the tricky part—allowing multiple presenters to co-host a show together while each in separate locations, without any noticeable delay. To do this, the tech team set up what was essentially a near-zero-latency audio link, meaning two or three people could chat "live" as if in the same room, and the audience wouldn't know the difference. As techie Ben Ryan points out, having multiple voices on air was a huge boost during isolation. If a listener was stuck at home alone, hearing their three favourite radio hosts laughing together might have been the most they'd "interacted" all day. "It was about being able to make those magical connections," he says. Grace Pashley confirms this. "We got lots of nice feedback at that time saying it's so good to be able to tune into Triple Zed and just feel a bit normal."

Administratively, the experience was intense. "I don't think people realise ... how much of a 'karate chop to the neck' the COVID pandemic was on admin at 4ZZZ," Programming Coordinator, Ian Powne says. "It took a real toll". With normal operations upended, staff had to manage everything remotely, from coordinating volunteers to figuring out new workflows for pre-recorded content. However, through trial and error, the 4ZZZ technicians built a system that has permanently improved the station's flexibility. Those remote broadcasting tools are still in use for contributors who can't make it to the station (for example during wild-weather events, but also for people who have accessibility limitations at Zed Towers). In a sense, COVID pushed 4ZZZ to innovate in ways it might never have otherwise.

By the time Brisbane emerged from the worst of the pandemic, 4ZZZ had proven its resilience. There were hiccups, of course—dodgy home internet connections or the occasional dog barking in the background—but overall 4ZZZ never went off air. In fact, it flourished. The station emerged with improved remote access and a higher profile. Many people who hadn't listened in years came back, and new folks discovered 4ZZZ while seeking local content during the pandemic. According to Stephen Stockwell (Jnr), who took over managing the station partway through the pandemic, "the station's Brisbane focus meant people came to us for news, music and company, which has been reflected with a rise in subscribers".[7] Indeed, while 2020 was rough financially for many organisations, 4ZZZ saw an uptick in support. The 2020 Radiothon met its target despite a recession, and by 2021 subscriptions were on a growth trajectory. The station became a lifeline for the community during lockdown. "Everyone's world got a bit smaller … people started looking around to their local community for support and found there were a lot of places and people there to help, including 4ZZZ," Stephen says.[8]

* * *

Running a community radio station is as much a financial juggling act as it is a creative endeavour. As Finance Coordinator Annie Ashton describes it, "[we are] always trying to make those dollars stretch from year to year, but I love it!". 4ZZZ's finances in 2025 are stable, and while the station isn't swimming in money, it continues to meet its needs. Triple Zed's income comes from a variety of sources, with subscriptions being the largest single slice of the fiscal pie. In the last financial year, subscriptions made up 36% of 4ZZZ's revenue. Close behind is sponsorship (on-air advertising from local businesses), contributing around 24.7%. The remaining income is rounded out by government grants (about 21%), donations, merchandise sales, and fundraising events.[9] This intentionally diversified mix protects the station from an over-reliance on any individual funding source. Treasurer Anthony Rutherford notes in the *Annual Report 2024* that revenues increased in comparison to 2023 thanks to rises in all avenues of funding except for sponsorships. However, expenses also have increased, particularly as some staff roles that were once grant-funded have transitioned to being paid out of

---

[7] A. De Luca-Tao, 'Positive Developments: Stephen Stockwell of 4ZZZ Radio', *Tone Deaf*, 11 June 2021, https://tonedeaf.thebrag.com/positive-developments-stephen-stockwell/, (accessed 3 June 2024).
4ZZZ, '4ZZZ Annual Report 2024'.*4ZZZ*, https://jeff.4zzz.org.au/sites/default/files/media/Annual%20Report%202024%20.pdf, (accessed 3rd April 2025).

[8] A. De Luca-Tao, "Positive Developments: Stephen Stockwell of 4ZZZ Radio", 11/6/21, https://tonedeaf.thebrag.com/positive-developments-stephen-stockwell/, accessed 3/6/24.

[9] 4ZZZ, "4ZZZ Annual Report 2024". https://jeff.4zzz.org.au/sites/default/files/media/Annual%20Report%202024%20.pdf, accessed 3/4/25.

Fig. 15.1 Photo of 4ZZZ's current transmitter tower at Broadcasting Park, Mount Coot-tha, taken by Gavin Unsworth; year unknown

4ZZZ's own pocket and significant investments have been made in new equipment (discussed below).[10] Overall, 4ZZZ's financial health can be described as sound but tight.

A recent major highlight for the station has been the upgrade of its broadcast infrastructure (Fig. 15.1). In 2024 4ZZZ invested in two brand new transmitters and associated gear—a large capital project that means the station has "the technology on hand to secure [its] broadcasting ability for the foreseeable future".[11] For a radio station that has often relied on ageing equipment, it is a game-changer in terms of signal reliability and audio quality. The

---

[10] 4ZZZ, "4ZZZ Annual Report 2024". https://jeff.4zzz.org.au/sites/default/files/media/Annual%20Report%202024%20.pdf, accessed 3/4/25.

[11] 4ZZZ, '4ZZZ Annual Report 2024', *4ZZZ*, https://jeff.4zzz.org.au/sites/default/files/media/Annual%20Report%202024%20.pdf, (accessed 3 April 2025).

transmitters essentially future proof the 102.1fm service. Up next on the technical wish list? Continued studio upgrades and expanding the station's digital capabilities.

4ZZZ has also notched up some community engagement wins. In the past year, the station hosted or participated in happenings like "Sounds Like Community Radio" (a live showcase of community music), Access All Areas (an inclusivity festival), and most recently a Youth Open Day in the 4ZZZ car park. These events strengthen ties with listeners and spread the word to folks who might not yet be part of the 4ZZZ family. The station's presence at marches, rallies, and local gigs continues to underscore its role as a grassroots media outlet.

What is 4ZZZ ultimately trying to achieve? In short, to empower alternative voices and build community. In its *2021–2024 Strategic Plan*, 4ZZZ set out a roadmap in two key areas: Engagement & Broadcasting (essentially programming and community outreach) and Organisational Capacity (the behind-the-scenes sustainability work). Under these banners were specific goals, for example to "Connect with people who need Zed but don't know they do" and "Develop a holistic Pay The Rent plan as a model for First Nations connections".[12] These efforts align with the concept of "making space," one of 4ZZZ's four core values (alongside Respect, Independence, and Creativity). In the station's words, "Making space is about making sure there are places for vulnerable and exploited communities to be heard, especially in a difficult and often discriminatory media environment".[13]

The *2024–2027 Strategic Plan* doubles down on community engagement and sustainability which aims to grow the audience and subscriber base, diversify revenue, invest in infrastructure, and strengthen 4ZZZ's role as a vital community hub.[14] The *4ZZZ Rights Framework* will also play an important role in guiding 4ZZZ's future development.[15] Recognising the complex power dynamics within a diverse volunteer-based organisation, the framework aims to promote proactive, flexible, and community-strength-based solutions while acknowledging that learning and revising these practices is ongoing. It applies to all staff and volunteers and is designed to work alongside 4ZZZ's broader social justice and governance commitments.

---

[12] 4ZZZ, '2021/2024 4ZZZ Strategic Plan', *4ZZZ*, https://jeff.4zzz.org.au/sites/default/files/media/Strategic%20Plan%202021%20-%2024.pdf, (accessed 3 April 2025).

[13] 4ZZZ, '4ZZZ Radio: Submission to Federal government's Community Broadcasting Sector Sustainability Review', *4ZZZ*, https://www.infrastructure.gov.au/sites/default/files/documents/cbssr-4zzz.pdf, (accessed 1 April 2025).

[14] 4ZZZ, '4ZZZ Strategic Plan 2024–2017', *4ZZZ* https://jeff.4zzz.org.au/sites/default/files/media/Strategic%20Plan%202024-2027.pdf, (accessed 16 April 2025).

[15] 4ZZZ, 'Rights Framework', *4ZZZ* https://jeff.4zzz.org.au/sites/default/files/media/4ZZZ%20Rights%20Framework.pdf, (accessed 1 April 2025).

Fig. 15.2 Photo of 4ZZZ's reception area at Zed Towers, Fortitude Valley, taken by Robert Broeders; 2025

In 2025, 4ZZZ stands as a living example of the power of community broadcasting. Its eclectic shows continue to champion local voices and music. Its volunteers and staff aim to foster an environment where its listeners are active members of the Zed family. The station's aims of independence, diversity, and making space for the unheard are lived out on air every day; there are challenges, sure, but also a clear sense of direction and optimism.

Everything the station does—be it launching a new youth hip-hop show or installing lighting that is kinder to neurodivergent brains—ties back to the *4ZZZ Rights Framework* and the station's values of Respect, Independence, Creativity, and Making Space. And unlike a commercial enterprise, success for 4ZZZ isn't measured in profit, but in participation and impact. As 4ZZZ's *2024 Annual Report* puts it, "numbers are not the be all and end all of any organisation—but they provide a picture of where that entity sits, how it arrived there, and where it is going". By those measures, 4ZZZ's numbers (subscriber growth, volunteer intake, community events, etc.) paint a picture of a station that is staying true to its radical roots while continually reinventing itself to meet the needs of Brisbane's next generation of listeners. As 4ZZZ heads toward its 50th birthday, the vibe around the station is one of celebration, not just of five decades past, but of what's yet to come. After all, a people-powered radio station that can survive half a century of ups and downs has plenty of mojo to spare. But, as Andrew Bartlett reminds us in the Foreword to this book, we should never take the warm inner glow for granted (Fig. 15.2).

Index

13-23 (4ZZZ show), xi, 219
2021–2024 Strategic Plan, 249
2024 Annual Report, 250
21st Century (song), 181
2SER, 194, 219
3ZZZ, 219
4AAA, Murri Country 98.9FM, 201
4EB, 86, 132, 219
4MBS, 86, 162
4ZZZ Breaks the Election (4ZZZ show), 212
4ZZZ car park (Fortitude Valley), 80, 115, 186, 249
   art, 115, 249
4ZZZ community, xi, 3, 46, 93, 131, 155, 171, 198, 207, 240, 244
4ZZZ journalists, 211, 213, 215, 228
   arrests, 213, 215
4ZZZ Newsroom, 210–212, 218
   activism, 211
   breaking stories, 212
   challenges, 210
   Convergent Community Newsroom (CCN), 218
   early days, 212
   headlines, 212
   pride, 211
   proposal, 218
   protests, 212
   trust, 211

4ZZZ Presents Beyond The Banana Curtain: A compilation of Brisbane bands 2000—2010, 177
4ZZZ studio (St Lucia campus), 66
   construction, 50
4ZZZ Studios (Fortitude Valley), 3, 8, 78–79, 115, 215
   history, 3
   paranormal activity, 93
   purchase, 8, 83, 237
   renovations and repairs, 24
4ZZZ studios (Mount Coot-tha), 54–55, 81, 86
4ZZZ studios (Toowong), 74, 79, 109, 217
4ZzZ's Hot 100 (CD), 183

A
Aarght Records, 9
Aarons, Eric, 83
Aberdeen, David, 25
Abolition, 193, 221, 241
Aboriginal and Torres Strait Islanders", 61
Aboriginal Councils and Associations Act 1976, 234
Abortion rights, 213
Access All Areas, 249

Accessibility, 4, 82, 92, 189, 206–207, 244, 246
Accessibility Coordinator, 206
Accessibility Reference Group, 206
Accessible Zed, 206–207
Acid World (band/artist), 120, 181
ACT (band/artist), 232–233, 235
Activism, 3, 14–15, 49–50, 80, 99, 171, 213, 215–216, 220–221
Adelaide, 10–13, 23, 125, 215, 219
Administration Coordinator, 148, 190
Agitate Educate Organise, 6
Air sound
  debates, 27, 166, 190
Airo-Farulla, Geoff, 192, 199, 227, 229
Albert Park, 118, 120–123, 125, 129, 131, 213
Alien Virus (band/artist), 235
Alliance Hotel, 107
Amyl and the Sniffers (band/artist), 5
Amyl's Nightspace, 107
Anarchy in the UK (song), 164
Anderson, Pam, 97
Anderson, Robert, 218
Anderson, Scott, 168
Announcing Coordinator, 166
Anthon, Bruce, 102, 167
Anthony, Doug, 27
Anthony (volunteer), 39, 146, 149
Armbruster, Stefan, 45, 55–56, 59, 68, 71, 74–76, 80, 183–184, 198, 215
Armstrong, Liz, 165
Art and About (4ZZZ show), 83
Art There Somewhere (4ZZZ show), 83
ARTache (4ZZZ show), 189
Ashton, Annie, 247
Audiences
  demographics, 129
  support, 35, 59, 173
Audio technicians, 6
  praise, 6
Aussie Nash, 107
Australian Broadcasting Act
  breaches, 56
Australian Broadcasting Corporation (ABC), 7, 50, 71, 151, 161, 184, 204, 212, 219
Australian Broadcasting Tribunal (ABT), 77, 171–172, 223

Australian Communications and Media Authority (ACMA), 171
Australian community radio sector, 22
Australian Defence Force (ADF), 156
Australian FM Radio Award for Best Community Service Program (1979), 191
Australian Journalists' Association, 214
Australian politics, 1975, 26
Australian Rules Football (AFL), 204, 219

B

Baines, Donna, 58, 198
Baird, Jon, 148, 152–153, 214, 216–217, 227–229, 238
Ballesteros, Shellah M, 197–198
Ballzzz in the Air, 205, 218–219
Banana
  award, 8
  mascot, 7
Banana Buffet, 113
Banshees Bar and Art Space, 240
Barb (volunteer), 231
Barry Crocker (band/artist), 176
Bartlett, Andrew, 41, 49, 63, 175, 185, 211, 250
Basmati (band/artist), 109–110
Batrider (band/artist), 134
Batswing Saloon (band/artist), 36
Bayles, Mundanara, 210
Bayles, Tiga, 210
Beach Boys (band/artist), 183
Beach, Wave, 122, 168
Beastman, 88–89
Beatson, Jay, 219
Beatson, Jim, 7–8, 15, 17–18, 20–27, 39, 83, 99–100, 122, 161, 217, 223
Beattie, Peter, 16
Beckingham, Clarrie, 80
Behan, Belle, 206–207
Behind the Bamboo Curtain, 217
Behind The Banana Curtain: 1975—2000 (2000), 177
Being Jane Lane (band/artist), 178, 185
Bell, Tamara, 132
Bertha Control (band/artist), 177
Bewes, Jan, 164

Beyond Brisbane (4ZZZ show), 217
Bicentenary, 200
Biggs, Tony, 5, 42, 56, 70, 100, 103–104, 164, 167–168, 174, 198
Birmingham, John, 142–143
Birthday celebrations, 1st, 8
Birthday celebrations, 30th, 134
Birthday celebrations, 35th, 88, 177
Birthday celebrations, 40th, 8, 221
Bjelke-Petersen
  death hoax, 67
  demise, 104
  Florence ('Lady Flo'), 223
  government, 67, 80, 98, 226
  government repression, 226
  interview, 105
  Johannes (Joh), 12
  phone calls, 223
  trial, 237
Black Nation Newspaper, 196
Blitz Babies (band/artist), 122
Bloodhound Gang (band/artist), 236
Blowhard (band/artist), 120, 123, 137, 140, 144, 177, 181–182
Blue (volunteer), 24, 144, 161, 209, 235, 239
Board of Directors, 10, 33–34, 43–44, 46, 86, 112, 166, 195
Bobir, Tessa, 203
Boggo Road Gaol, 226–228, 231, 233–234
  closure, 233
  conditions, 226, 231
  history, 226
  hunger strike 1983, 228
  hunger strike 1986, 230
  hunger strike 1988, 231
  Kennedy Report, 233
  Longland Inquiry, 229
  prison riots 1983, 228
  riots, 1983, 216
  riots, 1986, 230
  riots, 1988, 231–233
  smuggled recordings, 228
  Spider, 231
  State Prison for Women, 231
Bond, Danielle, 67, 216
Bones, Jay, 92
Bonner, Neville AO, 201

Bookkeepers, 44
Borallon Training and Correctional Centre, 235
Born and Bred (on Triple Zed) (song), 178
Bowden, Michelle, 35–36
Bowditch, Jo, 122
Brady, Qawanji Vincent, 234
Bragg, Billy (band/artist), 37
Brain Banana, 110–112, 134
Brazil, Victoria, 52–53, 55, 57–58, 60, 62–63, 72–73, 131, 232
Breaking the Unemployment Cycles Community Jobs Plan Scheme, 132
Brighten the Corners (4ZZZ show), 162
Brisbane Band Cricket Association, 204
Brisbane Blacks (song), 176
Brisbane City Council (BBC), 86, 122, 124, 127–128, 130, 152, 156
Brisbane Correctional Centre, 235
Brisbane Indigenous Media Association (BIMA), 201
Brisbane Line Extra, 217
Brisbane Line (4ZZZ Show), 14, 205, 210, 217, 221
Brisbane Pride Festival Queen's Birthday Community Awards, 195
Brisbane Spare Parts, 80, 88
Brisbane Women's Media Collective, 190
British Broadcasting Corporation (BBC), 12, 82
Broadcast
  inaugural, 11
Broadcast Act 1942, 25
Broadcast chain, 87
Broadcast technology, 91
Broadcasting
  Australian history, 170
  early tests, 22
  First Nations, 197, 199–203
  remote, 207, 246
Broadcasting Park, 86–87, 124
Broadcasting Services Act 1992, 33, 171
Bromley, Sid, 161
Brown, Barry, 221
Brown, Jackson, 163
Brown, Michelle, 6, 88, 177, 204
Brown, Mike, 47, 55–58, 232
Browne, Tony, 149

Buchanan, Cheryl, 196
Budd (band/artist), 123
Burke, Marty, 98, 103
Butcher Birds (band/artist), 134
Butt, Louise, 199, 209, 214, 227
Buzzcocks (band/artist), 164

C

Cairns, 196, 212–213
California Über Alles (song), 172
Camaraderie, 23, 38, 135, 162, 239
Cannonball (song), 181–182
Cappellone, Lorena, 168
Captain Burke Park, 117–118, 120
Caputo, Giordana, 88, 218, 220
Car park gigs, 115
Carmody, Kev (band/artist), 175, 198
Carroli, Linda, 42–43
Carroll, Emma, 219
Cass, Moss, 21
Cedar Bay police raid, 212
  coverage, 212
  fundraising, 213
Censorship, 13, 21, 49, 171–172, 174
  music, 21, 172
Central Australian Aboriginal Media Association (CAAMA), 200, 219
Chain (band/artist), 235
Challenges, 6, 24, 39, 104, 113, 171, 246, 250
Charlie (volunteer), 38, 72, 93, 193, 238
Cheverton, Jeff, 61
Children of the Privileged West (album), 181
Children (song), 233
Choo Dikka Dikka (band/artist), 175
Chopper Division (band/artist), 119
Circus Whore (song), 174
CJ (volunteer), 115, 225–226, 239–240
Clair, Frank, 155
Clapton, Richard (band/artist), 103
Clarke, Nicki, 238
Clarkson, Jeanette, 83
Cleveland Sands Hotel, 102
Cloudland Ballroom, 97–98, 103, 105
  demolition, 105
Coalition Against Police Violence, 127
Cold Chisel (band/artist), 102

Coleman, Stacey, 88, 91, 112, 134, 140, 143–144, 159
Collective, 39–46, 61, 63, 76–77, 81, 93, 120, 123, 129, 152, 165, 183, 191, 194, 199, 216, 221
  challenges, 41, 43
  collapse, 42, 45
Collinge, Amanda, 48, 191, 209, 216, 223, 227
Combat Wombat (band/artist), 112
Commonwealth Games (1982)
  protests, 196
  arrests, 213
  coverage, 196, 209
  radiothon, 36
Communist Party of Australia, 8, 78, 80–81
  Brisbane Headquarters, 8, 80
  bombing, 81
Community
  engagement, 220
  marginalised voices, 9, 222
  people living with disability, 206
  sport, 204
Community Broadcasting Association of Australia (CBAA), 170–171
Community Broadcasting Foundation (CBF), 177
Community Broadcasting Sector Sustainability Review, 87, 162
Community engagement, 9–10, 93, 115, 204, 239, 249
Community Engagement Coordinators, 93
Community Media Training Organisation, 203, 206
Community Radio Broadcasting Codes of Practice, 33, 169, 174
Community Radio Network, 219, 236
Community radio sector
  establishment, 27
Connor (volunteer), 78
Consensus-decision making, 39–43
  critique, 39–40
Constipation Blues (song), 173
Converse, Chris, 114, 205, 219
Cooke, Dave, 173
Cook-Long, Lizzie, 179
Cooper, Alice, 168

Cooper, Russell, 153–154, 231
Cosic, Branko, 87
Cosmic Psychos, 114
Country Party (Australian Country Party Queensland), 12
Covid-19 lockdowns, 207
Creative Broadcasters Ltd, 33
Crighton, Judy, 164
Crighton, Ross, 164, 167
Crilly, Cal, 51, 56, 63, 232
Criminal Justice Commission, 142, 154, 156
Croft, Warinkil Glenice, 196, 198
Crook, Michael, 166
Crossfire (band/artists), 99
Crucial Cuts (4ZZZ show), 121
Crystal Club, 107
Culture Vultures (4ZZZ show), 202
Curtis, Amanda, 67
Curtis, Gordon, 23, 25, 28–29, 100, 104, 171–172
Curtis, Paul, 117–118
Cybernana Riot Day: Whose Riot? The People … Or The Police? (2000), 177
Cyclone Hits Expo (song), 175

D
Daily Sun, 68, 223
Danika E (volunteer), 39, 45, 205
Dannecker, Ross, 18, 21, 25, 27
Darling, David, 101–103, 105, 112
Darren J (volunteer), 43, 45, 77
David McCormack and the Polaroids (band/artist), 134
Davies, Ian, 102, 107
Davies Park, 131–132
Davies, Stephen, 49, 104
Dead Flowers (band/artist), 121
Dead Kennedys (band/artist), 105, 172
Deafcult (band/artist), 178
Deanna (volunteer), 92
Deanna's Door, 92
Decolonisation, 199
Deen Brothers, 105
Defamation (Model Provisions) and Other Legislation Amendment Bill 2021, 222

Defamation threats, 221
Demo Show (4ZZZ show), 178
Dent, Andrew, 74
Derek and Clive, 172
Diamanda Galas (band/artist), 173
Dick Nasty (band/artist), 134
Die Yuppie Die (song), 69
Digital pigeonhole, 88
Diolene (band/artist), 139
Disability rights, 206
Diversity, 4, 11, 29, 159, 165, 168, 250
  incarcerated people, 226–228, 234
  listeners, 3–5, 12, 27, 31, 33–34, 36, 38, 51–52, 55–56, 59, 62, 71, 77, 88, 115, 123, 155, 166, 173, 183, 193–194, 213, 216, 220, 225, 236, 240, 244–245, 249–250
  media, 12, 29, 33
  music, 168
  people living with disability, 206–207
  programming, 11, 165
DIY attitude, 112
Doch (band/artist), 218
Doctor Strange (label), 168
Dogmachine (band), 139
Doherty, Mark 'The Colonel, 161
Don, Graham, 160
Doof Tent, 128, 130–131, 139, 147, 177
Dooleys Hotel, 107
Dos Santos, Ezarco, 193
Downs, Alex, 93
Dr Feelgood (band/artist), 104
Dr Ray-Gun, 93
Dream Poppies (band/artist), 120
Dreamkillers, 117, 126
Dreamworld, 104
Dregs of Humanity (band/artist), 139–140
Drugs, 14, 31, 60, 140, 150, 153, 227
Dub Day Afternoon, 109–110, 112, 134
Dykes on Mykes (band/artist), 195

E
Earache Records, 159
Earl, Anita, 47, 53–55, 67, 72, 76
East Leagues Club, 109

Echo and the Bunnymen (band/
   artist), 101
Eco Radio (4ZZZ show), 6, 90, 93, 220
Eddington, Ron, 15
Ekkythump, 110
El Cumbanchereo (song), 144
Electric Crush (4ZZZ show), 162
Electricity (Continuity of Supply) Act
   1985 (Qld), 215
Eleea (band/artist), 203
Elevation (band/artist), 139
Ellison, Quentin, 38
Em (volunteer), 239–240
Emergency broadcasts, 47, 54–56
Empty Records, 168
Emu Smugglers (band/artist), 178
Endicott, Daniel, 144, 157
Environmental issues, 214
Evan (volunteer), 226, 239–240
Evans, Jane, 190
Evans, Jason 'Evo', 204
Eviction attempt, 67, 74, 153
   eviction party, 72
   justifications, 67, 153
   listener support, 74
   occupation, 153
   political cartoon, 153
   resolution, 67
   response, 67
   t-shirt design, 67, 69
Exercise SUMAN WARRIOR, 148
Exit Stage Zed (4ZZZ show), 174
Exiting the Womb (song), 181
Expo 88 World Fair, 175

F
Fabok, Larysa, 86
Faithfull, Marianne (band/artist), 172
Falling Joys (band/artist), 70
Fat Juicy Cop (song), 181
Fat (band/artist), 122
Feminism, 190, 193
   anarcho, 193
   body image, 193
   critiques, 190, 193
   inclusion, 206
   intersectional, 193
   rape crisis workshops, 192

Ferguson, Guy, 76–78, 120, 122, 161
Festival Records, 172
Finance Coordinators, 49
Finance officers, 45
Financial health, current, 48, 248
Fingleton, Di, 141
Finucan, Michael, 104, 163–164, 167
Fiona P (volunteer), 43, 155
Firehouse (band/artist), 112
First Nations
   broadcasting, 199, 197, 202
   issues, 196, 198
   Pay the Rent, 249
   rights, 216, 233
   self-determination, 169
Fisher, Terry, 155
Flangipanis (band/artist), 186, 225
Flannery, Dan, 22, 40–41, 48, 104,
   213–214
Fletcher, Gordon, 53, 55, 69, 71, 74–75
Flicque, Dwayne, 163
FM radio, establishment, 12, 17–18
FM radio, technology, 25
FOCO Club, 99
Formal application for Issuing of a non-
   Commercial FM stereo Broadcasting
   Licence (1975), 21
Forster, Robert, 163, 178
Foster, Margot, 23, 28–29, 40, 100–101,
   104, 213
Foxall, Mike 'Fox', 129, 170
Frame, John, 195
Franklin River protests, (1982/3), 214
Fraser, Malcolm, 25–26
Free Radical (book), 162, 211
Free Speech protests, 215
Frenzal Rhomb (band/artist), 126
Friggin in the Riggin (song), 172
From A to Triple Zed (podcast), 184
From the Roots (4ZZZ show), 213
Front Desk Coordinator, 233
Front End Loader (band/artist), 112
Fryer, Greg, 47, 56–57, 75, 130, 197,
   232–234
Fuck U Symphony (song), 172
Fuck Your Dad (song), 174
Fundraising, 30–31, 33–34, 38–39, 43,
   48, 62, 67, 69, 84, 107, 112, 152,
   156, 247

challenges, 33–34, 62, 156
Fur (band/artist), 123

G
G20 summit, 2014, 216
Gardner, Ruth, 174, 195
Gay & Lesbian Radio Collective (early years), 194
Gay Rave (4ZZZ show), 194
Gay Waves (4ZZZ show), 194–195
Gazoonga Attack (band), 132
Generation Zed
 No Other Radio Like This, 36, 57, 71, 119, 129
Get Trucked
 32 Australian Trucking Songs (2000), 177
Gibbons, Denise, 193
Gizmo: A 4ZZZ Electronic Compilation (2001), 177
Gizzzmo 2 (2003), 177
Goebel, Christine, 128
Goldilocks Folk (4ZZZ show), 162
Good Vibrations (song), 183
Goodall, Julie, 190
Goss, Wayne, 59, 78
Governance models, 41, 45
 alternative, 45
Gravelrash (band/artist), 36, 120
Gravy Day, 225
Gray, Steve, 212–213
Green, Don, 234–236
Green, Tracy, 126
Greenhill, Anita, 55, 59, 67, 71–72, 74–75, 184
Greenhill, Brendan, 57, 150, 154, 156, 215, 238
Grenet, Claire, 49–50, 217, 230
Grigg, Jane, 121, 161, 165, 168
Groovy Things (band/artist), 36
Guinan, Josh, 92, 134, 166
Gunn, Donald, 118, 129

H
Hahn, Jeff, 144, 146
Hambling, Helen, 19–20, 26, 30, 48, 162, 190, 220

Harold and Maude (song), 36
HARPO (How about Resisting Powerful Organisations), 15, 99
Haslan, Dominique, 132
Hayes, Kevin, 23, 25
Heapz of Brisbane Punk Bands (2000), 176
Heavyweight Champion (band/artist), 177
Hecate, 190
Hell Metal (4ZZZ show), 165, 168
Henry, Kerryn, 83
Herriman, Allan, 54, 58, 74
Higgs, Gaye, 129
Hill, Phillip 'Basmati', 109
Hirst, Rob, 104
HITS (band/artist), 159
Hobby Horse Queensland Championships, 219
Hogar, Joe, 92–93
Holland, Chris, 131, 176
Hoodoo Gurus (band/artist), 107
Hoops (volunteer), 112
Horton, Sue, 14, 18, 29, 103, 160, 163
Hot 100, 3–5, 9, 130, 140, 159, 164, 176, 178, 181, 183–186, 226
 CD, 184
 critique, 5, 9, 130, 159, 178, 181, 183–185
 Hangout party, 4–5
 inaugural, 3, 181
 local music, 185
 voting system, 185
Hot Bin, 165, 167
House hunting (1989), 71
How Much is That Doggy in the Window (song), 144
How to Fly Kites (song), 225–226
How to Make Gravy (song), 225
Hoyt, Sean, 51
Hudson, Bob, 99
Hume, Jamie, 46, 173
Huml, Victor, 36, 109, 164, 179
Hunter, Alison, 190
Hunters and Collectors (band/artist), 101, 107

I

I am Vertical (band/artist), 185
I Want to Believe (song), 179
Ian Dury & the Blockheads (band/
    artist), 104
Iggy Pop (band/artist), 107
Igloo (song), 174
Import record shops, 167, 204
Incarcerated people, 226–227, 234
    rights, 226–227
Incarcerated People's Cultural Heritage
    Aboriginal Corporation
    (IPCHAC), 234–235, 238
Inclusion, 169, 194, 204, 206
    critiques, 169, 194, 206
    incarcerated people, 226–228, 234
    sport, 204–205
IncubatorZZZ (4ZZZ show), 207
Independent Inquiry into FM
    Broadcasting, 20
Indigenous, 169
Indigi-Briz (4ZZZ show), 201–203, 216
Information Technology, 91, 215, 248
Inside Information (4ZZZ show), 228,
    230–231, 235
International Police Association
    Conference, 157
Invasion Day, 200, 203–204
It's Not Fair (song), 174
I'm Stranded (song/album), 163

J

J4H Z3N (band/artist), 203
Jackson, Marc, 22, 27
Jason M (volunteer), 148
Jazz on Record (4ZZZ show), 161
Jerome, Paddy, 123
Jesus and the Mary Chain (band/
    artist), 107
Jetson, Judy, 92
Jimmy and the Boys (band), 105
JJ Speedball (band/artist), 128
Johnny Guitar Watson (band/
    artist), 168
Johnson, Hedley, 197
Johnston, Steve, 144–145, 149, 156
Joint Efforts, 99–103, 106–107,
    113–114
    first, 99
    security, 99, 106
Jones, Anne, 48, 52, 104–105, 107,
    172–173
Jones, Ignatius, 105
Joseph, Nicola, 196
Josephine (volunteer), 79
Journalism, 9, 17, 22, 77, 202, 211–212,
    214–215, 217–221
    activist, 9, 211
    anti-war, 220
    ant-nuclear coverage, 220
    Boggo Road, 216, 227, 234
    environmental issues, 90, 214, 245
    First Nations issues, 196, 198
    prison issues, 115, 222, 226, 228, 231
    sport, 191, 204, 219
    youth issues, 13
Jousif, Ray, 81, 130
Joy FM, 195
Joyner, Rona, 171
Jubilee Hotel, 110, 112, 114

K

Kafka (band/artist), 218
Kahoniz, Kelso, 112
Kate (volunteer), 231
Kathleen Turner Overdrive (band/
    artist), 179
Kelly, Candy, 212
Kelly, Paul, 225
Kempel, Randall, 178
Kempis, Paul, 230
Kent Records, 168
Kerlin, Cathy, 114
Kerr, John, 26
Kerrang, 159
Kids with Class Kicking Arse (4ZZZ
    show), 112, 205
Kidzone (4ZZZ show), 10
Killer Keller, Callum and Jack (band/
    artist), 176
King, Patrick, 6, 54, 88, 93, 243, 246
Kinniburgh, Jason, 124
Kitten Licks, 139
Kneipp, Tony, 175
Knight, Alan, 14, 17–18, 49, 161, 163,
    211

INDEX 259

Know Idea (4ZZZ show), 213
Know Your Product (song), 218
Kooii (band/artist), 177
Kosch, Angel, 221
Kowalski, Todd 'The Rod', 115
Kremlin (band/artist), 36
Kretschman, Sam 'DJ SLK', 110, 151
Kuepper, Ed (band/artist), 132, 134
Kylie G (volunteer), 168

L

Ladysmith Black Mambazo (band/artist), 124
Laughing Clowns (band/artist), 107
Law, Justin, 110
Lawlor, Jodie, 225
Le Goulon, Damien, 220
Le Plastrier, Teigan, 178, 185
Leah, Sean, 68
Leahy, Sean, 67–68
Led Zeppelin (band/artist), 163
Lee Harvey and the Oswalds (band/artist), 130
Legal threats, 221
Lemon, Gai, 194–195
Lennon, David, 31–32, 36, 38, 50–53, 55, 59, 63, 67, 72, 74–75, 120, 131, 197
Licence
  first, 171
  first application, 18–19, 25
  lobbying, 102, 171–173
  renewal, 77
  threatened, 25
Lily Allen (band/artist), 174
Lil' Fi (band/artist), 235
Lindsay, Kirstyn, 123, 130, 146, 149, 193
Lister, Harvey, 101
Little, Don, 23
Little Heroes (band/artist), 107
Live music, 9, 24, 36, 48, 98–99, 109, 112–113, 115, 118–119, 144, 155, 222
  benefits, 24, 99, 113, 119
  pub rock, 101
  touring bands, 104, 109, 132
Livestreaming, 87

Live-to-airs, 59, 76
Lloyd, Kellie, 125, 140, 143, 178, 185
Local music, 3, 6, 9, 48, 99, 102, 124, 169, 175, 177–178, 181
  Hot 100, 185
  pride, 185
  support, 9, 102
Locked In (4ZZZ show), 115, 225–226, 236–241
  artwork, 240
  community engagement, 239
  Crew, 240
Locked In (national program), 115, 225–226, 236, 238–241
Loki (volunteer), 112
London Line (4ZZZ show), 217
Longland, David, 229
Lots of Brisbane Punk Bands (1998), 176
Louttit, Mark, 28, 103–104
Luckus, Irena, 24, 74, 164
Lyall, Tobin, 121, 130, 135

M

Mack (volunteer), 218
Mackie, Kate, 195
Maginnis, Tom, 75, 199–200, 235
Manning, Phil, 235
Manser, Bruno, 220
Marga (band/artist), 99
Marginalised voices, 9, 222
Market Day, 9, 35–36, 77, 81, 107, 118–120, 122, 124, 126, 128–132, 134–135, 139–141, 145, 152, 154, 156, 166
  All-Stars Tattoo Tent, 132
  AM radio throwing, 35–36
  arrests, 127–128
  Bananageddon, 133
  challenges, 36, 77, 107, 118, 123–124, 126, 128, 130–132, 134
  Coordinator, 120, 126, 128, 130, 132, 137, 142–143, 149
  Criminal Justice Commission (CJC), formal complaint, 9
  Cybernana, 9, 129, 137
    aftermath, 123–124, 157
    arrests, 140, 152

media coverage, 152
military police, 157
police violence, 134
response, 129, 154
theories, 156
legal support, 155–156
storm, 137
violence towards police, 140–141, 148
Day of the Living Dead, 131
Doof Tent, 128, 130–131, 139
early, 36, 107, 118–120, 122, 129–131
Elect-O-Cution, 120
Ethno Super-Lounge, 130
legal support, 129, 157
logistics, 139
Octobanana, 120
police violence, 127, 134
Promised Land, 117–119, 122
Return of the Living Zed, 131–132
storm, 9
The Dance Out, 121
TV smashing, 36
violence towards police, 129, 140–141, 148
West End Of The World, 123–124
Zed Beat, 126
Zed Bubble, 130, 157
Zed Rox, 126–127
Zed World, 121
Zedification, 130–131
Zed-O-Matique, 125
Zed-O-Mitter, 128–129
Zed-O-Vision, 122
Market Day 2005, 8
Market Day 2006, 8, 134
Market Days, 1980s, 107, 118
Marston, Darren, 128, 130
Martin, Blair, 38, 195
Masochist (band/artist), 115
Matchett, Stuart, 164
Mawson, Matt, 7, 70, 85, 176
Maximum Rock n Roll, 159
McCallum, Doug, 76, 81, 84, 87
McDonnell, Jack, 46, 91, 218, 243–245
McEvoy, Owen, 234
McIntosh, Celeste, 203
McKinnon, Lauren, 194

McLean, Chris, 148, 157
McLeod, Fiona, 190–191
Medew, Mick, 4, 174, 186
Media diversity, 12, 29, 33
Media Monitors, 151
Megahers (4ZZZ show), 191
early years, 191
history, 191
Megaherz (*See Megahers, Megaherzzz*), 10
Megaherzzz, 162
Mental As Anything (band/artist), 37
Mercer, John, 134, 222
Merritt, Ashleigh, 164
Mick Medew and Ursula (band/artist), 4, 186
Midgley, Jonathon, 124
Midnight Oil (band/artist), 104
Military police, 145, 148–149, 156
Millie Jackson (band/artist), 172
Milpera Airspace Radio Project, 220
Misery (band/artist), 123, 139
Mi-Sex (band/artist), 102
Mogg, Peter, 121
Monsour, Phil, 179
Monster Zoku Onsomb! (band/artist), 177
Moonlight State (documentary, 1987), 51
Moonlite (band/artist), 99
Moore, Bec, 45, 120
Moore, Lucas, 113, 134, 218–220
Mop and the Dropouts (band/artist), 176
Moral panic, 13
Morrison, Lindy, 163–164, 178
Motherfuckers from the Bowels of Hell, 159
Mount Coot-tha, 53–55, 65, 74, 81–82, 84, 86, 243
Mount Coot-tha caravan, 65, 74, 81
Mount Coot-tha Caravan, challenges, 65, 74
Mouthguard (band/artist), 179
Moynihan, Josie, 83
Moynihan, Ray, 83
Mudhoney (band/artist), 109
Multiplexing, 77
Muntz, Geoff, 228
Murphy, Josh, 115, 182, 186

Murri community, 123, 139, 199, 234
Murri Hour
  challenges, 199
  early days, 201
  growth, 200
Murri Hour (4ZZZ show), 197–201, 234, 236
Musgrave Park, 123–126, 128, 137–139, 142, 147–149, 152–153, 209, 214, 216
Music
  4ZZZ releases, 102, 175, 177, 184
  acquisition, 24
  alternative, 5, 9, 15, 102, 138, 183, 194
  carts, 175
  censorship, 21, 172
  curation, 169, 177, 183, 240
  demos, 175
  diversity, 168
  independent, 3, 6, 8, 56
  labels, 168
  library, 167
  local, 3, 6, 9, 48, 99, 102, 124, 169, 175, 177–178, 185, 245
  obscenity complaint, defence, 172
  obscenity complaints, 171
  policy, 161
  programming, 195, 206, 217, 236, 245–246
  quotas, 169–170
Music Broadcasting Societies (MBS), 12
Music Coordinators, 168
Music genre
  blues, 122, 161, 165, 235
  classical, 161–162
  country, 42, 161, 199
  disco, 121, 165
  electronica, 4, 110, 177
  jazz, 4, 121, 161, 168
  metal, 165
  punk, 4, 36, 77, 98, 102, 107, 109, 111, 115, 122, 124, 150, 163–165, 167, 183, 218, 231
  reggae, 162, 109–111, 121, 168, 177
Music promotions, 101
  challenges, 101
Mystery of Sixes (band/artist), 36, 178

N
Nam Shub of Enki (band/artist), 112, 131, 165
Nancy Vandal (band/artist), 129, 170
National Party (Queensland), 51–52, 56
  demise, 67, 74
National Youth Media Awards, 219
Nehl, Andy, 31, 40, 172–174, 183–184
Netherworld, 38, 40
New Import Releases Show (4ZZZ show), 168
New Releases Show (4ZZZ show), 221
New Zealand Show (4ZZZ show), 6
News and Current Affairs, 9, 14, 196, 204, 210, 217, 219–220, 236, 245
  early days, 9, 204, 217
  marginalised voices, 9, 222
  politics, 9, 14
News Coordinators, 83, 212
Nick Cave and the Bad Seeds (band/artist), 107
Nikko (band/artist), 177
Nilson, Jo, 134
Noddy No Mask (band/artist), 115
Non-Indigenous News Show (4ZZZ show), 234
Noonan, Fred, 177
Noonuccal, Oodgeroo, 234
Noose (band/artist), 120
Nothin' but the Blues (4ZZZ show), 161
Nowland, Don, 229, 237
Nunya, Leah, 236
Nyx Fullmoon, 92

O
Objectionable Literature Act of 1954, 14
Oliver, Alex, 91, 93
Olle, Andrew, 212
On- Air sound, 27, 190–191
On-Air sound
  block programming, 162
  dissatisfaction, 166
  diversity, 27, 191
  news and current affairs, 9, 14, 21, 196, 210, 219, 236, 245
  strip programming, 162, 194
Only Human (4ZZZ show), 206–207
Open Days

First Nations, 115, 203
  Youth Week, 115
Orange Crush (song), 53
Otton, Salty, 92, 162, 205
Outer Limits (band/artist), 107
Outside broadcasts, 4, 130, 203, 216
  Commonwealth Bank of Australia, 215
  First Nations, 216
  G20 summit 2014, 216
  Invasion Day, 200, 203–204
O'Brien, Patrick, 76, 173, 178
O'Connor, Terry 'Oofus', 125, 127, 132, 141–142, 147, 151, 153, 156, 177, 184
O'Gorman, Terry, 142, 155
O'Keefe, Maisy, 126, 152
O'Rourke, Kerry, 209
O'Ryan, Gabrielle, 191
O'Sullivan, Eugene, 106

P
Pace, Davey, 69
Pacifica Radio Network, 33
Padovan, Michelle, 204–205
Paine, Andy, 221
Paint Factory, 118
Paint the Town Zed, 88
Painters and Dockers (band/artist), 69, 114
Palen Creek Correctional Centre, 234
Palestine, 174
Parameters (band/artist), 178, 183, 185
Parliament Funkadelic (band/artist), 168
Pascoe, Ricky, 197, 230
Pashley, Grace, 91, 93, 169, 202, 246
Pass the Aux (4ZZZ Show), 115
Pass the Mic, 203
Peachey, Andy 'Chopper/Snappa', 126
Pennings, Ben, 150
Petrou, Leon, 201
Pfingst, Jason, 44–45, 125
Physical Graffiti, 163
Pig City (book), 51
Pig City (song), 175, 185
Pine Gap protests, 2002, 220
Pineapples From The Dawn Of Time (band/artist), 177
Pink, Alexis, 211–212

Pirate radio, 17, 211
Police, 9
  horses, 147–148, 153
  military, 145, 148–149, 156–157
  surveillance, 15
  Violence, 14, 16–17, 127, 134, 151, 154, 156
Police Behaviour at a 4ZZZ Market Day Function, 142, 155
Political reportage, 211
  election coverage, 212
Ponting, Larry, 69
Pope, Kathy, 56, 58
Powderfinger (band/artist), 126
Powne, Ian, 166, 169–170, 189, 244–246
President's XI (band/artist), 185
Primary (song), 185
Prison issues, First Nations, 196, 198, 203, 234
Prison rights, 226
Prisoners Action Group (PAG), 227
Production Coordinators, 31, 35, 227
Program Coordinators", 53
Program Director, 165
Program Review Team, 166
Programmimg Coordinators, 166
Programming, 3, 9, 20–22, 42, 109, 162, 165–167, 171, 174, 189, 194–195, 197, 202, 206–207, 217, 221, 236, 244–246, 249
  activist, 221
  Bicentenary, 200
  complaints, 42, 103–104, 125, 155
  decision-making, 39, 43
  disability issues, 207
  diversity, 11, 165
  feminist, 189, 191, 193
  First Nations, 170, 201–202
  Invasion Day, 200, 203
  news and current affairs, 9, 14, 217, 236, 245
  prison issues, 115, 231
  spoken word, 162
  transgender, 193–194
Programming committee, 166
Programming coordinator, 166, 169, 189, 244–246

Promotions Coordinators, 18, 51, 67, 101–102, 120, 124, 128, 161, 169, 173, 175
Propagandhi (band), 115
Protest, 12, 18, 32, 39, 56, 103, 123, 147, 157, 196–197, 203, 209, 213, 215–216, 220, 227–228, 230, 232, 245
  Bicentenary, 200
  G20 summit 2014, 216
  Springboks, 15–16
Protests, 14–15, 17, 26, 73, 147, 196, 210, 213–216, 220–221, 226, 231, 237
Public Broadcasting Association of Australia", 20
Public Radio Party (1989), 69
Public Safety Response Team (PSRT, riot police), 9, 142
Puhakka, Heli, 120
Puhakka, Tony, 124
Punk Grandma (song), 4, 186
Punkfest, 114
Punks, 5, 36, 56, 102, 106, 129, 139, 222

Q
Q-Music, 204
Quasar (band/artist), 99
Queensland Communist Party, 15
Queensland Corrective Services, 228
Queensland Council for Civil Liberties, 142, 155
Queensland Folk Federation, 81
Queensland in Quarantine: *A compilation of diseased music* (1984), 175
Queensland Jewish Board of Deputies, 174
Queensland Licensing Commission, 102
Queensland Music Awards (QMA), 88
Queensland Police Service, 129, 143, 145, 216
  arrests, 145
  mounted, 145
  surveillance, 80
  violence, 145
Queensland politics, 51

corruption, 12
Queensland University of Technology Student Union, 48
Queer broadcasting, 194
  early days, 194
Queer Radio (4ZZZ program), 6, 38, 113, 178, 195–196
Queer rights, 194, 245
Quinn, Carole, 164
Quotas
  Australian music, 169–170
  debates, 4, 169–170
  female content, 169
  First Nations music, 169
  local music, 169
  new releases, 4, 170

R
Rachel (volunteer), 165, 168
Radical Brisbane (book), 16
Radical Radio, 220
Radio Adelaide, 13, 219
Radio Democracy, 220
Radio Redfern, 200, 210
Radio Reversal (4ZZZ show), 221, 241
Radio Skid Row, 69
Radio Times, 33–35, 43, 85, 98, 112, 118, 123, 156, 161, 163, 174, 183, 189–190, 193–194, 196, 217
Radiothon, 31–32, 35–39, 55, 59, 109, 166, 213, 215, 244–245, 247
  A Street Kid Named Zed Radiothon (1989), 69, 118
  history, 32
  No Choice Radiothon (1982), 36
  Priority 102-1 (1986), 32
  prizes, 38
Railroad Gin (band/artist), 99
Raparations (4ZZZ artist), 202
Rave Magazine, 139
Razar (band/artist), 36, 98, 101, 103, 165, 178
Real Life (band/artist), 107
Reclink Australia, 204
Reclink Community Cup, 204–205
  Foster McLennan Award, 204
  The Brisbane Lines, 204–205
  The Rocking Horses, 204

Record labels, 9
Record library, 59, 71, 76, 160, 167–169
Regan, Gemma, 92
Regurgitator (band/artist), 112
Reilly, Justine, 204
Report on the inquiry into the Australian music industry, 170
Resilience, 26, 247
Resin Dogs (band/artist), 134
Rhinestone Cowgirl (4ZZZ show), 162, 213
Rialto Theatre, 5
Richards, Anne, 13, 16
Richards, 'Evil' Dick, 159
Riethmuller, Ted, 80–81
Riff Patrol (4ZZZ show), 112
Right Here, Right Now (4ZZZ show), 245
Riner, Bill, 163, 167
RNA Showgrounds, 134
Roberts, Alan 'Schleke', 92, 109
Roberts, Mikey, 150
Rock 'n' Roll Circus, 36
Rocking Horse Records, 160, 167
Rohweder, Peter, 45, 86–87, 123, 125, 127, 129–132, 142–143, 149, 153
Rollason, Brentyn 'Rollo', 122, 176
Rolling Stone Magazine, 184
Rolling Stone Magazine, 142–143
Rollo, 144
Rose, Linda, 220–221
Rough Trade, 167
Rowen, Thomas, 126
Rumble Rock, 112–113
Rutherford, Anthony 'The Accountant', 205, 219
Ryan, Ben, 87, 91, 93, 216, 243, 246

S
S11 protests, 2000, 220
Sadler, Own, 92, 206–207, 244
Samedi Sound System (band/artist), 112
Sarah (volunteer), 146, 193
Saturday Night Request Show, 163
Saunders, Tabatha, 202–203
Scandrett, Charlie, 72
Schiavone, Shane, 139–140
Schonell Theatre, 24

Scott, Adam, 222
Screamfeeder (band/artist), 125, 139–140, 143, 177–178, 185
Screaming Tribesman (band/artist), 174
Screamin' Jay Hawkins (band/artist), 107, 173
Scrumfeeder (band), 128
Search Foundation, 78, 83
Sekiden *(band)*, 131
Semper Floreat (newspaper), 16, 57, 61–62, 73, 106
  editorial interference, 61
Sensoria, 107
Serantak, Will, 129, 138
Sex Pistols (band/artist), 164, 172, 183
Seymour, Mark, 101, 107
Sharp, Steve, 31
Shaw, Nikola, 144
Shield Wars, 157
Shillingsworth, Alfie, 197
Shock Records, 168, 184
Sinclair, Belinda, 117–118
Sinclair, Lance, 120
Siouxsie and the Banshees (band/artist), 164
Sisi (volunteer), 193
Six Days on the Road (song), 176
SixFtHick (band/artist), 177
Ska Show (4ZZZ show), 177
Sky News, 174
Skyhooks (band/artist), 102
Smith, Denis, 221
Smith, Kelly, 146
Smudge (band/artist), 120
Snaith, Ben, 206
Snappahead (band/artist), 126
Snowdon, Gemma, 92, 219
Society for Democratic Action (SDA), 15
Society to Outlaw Pornography (STOP), 171
Solidarity Infoshop, 80
Solway, Mark, 52, 68
Something for Kate (band/artist), 137, 143
Soorley, Jim, 122, 151–152
SoulJah Sistars (4ZZZ show), 201–204
Sound Surgery (band), 123
Sounds Like Community Radio, 249

South Brisbane Community Arts Centre Alliance, 78
South Leagues Club, 107
South-East Queensland Electricity Board [SEQEB] dispute, 215
Special Branch, 26, 80–81, 103, 216–217
Spenceley, Cameron, 62
Spiderbait (band/artist), 132
Sponsorship, 27, 30, 33, 39, 99, 112, 247
Sponsorship Manager, 112
Sport, 191, 204–206, 218–219
Sporting Wheelies, 219
SportsLine (4ZZZ show), 219
Springbok protests, 17
Square Tug (band/artist), 179, 186
Stamp Out Disco (song), 165
Stanley, Richard, 9
Stanwell, John, 7, 15–16, 18, 23–24, 26–30, 34–35, 39, 41, 99–101, 167
State of Emergence (1986), 175, 176
State of Emergency, 15–16, 209
Station Coordinators", 77
Station Managers", 6
Station Policy, 171, 203
   accessibility, 171, 203
   First Nations, 203
   mission, 171, 203
   Rights Framework, 241, 249
   Strategic Plan, 206, 249
Steely Dan (band/artist), 164
Stephen P (volunteer), 40–41, 44
Steward, Robin, 168
Stewart, Kim, 206–207, 216, 220
Stewart, Paulie, 69
Stockwell, Stephen, Jnr, 18, 35, 37–38, 80, 88, 91, 161, 165, 167, 183, 227
Stop Wondering Now (2005), 177
Strategic Plan 2021–2024, 206
Strutt, Deb, 41, 107, 169, 175, 191, 194
Strutter (band/artist), 159
Student politics, 52
Students for a Democratic Union (SDU), 73
Stumm, Harley, 175, 215, 223
SubNovo (4ZZZ show), 179
Subscription model, 34
Subscriptions Coordinator, 126, 152

Summer Vacation (song), 185
Summerville, Gary, 194
Sunday Sun, 105
Surfair Hotel, 102
Susie Bright (band/artist), 174
Sydney Gay and Lesbian Mardi Gras Parade, 195
Sympathy for the Devil (song), 163

T
Talkback Show (4ZZZ show), 157
Talking Heads (band/artist), 164
Talking Zeds (4ZZZ show), 10
Tall, Ingrid, 194
Tall Tales and True (band/artist), 70
Tape/Off (band/artist), 87
Task Force (Undercover Cops) (song), 103
Taylor, Amy, 5
Technical innovation, 207
Technical Manager, 54, 246
Test transmissions, 22
The Aampirellas (band/artist), 160
The Anarchy Show (4ZZZ show), 220
The Angels (band/artist), 104
The Australian Broadcasting Tribunal Annual Report (1980-81), 172
The Better Alternative, demise, 61, 73
The Better Alternative (TBA), 52, 60–61, 73
The Black Assassins (band/artist), 5, 70, 105, 167
The Booze Blues & Boogie Band (band/artist), 99
The Breeders (band/artist), 181
The Brisbane Line
   early days, 14, 204
   origin of name, 14
The Brisbane Line (4ZZZ show)", 15
The Brisbane Line (newspaper), 14–15, 204–205, 210, 217
The Brown Couch (4ZZZ show), 178
The Carol Lloyd Band (band/artist), 99
The Celibate Rifles (band/artist), 132, 176
The Clash (band/artist), 98, 104, 150
The Colours *(band)*, 107
The Courier Mail, 17, 56, 58, 62, 67, 72, 83, 130, 148, 152–153

266 INDEX

The Cure (band/artist), 101, 185
The Custodian (4ZZZ show), 202–203
The Distained (band/artist), 4
The Dwarves (band/artist), 159
The Environment Show (4ZZZ show), 220
The Exchange Hotel, 102
The Fitzgerald Report, 73
The Frog and Peach, 93
The Gay Radio News (4ZZZ show), 194
The Go-Betweens (band/artist), 107
The Hekawis (band/artist), 76
The Herd (band/artist), 113–114
The Home Show (4ZZZ show), 189
The Jazz Show (4ZZZ show), 161, 213
The John Citizens (band/artist), 218
The Lesbian Show (4ZZZ show), 195
The Litanies of Satan, 173
The Little Red Schoolbook (book), 14
The National Hotel, 103, 107
The New Christs (band), 107
The New York, 25, 103
The Paradigm Shift (4ZZZ show), 221
The Peace and Environment Show (4ZZZ show), 90, 221
The People's Bookshop, 80
The Pits (band/artist), 36
The Prisoners' Show (4ZZZ show), 231, 236–238
The Psychedelic Furs (band/artist), 164
The Punk Show (4ZZZ show), 9, 115, 160, 186
The Queen's Hotel, 102
The Rev, 218
The Riptides (band/artist), 177
The Roof is on Fire (song), 236
The Saints (band/artist), 109, 163, 177–178, 218
The Sparklers (band/artist), 70
The Specials (band/artist), 99, 164
The Subteraneans (band/artist), 139
The Sunday Mail, 127
The Survivors (band/artist), 101–102
The Triffid, 4
The Who (*band*), 29
The Wire (national show), 219
The Witching Hour (4ZZZ show), 93
The Worm Turns (band/artist), 36
The Yard (4ZZZ show), 162

The Zoo, 177
This! (4ZZZ show), 218
Thomson, Phil, 131
Thorpe, Gary, 86, 162
Thou Shalt Not Steal (song), 197–198
Through the Looking Glass (4ZZZ show), 189–190
Thug (band/artist), 174
Tigwell, Craig, 170
Time Off Magazine, 129
Tina & the Hams (band), 170
Today Tonight, 221
Too Drunk to Fuck (song), 172
Toothfaeries (band/artist), 129
Tower Mill Motel, 15–16
Townshend, Pete, 29
Toy Watches (band/artist), 102
Tracey, John, 234–235
Tracey (volunteer), 121
Training
  accessibility, 206
  announcer, 10, 92, 174, 206
  announcing, 170
  community development, 132, 189
  First Nations, 202–203, 233
  newsroom, 10, 239
  Pass the Mic, 203
Transgender rights, 32, 193
Transglobal, 125–126
Transmission site, Mt Coot-tha, 86
Transmitter
  erection, 84
  first, 22
  interim, 27
  lost, 54
  new, 27, 248
  problems, 65, 84, 86
Tranzmission (4ZZZ show), 93, 193
Tresidder, Julia, 199
Triple J, 31, 160, 176, 183–185, 191, 219
  challenges, 184
  Hottest 100, 184–185
  national rollout, 183–184
Tropical cyclone Alfred, 243
Tropical cyclone Debbie, 91
Trott, Abbie, 44
Trucks (song), 177
Tug, Dave, 179, 186

Tulloch, Ilana 'Ili', 115
Turnpike (band/artist), 177
Turtlebox (band/artist), 143
Tyers, Darren, 52, 55, 68
Tylea (band/artist), 125

U
Unemployed People's Theatre Group, 223
University of Queensland (UQ) (*See* also UQ Student Union), 8, 14
   conflict, 16, 19, 48, 106, 192
   student occupation, 37
University of Queensland Media Committee (UQMC), 18
University of Queensland Student Union, 53, 99
   challenges, 55
Unlocked art exhibition, 2023, 240
Unsworth, Gavin, 81–82, 86–87, 131, 248
Ups and Downs (band/artist), 70, 185
UQ Student Union, 16, 22, 26, 33, 49, 52–53, 56, 62, 71, 73, 109, 131

V
V8 Rock n Roll (song), 181
Van Der Beek, Nils, 194
Van Vuuren, Kitty, 237–238
Velvet Hammer (band/artist), 120
Vlatkovic, Michelle, 151, 202
Vogel, Seja, 131
Voltron and Charlie Show (4ZZZ show), 222
Volunteer Coordinators, 92, 162, 205
Volunteering Queensland, 206

W
Waiting for the Great Leap Forward (song), 37
Walker, Bejam Denis, 234–235
Walker, Brett, 81
Walsh, Gay, 162, 194, 211
Wang Building, 82
Warm Inner Glow, 32, 34, 250
Wasted Days (band/artist), 101

Watson, Maureen, 209
Watson, Ross, 196–197, 200, 209, 233
Watson, Yudin Dali Ted, 234
Webster (band/artist), 143
Weiland, John, 148
West, Rod, 124
Westerman, Nancy, 5, 173, 192
Wests Rugby Union, 118
Whalley, Jay, 126
Whatever Floats Your Boat Cruise, 113
White Riot (song), 150
Whitlam, Gough, 19, 26, 67
   dismissal, 29
   government, 19–20, 25–26
Whitman, Patrick 'DJ No MC', 109, 223
Why D'Ya Do It (song), 172
Wightman, Alex, 39, 43, 59, 122, 135, 147
Wilkinson, Gary, 152
Wilkinson, Marian, 14, 17–18, 20–21, 23, 28–29, 211
Williams, Garry, 119–121, 123, 139, 177
Williamson, Donna, 122, 126–127, 130, 147, 149–150, 155, 235–236
Williamson, Peter, 101, 105
Williamson, Sue, 42
Willis, Liz, 5, 40, 42, 69, 71, 191, 199
Willsteed, John, 101
Wilson, Geoff, 44, 134, 178
Wilton, Rohan, 58
Winter, Annie, 45, 128, 130, 147, 157
Wishing Chair (band/artist), 140, 143
Witt, Liz, 93
WOMADelaide, 125
Women's House, 192
Won't Get fooled again (song), 29, 58
Wood, Geoff, 165, 174
Woodford Correctional Centre, riots 1997, 236
Woods, Charlie, 38, 93
Woods, John, 11, 23, 28–29, 194
Woodward, Linden, 40–41, 211
Workers' Power (4ZZZ show), 189
Working Party on Public Broadcasting (WPPB), 21
WorldBeat (4ZZZ show), 124
Wrestling, 112

X
XTC (band/artist), 104

Y
You Am I (band/artist), 121
Yalga Bindi (4ZZZ show), 234–235
Youth Show (4ZZZ show), 205

Z
Zed Digital, 160, 206, 217, 240
Zed Games (4ZZZ show), 193
Zed Hed Recordings, 176
Zed Towers, 8, 79, 82, 84, 87–89, 91–93, 115, 161, 167, 207, 217, 240, 243, 246
Zedlines (4ZZZ show), 204, 218, 239
Zero (band/artist), 101, 163, 178
Zim (volunteer), 238–239
Zion, Laurie, 184

GPSR Compliance

The European Union's (EU) General Product Safety Regulation (GPSR) is a set of rules that requires consumer products to be safe and our obligations to ensure this.

If you have any concerns about our products, you can contact us on

ProductSafety@springernature.com

In case Publisher is established outside the EU, the EU authorized representative is:

Springer Nature Customer Service Center GmbH
Europaplatz 3
69115 Heidelberg, Germany

www.ingramcontent.com/pod-product-compliance
Lightning Source LLC
LaVergne TN
LVHW020136080526
838202LV00048B/3956